Slum Health

Slum Health

From the Cell to the Street

EDITED BY
Jason Corburn and Lee Riley

UNIVERSITY OF CALIFORNIA PRESS

University of California Press, one of the most distinguished university presses in the United States, enriches lives around the world by advancing scholarship in the humanities, social sciences, and natural sciences. Its activities are supported by the UC Press Foundation and by philanthropic contributions from individuals and institutions. For more information, visit www.ucpress.edu.

University of California Press
Oakland, California

Library of Congress Cataloging-in-Publication Data

Names: Corburn, Jason, editor. | Riley, Lee W., editor.
Title: Slum health : from the cell to the street / edited by Jason Corburn and Lee Riley.
Description: Oakland, California : University of California Press, [2016] | 2016 | Includes index.
Identifiers: LCCN 2015042220 | ISBN 9780520281066 (cloth : alk. paper) | ISBN 9780520281073 (pbk. : alk. paper)
Subjects: LCSH: Slums—Health aspects. | Urban health—Brazil. | Urban health—India. | Urban health—Kenya—Nairobi. | Cities and towns—Health aspects. | Urban ecology (Sociology)
Classification: LCC HV4028 .S575 2016 | DDC 614.09173/2—dc23

LC record available at http://lccn.loc.gov/2015042220
Manufactured in the United States of America

25 24 23 22 21 20 19 18 17 16
10 9 8 7 6 5 4 3 2 1

In keeping with a commitment to support environmentally responsible and sustainable printing practices, UC Press has printed this book on Natures Natural, a fiber that contains 30% post-consumer waste and meets the minimum requirements of ANSI/NISO Z39.48-1992 (R 1997) (*Permanence of Paper*).

Contents

Illustrations

MAPS

FIGURES

PHOTOGRAPHS

BOXES

Tables

Prelude

MEMOIRES OF A KENYAN SLUM DWELLER

(The subject's name is withheld to protect confidentiality. Reproduced with permission from Memoirs of a Kenyan Slum Dweller, ageofzine.com/memoirs-of-a-kenyan-slum-dweller/.)

I recall my early life with somberness. This was a time when my mother, a single mother, had just migrated into the city of Nairobi.

Our first rental house in Kariobangi was made of mud lumped onto a frame of wattle poles, and had a tin sheet roof. The room we, the children, occupied was divided into two sections: one side for the nine of us, and on the other side we had space for our family's goats.

Later, when I was eleven, going on to class four, my mother managed to get a piece of land to construct her own house in Korogocho slum. She did this through her "Nyakinyua" group. Nyakinyua women dancing groups were formed purposely to perform during government functions or other gatherings that required entertainment.

Though our house was built under the high voltage power line, we lived there for over 20 years oblivious of the danger. We, and all the goats and some chicken, lived in that house without threat from the power company or the government. The construction of our first house involved us all. It did not require a lot of expertise in the construction, as I recall vividly the activities. All we needed were wattle poles that were plenty in Korogocho. With the poles we mixed grass and mud and covered the walls. For the roof, it was improved later; we only used sheets of polythene. There was plenty of waste polythene and PVC in the city's dumping site that shares a fence with Korogocho.

Later the house was improved as we continued staying there. It never got to the stage where it required an architect or a design approved by the City Council. To this day the quality of houses in Korogocho remain largely unchanged. However, the slum now has a good tarmac road network and better electricity and water supply.

It was much later, when we were older, that we fully understood how tough life was and how wise my mother was in shielding us from the full impact of our situation. Many evenings, the pot would be set to boil for the evening meal. After some time my mother would say that firewood had run out and send us out to get any flammable material outside. We would come back and the fire would be started again and the food would continue bubbling.

Occasionally my mother would stir the food or add fuel to the fire. Eventually we would get drowsy and nod off in the comfort that when the food was ready we would be woken up to eat. Our young minds never suspected that all that the pot had was boiling water. We all thought that we kept falling asleep before the evening meal was ready. Today, I understand the power that hope brings.

How does a journey of a thousand miles begin? Perhaps the same way the journey of becoming an alcoholic or drug user begins.

The story of my mother as a brewer who never drank alcohol, to many people who I have shared this story with, tells the story of the morality of survival. My mother was introduced into brewing by her stepsister, who had also shown her the way to get around city life.

Our first brew was called busaa. It was a traditional brew mainly consumed by the people of Western Kenya. The brew was prepared using millet and yeast. The mixture of millet and water was fermented for a couple of days to produce thick coarse paste. The paste was fried using a big metallic pan outside the house. The fried or, if you prefer, cooked matter would be put into a drum and mixed with water to ferment again for another couple of days to produce the alcohol.

Busaa is preferred hot and is considered to be a social drink. Most customers drank and socialized in our house. Due to its cumbersome nature my mother abandoned the busaa business and entered into the distillation of "Changaa." Unlike busaa, Changaa is not associated with any customary brews. It is far more potent and is considered to be "more illegal" than busaa.

And therefore it fetched more. With her experience and with ready customers my mother started brewing Changaa or the "African Gin." It is as clear as ordinary gin.

Brewing Changaa was a different game from the busaa service. You had to have your wits around you. In order to make it as a Changaa brewer, you first need to be well protected by law enforcers.

This requires the brewer to set aside some cash to pay off policemen, the administration police, and sometimes the local area chief. Then the recipient of this bribe offered instructions as to what one should do to avoid being arrested or being caught with the alcohol.

For a Changaa manufacturer you will require an industry or physical space. Now for a single unit dweller like my mother this was tricky. Therefore it required innovation.

The brewing process started with fermenting molasses mixed with yeast and water and closed in a drum (a cylindrical container normally used to store chemicals or liquids measuring around 100 liters). The fermentation process takes not less than seven days and produces a very distinct smell of alcohol.

This can easily attract attention. To get around the risk of being smelled out or the drum being seen, a smart brewer like my mother had to bury the drum under my bed. This actually meant me getting the feel of a ready matured brew before anyone else. Anyway, after fermentation the result is a thick dark liquid. This is put into another drum ready for distillation. The distillation process could be done in two ways. One required a pipe that would bring out vapor that is cooled using water or a distillation process where the vapor cools off into an aluminum pot inside the drum.

The result is a clear and very strong alcohol. To test its alcoholic nature most of the customers would light it using a match box and its blue flame represented a clear alcohol substance. All the brewing activities took place very early in the morning between 3 AM and 5 AM so as not to attract attention from the neighbors or the police patrolling the area.

I was trained how to brew and keep watch so as not to have ourselves arrested. I remember I was caught several times while brewing, but given my young age, I could not be arrested. Cleverly, my mother recruited some of us in the family to be brewers. My younger sister would later pick up this business soon after my mother's retirement.

The most valuable lesson that I drew from my mother during her brewing days is that one can brew, sell, and never drink the alcohol. She did this amazingly as a "Mukurino" (this is a Christian-cum–traditional spiritual religion that believes in prophesies). The religion is recognized for extremism, which at times forces its followers not to mix or eat from those they consider "unclean" spiritually.

This brought out the contrast of who my mother was, as a believer and also as a hustler who required earthly money to keep us in school, fed, and clothed. She confesses that she stopped her involvement with the alcohol business the day I completed my secondary education. Her resolve was that we, her children, would never fail to study due to lack of school fees—unless we failed to see the importance of studying.

To her, educating a child was worth committing crime. I am not convinced that brewing and selling alcohol constitutes a crime when more than half the city's population cannot afford legally brewed alcohol.

. . .

The time is around 12:30 PM and the normal Mau Mau road (the road that cuts across the Mathare valley and runs adjacent to Juja road right from Kiamutesya all the way to Mabatini) is covered with a buzz of activities, mainly food vendors, firewood sellers, greengrocers. The street at this hour was busy with mainly school children who were grabbing fast food from the "Mama nitilie" (Tanzanian Swahili referring to women food vendors). We were having a visit to a community toilet project that was being renovated in the settlement, and our team was composed of a few community members mainly from the federation in charge of the project and some of the youths who were to be the beneficiaries of the project as their income-generating project.

As our team walked basically from the toilet to the road, we observed from one end of the road a group of youths numbering close to eight smartly dressed in suits or rather in an official manner to the point of attracting attention in the settlement. Their walk, dress, confidence, and persona suggested they were not ordinary visitors or strangers to this settlement. As a matter of fact, one would have thought they were guys out on a promo, working for a sales company, or special branch from the police or a very important entourage of government or diplomatic corps.

We immediately noticed that the busy activities that were going on along that section of the road where the group was visible almost came to a pause, like a sudden stop to loud music playing. The quietness came with a chilling fear that I personally felt gripping me and causing nervousness among our team members, and even the community leaders from the federation remained frozen for a moment; and at that time, as the group of youths approached us, we noticed some three policemen who were on patrol in the settlement diverting and taking a different route as if avoiding to meet the oncoming group of youths . . . this happened very naturally, so that a stranger one would not have suspected or understood what was happening.

As they approached I could not hold back my curiosity to want to know who the young men were, and to my own comfort and surprise I was able to spot at least three of them whom I had seen in the area before and had interacted with through the youth organization we had started engaging on waste management. I got further relief when they greeted us as they passed us and entered into a congested lane within the settlement and, whoop! they vanished. Immediately they were out of the road, life naturally returned to normal as if nothing had happened. Being a community organizer and with my slum life experience, I realized I was relieved just like the rest of the team the moment they left, meaning all of us had been captives of that fear. This was naturally followed up with lots of questions in my mind. Where were they coming from, all eight dressed in such an official manner at that time of the day? Why was everyone including the federation members scared? What about the police taking a different route and pretending they did not see them? Who were they? What was really happening?

I became curious and followed the story deeper. . . . As a start the community federation team reminded us that there was nothing to be afraid of since the young men meant no one in the community any harm. Then they told us that they were coming from town (basically the city center) and that this was when they were coming back to the settlement. The explanation continued to state that the group was a professional group of criminals and that their "game," or rather their job, is highly regarded and respected (literally) by some of the community members. Yes, any youth involved in crime was highly glorified by the rest of the community members. In fact one member of the federation told me that in the settlement of Kiamutesya you can find a family where three of its generations have been actively involved in crime. That is to say, some of the young men we saw had fathers and grandfathers who were all actively involved in crime. Hence, committing crime is normal family business as well as a community way of life.

Acknowledgments

JC would like to thank his students from the Urban Health Equity seminar and the Center for Global Healthy Cities at the University of California, Berkeley, for commenting on various chapters and sitting through presentations of draft material; Guillermo Jaimes for research in Pau da Lima Brazil; and Chantal Hildebrand, for her research and writing on women's health and sanitation in Nairobi, and Alice Sverdlik, on slum upgrading and health. He is grateful to all the partners in Kenya who are committed to improving the well-being and power of the urban poor, including Professor Peter Ngau (University of Nairobi) and his students. Thanks to the leaders and on-the-ground planners in Kenya, including Jane Weru, Jack Makau, Irene Karanja, Jason Weweru, David Mathenge, Baraka, and countless others within the Muungano and Shack/Slum Dwellers International (SDI) family—Asante Sana! Also a big thank you to Dr. Siddarth Agarwal for being so generous with his time and sharing his work with the Urban Health Research Center (UHRC) for this book.

LR would like to thank the students at UC Berkeley, Weill Medical College of Cornell University, University of California at San Francisco, and Federal University of Bahia, and at the Gonçalo Moniz Research Center of the Oswaldo Cruz Foundation in Salvador, Brazil, who have participated in our field studies since the early 1990s. He thanks the PhD and medical students Brendan Flannery, Michele Barocchi, Sara Tartof, Robert Snyder, Alon Unger, Guilherme S. Ribeiro, and postdoctoral fellow Mariel Marlow for their work in the informal settlements of Salvador and Rio de Janeiro; the many collaborators who made it all possible to do the work that led to many of the ideas expressed in this book, including Albert Ko, Mitermayer Galvao Reis, Beatriz Moreira, Edson Moreira, and Claudete A. Cardoso. He thanks Eva Raphael for reviewing and proofreading a draft of this book's chapters. Lastly, he thanks the Pau da Lima Urban Health Team and all the urban slum dwellers who struggle in their communities every day to make them a healthy place to live.

The following chapters in this volume have been adapted from previously published material:

Chapter 2: *PLoS Med.*, 4.10 (2007): e295.
DOI: 10.1371/journal.pmed.0040295.

Chapter 4: *Journal of Urban Health*. 84.1 (2007): 7–15.
DOI: 10.1007/s11524-007-9191-5.

Chapter 7: *PLoS Negl Trop Dis.* 2.4 (2008): e228.
DOI 10.1371/journal.pntd.0000228.

Chapter 8: *BMC Infectious Diseases,* 10:327 (2010).
DOI: 10.1186/1471-2334-10–327.

Chapter 12: *Environment and Urbanization,* 23.1 (2011): 13–28.
DOI: 10.1177/0956247811398589.

Chapter 13: *Social Science & Medicine,* 71.5 (2010): 935–40.

Introduction

JASON CORBURN AND LEE RILEY

Mjondolos, bustees, favelas, ghettos, slums. Different as they are by name, living conditions, and social and political factors, the populations living in these urban communities all face serious challenges to their safety, getting access to adequate medical care, and living lives free of disease-related disabilities. The people in these neighborhoods and the organizations they often form are among the twenty-first-century public health innovators. Slum dwellers in partnership with researchers, nongovernmental organizations (NGOs), and medical professionals are blazing new trails to access greater opportunities for their families to be healthy. Slum dwellers are building a new kind of urban health system, overcoming exclusion from economies and many basic services, and building new kinds of institutions and social arrangements that are changing not just their own lives but those of billions of people living in cities everywhere. This book aims to help tell their stories.

Addressing the human health challenges facing the millions of urban poor living in informal settlements or slums of the global South can seem overwhelming. Yet we were inspired to write this book by our work with slum dwellers. Time and again, from Salvador to Nairobi to India, slum dwellers would let us know that their health and that of their children formed a major impediment to improving their lives in so many other ways. Thus, we aimed for *Slum Health* to be responsive to and offer a practical guide for all those interested in improving the lives of the urban poor around the world.

As of 2015, not only does a majority of the world's population live in cities, but global poverty is increasingly moving from rural to urban areas. Wealth is increasingly concentrated in the hands of a few, and the percentage of the metropolitan-area population living in poverty is rising. In the growing cities of Latin America, Africa, and Asia, urban poverty is often associated with insecure living conditions—what we call slums in this book—and lack of basic services, political rights, and health care. These forces combine to coproduce poor health for many urban slum dwellers. Yet these generalizations are not the same from city to city or even within the same city; slums and the risks and opportunities slum dwellers face vary from place to place and over time. In this book we set out to dispel the all too common assumption that all slum dwellers need similar interventions—more care, more services, more rights, more economic opportunities, and so forth—and offer details concerning the nuances and challenges facing slum health in specific places: Salvador, Brazil, Nairobi, Kenya, and urban India.

We also want to acknowledge here (and we return to this point throughout the book) that recognizing the differences and unique characteristics of urban poor communities and the populations that live there involves questioning the word "slum" itself. We recognize the term "slum" is loaded with historical baggage that tends to be linked to dirty, disorganized, and dysfunctional places and people. "Slums" too often are assumed to be one thing: unhealthy places and people; and the term fails to acknowledge the assets, resources, and cultures of urban poor places and populations that can contribute to health and well-being. Some would prefer to use alternative, less emotive phrases to describe urban poor communities, such as "low-income communities," "informal settlements," "squatter colonies," "shantytowns," "self-built communities" or, depending on the country, "bustee," *bidonville,* "favela," *katchi abadi,* "barrio," or *kampung*. While we purposely use the term "slum" throughout this book to call attention to the inequities faced by many places and people, we by no means intend it to carry any derogatory associations. In short, "slum" here is used as an entry point for the reader to explore the variegated characteristics of places, populations, and practices that can all contribute to improved health and well-being for the millions of urban poor in the world.

We are not romanticizing the term "slum" or the living conditions faced by slum dwellers; nor are we blaming the poor for the living conditions they face; nor are we blaming the slum for "creating" unhealthy people. We recognize that forces often beyond the control of the urban poor continue to contribute to the formation and perpetuation of urban slums: from an anti-urban bias among national governments, or a retreat of the state from engaging with the complex issues of urban poverty, to political corruption that profits from urban poverty, to global neoliberal economic pressures that have weakened or privatized government services. This book aims not to grapple with all the forces that have created and perpetuate urban slums, but rather to recognize the human right of the urban poor to lead a healthy life and to offer some strategies toward this goal.

Some have viewed urban slums as natural and inevitable; as the rural poor move to cities, they seek low-cost housing near employment. Yet many urban slums around the world have expanded in the absence of economic growth in these same cities. Slums can grow in cities with declining as well as emerging economies. Similarly, others view urban slums as a stage in the development process; according to this theory, as the economic status of the urban poor improves, they move out of slums into other, presumably healthier neighborhoods. Yet there is a disturbingly low degree of intergenerational socioeconomic mobility for households living in urban poor neighborhoods and slum settlements around the world. As we highlight throughout this book, slum conditions are fundamentally a manifestation of institutions underinvesting in housing, infrastructure, and life-supporting services for the urban poor, not an inevitable consequence of urban growth. At the same time, understanding how the institutions of public health, city development, and other policy decisions have underdeveloped cities to coproduce slum conditions demands a critical look at the histories of colonialism, the "export" of urban planning decisions from the global North to the South, and the emergence of an anti-urban bias in international development. We briefly engage in these histories in chapter 1 and remain cognizant of the legacies of these decisions in efforts to promote slum health today.

While we focus on three regions of the world, some material in this book can be generalized to other urbanizing areas. However, we emphasize a bit of caution here since culture, political processes, and acceptable healthy living conditions do vary from place to place. Interventions should always be mindful of the histories of places and the biographies of the people living in urban areas. Thus, historical and contemporary context is a crucial factor in slum health and must never be ignored for some seemingly universal "best practice."

OUTLINE OF THE BOOK

This book is divided into five parts. Part I introduces the basic concepts and approaches to slum health research and action, and the challenges that need to be addressed. Chapter 1 discusses various definitions and nuances of the term "slum." It provides an overview of the contemporary slum health issues that were shaped by historical evolution of urban informal communities in the global South and the global North, including the United States. We explore how the health challenges of slums in cities of the global South in the twenty-first century often cannot be divorced from the legacies of institutions and policy decisions from the past 150 years in rich, global North countries. Part I introduces the coproduction approach to addressing slum health, which is expanded by specific applications of the approach in subsequent parts. Chapter 2 is a reprint of a paper that discusses suggestions for intervention and actions that may be taken based on better knowledge and research regarding slum-specific biological, structural, social, economic, and political factors that engender adverse health outcomes in slums. Chapter 3 describes five frameworks toward slum health equity: (1) coproduction of slum health, (2) a relational view of slum places, (3) ecosocial epidemiology, (4) urban systems science for the city, and (5) adaptive city management. We explore the extent to which the features of these frameworks exist in the research and practice discussed in each of the three sections on Brazil, Kenya and India. The last two chapters of this section discuss the challenges of slum health in the larger context of urban poverty and upgrading programs. Chapter 4 is a reprint of an article produced by a team of World Health Organization leaders articulating the challenges of urban health promotion. Chapter 5 is an original paper reviewing the health challenges and opportunities associated with urban slum upgrading.

Parts II–IV compare and contrast contemporary slum health issues in three regions of the world that serve as paradigms for major concepts and approaches to understanding slum health that we believe relevant to most regions of the world. We focus on urban Brazil, Kenya, and India because these are regions of the world shaped by different urbanization pressures, political changes, and economic conditions. Brazil is now a middle-income nation with an increasingly strong social support system. Social policies in Brazil—from wealth distribution to social security programs such as Bolsa Familia—are perhaps some of the most promising in the world for reducing urban poverty and addressing social and economic inequalities that contribute to health inequities in urban Brazil.

Yet, even with progressive policies, the number of urban poor in most Brazilian cities is on the rise, according to the 2010 Brazilian census. In Kenya, a new constitution in 2010 guaranteed the right to health, housing, and adequate sanitation. Part III explores the multiple ways slum dwellers and researchers are leading the way toward implementation of these human rights. Nairobi, Kenya's capital, is known for having some of Africa's largest and most unhealthy slums, so investigating the ways civil society groups are working to change living conditions, planning, and policy can offer insights for how to grapple with similar challenges in sub-Saharan Africa. Specifically, we explore how lack of secure land tenure—a chronic condition in urban slums and one that can limit investment in health-supporting infrastructure—does not have to be a barrier to slum health, and how resident-driven improvement projects focused on health can increase the security and legitimacy of settlements and slum dwellers. In India, the worlds' largest democracy, with some of the most polluted and unhealthy urban slums, we highlight the importance of comparative data and community innovation for slum health. The examples from urban India offer suggestions for how health infrastructure can both support community organizing and coproduction strategies that involve researchers and state institutions in urban health promotion. For instance, we highlight a case in urban India where community groups and state institutions negotiated a sanitation intervention that bypassed official infrastructure standards to meet both local needs and cost-effectiveness goals, ultimately ensuring that healthy infrastructure development was embedded in a broader poverty alleviation agenda.

In addition to organizing this book by three geographic regions of the world, a major theme this book explores is the interaction between the biology of disease ("the cell") and the structural, historical, social, economic, and political forces ("the street") that ultimately affects disease outcome and distribution in slums. A recent catastrophic world event illustrates the need for this type of exploration—the Ebola epidemic in West Africa. As of February 2015, more than 23,000 confirmed, probable, and suspected cases of Ebola and more than 9,300 Ebola-related deaths had been reported.[1] Although the Ebola epidemic was recognized as early as 1976, the magnitude of the 2014–2015 epidemic is unprecedented. In the early phase of this West African epidemic, a variety of factors were blamed: local cultural practices, poverty, inadequate health infrastructure, and political strife. However, these factors have always been known to be associated with Ebola epidemics. What was rarely mentioned in the international discourse concerning this epidemic was the fact that this was the first time in history that Ebola entered urban centers largely comprised of informal settlements. Slums were the "elephant in the room."[2] When a highly transmissible virus enters urban slums, the disease epidemic takes on a different characteristic, and its control requires understanding both the biology of the virus and the environmental and community social context in which this virus transmits itself. This observation is not limited to the Ebola virus. The world will witness and experience many other episodes of epidemics like this, caused by other highly transmissible agents (e.g., the Zika virus in Brazil), as well as noncommunicable diseases. This book discusses these interactions in chapters that focus on slum-specific infectious and noncommunicable diseases.

Part II, "From the Cell to the Street: Slum Health in Brazil," focuses on Salvador, Brazil, the third-largest city and the first colonial capital of Brazil. We explore how scientists and residents have built an action research program aimed at improving the health of residents Pau da Lima, one of the city's largest favelas. We examine how clinicians working in a local hospital discovered a disproportionate number of cases of leptospirosis, an infectious disease caused by the spirochete bacteria *Leptospira*, transmitted by rat urine. We highlight how clinical and community research was crucial for understanding this disease and other health issues faced by slum dwellers. We show how clinical and biomedical researchers and slum dwellers can combine their expertise to coproduce improvement in slum health.

In Part III, "Urban Upgrading and Health in Nairobi, Kenya," we focus on slum upgrading in Nairobi, Kenya. Kenya and Nairobi have a different colonial and cultural legacy than Brazil, one that presents this region with different challenges. While slavery and racism defined significant aspects of urbanization and health in Brazil, British colonialism in Nairobi organized the city into segregated land uses, with the largest and most productive areas reserved for Europeans, and marginalized land left for Indians and Africans. The infrastructure of colonial Nairobi was built to extract resources, not to facilitate internal movement or provision of services. Thus, the legacy of colonial land segregation and development decisions shapes Nairobi's slums today. In Mathare, the slum we focus on, residents live on steep slopes and flood-prone land sandwiched between rivers and highways. Almost all supporting services, including water, sewer, electricity, and health care, are "informal"—meaning that they are not provided by the state. Yet we highlight how slum dwellers and academic partners have gathered data to replan the community and successfully advocate for state-supplied services, primarily infrastructure. That story alone would be welcome among the many, more frequent cases of evictions and demolitions that slum dwellers face across the world. However, in Nairobi, the research and advocacy process also contributed to a new regional plan that includes Mathare within the larger fabric of the city and now acts as a model for inclusive urban development. Further, slum dwellers in Nairobi have participated in and significantly shaped new national policy on slum upgrading and prevention, ensuring that all slum dwellers will benefit from legal protections from evictions and human rights to water, sanitation, and health, just to name a few. In this section, we highlight how slum dwellers coproduce knowledge and action for their health and well-being, sometimes with and sometimes antagonistic to the state.

In Part IV, "Indian Cities and Slum Health Planning," we turn to India and the challenges faced in one of the world's largest and fastest-growing economies. India's 2010 census reported that about 93 million people, or about 21 percent of the total urban population, live in slums, and a substantial proportion of the slum population consists of squatters, migrant colonies, pavement dwellers, families living on construction sites, street children, and other vulnerable populations. Since at least 2011, India has been developing the National Urban Health Mission (NUHM), focused on the implementation of a healthy city framework in Indian cities and towns with the cooperation of local municipal bodies. The NUHM seeks to improve the health of the urban poor by facilitating equal access to available health services and strengthening the existing capacity of health delivery. The NUHM has designated 430 cities and towns across India for program implementation. In this section, we highlight the challenges Indian slum dwellers face in terms of access to basic infrastructure and services, including primary care. We emphasize the gendered dimensions of these inequalities and highlight the work of the Urban Health Resource Center (UHRC) in Delhi and how it has helped organize slum-dwelling women to identify core health issues and advocate for services.

Part V, comprising the final chapter of this book, addresses some of the gaps and future considerations regarding slum health. In particular, we highlight the need for more research especially in the area of noncommunicable diseases emerging in slum communities and their interaction with prevalent infectious diseases; development of new metrics designed to assess the disease burden in slums; new international, national, regional, and local policies directed at maximizing health in slums; and training in research and action to address the major gaps that persist in slum health coproduction.

Throughout this book, we seek to combine the viewpoints and voices of slum dwellers and outside professionals. We use interview and ethnographic data along with survey statistics, spatial mapping, and biological measures. We include discussions of science and medicine along with those of planning and policy. For us, this combination of methods, data, and viewpoints values multiple forms of expertise and recognizes that slum health science is as much political as technical.

The prelude narrates a brief reflection from one of our Kenyan slum-dwelling partners. The hope is to situate the reader in the everyday life of the slum dweller and to recognize the multiple challenges and even opportunities he or she might face for being healthy. We also aim to highlight that no slum dweller should be blamed for her or his lot in life and that those of us with privileges—in education, politics, resources, culture, or the like—can and must work in partnership with slum dwellers to improve their lives and living conditions. We hope this book inspires you to act.

NOTES

1. Centers for Disease Control (2015). *Morbidity and mortality weekly report* 64(7; February 27):186–87.

2. Snyder, R.E., Marlow, M.A., & Riley, L.W. (2014). Ebola in urban slums: The elephant in the room. *Lancet Glob Health* 2(12; December):e685.

PART I

Slum Health

Framing Research, Practice, and Policy

CHAPTER 1

From the Cell to the Street

Coproducing Slum Health

JASON CORBURN AND LEE RILEY

The first comprehensive report on the demographic, spatial, economic, legal, and social indicators of informal human settlements defined by the United Nations Expert Group as "slums" was published by UN-Habitat in 2003.[1] According to the UN, slums are human settlements that have the following characteristics: (1) inadequate access to safe water, (2) inadequate access to sanitation and other infrastructure, (3) poor structural quality of housing, (4) overcrowding, and (5) insecure residential status.[2] Yet, as we emphasize throughout this chapter, no single definition adequately captures the characteristics of "informal settlements" that contribute to poor health or well-being. For instance, the UN also defines informal settlements as unplanned squatter areas that lack street grids and basic infrastructure, with makeshift shacks erected on unsanctioned subdivisions of land. As we suggest in this chapter, to engage with slum health means to explore not just how physical deprivations in slums might influence disease and death, but also how economic poverty, social inequalities, and political disenfranchisement act to stymie well-being or support resilience.[*3] In short, we

* We draw from a range of works on slum and informal urbanization, including AlSayyad, N. (2004), "Urban informality as a 'new' way of life," in *Urban informality: Transnational perspectives from the Middle East, Latin America, and South Asia,* ed. A. Roy & N. AlSayyad (Lanham, MD: Lexington Books), 7–30; Arabindoo, P. (2011), "Rhetoric of the 'slum': Rethinking urban poverty," *City* 15:636–646; Turner, J. (1976), *Housing by People: Towards Autonomy in Building Environments* (New York: Pantheon

are interested in the combinations of knowledge and "expertise" needed to coproduce slum health. We expand on these ideas throughout this chapter.

In this chapter, we introduce the concept of coproducing slum health and how coproduction demands knowledge creation that integrates the laboratory and the street—or biological and community-based expertise. We first explore the importance of moving "from the cell to the street" for slum health using the example of rheumatic heart disease in the favelas of Brazil. We suggest that this disease, like so many others that are more prevalent in urban poor populations than nonpoor populations and communities, demands a multidisciplinary response and intervention strategy. This new polycentric knowledge-for-action process is a central feature of what we call coproducing slum health.

The chapter also suggests that moving toward slum health requires an understanding of how contemporary health issues may have come to be in urban slums. Thus, we offer a brief review of how medicine and public health "treated" urban slums from the late nineteenth through the end of the twentieth century. We suggest that public health justifications were often used to segregate the urban poor from other groups and often combined with racist views of slums and slum dwellers that blamed the poor for disease and "dirty" living conditions. We also suggest that this legacy remains with us today and is something slum health advocates must acknowledge and take on in their work. Unfortunately, most urban development in the twenty-first century, as proposed by governments, the private sector, and large international organizations, does not seem intent on addressing the health and living-condition needs of slum dwellers. Thus, we recognize that coproduction must always include the participation and expertise of slum dwellers and their civil society organizations. In this way, slum health ought to be understood as one important component of the "right to the city," whereby services, land, and the decision-making processes of the state act to serve, not sever, the well-being of the urban poor. We conclude the chapter with some principles of slum health that act to guide research and action.

Books; London: Marion Boyars); Gilbert, A.G. (2007), The return of the slum: Does language matter? *International Journal of Urban and Regional Research* 31:697–713.

FROM THE CELL TO THE STREET

City living can be beneficial for human health, since urban areas generally offer greater economic and educational opportunities, medical services, political and gender rights, affordable housing, and cultural, political, and religious expression. This holds true in both rich and poor cities of the global North and global South. Yet not everyone in cities can take advantage of these socially produced resources, and the poor and socially marginalized often experience health inequities, or differences in access to health-promoting resources that are unnecessary, avoidable, and unfair. As UN-Habitat and the World Health Organization (WHO) stated in their 2010 report *Hidden Cities: Unmasking and Overcoming Health Inequities in Urban Settings:*

> Health inequities are the result of the circumstances in which people grow, live, work and age, and the health systems they can access, which in turn are shaped by broader political, social and economic forces. They are not distributed randomly, but rather show a consistent pattern across the population, often by socioeconomic status or geographical location. No city—large or small, rich or poor, east or west, north or south—has been shown to be immune to the problem of health inequity.

Slum health is one way to begin to chip away at urban health inequities, such as those between urban, rural, and slum dweller populations.

As used in this book, "slum health" refers to the continual improvement of well-being, living conditions, access to life-affirming services and opportunities, and the reduction of risk, disability, danger, and disease for the urban poor, especially but not limited to the global South. Ensuring the conditions in which the urban poor and slum dwellers can be healthy requires the sharing of existing, and creation of new, knowledge across social and natural science disciplines, not just in medicine or public health. The actors in slum health must include governments, scientists, nongovernmental organizations, international institutions, the private sector, community-based organizations, and most important, slum dwellers and the urban poor themselves. Our view of slum health is consistent with the 1986 Ottawa Charter for health promotion, which emphasized that health is a "resource for everyday life, not the objective of living" and "is a positive concept emphasizing social and personal resources, as well as physical capacities."[4] Slum health aims to address the forces that contribute to the *distribution* of disease and well-being across populations and places, and the drivers of current and changing patterns of inequalities in well-being across population groups and places. By emphasizing *distribution* as distinct from *causation,* slum health investigates how social, political, and economic forces—from discrimination to economic policies and neighborhood environments—get "into our bodies" to shape which groups get sick, die earlier, and suffer unnecessarily.

Moving toward slum health demands deliberate action-research into the context-specific factors that might be making particular slum dwellers unhealthy and more susceptible to disease, disability, and death, and requires that this work must privilege partnerships, participation, and power-sharing between and among scientists, slum dwellers, and state-level decision makers. There is no one-size-fits-all approach. We call this collaborative approach *coproduction.*[5] In the coproduction of slum health, science is understood as dependent on the natural world, as well as historical events, social practices, material resources, and institutions that contribute to the construction, dissemination, and use of scientific knowledge. Political decision making, in the coproduction framework, does not take "scientific knowledge" as a given, but seeks to reveal how science is conducted, communicated, and used. The coproduction model problematizes knowledge and notions of expertise, challenging hard distinctions between expert and lay ways of knowing. Acting to improve slum health, under the coproduction approach, requires negotiation among the always partial and plural positions of professionals and laypeople. The coproduction model also destabilizes the dominant view in science policy making that scientific findings can be uncritically accepted as "fact" or "truth." The destabilizing stories and emphasis on the need for "negotiating expertise" suggest that a deliberative science is necessary for the coproduction of slum health knowledge for action.

Before going into greater detail on coproduction in practice, we offer an example below from our own research on the importance of linking "the cell to the street" and why a coproduction framework is crucial for slum health.

Rheumatic Heart Disease

Rheumatic heart disease (RHD) is a chronic heart condition triggered by multiple episodes of pharyngitis (sore throat) caused by the bacterium *Streptococcus pyogenes* or Group A streptococcus (GAS). It is an autoimmune disease in which the host immune response mounted against the bacterium causes collateral damage to the heart valves. RHD is a paradigm of a disease of urban slums. Pankaj Mishra once commented,

"Migrants from impoverished hinterlands, living without security, public health, and, often, clean water in the shantytowns of São Paulo, Lagos, Karachi, Dhaka, and Jakarta, have as much in common with each other as 'People Like Us'—the global class of businessmen, journalists, academics, and anti-terrorism experts—do among themselves."[6] In studying pharyngitis caused by GAS in children living in slum versus nonslum communities in Salvador, Brazil, Tartof, and colleagues (chapter 8) describe differences in the diversity of genotypes of GAS isolated in these children.[7] The study found that GAS strains that infect children of slums are more diverse and resemble the genotypes and level of diversity of strains found in low-income countries in Africa and the Pacific region, while strains that infect children attending the private clinic have genotypes and diversity that resemble those reported from high-income Western countries.[8] These children live in communities located within a few kilometers of each other, yet the GAS strains isolated from children residing in the slums versus nonslums were, respectively, more similar to those that occur in low-income and high-income countries in other continents of the world rather than to each other in the same city.[9, 10]

This difference in strain diversity may be contributing to the higher prevalence of RHD in the slums of Salvador, and may itself result from social disparity unique to the slum community. Addressing the social disparity issues only, however, may not be sufficient to correct the problem of RHD that results directly from the biological disparity revealed through rigorous molecular epidemiological studies.

Often, discussions related to social determinants of disease do not address the biological factors that actually cause the disease. We discuss RHD as an example of a disease of urban slums to demonstrate why biological determinants of disease must be included as part of a discourse on social determinants of disease to understand how social and biological disparity interacts to affect disease occurrence and distribution in different communities.

Sore throat, of course, is an infection that everyone experiences many times during childhood and adult life. GAS pharyngitis is one of the most common infectious diseases among children everywhere in the world, including developed countries. While most pharyngitis episodes are caused by viruses, those caused by GAS require antibiotic treatment. Without treatment, the infection, especially after multiple such episodes, can trigger immunologically mediated complications including rheumatic fever (RF) and RHD. RHD, which follows repeated bouts of RF, is characterized by progressive damage to the heart valves, leading to complications such as congestive heart failure (CHF), stroke, and even death. The damaged heart must be surgically repaired or replaced with artificial valves. RHD is rarely diagnosed today in developed countries, but the disease is responsible for 12 to 65 percent of hospitalizations for cardiovascular disease in developing countries, and is the leading cause of valvular damage requiring surgery in China.[11] The mean age of those with RHD in Brazil who develop complications such as CHF and mitral valve regurgitation was 9–12 years in the early 2000s.[12,13] These valvular damages that require surgical repair may have to undergo repeated repairs later in life. Fifteen years ago, it was estimated that the societal cost just of RF for Brazil was over $51 million a year.[14] A large proportion of RF and RHD in the world occur among children residing in informal settlements.[15,16,17] Thus, a simple sore throat, when it occurs in slums, affects these communities in a substantially disparate manner.

The motivation behind the study of GAS pharyngitis in Salvador was to address one hypothesis about RHD occurrence: that GAS strain differences contribute to RHD pathogenesis.[18] In a follow-up study, the same group of investigators attempted to assess the burden of RHD in Salvador.[19] An echocardiographic survey of the entire population would have been the ideal way to make such an estimate, but it would have been impractical and tremendously costly. Instead, the investigators reviewed medical charts of patients who underwent cardiac valvular surgical procedures performed by cardiac surgeons in all the hospitals of Salvador between 2002 and 2005.[20] Of 491 valvular heart surgery patients identified, RHD accounted for 60 percent of the surgeries.[21] The mean age of those with RHD was 37 years (25–48), compared to 69 (63–77) for degenerative valve disease and 49 (38–68) for endocarditis.[22] The surgery was paid for by the public sector in 71, 32, and 18 percent of cases, respectively.[23] Thus, a large proportion of the RHD patients who underwent valvular surgery were young adults from low-income communities in Salvador. Since RHD requiring surgery is only the "tip of the iceberg," this observation suggests that a large number of people in Salvador live with RHD, most of whom likely reside in slum communities. Clearly, RHD is a disease that disproportionately affects low-income residents of Salvador.

Social and Environmental Determinants of Disease

We recognize that structural, economic, legal, and environmental differences between urban slums and nonslums contribute to many differences in health outcomes in these communities.[24] It should be stressed, however,

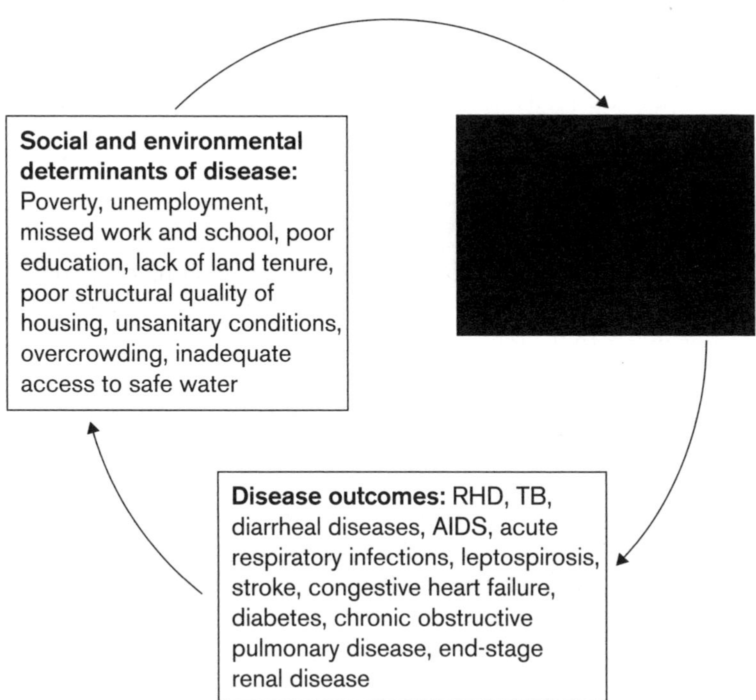

Social and environmental determinants of disease:
Poverty, unemployment, missed work and school, poor education, lack of land tenure, poor structural quality of housing, unsanitary conditions, overcrowding, inadequate access to safe water
Disease outcomes: RHD, TB, diarrheal diseases, AIDS, acute respiratory infections, leptospirosis, stroke, congestive heart failure, diabetes, chronic obstructive pulmonary disease, end-stage renal disease

FIGURE 1.1. Cycle of social and environmental determinants of disease, the "black box," and disease outcomes predominant in informal settlements. The "black box" represents biological determinants of disease that are not often known. Opening this black box may identify new intervention strategies that complement those based on addressing the social and environmental determinants of disease.

that these disparities do not *cause* disease but do explain their distribution across populations and places. Bacteria, viruses, parasites, fungi, and immunological responses to these infectious agents cause diseases. Mutations that occur in human genes contribute to other diseases. Disease is a biological process resulting from disruption of a homeostatic state of a healthy body. Resiliency is the ability of the human body to maintain an equilibrium state despite its exposures to external stresses. One of the major gaps in our knowledge regarding social determinants of disease is this biological process—often a "black box"—that lies in the pathway between social disparity and disease outcome (fig. 1.1). What are the biological and social mechanisms through which poverty, social disparity, and injustice influence RHD, or for that matter, tuberculosis (TB), HIV-AIDS, diarrheal diseases, acute respiratory infections, leptospirosis, and many other infectious diseases, as well as complications of chronic noncommunicable diseases common in urban slums? Tartof et al. addressed the "black box" standing in the way between living in slum communities and pharyngitis and found disparity at the bacterial cell level among GAS strains circulating in Salvador. This biological disparity may influence who develops RHD and who does not.[25] How does this happen? How do bacteria "decide" which children to infect with which strain?

Although there is no conclusive evidence, the great diversity of GAS strains in Salvador observed among slum children may be one factor that contributes to the increased occurrence of RHD in slum communities. Streptococcal organisms are prone to high frequency of horizontal gene transfers. Such transfers may be facilitated by crowding, one of the defining conditions of urban slums.[26] Exposure to a wider variety of strains may induce a wider spectrum of immune responses, some of which may be detrimental to the infected host. Thus, crowding may directly affect the selection of rheumatogenic strains. In this way, social disparity can be connected to the biological disparity observed among the slum children of Salvador.

Vicious Cycle of Disparity

Unfortunately, this chain of disparity does not end with RF or RHD. Fifteen years ago, Terreri and colleagues assessed the socioeconomic impacts of RF on 100 low-income subjects under 18 years of age with RF in São Paulo, Brazil.[27] During a follow-up of at least one year, these patients had 1,657 medical consultations, 22 hospital admissions, and 4 admissions to intensive care unit.[28] Cumulative workdays missed was calculated to be 901, and about 5 percent of their parents lost their jobs. RF patients showed a high rate of school failure (22%). Overall, the cost of RF for the family was estimated to be about 1.3 percent of the annual family income.[29] If RF can cause this level of socioeconomic disruption, RHD is likely to exert even more of a burden in communities where this disease is prevalent. The socioeconomic disruption caused by these diseases further exacerbates the structural and environmental conditions that facilitate GAS transmission, which then creates conditions that favor immunological complications characterized by RF and RHD, which, in turn, causes more socioeconomic disruption, and so forth in an endless cycle (fig. 1.1).

The biological disparity unmasked by Tartof et al. in Salvador has implications for public health intervention. An experimental multivalent vaccine formulation against GAS has been developed to include coverage against predominant *emm* types circulating in high-income Western countries (USA, Canada, and Europe). Steer and colleagues described GAS *emm* type global distribution and found that the experimental vaccine formulation would have poor efficacy in Africa and the Pacific, where the *emm* types covered by the vaccine were found to be uncommon.[30] Interestingly, Tartof et al. found that 36 percent of all the *emm* types isolated from children attending the private clinic were *emm* types 1 and 12, the predominant types in high-income countries included in the experimental vaccine formulation; these *emm* types comprised less than 20 percent of the isolates from slum children. If this vaccine were to be introduced into Salvador, it would show differential efficacy in the two communities of the same city. Thus, even an intervention against a disease could exhibit disparity in efficacy that is biologically determined. This means that attempts to enhance vaccine coverage, increase health care service access, provide better health education, and other types of public health intervention in the vulnerable population would have a limited effect on disease control if this biological disparity is not addressed. These attempts to correct the social and structural disparity are all well intentioned, even evidence based, and may eventually be effective, but they may miss the opportunity for a speedier correction of the health outcomes in question.

However, the observation that there is this disparity at the molecular level creates an opportunity to develop new strategies to address this health problem that is almost exclusively a problem of people residing in urban informal settlements. With this new knowledge, a vaccine formulation against GAS can now be designed to include those *emm* types circulating in slum communities. Such a vaccine formulation would be effective against GAS pharyngitis not only among slum-dwelling children in Salvador, Brazil, but also among children in low-income countries of Africa and the Pacific region. By decreasing GAS pharyngitis incidence, the vaccine could reduce RF and RHD, which in turn could prevent the spiral descent into poverty and social disparity. Opening the "black box" with better science and epidemiology might break this vicious cycle. Such an approach is a major component of slum health research and coproducing slum health.

COPRODUCING SLUM HEALTH IN PRACTICE

As noted above, coproduction entails scientific and medical professionals and laypeople working together to generate good data, understand challenges, generate appropriate interventions, and monitor and evaluate what is working, for whom, and over what time period. Elinor Ostrom defined coproduction as "a process through which inputs from individuals who are not 'in' the same organization are transformed into goods and services."[31] Ostrom noted how communities in northeastern Brazil contributed to the design and implementation of a condominial sewer system and, by doing so, dramatically improved urban services in the poorest neighborhoods in Brazilian cities.

One health-promoting "resource" that emerges in this idea of coproduction is social capital—both bonding and bridging capital. Bonding social capital results when community members come together to work on a common challenge and together their collective knowledge and power work as "capital" to deliver more than individuals working independently. Bridging capital is created when community members who already know or work with one another build alliances and working partnerships with unlikely allies, such as a community partnering with an academic scientist or a slum dweller organization working with state-run water and sewer companies. The networks created through co-researching, coplanning, and co-delivery of services may also shift from a top-down centralized model to one that is more polycentric and adaptive, as it must then respond to different needs and expertise.[32] A key goal in slum health coproduction is to ensure community residents are able to participate in and shape the technical and political processes that can deliver immediate service and health needs, while at the same time begin to change and decentralize professional and state institutions to ensure greater long-term resident control over resources and decision making.[33]

A major challenge in coproduction is that the process often assumes what may not necessarily be the case: that all community members and households have equal access to the process and resulting services, that there is no exclusion on the grounds of income, gender, or ethnicity, and that the relationships between professionals and the urban poor will be fair, consensual, and not corrupted. In other words, power must be taken seriously into account and managing conflicts must be part and parcel of coproduction.[34] However, coproduction also acknowledges that too often some resources and technologies for improving slum health rely on investments at a scale best handled by governments (e.g., municipal waste water treatment), while other resources may best be delivered by local people.

Coproduction can happen in the laboratory setting when disease sufferers inform scientists' experiments and hypotheses. Coproduction

Exposed Populations in the Urban Setting

- There are 150 million street children worldwide. Forty percent of them are homeless.[1]
- A study in Zambia shows that two-thirds of urban households have lost their breadwinner to HIV-AIDS.[2]
- At least once every five years, 60 percent of those living in cities of 100,000 inhabitants or more are victims of one form of crime or another.[3] Violent crime is particularly prevalent in Latin America's large cities, disproportionately affecting men in low-income neighborhoods,[4] with relative risk of 5.1 in the lowest versus the highest measure of living standards.[5]
- In Nairobi, where 60 percent of the city's population lives in slums, child mortality in the slums is 2.5 times greater than in other areas of the city.[6]
- In Manila's slums, up to 39 percent of children between ages 5 and 9 are already infected with TB—this is twice the national average.[7]
- In Latin America, the average urban woman's employment income is only 58 to 77 percent of men's.[8]

1. Pangaea. Street Children—Community Children. http://pangaea.org/street_children/kids.htm (accessed February 15, 2007).
2. UNICEF. (2003). Africa's Orphaned Generations. New York: United Nations Children Emergency Fund.
3. Vanderschuren, F. (1996). From violence to justice and security in cities. *Environ Urban* 8(1):93–112.
4. Barata, R.B., Ribeiro, M.C., Guedes, M.B., & de Moraes, J.C. (1998). Intra-urban differentials in death rates from homicides in the city of Sao Paulo, Brazil, 1988–1994. *Soc Sci Med* 47(1):19–23.
5. Macedo, A.C., Paim, J.S., Silva, L.M., & Costa, M.M. (2001). Violence and social inequalities: Mortality rates due to homicides and life conditions in Salvador, Brazil. *Rev Saude Publica* 35(6):515–522.
6. UN-Habitat Features. The urban penalty: The poor die young. United Nations Human Settlements Programme. http://www.unhabitat.org/documents/media_centre/sowcr2006/SOWCR%2022.pdf (accessed 2007).
7. Wallerstein, C. (1999). Tuberculosis ravages Philippines slums. *Br Med J* 319(7202):402.
8. PAHO. (2005). Gender, health, and development in the Americas: Basic indicators 2005. Washington, DC: Panamerican Health Organization.

can occur at the bedside when clinicians take seriously the social, economic, and everyday "exposures" described by their patients. Coproduction can occur in government policymaking when slum dwellers help design budget priorities and appropriate rules and enforcement strategies for ensuring all city dwellers, no matter their economic status or ethnicity, have adequate access to services and life-supporting resources.

STRUCTURE AND EVOLUTION OF SLUMS

A Brief History of Slum Health

In practice, every city in the world seems to define slums differently. In Victorian England the term "slum" was used to describe low-quality, working-class housing and evolved over time to include settlements built on cheap or marshy land.[35, 36] Nineteenth-century city governments and law, in particular the UK's Artisans' and Labourers' Dwellings Improvement Act 1875, legislated the clearing of slums because they were labeled as "unhealthy areas."[37] By the turn of the twentieth century, Sir Ebenezer Howard, a British social reformer, published *Garden Cities of Tomorrow,* which advocated the removal of "unhealthy" urban slums and the construction of green suburbs.[38] Howard's ideal was his antidote to the growing concern of unhealthy urban slums; based on his designs, he founded the Garden City Movement. The ideals of European and North American urban planning—particularly those aimed at reducing epidemics of urban disease—would lead to the export of slum planning under the guise of human health protection around the world.

Colonialism and Slum Health

Colonial powers around the world frequently used public health knowledge to discriminate against indigenous populations living in urban slums. Almost all migrants to colonial cities had to make or find their own housing. Laws pertaining to private property were almost nonexistent for indigenous peoples in colonialized Asia, Africa, and the Caribbean in the nineteenth century. Doctors became all-purpose experts, and authorities frequently put them in charge of everything from "native affairs" to town or city planning.[39]

By the end of the nineteenth century the cities of Bombay and Calcutta were among the largest in the world, with burgeoning slum populations and mortality rates three to four times those in England, the seat of colonial power.[40] According to some estimates, more than 2,800 people per week were dying of the plague in Bombay.[41] Even though very little was known about the causes of and reasons for the spread of the plague at the time, colonial medical authorities tended to blame the racial characteristics, living conditions, and practices of the indigenous populations. Yet many indigenous populations had devised sophisticated drainage and water supply systems in cities, particularly in India, that kept them healthy for generations before colonial powers enforced widespread neglect of traditional methods.[42]

Medical attention focused on protecting the health of Europeans and reducing threats to trade and commerce. A report from the Liverpool School of Tropical Medicine in 1900 addressed the malaria epidemic in Lagos:

> So closely associated indeed are malaria and the native in Africa, and so wonderfully constant is the presence of anopheles where natives are collected in numbers, that we doubt whether any operations, now possible, directed against anopheles will do much to diminish the danger of malarial infection. In fact, in Africa the primary aim should be to remove susceptible Europeans from the midst of malaria. To stamp out native malaria is at present chimerical, and every effort should be turned to the protection of the Europeans.[43]

British sanitary engineers were sent to such colonial cities as Singapore, Calcutta, Pune, Lagos, and Cape Town to help control infectious disease outbreaks. In practice, sanitarians tended to subject indigenous customary practices to inspection, regulation, and disciplinary action—including razing homes and markets to "ventilate" slums of their "unhealthy" dark, dirty, and smelly conditions.[44] The increased colonial control over local practices prompted indigenous populations to resist the limited sanitary, hygienic, and medical interventions colonial authorities offered them.[45]

Miasma—foul or dirty air—was the leading theory of disease causation among the colonial sanitarians. One popular remedy was new road construction and widening, since these physical interventions were thought to increase the free passage of air, thereby reducing the spread of disease.[46] Some colonial authorities and planners questioned the rationality and morality of slum clearance as a sustainable hygienic policy. Scottish town planner Patrick Geddes, working in India, wrote that "the policy of sweeping clearances should be recognized for what I believe it is; one of the most disastrous and pernicious blunders in the chequered history of sanitation."[47] Yet urban renewal of "unsanitary" slum housing remained a common practice.[48] These strategies also helped justify the physical separation of Europeans from indigenous populations—or racial residential segregation.

Biomedical Research in the Tropics

Today, several research institutions and journals bear the phrase "Tropical Medicine" in their title. Much of so-called "tropical medicine" deals with infectious diseases that were or are still prevalent in the world's tropical regions. Clearly, it is a terminology introduced by researchers from the global North working in the global South. (Interestingly, research on infectious diseases of high prevalence in the global North, such as Lyme disease, is not referred to as "temperate zone medicine.")

Biomedical research in the tropics coevolved with many of the public health interventions introduced into these regions described above. It was in the latter half of the 1800s that the "germ theory" of infectious disease, first proposed in the sixteenth century, came to be widely accepted by the biomedical community and to be applied to the study of highly prevalent diseases, including those that exerted a heavy economic toll on Europeans and European-Americans extracting natural resources in Africa, the Americas, and Asia. These diseases included cholera (which occurred in epidemics that spread across the globe, including large European and North American cities), malaria (which may have contributed to the expansion of African slavery in the Americas), yellow fever (the control of which was critical for the construction of the Panama Canal), and what are now considered "neglected tropical diseases," including schistosomiasis, leishmaniasis, American trypanosomiasis (Chagas disease), African trypanosomiasis (African sleeping sickness), and other protozoan and helminthic diseases. The early biomedical research on these diseases focused on identifying their causes, life cycle, and modes of transmission and on development of drugs to treat them.

Today, we know a lot about these diseases. Contemporary biomedical research on them involves pathogenesis, immunology, microbial genetics, drug-target identification, rational vaccine design, and host susceptibility genetics. Much of this research takes place in the global North, but in the past thirty years, North-South collaborative research projects have become increasingly common, supported by government institutions such as the US National Institutes of Health, foundations such as the Bill and Melinda Gates Foundation and the Burroughs Wellcome Trust, the World Health Organization, and nongovernmental organizations (NGOs).

Despite the new knowledge and billions of dollars spent, however, the above-mentioned diseases remain important causes of morbidity and mortality among vulnerable populations, especially in the global tropical South. In fact, a licensed vaccine is available today for only two of the diseases mentioned above—cholera and yellow fever. Furthermore, the rise of urban informal settlements has created new challenges for biomedical research beyond the traditional, so-called tropical diseases described above. These include infectious diseases such as tuberculosis, childhood diarrhea, acute respiratory infections, leptospirosis, rheumatic heart disease, and, of course, HIV-AIDS. Later chapters highlight the need for new biomedical research to address the rising prevalence of noncommunicable diseases and their interaction with existing infectious diseases in slum communities of the global South. Throughout, we emphasize that the challenges of biomedical research are not just the basic science obstacles associated with these diseases but the slum-specific context in which diseases occur.

Haiti was a cholera-free nation for more than one hundred years until October 2010, when, after a major earthquake, a cholera epidemic exploded in the country, killing, to date, more than eight thousand people. Like the Ebola epidemic in West Africa, the Haitian cholera epidemic was largely exacerbated by the introduction of the agent of cholera, *Vibrio cholerae,* into large urban informal settlements that existed prior to the earthquake but were disrupted further by this natural disaster. The epidemic occurred despite the availability of vaccines, effective drugs, and knowledge about how to control the disease. Both the cholera epidemic in Haiti and the Ebola epidemic in West Africa dramatically demonstrate that the challenges of slum health are not only the biomedical research of the pathogens that cause disease but also the community dynamics of these diseases shaped by slum conditions. Below we discuss these other challenges.

Institutional Racism and Slum Health

Understanding the spatial segregation of the urban poor and related health outcomes demands an engagement with structural racism, or the ways multiple institutions and decisions—affecting housing, transportation, medicine, citizenship, employment, and education—disadvantage and marginalize groups based on race, ethnicity, caste, religion, tribe, or whatever socially constructed category. Slum clearance and evictions of the urban poor from their communities from the nineteenth through twentieth century cannot be linked to medical and public health beliefs alone. In the nineteenth and the first half of the twentieth century, scientific racism also justified action (or inaction) against slum dwellers. Eugenics was the pseudoscience arguing that slum dwellers' poverty, lack of resources, disease, and early death were due to their inherent racial inferiority, not the result of deliberate policies or social and political discrimination.[49] Francis Galton coined the term "eugenics," and the movement argued that the "feebleminded" and destitute segments of urban society suffered from inherited genetic defects.[50] One solution of the eugenic societies that emerged in cities around the world was to control reproduction of slum dwellers, generally through forced sterilization. Eugenics advocates challenged the sanitarian ideas that reducing poverty and improving environmental and housing conditions would actually improve the health of the poor and were worth the expense.[51]

Sir William John Ritchie Simpson (1855–1931) was one of the most influential tropical medicine physicians and colonial public health authorities in the early twentieth century. A founder of the London School of Medicine and Tropical Medicine, Simpson served on public health commissions in South Africa, Hong Kong, Calcutta, West Africa, East Africa, and Northern Rhodesia. His classic text, *Maintenance of Health in Tropics* (1916), blamed the "customs of the local people" for the spread of many diseases and recommended that European housing should "not be close to native huts."

In North America, W.E.B. Du Bois, among others, challenged the eugenic medical and scientific view that inherent racial inferiority was to blame for the health of the urban poor, particularly African Americans. In his 1906 edited volume, *The Health and Physique of the Negro American,* Du Bois used statistics from northern and southern cities to argue that health inequities facing African Americans were a consequence of their poorer economic, social, and sanitary conditions as compared to those of whites. Du Bois noted:

> If the population were divided as to social and economic condition the matter of race would be almost entirely eliminated. Poverty's death rate in Russia shows a much greater divergence from the rate among the well-to-do than the difference between Negroes and white Americans. . . . Even in consumption all the evidence goes to show that it is not a racial disease but a social disease. The rate in certain sections among whites in New York and Chicago is higher than the Negroes of some cities.[52]

Du Bois directly challenged Frederick Hoffman's widely read text *Race Traits and Tendencies of the American Negro.* Hoffman enlisted science to claim that "it is not the conditions of life, but in race and heredity that we find the explanation of the fact to be observed in all parts of the globe, in all times and among all people, namely the superiority of one race over another, and of the Aryan race over all."[53] Du Bois replied directly to these claims:

> The undeniable fact is, then, that in certain diseases the Negroes have a much higher rate than the whites, and especially in consumption, pneumonia and infantile diseases. The question is: Is this racial? Mr. Hoffman would

> lead us to say yes, and to infer that it means that Negroes are inherently inferior in physique to whites. But the difference in Philadelphia can be explained on other grounds than upon race. The high death rate of Philadelphia Negroes is yet lower than the whites of Savannah, Charleston, New Orleans and Atlanta.[54]

While eugenics was discredited, structural racism persisted within many urban policy decisions.†

By the 1940s, the United States Housing Authority and New York City's Public Health Department blamed slums for crime and infant mortality and were advocating removing slums and replacing them with modern, high-rise buildings. The American Public Health Association published a guide titled "Planning the Neighborhood" in 1948 that also recommended removing older slums in cities and suggested that the model of healthy housing was new, suburban-style development.[55] Slums and slum dwellers became synonymous with unhealthy places and populations. As Gilbert notes: "The most worrying ingredient in most people's use of the word 'slum,' therefore, is the survival of these wholly negative connotations. Slum dwellers are not just people living in poor housing; they are considered by others to be people with personal defects. In Brazil, a *favelado* is not just someone who lives in a favela, he or she is thought to be someone who deserves to live there."[56] Slums often generated fear in the minds and actions of those who do not live there, and the institutional response was largely to eliminate, not improve, slums. "Slum" had effectively become a pejorative, associated with unhealthiness, no matter the context or time period.[57]

American federal housing policies instituted by the Federal Housing Administration (FHA) from the 1930s through the 1950s focused on developing new, single-family suburban homes by offering mortgage insurance for new homes but not older ones in cities. The FHA also issued technical guidelines for neighborhood design, rejecting the urban

† By "structural racism," we mean that seemingly neutral policies and practices can function in racist ways by disempowering communities of color and perpetuating unequal historical conditions. Powell notes that a structural racism lens helps us analyze: how housing, education, employment, transportation, health care, and other systems interact to produce racialized outcomes. Such a model allows us to move beyond a narrow merit-based, individualized understanding of society to show how all groups are interconnected and how structures shape life chances. At the level of cultural understanding, the structural model shows how the structures we create, inhabit, and maintain in turn recreate us by shaping identity and imparting social meaning. Chief among the processes in a structural model that connect institutions to identity formation is the relationship between racial identity and geography . . . the racialization of space (Powell 2007, 793).

grid pattern and instead mandating that new residential subdivisions, in order to take advantage of federally insured mortgages, be designed using cul-de-sacs and curvilinear streets. These federally mandated suburban design patterns would set the stage for late-twentieth-century suburban sprawl. The Housing Act of 1949 institutionalized urban renewal, whereby municipalities began razing "slum" neighborhoods and displacing thousands of poor, mostly African American residents. Urban renewal was a program and theory that aimed to remove downtown blight—still viewed as the cause of moral evil and the breeding ground for disease—and rebuild whole sections of the city using the best of modern technology and scientifically rational design. Yet urban renewal tended to only increase poverty for residents of poor neighborhoods, because either their homes were replaced with inadequate public housing or, as was more often the case, private real estate developers acquired the downtown land cheaply and opted not to build new housing, but instead expensive high-rise office towers. Not only were neighborhoods physically fractured, but social and emotional ties, trust, and notions of collective efficacy were also severed by urban renewal, further diminishing the health-promoting resources available for African Americans. Shut out from most new suburbs, African Americans were denied other health benefits that can come with home ownership, such as capital accumulation, access to better-funded schools, and participation in the growing economy.[58]

Cities with Slums: A Right to the City for All

While the 2015 UN Sustainable Development Goal (SDG) 11 aims to "make cities inclusive, safe, resilient and sustainable" and upgrade slums by 2030,[59] many cities in the global South continued to evict squatters and demolish slums, rather than develop strategies to improve the health and well-being of the urban poor.‡[60] Yet international institu-

‡ Cf. Africa: Slum dweller representatives denounce forced evictions, IRIN Humanitarian News and Analysis, March 22, 2012, http://www.irinnews.org/report/95131/africa-slum-dweller-representatives-denounce-forced-evictions (accessed November 18, 2015); Slumdwellers evicted by railway officials, *The Hindu,* July 13, 2014, http://www.thehindu.com/news/cities/Visakhapatnam/slumdwellers-evicted-by-railway-officials/article6206320.ece (accessed November 18, 2015). Egypt: Stop forced evictions and consult slum dwellers, Amnesty International, August 23, 2011, http://www.amnestyusa.org/research/reports/egypt-stop-forced-evictions-and-consult-slum-dwellers-to-resolve-housing-crisis (accessed February 13, 2016); Dhaka slum dwellers live under threat of eviction, *The Guardian,* April 11, 2012, http://www.theguardian.com/global-development/2012/apr/11/dhaka-bangladesh

tions and governments have changed their approach to urban slums in the global South, and the impacts on health can be significant. For instance, from the 1960s through the 1970s, newly independent countries often continued the colonial governments' approach to slums and slum dwellers, which viewed the settlements as illegal and the temporary result of rural-to-urban migration. Slums and informal urban settlements were often omitted from land use maps, instead being shown as areas of undeveloped land.[61] Governments often responded to slums with widespread evictions and razing of squatter settlements.

International institutions such as the World Bank began to have a significant influence on slums in the 1970s as they financed large-scale urban development and slum clearance as part of what were often called "sites and services" schemes.[62] These large projects turned out to be a major challenge for emerging governments in the South, since their scale and costs tended to put countries in significant debt to international institutions and were difficult to manage.[63] A second generation of slum upgrading in the 1980s and into the '90s emerged that argued that governments should be "enablers" of affordable housing and community development, rather than providers.[64]

Yet the grip of international debt often forced governments in the global South to prioritize loan repayments over constructing, delivering, and effectively managing basic urban services.[65] The UN's Cities Without Slums Action Plan and 2003 *Challenge of Slums* reports emphasized reversing the pressures on governments in the South to attend to priorities of international financial institutions and instead provide for the needs of the urban poor: "The main single cause of increases in poverty and inequality during the 1980s and 1990s was the retreat of the state. The redirection of income through progressive taxation and social safety nets came to be severely threatened by the ascendancy of neoliberal economic doctrines that explicitly 'demanded' an increase in inequality."[66] As civil society and NGOs gained a larger voice in development decisions in the 1990s, they challenged the eviction-relocation and "sites and services" approaches to slums. Instead, this new approach was fostered by increased awareness at the international level of the right to housing and protection against forced eviction and the definition of new national

-slum-dwellers-eviction (last accessed November 18, 2015); Slum dwellers are defying Brazil's grand design for Olympics, *New York Times,* March 4, 2012, http://www.nytimes.com/2012/03/05/world/americas/brazil-faces-obstacles-in-preparations-for-rio-olympics.html?pagewanted=all&_r=0 (last accessed November 18, 2015).

and local political agendas in the context of an emergent civil society as well as processes of democratization and decentralization. By 2009, the World Bank's urban strategy set forth in *Systems of Cities: Harnessing Urbanization for Growth and Poverty Alleviation* articulated a shift in focus to in situ slum upgrading, which emphasized improving urban slums while current residents stayed in their communities and were supported to improve their own housing, infrastructure, and social and economic conditions.[67] The World Bank report also launched its "decade of the city," in which inclusive or "pro-poor" urban growth was viewed as an essential aspect of human development.

PARTICIPATORY SLUM UPGRADING FOR HEALTH

Participatory slum upgrading, advanced by NGOs and international organizations in the early 2000s, consists of physical, social, economic, organizational, and environmental improvements undertaken cooperatively and locally among citizens, community groups, businesses, and local authorities. The Cities Alliance defines slum upgrading as a physical, social, and political transformation:

> Slum upgrading is a process through which informal areas are gradually improved, formalised and incorporated into the city itself, through extending land, services and citizenship to slum dwellers. It involves providing slum dwellers with the economic, social, institutional and community services available to other citizens. These services include legal (land tenure), physical (infrastructure), social (crime or education, for example) or economic. Slum upgrading is not simply about water or drainage or housing. It is about putting into motion the economic, social, institutional and community activities that are needed to turn around downward trends in an area. These activities should be undertaken cooperatively among all parties involved—residents, community groups, businesses as well as local and national authorities if applicable. The activities tend to include the provision of basic services such as housing, streets, footpaths, drainage, clean water, sanitation, and sewage disposal. Often, access to education and health care are also part of upgrading. In addition to basic services, one of the key elements of slum upgrading is legalising or regularising properties and bringing secure land tenure to residents. Ultimately, upgrading efforts aim to create a dynamic in the community where there is a sense of ownership, entitlement and inward investment in the area.[68]

The implication of participatory slum upgrading is that all urban residents, but particularly those historically excluded and marginalized, ought to have a right to the social, economic, political, and health benefits that city living offers.

Delivering the benefits of urban living and city management to all is the main idea behind the concept of the right to the city. The "right to the city" idea was first articulated by the urban theorist Henri Lefebvre but has gained increased attention as a framework for improving the health of the urban poor.[69, 70] The right to the city has been described as more than just individual rights, extending to the collective power to influence decisions and direct resources of the state to those most in need:

> The right to the city is far more than the individual liberty to access urban resources: it is a right to change ourselves by changing the city. It is, moreover, a common rather than an individual right since this transformation inevitably depends upon the exercise of a collective power to reshape the processes of urbanization. The freedom to make and remake our cities and ourselves is . . . one of the most precious yet most neglected of our human rights.[71]

The World Charter on the Right to the City defines the right to the city as "the equitable use of cities within the principles of sustainability, democracy, equity, and social justice. It is the collective right of the inhabitants of cities, in particular of the vulnerable and marginalized groups, that confers upon them legitimacy of action and organization, based on their uses and customs, with the objective to achieve full exercise of the right to free self-determination and an adequate standard of living."[72]

In Brazil, these concepts helped form Federal Law No. 10.257, or the "City Statute," enacted in 2001. Brazil's City Statute emerged as a result of widespread participation by civil society organizations in the drafting of its 1988 constitution. The City Statute was groundbreaking in that it articulated the social functions of cities and the responsibilities of municipal governments to deliver land rights and essential services to all residents and to prioritize urban sustainable development.[73] While not a set of individual rights per se, the Brazilian City Statute can be seen as an important policy for slum health since it aimed to address the social determinants of health[74] through such provisions as

Redefining the concept of land ownership so that all urban property must have a social-service function

Requiring the incorporation of informal settlements into the fabric of the entire city

Directing a new National Ministry of Cities to strengthen urban management

Developing a program, called Papel Passado, to support land regularization

Investing federal resources into the rehabilitation of cities[75]

The Brazilian City Statue offers one set of strategies for moving toward greater slum health by linking resources and expertise from the nation to the neighborhood.

Thus, policymaking at multiple levels—national to local—can ensure that slum dwellers and their needs are recognized and that they have a right to remain in place and experience the benefits of urban living. As we explore in later chapters, achieving slum health will involve as much science as it does policy and will require community residents to participate in both processes to redirect resources to best support their well-being and inclusion in the city's functioning.

WORKING TOWARD SLUM HEALTH: KEY PRINCIPLES

This chapter introduces our approach to slum health, which is expanded upon in more detail in the chapters that follow. Our overarching approach is to encourage action-research that moves from the cell to the street, or is simultaneously legitimate inside the laboratory and credible in and with community residents. We recognize this will be at the frontier of many fields and will challenge disciplinary boundaries and current assumptions about slums and slum dwellers. Thus, in conclusion, we offer fundamental principles to guide collaborative inquiry and action that moves toward greater slum health. These principles should act as a starting point and always be adjusted for particular contexts. Our principles include:

Slums and those who live there are not synonymous with pathology, deficits, crime, dirt, or unhealthy behaviors in need of fixing; rather, health promotion can take advantage of the wealth of untapped social resources within informal settlements and what is already working that can support health and improve access to care.

Evicting, gentrifying, or resettling existing urban slum dwellers far from their existing social and economic networks will not contribute to population health. Instead slum health should explore new inclusive rights and access to and opportunities in the entire city for the poor and marginalized.

Since the urban poor do not wait for professionals or governments to help them, health promotion in slums should seek respectful and meaningful partnerships with these local experts.

Slum improvement has been too narrowly framed in economic terms, and healthy urban development too narrowly focused on Northern and Western notions of "formal" and "developed" and too wedded to the assumption that informal settlements in the global South are inherently "underdeveloped." Slum health must redefine accepted categories and take a critical stance toward established scientific and developmental discourses.

Slum health is not gender neutral but instead must recognize that slum living and environments often place a disproportionate burden on women's health such as through the stress of poverty, discrimination in clinical settings that denies them basic well-women and maternal health care, exposure to pathogens in open sewage, caring for sick children, vulnerability to sexual violence, and the indignity of having to defecate in the open.

Coproducing slum health must link medical, biological, and public health fields currently disconnected from the fields of urban planning, policy, and development.

Slum health cannot just improve the built environments of the urban poor, but must also improve the institutions, rules, and laws that govern the places where the poor live and work to ensure they are healthy and safe now and in the future.

Slum health does not impose outsider values on the urban poor and must be open to, but not romanticize, the possible health advantages that low-income settlements might provide for the poor, such as affordability, location, flexible housing designs, and community cohesion.

Slum health research is not a one-off pilot or boutique project but rather must become a priority of government policy, international finance and health organizations, civil society and grassroots groups, the private sector, and university researchers.

NOTES

1. United Nations Human Settlements Programme (2003). *The challenge of slums: Global report on human settlements, 2003*. London: Earthscan Publications.

2. Ibid.

3. Legg, S., & McFarlane, C. (2008). Ordinary urban spaces: Between postcolonialism and development. *Environment and Planning A* 40(1):6–14. Mehrotra, R. (2010). "Foreword" in F. Hernández, P. Kellett, & L.K. Allen (eds.). *Rethinking the informal city: Critical perspectives from Latin America*. New York: Berghahn, xi–xiv. Roy, A. (2011). Slumdog cities: rethinking

subaltern urbanism. *International Journal of Urban and Regional Research* 35:223–38. Simone, A. (2008). The politics of the possible: Making urban life in Phnom Penh. *Singapore Journal of Tropical Geography* 29:186–204.

4. World Health Organization (1986). *The Ottawa Charter for Health Promotion.* http://www.who.int/healthpromotion/conferences/previous/ottawa/en / (accessed November 16, 2015).

5. Jasanoof, S. (2004). *States of knowledge: The co-production of science and social order.* London: Routledge.

6. Mishra, P. (2004). Bombay: The lower depths (review of *MaximumCity: Bombay Lost and Found,* by Suketu Mehta, 2004). *New York Review of Books* 51(18).

7. Tartof, S.Y., Reis, J.N., Andrade, A.N., Ramos, R.T., Reis, M.G., & Riley, L.W. (2010). Factors associated with Group A Streptococcus *emm* type diversification in a large urban setting in Brazil: A cross-sectional study. *BMC Infectious Diseases* 10:327.

8. Steer, A.C., Law, I., Matatolu, L., Beall, B.W., & Carapetis, J.R. (2008). Global *emm* type distribution of group A streptococci: Systematic review and implications for vaccine development. *Lancet Infectious Diseases* 9(10):611–16.

9. Tartof et al. (2010).

10. Steer et al. (2008).

11. Baoren, Z. (2001). Heart valve surgery in China: Yesterday and today. *Heart Lung Circulation* 10(2); A11–A16.

12. Camara, E.J., Braga, J.C., Alves-Silva, L.S., Camara, G.F., & da Silva Lopes, A.A. (2002). Comparison of an intravenous pulse of methylprednisolone versus oral corticosteroid in severe acute rheumatic carditis: A randomized clinical trial. *Cardiol Young* 12(2):119–24.

13. Camara, E.J., Neubauer, C., Camara, G.F., & Lopes, A.A. (2004). Mechanisms of mitral valvular insufficiency in children and adolescents with severe rheumatic heart disease: An echocardiographic study with clinical and epidemiological correlations. *Cardiol Young* 14(5):527–32.

14. Terreri, M.T., Ferraz, M.B., Goldenberg, J., Len, C., & Hilario, M.O. (2001). Resource utilization and cost of rheumatic fever. *J Rheumatol* 28(6): 1394–97.

15. Vashistha, V.M., Kalra, A., Kalra, K., & Jain, V.K. (1993). Prevalence of rheumatic heart disease in school children. *Indian Pediatrics* 30(1):53–56.

16. Longo Mbenza, B., Bayekula, M., Ngiyulu, R., Kintoki, V.E., Bikangi, N.F., Seghers, K.V., et al. (1998). Survey of rheumatic heart disease in school children of Kinshasa town. *International J Cardiology* 63(3):287–94.

17. Ibrahim-Khalil, S., Elhag, M., Ali, E., Mahgoub, F., Hakiem, S., Omer, N., et al. (1992). An epidemiological survey of rheumatic fever and rheumatic heart disease in Sahafa Town, Sudan. *J Epidemiol Community Health* 46(5):477–79.

18. Meira, Z.M., Goulart, E.M., Colosimo, E.A., & Mota, C.C. (2005). Long term follow up of rheumatic fever and predictors of severe rheumatic valvular disease in Brazilian children and adolescents. *Heart* 91(8):1019–22.

19. Ribeiro, G.S., Tartof, S.Y., Oliveira, D.W., Guides, A.C., Reis, M.G., Riley, L.W., et al. (2012). Surgery for valvular heart disease: A population-based study in a Brazilian urban center. *PLoS One* 7(5).

20. Ibid.
21. Ibid.
22. Ibid.
23. Ibid.
24. Unger, A., & Riley, L.W. (2007). Slum health: From understanding to action. *PLoS Med* 4(10):1561–66.
25. Tartof et al. (2010).
26. United Nations Human Settlements Programme (2003).
27. Terreri et al. (2001).
28. Ibid.
29. Ibid.
30. Steer et al. (2008).
31. Ostrom, E. (1996). Crossing the Great Divide: Co-production, synergy and development. *World Development* 24(6):1073–87.
32. Bovaird, T. (2007). Beyond engagement and participation: User and community co-production of public services. *Public Administration Review* 6(5):846–60.
33. Mitlin, D. (2008). With and beyond the state: Co-production as a route to political influence, power and transformation for grassroots organizations. *Environment and Urbanization* 20(2):339–60.
34. Patel, S., Baptist, C., & D'Cruz, C. (2012). Knowledge is power: Informal communities assert their right to the city through SDI and community-led enumerations. *Environment and Urbanization* 20:339–60.
35. Prunty, J. (1998). *Dublin slums, 1800–1925: A study of urban geography*. Dublin: Irish Academic Press.
36. Garside, P.L. (1988). Unhealthy areas: Town planning, eugenics and slums, 1890–1945. *Planning Perspectives* 3:24–46.
37. Ibid., 24.
38. Howard, E. (1902). *Garden cities of tomorrow.* London: S. Sonnenschein & Co.
39. Home, R. (1997). *Of planting and planning: The making of British colonial cities.* London: Routledge.
40. Ibid.
41. Ibid.
42. Melosi, M. (1999). *Sanitary city: Urban infrastructure in America from colonial times to the present.* Baltimore: Johns Hopkins University Press.
43. Reports of the Malaria Committee of the Royal Society, as quoted in Curtain, P. (1985). Medical knowledge and urban planning in tropical Africa. *American Historical Review* 90(3):598.
44. Home (1997), 78.
45. Garside (1988).
46. Scott, H.H. (1939). A history of tropical medicine: Based on the Fitzpatrick Lectures delivered before the Royal College of Physicians of London, 1937–38. London: E. Arnold & Co.
47. Tyrwhitt, J. (1947). *Patrick Geddes in India.* London: Lund Humphries, 40, 45.
48. Curtain (1985).

49. Freeden, M. (1979). Eugenics and progressive thought: A study in ideological affinity. *Historical Journal* 22(3):645–71.

50. Mazumdar, P.M.H. (1980). The eugenists and the residuum: The problem of the urban poor. *Bulletin of the History of Medicine* 54(2):204–15.

51. Ibid.

52. Du Bois, W.E.B. (1906). *The health and physique of the American Negro: A sociological study made under the direction of Atlanta University by the Eleventh Atlanta Conference*. Atlanta, GA: Atlanta University Press.

53. Hoffman, F. (2004 [1896]). *Race traits and tendencies of the American Negro*. Clark, NJ: Lawbook Exchange, 312.

54. Du Bois (1906).

55. American Planning Association (1948). *Planning the neighborhood*. Washington, DC.

56. Gilbert, A. (2007). The return of the slum: Does language matter? *International Journal of Urban and Regional Research* 31(4):697–713.

57. Rao, V. (2006). Slum as theory: The South/Asian city and globalization. *International Journal of Urban and Regional Research* 30(1):225–32.

58. Corburn, J. (2009). *Toward the healthy city: People, places, and the politics of urban planning*. Cambridge, MA: MIT Press.

59. United Nations (2015). Goal 11: Make cities inclusive, safe, resilient and sustainable. In Sustainable Development Goals: 17 goals to sustain our world. http://www.un.org/sustainabledevelopment/cities/ (accessed February 13, 2016).

60. Valladares, L. (1978). Working the system: Squatter response to settlement in Rio de Janeiro. *IJURR* 2:12–25.

61. Gilbert, A. (1992). Third World cities: Housing, infrastructure and servicing. *Urban Studies* 29:435–60.

62. World Bank (1974). *Sites and Services working paper.*

63. Davis, M. (2007). *Planet of slums*. New York: Verso.

64. Mayo, S.K., & Angel, S. (1993). *Housing: Enabling markets to work*. World Bank.

65. Gilbert, A. (2009). Extreme thinking about slums and slum dwellers: A critique. *SAIS Review* 29(1):37–38.

66. United Nations Human Settlements Programme (2003), vol. 3, p. 45.

67. World Bank (2009*). Systems of cities: Harnessing urbanization for growth and poverty alleviation.* http://siteresources.worldbank.org/INTURBANDEVELOPMENT/Resources/336387-1269651121606/FullStrategy.pdf (accessed August 1, 2015).

68. Cities Alliance (2014). *About slum upgrading*. Brussels, Belgium. http://www.citiesalliance.org/About-slum-upgrading (last accessed November 18, 2015).

69. Purcell. M. (2002). Excavating Lefebvre: The right to the city and its urban politics of the inhabitant. *GeoJournal* 58:99–108.

70. Sugranyes, A., & Mathivet, C. (eds.) (2010). *Cities for all: Proposals and experiences towards the right to the city*. Santiago, Chile: Habitat International Coalition.

71. Harvey, D. (2008). The right to the city. *New Left Review* 53:23–40.

72. Ortiz, E. (2005). Toward a world charter for the right to the city. Habitat International Coalition. http://www.hic-gs.org/articles.php?pid=2296 (accessed February 13, 2016).

73. Fernandes, E. (2007). Constructing the "Right to the City" in Brazil. *Social Legal Studies* 2007 16:201–19.

74. World Health Organization (2013). Progress on the implementation of the Rio Political Declaration on the Social Determinants of Health. http://www.who.int/social_determinants/en/ (last accessed November 19, 2015).

75. Carvalho, C.S., & Rossbach, A. (2010). *The City Statute: A commentary*. São Paolo, Brazil: Cities Alliance and Ministry of Cities. http://www.citiesalliance.org/node/1947 (last accessed November 19, 2015).

CHAPTER 2

Slum Health

From Understanding to Action

ALON UNGER AND LEE RILEY

Slums are a manifestation of the two main challenges facing human settlements development at the beginning of the new millennium: rapid urbanization and the urbanization of poverty.

—Anna Kajumulo Tibaijuka, Executive Director, United Nations Human Settlements Programme[1]

Jo lives—that is to say, Jo has not yet died—in a ruinous place, known to the like of him by the name of Tom-All-Alone. It is a black, dilapidated street, avoided by all decent people. . . . Now, these tumbling tenements contain, by night, a swarm of misery. . . . As, on the ruined human wretch, vermin parasites appear, so, these ruined shelters have bred a crowd of foul existence that crawls in and out of gaps in walls and boards; and coils itself to sleep, in maggot numbers, where the rain drips in; and comes and goes, fetching and carrying fever.

—Charles Dickens, *Bleak House*[2]

As we enter the twenty-first century, a majority of the world's population lives in cities.[3] The United Nations projects that the world's urban population will grow by two billion before 2030. More than 90 percent of this growth will take place in the least-developed countries[4] and will be concentrated in the bleakest parts of the city—human settlements known as slums. Already nearly a third (32%) of the world's population and more than three-fourths (78%) of the least-developed countries' urban population live in slums.[5]. Today's slums are unprecedented in their sheer magnitude, their rapid growth, and their worldwide distribution.[6,7] They represent a fundamental transformation of the physical and social environment of urban life and human health.

Like Dickens's Tom-All-Alone, slums are synonymous with squalid living conditions. A visit to the favelas of Rio de Janeiro, the shantytowns of Nairobi, or the *jhopadpatti* of Mumbai shows that a slum, by any name, is an unhealthy place to live. Many health outcomes are worse in slums than in neighboring urban areas or even rural areas.[8,9,10] Moreover, the formal health sector encounters slum residents only when they develop late-stage complications of preventable chronic diseases. This takes a costly toll on these neglected communities and already limited health care resources.

DEFINING SLUMS AND THE CHALLENGE OF SLUM HEALTH

In 2002, the UN operationally defined slums as those communities characterized by insecure residential status, poor structural quality of housing, overcrowding, and inadequate access to safe water, sanitation, and other infrastructure (table 2.1)[11].

The 2003 UN report *The Challenge of Slums* is the most comprehensive account of the demographic and socioeconomic indicators of slums worldwide.[12] It details not only the high concentration of poverty and substandard living conditions in slums, but also the insecurity of tenure and marginalization from the formal sector, including basic health services.

Conditions of Slum Life and Health Using the UN Operational Definition

Slums are areas of "concentrated disadvantage."[13] The physical and legal characteristics enumerated by the UN are intimately related to population composition and dynamics, social environment, poverty, and marginalization. Health comparisons of rural versus urban areas, or emphasis on the urban health "penalty" or "advantage," do not highlight the specific health determinants of slums.[14] Here, we use the UN operational criteria to show that the conditions of slum life have a direct impact on the health and well-being of these communities (table 2.1).

TABLE 2.1 UN OPERATIONAL DEFINITION OF SLUMS AND ASSOCIATED PHYSICAL, LEGAL, AND ADVERSE HEALTH OUTCOMES

Characteristic	Physical or legal definition	Physical/legal outcome	Adverse health outcomes
Insecure residential status	Households without • formal title deeds to either land or residence • enforceable agreements as proof of tenure	• Eviction • Exposure to toxic/chemical waste and pollution • Low service utilization	• Poor access to health care services, traffic injuries • Acute poisoning, respiratory diseases, cancer • Intentional injuries, STDs/HIV-AIDS, unwanted pregnancy, substance abuse–related diseases
Poor structural quality of housing	Households residing in hazardous sites: • geologically hazardous (landslide/earthquake/flood areas) • industrial pollution • unprotected hazards (e.g., dumps, railroads, power lines) Households living in temporary and/or dilapidated structures: • inferior building materials (cardboard, corrugated tin, mud, low-grade concrete/bricks) • substandard construction (e.g., lack of adequate foundation or support structures, insecure joints/connections)	• Land and mud slides • Flooding • Fire • Vertical, multistory housing construction • Residence in or near dumps; spontaneous combustion of garbage	• Unintentional injuries • Leptospirosis, diarrheal diseases, cholera, malaria, dengue, hepatitis, drowning • Falling injuries • Burn injuries
Overcrowding	Households with more than two persons per room or less than 5 square meters per person	Enhanced opportunity for disease transmission	Tuberculosis and other respiratory illnesses, meningitis, scabies, skin infections, bacterial pharyngitis, rheumatic heart disease

Inadequate access to safe water	Less than 50% of households have access (20 liters/person/day, acceptable collection distance) to • household connection • public stand pipe • rainwater collection	• Contaminated water sources • Water scarcity	• Diarrheal diseases, cholera, typhoid, hepatitis • Scabies, bacterial skin infections, acute glomerulonephritis
Inadequate access to sanitation and other infrastructure	Less than 50% of households have improved sanitation (shared by maximum of two households), defined as • public sewer • septic tank • pour-flush latrine • ventilated improved pit latrine	• Increased rat density • Open or broken sewers • Suboptimal schools • Inadequate/inappropriate health care services	• Typhus, leptospirosis, diarrheal diseases, cholera, malaria, dengue, hookworm, hepatitis, chronic respiratory diseases, growth retardation • Underutilization of services, maternal health complications, vaccine-preventable diseases, perinatal diseases, rheumatic heart disease, suicide • Poor access to health education • Drug-resistant infections, poorly controlled hypertension, diabetes, and other chronic illnesses

NOTE: Operational definition of slums adapted from UN sources.

Insecure Residential Status

The lack of secure land or housing tenure forces residents to occupy unused or undesirable land. For example, between 1991 and 1997, 1.5 million were evicted from central areas of Shanghai, and 1 million people from Beijing.[15] Such dislocations out of the city center force large numbers to commute longer distances to their original place of work, braving the roads by foot or in overcrowded and dangerous vehicles and thus putting themselves at risk for road traffic injuries.[16] Slum locations may be unused or undesirable because of their hazardous geography, such as landslide- or flood-prone areas, or their unsafe or polluted environments. Moreover, slum dwellers' residential status limits their ability to fight for the right to a safe environment. In 1984, the accidental release of methyl isocyanate from a pesticide factory in Bhopal, India, killed more than 20,000 slum residents; the factory was built after the settlement had come into existence.[17] Even in the United States, Hurricane Katrina unmasked the vulnerability of residents of poor neighborhoods in flood-prone areas and also the neglect of this population by political institutions.[18, 19]

Poor Structural Quality of Housing

Slum housing is densely packed and poorly built with substandard and even flammable materials. Houses built against hillsides are subject to landslides during heavy rain, and inferior building standards cause many thousands of deaths from earthquakes, especially where urbanization and poverty collide.[20] In Bam, Iran, poor structural quality of housing played a major factor in the earthquake-related deaths of 32,000 people in 2003.

The built environment is also directly related to accidental injuries, such as falls and burns.[21] Physical characteristics of slums not only magnify the consequences of natural or man-made disasters but also hinder rescue efforts.[22]

Overcrowding

Slum dwellings have high occupancy rates in all-purpose rooms. Packing the cooking, sleeping, and living of an average of 13.4 people per 45 square meter room, as in the slums of Kolkata, India,[23] places residents at risk of respiratory infections, meningitis, and asthma.[24, 25] In Manila, the Philippines, children living in squatter settlements are nine times more likely than other children to have tuberculosis (TB).[26] Epidemic-prone infections such as pertussis cluster in areas of urban poverty,[27] and overcrowding may even fuel potentially emerging epidemic diseases such as SARS or influenza.[28] Crowding is also associated with rheumatic heart disease, a chronic and debilitating disease facilitated by increased transmission of group A *Streptococcus pyogenes* infections and lack of early treatment.[29]

Inadequate Access to Safe Water

Poor water quality is a leading cause of morbidity and mortality worldwide and a defining danger of living in slums.[30] Many life-threatening infectious diseases are associated with contaminated water in slums, such as cholera and hepatitis (table 2.1).[31] Lack of access to water also restricts water intake, sources for infant formula, and cooking, bathing, and personal hygiene. Infrequent bathing is associated with scabies and bacterial skin infections, a subset of which (i.e., group A *Streptococcus*) can lead to acute glomerulonephritis.[32]

Inadequate Access to Sanitation and Other Infrastructure

Lack of infrastructure affects all aspects of life, including waste collection and sewers, public transportation, policing, education, and electricity supply. Five million slum residents live without toilets in Mumbai; if each person defecates half a kilogram per day, 2.5 million kilograms of human waste contaminate their environment each day.[33] While diseases such as leptospirosis generally occur in developed countries as a result of recreational water sports,[34] 95 percent of severe manifestations of this disease in Salvador, Brazil, occur among slum residents living in areas in close proximity to open sewers and high rat density.[35] Slums are also excluded from the benefits of formal policing, and young men in the favelas of Brazil are up to five times more likely to die from homicide than their urban counterparts.[36] Violence associated with drug traffic between gangs or with the police creates unsafe conditions for all residents and pose a major barrier to provision of public health interventions.[37] Violence toward women is also associated with the absence of basic services like street lighting.[38]

Available health services often comprise an inconsistent patchwork of public, private, and charity-based providers. Inadequate or inappropriate care at these places permits the progression of preventable diseases, such as hypertension and diabetes, and increases the risk of drug-resistant infections, such as multi-drug-resistant TB.[39] Vaccination coverage in slums is markedly lower than in other urban areas due to inadequate infrastructure and a lack of community awareness and mobilization.[40] Appropriate interventions and treatments are effective only when provided in the context of accessible and utilized health care services.

Meeting the Challenge of Slum Health

The determinants of slum health are too complex to be defined by any single parameter. Yet they arise from a common physical and legal pedigree that concentrates the ill effects of poverty, unhealthy environments, and marginalization from the formal sector. The promotion of urban health in the twenty-first century must take neighborhood-centered as well as person-centered approaches. We recognize that broad economic, social, and political forces play an important role in the creation and growth of slums and that addressing these forces will take time. However, we represent clinicians and public health specialists, and therefore our approach focuses on immediate solutions that can dramatically improve health and health disparities (box 2.1).

Gathering Data on the Slum Disease Burden and Intraurban Health Disparities

Accurate health statistics in slums are difficult to obtain, and health statistics rarely report intraurban differences. The inability to collect or analyze detailed urban health data masks gross health disparities within cities. Currently, most slum disease burden and mortality data are based on clinic, hospital, or national mortality registry data. This grossly underestimates the underlying medical conditions, such as hypertension, that give rise to the complications observed by the formal health sector, such as stroke.[41] The absence of detailed accurate data limits the ability of officials to detect health threats or appropriately allocate resources. Prompt identification of local health concerns is the first step in any intervention.

There is a pressing need for a new analytic framework to understand health in slums. Standard health metrics, such as disability-adjusted life years (DALY) lost, do not account for the context in which diseases

Meeting the Challenge of Slums

Gather data on the slum disease burden and intraurban health disparities

- Establish routine disease surveillance within slum communities or at local clinics
- Ensure a safe environment for disease surveillance and reporting of illegal or informal residential status, without fear of reprisal
- Organize community planning groups for health care prioritization made up of community leaders, local health professionals, and representatives of high-risk groups, community-based organizations, and nongovernmental organizations
- Develop a new analytical framework for understanding health outcomes in slums, including new metrics for disease burden estimates based on slum-specific social and physical parameters

Identify and target relevant and modifiable conditions of slums life

- Focus on slum-specific health care needs, which may be very different than those in neighboring urban areas
- Target immediately modifiable health risks, such as diverting sewage or runoff, providing waste disposal, installing public lighting, offering soap and hygiene education, and improving traffic safety
- Involve auxiliary health care providers, such as private pharmacies and traditional healers

Take action

- Use existing structures and social capital in slums, such as community groups or religious institutions, and involve residents in design and provision of services
- Engage in multisectoral interventions, including professionals from urban planning, public works, engineering, and health sectors
- Advocate for patients through public advocacy and political institutions and by reporting study results in internationally distributed professional journals

occur. The DALY for TB for a 25-year-old man in New York City is different than that for a 25-year-old man in the Dharavi slum of Mumbai. Accepted indicators of socioeconomic status (e.g., income, education, occupation) are inadequate in areas of generalized poverty and informal residence or work.[42] The social gradient within slums may be better indicated, for instance, by the difference in building materials (i.e., mud versus brick) or number of meals per day. Slums are complex, and our efforts must match this complexity. Once they do, we can better focus scarce resources on the most modifiable and relevant factors for improving health. This will save time, money, and lives.

Targeting Relevant and Modifiable Conditions of Slum Life

Slum-specific information may reveal that health priorities in slums should be very different than national or even local urban ones. Improving health status in slums may simply require closing open sewers to limit diarrheal disease, lighting footpaths to deter violence, constructing barriers to prevent falling injuries, or diverting run-off or reinforcing dams to lessen loss of property and life from heavy rains. Some priorities, such as addressing high rates of HIV-AIDS in slums, may be the same as for other communities; however, the solutions must be slum-specific.[43] These efforts can be made without awaiting poverty alleviation. Intervention trials in poor-urban or slum areas have already demonstrated that hand washing with soap can reduce the risk of diarrheal diseases by up to 47 percent and could save a million lives.[44] Compelling data like these can be used to advocate for improved sanitation infrastructure and basic hygiene supplies.

From Understanding to Action

Health officials, doctors, and public health specialists can take advantage of existing structures and social capital in slums. Dense populations may pose not only a risk but also an opportunity—to efficiently reach a large, vulnerable proportion of the population. We can minimize the lack of access to health services through innovative programs such as school-based vaccination or outreach via churches, temples, and mosques. This approach means finding people where they congregate, be it bars in Venezuela or dance halls in Kenya. In particular, private pharmacies are central to health care in slums and can play an important role in monitoring chronic diseases (e.g., hypertension and diabetes) and delivering health education in slums.[45] It is more important than ever to enlist residents of slums as partners. In Mumbai, residents are instrumental in managing community toilets in a nationwide project supported by the World Bank.[46] In Rio de Janeiro, community members educate their neighbors about HIV infection and hand out condoms in markets.[47] Involving residents is also an important step in redressing the social exclusion, inequity, and disempowerment that characterize their situation.

Interventions to improve the health of slum dwellers are not cutting-edge science. Effective interventions involve not only treating disease but also addressing the underlying social and living conditions of slums. Many solutions will require significant multisectoral effort and resource mobilization, which may be beyond our traditional role as health professionals. This will require us to be students of problems, not disciplines, and to work closely with urban planners, engineers, and politicians to make the necessary changes. Health professionals can also make important contributions as civic leaders when they organize neighborhood associations and resident advocacy groups or when they themselves act to represent the billion unheard voices of slum dwellers.

MOVING FORWARD

This brief chapter describes the interrelated conditions confronting the health of slum dwellers around the world. The remainder of this book looks in-depth at how research and action have embodied the ideas offered here, specifically in Brazil, India, and Kenya. We hope to offer concrete solutions for making the lives of the poorest urban residents living in some of the harshest conditions more equitable and healthy.

NOTES

1. UN-Habitat (2003). *The challenge of the slums: Global report on human settlements.* Nairobi, Kenya: United Nations.
2. Dickens, C. (1853). *Bleak House.* London: Penguin Books.
3. United Nations Population Division (2004). World urbanization prospects: The 2003 revision. New York: United Nations. http://www.un.org/esa/population/publications/wup2003/WUP2003Report.pdf. Accessed 6 September 2007.
4. United Nations Population Division (2002). World urbanization prospects: The 2001 revision. New York: United Nations. http://www.un.org/esa/population/publications/wup2001/WUP2001report.htm. Accessed 6 September 2007.
5. UN-Habitat (2003).
6. UN-Habitat (2003).
7. Davis, M. (2006). *Planet of slums.* New York: Verso.
8. Szwarcwald, C.L., Andrade, C.L., & Bastos, F.I. (2002). Income inequality, residential poverty clustering and infant mortality: A study in Rio de Janeiro, Brazil. *Soc Sci Med* 55:2083–92.
9. Sclar, E.D., Garau, P., & Carolini, G. (2005). The 21st century health challenge of slums and cities. *Lancet* 365:901–3.

10. Fotso, J.C. (2006). Child health inequities in developing countries: Differences across urban and rural areas. *Int J Equity Health* 5:9.

11. UN-Habitat (2002). *Defining slums: Towards an operational definition for measuring slums.* Background Paper 2, Expert Group Meeting on Slum Indicators, October. Nairobi, Kenya: United Nations.

12. UN-Habitat (2003).

13. Vlahov, D., Freudenberg, N., Proietti, F., Ompad, D., Quinn, A., et al. (2007). Urban as a determinant of health. *J Urban Health* 84:16–26.

14. Freudenberg, N., Galea, S., & Vlahov, D. (2005). Beyond urban penalty and urban sprawl: Back to living conditions as the focus of urban health. *J Community Health* 30:1–11.

15. Zhang, Y., & Fang, K. (2004). Is history repeating itself? From urban renewal in the United States to inner-city redevelopment in China. *J Plann Educ Res* 23:286–89.

16. Ameratunga, S., Hijar, M., & Norton, R. (2006). Road-traffic injuries: Confronting disparities to address a global-health problem. *Lancet* 367: 1533–40.

17. Dhara, V.R., & Dhara, R. (2002). The Union Carbide disaster in Bhopal: A review of health effects. *Arch Environ Health* 57:391–404.

18. Nates, J.L., & Moyer, V.A. (2005). Lessons from Hurricane Katrina, tsunamis, and other disasters. *Lancet* 366:1144–46.

19. McLellan, F. (2005). Hurricane Katrina: "A speaking sight," or, washday in Durant. *Lancet* 366:968–69.

20. Jackson, J. (2006). Fatal attraction: Living with earthquakes, the growth of villages into megacities, and earthquake vulnerability in the modern world. *Philos Transact A Math Phys Eng Sci* 364:1911–25.

21. Bartlett, S.N. (2002). The problem of children's injuries in low-income countries: A review. *Health Policy Plan* 17:1–13.

22. Sapir, D., & Lechat, M. (1986). Reducing the impact of natural disasters: Why aren't we better prepared? *Health Policy Plan* 1:118–26.

23. Kundu, N. (2003). *Urban slum reports: The case of Kolkata, India.* Nairobi, Kenya: United Nations.

24. Sharma, S., Sethi, G.R., Rohtagi, A., Chaudhary, A., Shankar, R., et al. (1998). Indoor air quality and acute lower respiratory infection in Indian urban slums. *Environ Health Perspect* 106:291–97.

25. Benicio, M.H., Ferreira, M.U., Cardoso, M.R., Konno, S.C., & Monteiro, C.A. (2004). Wheezing conditions in early childhood: Prevalence and risk factors in the city of São Paulo, Brazil. *Bull World Health Organ* 82: 516–22.

26. Fry, S., Cousins, B., & Olivola, K. (2002). *Health of children living in urban slums in Asia and the Near East: Review of existing literature and data.* Environmental Health Project, U.S. Agency for International Development. http://www.ehproject.org/PDF/Activity_Reports/AR109ANEUrbHlthweb.pdf. Accessed 6 September 2007.

27. Siegel, C., Davidson, A., Kafadar, K., Norris, J.M., Todd, J., et al. (1997). Geographic analysis of pertussis infection in an urban area: A tool for health services planning. *Am J Public Health* 87:2022–26.

28. Davis, M. (2005). *The monster at our door: The global threat of avian flu.* New York: The New Press.

29. World Health Organization (2004). *Rheumatic fever and rheumatic heart disease.* http://www.who.int/cardiovascular_diseases/publications/trs923/en/. Accessed 19 November 2015.

30. World Health Organization (2003). *Emerging issues in water and infectious disease.* http://www.who.int/water_sanitation_health/emerging/emergingissues/en/. Accessed 6 September 2007.

31. UN-Habitat (2003). *Water and sanitation in the world's cities: Local action for global goals.* London: Earthscan.

32. Heukelbach, J., Wilcke, T., Winter, B., & Feldmeier, H. (2005). Epidemiology and morbidity of scabies and pediculosis capitis in resource-poor communities in Brazil. *Br J Dermatol* 153:150–56.

33. S. Mehta. (2004). *Maximum city: Bombay lost and found.* New York: Knopf.

34. Dziuban, E.J., Liang, J.L., Craun, G.F., Hill, V., Yu, P.A., et al. (2006). Surveillance for waterborne disease and outbreaks associated with recreational water—United States, 2003–2004. *MMWR Surveill Summ* 55:1–30.

35. Ko, A.I., Galvao Reis, M., Ribeiro Dourado, C.M., Johnson, W.D., Jr, & Riley, L.W. (1999). Urban epidemic of severe leptospirosis in Brazil. Salvador Leptospirosis Study Group. *Lancet* 354:820–25.

36. Montgomery, M.R., Stren, R., Cohen, B. & Reed, H.E. (eds.) (2003). *Cities transformed: Demographic change and its implications for the developing world.* Washington, DC: National Academies Press. http://www.nap.edu/catalog.php?record_id=10693. Accessed 6 September 2007.

37. Loewenberg, S. (2005). Tackling the causes of ill health in Rio's slums. *Lancet* 365:925–26.

38. Krishnakumar, A. (2003). Issues in focus: A sanitation emergency. *Frontline* 20(24). http://www.hinduonnet.com/fline/fl2024/stories/20031205002510100.htm. Accessed 6 September 2007.

39. Bates, I., Fenton, C., Gruber, J., Lalloo, D., Lara, A.M., et al. (2004). Vulnerability to malaria, tuberculosis, and HIV/AIDS infection and disease, Part II: Determinants operating at environmental and institutional level. *Lancet Infect Dis* 4:368–75.

40. Agarwal, S., Bhanot, A., & Goindi, G. (2005). Understanding and addressing childhood immunization coverage in urban slums. *Indian Pediatrics* 42:653–63.

41. Riley, L.W., Ko, A.I., Unger, A., & Reis, M.G. (2007), Slum health: Diseases of neglected populations. *BMC Int Health Hum Rights* 7:2.

42. Ompad, D.C., Galea, S., Caiaffa, W.T., & Vlahov, D. (2007). Social determinants of the health of urban populations: Methodologic considerations. *J Urban Health* 84:42–53.

43. Amuyunzu, M., Okeng'o, L., Wagura, A., & Mwenzwa, E. (2007). Putting on a brave face: The experiences of women living with HIV and AIDS in informal settlements of Nairobi. *AIDS Care* 19:S25–S34.

44. Curtis, V., & Cairncross, S. (2003). Effect of washing hands with soap on diarrhoea risk in the community: A systematic review. *Lancet Infectious Diseases* 3:275–81.

45. Amuyunzu-Nyamongo, M., & Nyamongo, I.K. (2006). Health-seeking behaviour of mothers of under-five-year-old children in the slum communities of Nairobi, Kenya. *Anthropology and Medicine* 13:25–40.

46. Chinai, R. (2002). Mumbai slum dwellers' sewage project goes nationwide. *Bull World Health Organ* 80:684–85. http://www.archidev.org/IMG/pdf/v80n8a15.pdf. Accessed 7 September 2007.

47. Loewenberg (2005).

CHAPTER 3

Frameworks for Urban Slum Health Equity

JASON CORBURN

Urban slum health equity demands new frameworks for integrating the "cell" and "street" into research and action. Cities have many unpredictable parts and are variegated, and the sum of their parts rarely equates easily with the functioning of the whole. People in cities find ways to interpret and assign meaning to places in surprising and unexpected ways, even when certain aspects of the city, such as roads and parks, are "hard-wired" for a particular function. Cities are constantly built and rebuilt socially, physically, and interpretively. The interpretations and possibilities of cities are influenced not only by forces from within their neighborhoods and municipal boundaries, but also by policies and institutions outside at the national and international scales. With all this complexity, I suggest that a machinelike fix-it approach to urban health for the poor is inadequate. Instead, I offer new frameworks that borrow from epidemiology and the policy sciences for approaching slum health.

This chapter argues that cities are complex systems characterized more by uncertainty, indeterminacy, and ignorance than by certainty, function, and rationality. A complex system must develop processes of constant inquiry, learning, and adapting to change, since it is nearly impossible to model and predict the future of complex systems. To make the abstraction of complex systems more concrete, this chapter turns to existing frameworks in the social sciences to offer details of the processes and practices that must underwrite urban slum health equity. I build upon existing ideas from the coproduction of scientific knowledge, a relational view of place, ecosocial epidemiology, sustainability science, and adaptive ecosystem management in order to frame how researchers and practitioners ought to approach urban slum health equity.

FRAMEWORK 1: COPRODUCING SLUM HEALTH

One emerging science policy frame, called coproduction, questions institutionalized notions of expertise from the outset and hard demarcations between nature and society.[1] The frame of coproduction seeks to open up how authoritative technical knowledge is produced in society and gets stabilized and institutionalized over time, so that it becomes a "given" or "taken-for-granted truth." Coproduction aims to problematize the origins and substance of the meanings of science policy issues—who was included in or excluded from generating these meanings—and aims to emphasize that scientific legitimacy is simultaneously a social, political, and material phenomenon, none of whose aspects can be disentangled from the others. The notion of coproduction also aims to extend analyses within the interpretive turn in the social sciences, particularly post-structuralist frameworks, by highlighting the often invisible role of knowledge, expertise, technical practices, and material objects in shaping, sustaining, subverting, or transforming relations of authority, particularly that of the state.[2]

Coproduction as used here should not be viewed as a full-fledged theory—claiming lawlike consistency and predictive power—but rather as an *idiom,* or a way of interpreting and accounting for complex phenomena so as to avoid the strategic deletions and omissions of most other approaches to understanding the role of the public in science policy.[3] For example, Ian Hacking describes how the American legal and policy processes created new "social kinds" of child abuse and "recovery memory" in response to specific cultural anxieties of the 1980s and, in the process, generated "objective" evidence of these phenomena.[4] In another example of coproduction, Evelyn Fox Keller showed how concepts central to the practice of science, such as objectivity and disinterestedness, came to be gendered as masculine through centuries of rhetorical usage, and that the construction of the "laws of nature" have political origins.[5] Thus, a central aim of the coproductionist framework is to help clarify how power originates, where it gets lodged, who wields it, by what means, and with what effect within the complex network of science policy making.

Coproduction can also be understood by contrasting it with two other, perhaps more dominant modes of lay-professional interaction in public health, namely the deficit and complementarity models.[6] According to the deficit model, professionals view laypeople as not having sufficient knowledge about scientific and technological problems and needing to be educated in order to see the world more like professional scientists. The deficit model also assumes that scientists will agree on the "correct" information that laypeople need to know so they understand technical problems from the professional's vantage point. This model perpetuates the notion that "science speaks truth to power," or the idea that technical input to policy problems has to be developed independently of political influences in order to act as a constraint on political power.

The complementarity model rejects the notion that only professional knowledge should inform science discourse and instead invites laypeople into the process to raise issues of "risk perceptions" and value questions. While laypeople offer values and weigh in on questions of fairness, according to the complementarity model, professionals retain autonomy over technical analyses and policy decisions. Science, in the complementarity model, is still viewed as offering disinterested and apolitical "facts" to policy processes. The major difference between the deficit and complementarity models is that in the latter, lay publics are given an opportunity to comment on the fairness or relevance of predetermined facts—not, for instance, on whether or not the *original framing* of the issue may appear one way to those in power and quite another way to the marginal or excluded.

Both the deficit and complementarity models tend to view lay or nonprofessional knowledge with skepticism, noting its populist, anti-intellectual, majoritarian, and moralistic tendencies. Populist political movements are criticized for "get the government off my back" economic libertarianism, xenophobia, and ethnocentric nationalism. The same critics characterize local knowledge in environmental and health controversies as parochial and confined to "the neighborhood," and this particularism, they say, violates core scientific values of universality, replicability, and objectivity.

The coproduction model responds to these critics by suggesting that science and technology are not "contaminated" by society, but rather are embedded in social practices, identities, norms, conventions, discourses, instruments, and institutions—in short, in all the building blocks of what we term the social.[7] Coproduction aims not only to bring the social back into science policy making but also to explore how this knowledge is applied, stabilized, and institutionalized over time. Thus, coproduction is both a reaction to the incompleteness of the deficit and complementarity models and a critique of the realist ideology that persistently separates the domains of nature, facts, objectivity, and reason from those of culture, values, subjectivity, and emotion in policy and politics more generally.

FRAMEWORK 2: SLUMS AS PLACES—A RELATIONAL APPROACH

The term "slum" often conjures up images of a certain type of space, as we discuss in chapters 1 and 2. According to Mike Davis in his popular book *Planet of Slums,* "Much of the twenty-first century urban world squats in squalor, surrounded by pollution, excrement, and decay."[8] Robert Neuwirth, in his book *Shadow Cities: A Billion Squatters, a New Urban World,* which recounts his experiences in slums of Rio de Janeiro, Nairobi, Mumbai, and Istanbul, emphatically states that the term "slum"

> is laden with emotional values: decay, dirt and disease. Danger, despair and degradation. Criminality, horror, abuse and fear. Slum is a loaded term, and its horizon of emotion and judgment comes from the outside. To call a neighbourhood a slum immediately creates distance. A slum is the apotheosis of everything that people who do not live in a slum fear. To call a neighbourhood a slum establishes a set of values—a mortality that people outside the slum share—and implies that inside those areas, people don't share the same principles.[9]

Yet slums are places too, and the definitions of place and slum, as with any concept, are contested. Place is more than just a space; places are locations with meaning. Place helps us understand how the world looks, how it functions, and how it feels. For instance, we might use expressions such as "knowing one's place" or being "put in one's place" to suggest a more abstract and less locatable interaction of the social and the geographical. Places include the experiences that happen in a particular location and give our lives a sense of boundaries, however permeable. In short, place is where we connect to everyday life and should never be framed essentially.

In this book, we suggest that both people and places matter for slum health. This is a central part of the second framework: *a relational view of place for slum health.* The relational view of place is understood as having physical and social characteristics that are given meaning through the interactions among the people living in a place. A space becomes a place as meanings are assigned through social relations and as these social meanings, in turn, act to reshape places and the opportunities and well-being of the people in those places.[10] The meanings of places are, in turn, shaped by social and political institutions—or the established rules, norms, and practices emerging from governmental and cultural organizations.

The relational interplay between slum place characteristics and meaning making, however, is always contingent and contested, such as when new squatters with new cultural orientations move into a slum. Meanings are also essential for "making sense" of evidence and act as a form of evidence in themselves. The relational view of place is a crucial framework for slum health because social processes, such as power, inequality, and collective action, are often revealed through the construction and reconstruction of the material forms and social meanings of places.[11]

The meanings and interactions in urban places are crucial for understanding how slums shape human well-being.[12] For example, a "sense of place" might invoke feelings of inclusion and connections with others, while a "lack of place" might induce loneliness and depression. People and organized groups or coalitions actively accomplish places, and the process is rarely the same from place to place. There are real winners and losers in the political struggles of place making, and static definitions of physical and social variables rarely capture this dynamic of place making.

Places also take on monetary value, as through ownership and control of land, further distributing power. Places are sites of politics since social movements often organize in places but governments also organize electoral and representational politics by creating place-based political districts. State-defined places take on further power distribution roles through taxation of land and catchment areas for such services as schools, hospitals, fire and emergency services, and sanitary districts. Place politics is increasingly about boundary making—who and what is invited in—as competing metropolitan areas replace nation-states for business, cultural, and other investments.

In slum health, a relational view of place demands multidimensional research and analysis that combines multiple ways of characterizing and understanding places, including resident narratives, systematic observation, and quantitative and qualitative measures of the location and spatial accessibility of resources.

FRAMEWORK 3: ECOSOCIAL EPIDEMIOLOGY

The third framework for slum health equity is ecosocial epidemiology. First articulated by Nancy Krieger in 1994, ecosocial epidemiology explicitly asks "who and what drives current and changing patterns of social inequalities in health?"[13] Krieger describes ecosocial epidemiology as having four core constructs that together direct inquiry and action.

Embodiment

The first concept of ecosocial epidemiology is embodiment, which suggests that "we literally embody, biologically, our lived experience," particularly the material and social worlds in which we live, "thereby creating population patterns of health and disease."[14] Thus, the foundation of understanding and acting to reverse health inequities is knowing the histories of people, groups, places, and the social, political, and economic decisions that over time have shaped these histories. Embodiment is not a static concept but rather a dynamic ongoing event, much like urban slums. For instance, ecosocial embodiment emphasizes the constant interactions between genes and ever changing social environments—the expression of genes rather than just the presence of a particular genetic sequence. As Krieger emphasizes, embodiment is a *verb* for "our bodily engagement (soma and psyche combined), individually and collectively, with the biophysical world and each other."[15] People and the world they help shape are always active participants, not passive subjects, in the processes of embodiment.

Embodiment can link epidemiology to slum health in currently underhypothesized ways. Public health and urban development activities regularly shape the physical, cultural, and social worlds of urban slum dwellers, but the field has not engaged with the bodily implications of its practices as much as fields like sociology and anthropology have.[16] Krieger explains the far-reaching intentions of ecosocial embodiment and the potential for linking currently disparate disciplines, describing it as

> a useful bridge to novel twenty-first century research in the cognitive and neurosciences, which are providing new evidence on the centrality of bodily sensory-motor experiences and interactions (with both organisms and the broader biophysical context) to the development and expressions of both cognition and behavior. Thus, embodiment conceptually stands as a deliberate corrective to dominant disembodied and decontextualized accounts of

"genes," behaviors and mechanisms of disease causation, offering in their place an integrated approach to analyzing the multilevel processes, from societal and ecological to subcellular, that co-produce population distributions of health, disease and well-being.[17]

Thus, for slum health, understanding history and context must be the starting points for exploring the relational interactions between society and biology.

Structural Racism

The biographies of urban populations and the histories of communities, and how these might become embodied, cannot be divorced from inequitable and often racist urban health and development decision making. Seemingly neutral policies and practices can function in ways that disempower communities of color and perpetuate unequal historical conditions. This is what is known as structural racism, a concept that, Powell notes, helps us analyze how the multiple characteristics of urban living can influence groups' opportunities for well-being. Powell suggests that a structural racism lens allows us to simultaneous understand

how housing, education, employment, transportation, health care, and other systems interact to produce racialized outcomes. Such a model allows us to move beyond a narrow merit-based, individualized understanding of society to show how all groups are interconnected and how structures shape life chances. At the level of cultural understanding, the structural model shows how the structures we create, inhabit, and maintain in turn recreate us by shaping identity and imparting social meaning. Chief among the processes in a structural model that connect institutions to identity formation is the relationship between racial identity and geography . . . the racialization of space.[18]

Health inequities experienced in cities by people of color are increasingly associated with structural racism.[19] Researchers have noted that addressing the health impacts of structural racism requires going beyond increasing access to medical care or "lowering the public's cholesterol level" to planning for reducing poverty, inequalities, and discrimination.[20] The past practices of governments and public health professionals can be relevant since seemingly inexplicable disadvantages that persist across conditions, subpopulations, and time may be attributable to historical traumas, or to what some have called intergenerational drag. The intergenerational drag hypothesis posits that "ethnic or racial groups pass social assets and liabilities on to their descendants" and views contemporary health disparities as the cumulative effects of macrolevel systems interacting with one another in ways that generate and sustain racial inequalities.[21] Applying an intergenerational-drag approach to slum health might help reveal how contemporary disease and mortality differences between groups and communities might reflect the "cumulative accrual" of advantages and disadvantages from one generation to the next.

Multiple Pathways of Embodiment

Like structural racism, ecosocial epidemiology emphasizes that there are always multiple pathways of embodiment. Too often in public health and medicine we look for the "one big cause" that can explain illness or promote well-being, such as sugar, dietary fats, smoking, or insufficient physical activity. Public health also tends to model just one exposure at one point in time, often discounting multiple exposure pathways that change over one's lifetime. Ecosocial epidemiology posits that multiple exposures happen at a range of scales, from the individual to the city and region to the global, and can include such pathogens as social and economic deprivation, environmental pollutants and toxins, discrimination and trauma, targeted marketing of harmful commodities, inadequate health care, and the degradation of life-supporting ecosystems.[22] Here again, city planners must understand how urban policies, institutions, and practices shape and influence these factors, such as policies promoting racial residential segregation, taxation and government spending, infrastructure, transport and environmental policies, and inclusive or exclusive decision-making processes.

Toxic Stress

One hypothesis that can help link slum health from the cell to the street is the notion of toxic stress.[23] Toxic stressors on the body include social, economic, political, and environmental deprivation and pathogens. We can be exposed to these "stressors" from in utero throughout the life course. The toxic stressors constantly wear down or "weather" the immune and neurologic systems, leading to a range of diseases and possibly premature death.[24] The idea of "weathering on the body" is like the weathering effect that sea salt–laden air might have on the paint on a building's exterior—a constant wearing away that reduces the paint's ability to protect the surfaces underneath and ultimately the building's

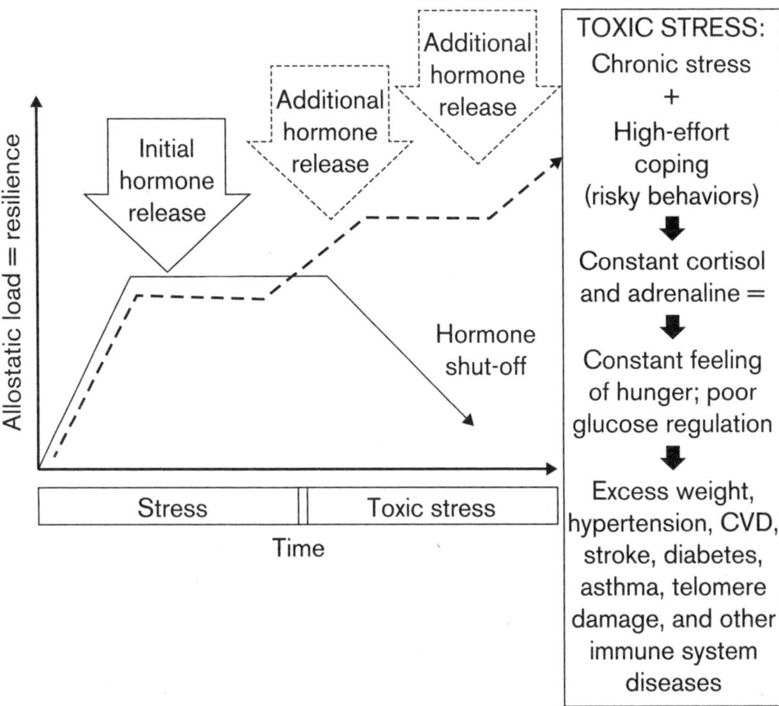

FIGURE 3.1. Toxic stress and biological embodiment.

inhabitants. However, human weathering affects not the surface but the human body's neuroendocrine system, which reacts to socially produced, unnatural stressors such as chronic unemployment, poverty, housing instability, lack of medical care, and the fear of crime.[25]

Under "normal" stressful situations, the human body has a range of physical and chemical responses, but primarily releases epinephrine (adrenaline) and cortisol to bring the endocrine and immune systems back to homeostasis. Through this adaptation, called allostasis, the body is able to maintain stability under change (fig. 3.1, solid line). The weathering hypothesis states that under constant stressors the "allostatic load" continues to increase and the chemical release of fight-or-flight hormones does not properly regulate or shut off (fig. 3.1, dotted line). According to the hypothesis, increased allostatic load wears away at the immune system as it overworks to manage the hormonal releases and attempts to return to homeostasis. Toxic stress can trigger other biological responses, such as poor glucose regulation and constant feelings of hunger that can contribute to chronic diseases such as excessive weight and obesity, diabetes, hypertension, cardiovascular disease, stroke, asthma, and other immune-related illnesses. Slum health research from the cell to the street demands investigating how a range of potentially toxic stressors might be driving disease, suffering, and premature mortality among urban slum dwellers.

Resilience and Slum Health

Another construct in ecosocial epidemiology is that there is constant "interplay between exposure, susceptibility and resistance, at multiple levels (individual, neighborhood, regional or political jurisdiction, national, inter- or supra-national) and in multiple domains (e.g., home, work, school, other public settings)."[26] What this means is that slum health researchers cannot be content with studying only morbidity and mortality but must also take seriously the institutional and individual forces that promote resilience and decrease susceptibility to illness for people in particular urban places. Too often public health researchers assume that if they reveal forces that seem to contribute to vulnerability and susceptibility to disease, eliminating these forces will result in greater resilience and even reduce health inequities between groups. Yet, just as public policy and behavioral economists have emphasized that reducing "negative" behaviors is very different from inducing "positive" ones, urban public health must focus on appreciative inquiry. No place, no matter how harsh the conditions, is all bad; people find ingenious ways to survive and thrive in unexpected ways, and slum health must investigate this type of resilience and integrate it into research and practice.

Accountability and Agency: Identifying Responsible Institutions

Accountability and agency, both for the actual health inequities and for ways in which they are monitored, analyzed, and addressed, is a fourth concept in ecosocial epidemiology. Agency can apply to researchers framing issues, defining problems, and emphasizing certain evidence over other evidence; to community organizations and civil society groups more generally that mobilize to reframe science policy issues; to corporations that use the inherent uncertainties of science to pollute and kill; and to governments and intergovernmental institutions that legislate, regulate, enforce, and reinterpret the rules that govern society. Slum health must identify the agents and institutions responsible for helping to create the social inequalities that contribute to health inequities experienced by slum dwellers.

This ecosocial construct also emphasizes *monitoring*. Surveillance is already a recognized function of public health, and planners regularly collect reams of data on land use, sociodemographics, and so on. However, turning data into monitoring indicators requires value judgments concerning what is important to measure, at what frequency, and to what end. Monitoring can also imply assigning responsibility for a particular trend, and this too is rarely done in current planning and public health practice.

For example, burden-of-disease estimates have tended to focus on the whole world or specific geographic regions. These data can mask intracity differences, and global data may not be relevant for informing national or municipal policy making. Public health has developed metrics for single pathogenic exposures or risk factors, but these measures often ignore both community assets that promote health equity and cumulative impacts on health from exposure to a range of urban environmental, economic, and social stressors that characterize twenty-first-century urban health inequities in the global North and South. Recognizing these population health challenges, the Commission on Social Determinants of Health in 2008 called for "health equity to become a marker of good government performance" and for the UN to "adopt health equity as a core global development goal and use a social determinants of health indicators framework to monitor progress."[27]

Yet the danger of indicator efforts is that they portray a too simplified picture of a complex reality, and policy solutions based on them may suffer the same defects. For example, indicators of single chemical exposures cannot produce policy-relevant knowledge about the environmental health consequences of multiple exposures. In a similar way, cross-sectional measures of single built and social environmental features of urban neighborhoods tend to ignore the cascading and relational effects of inequalities in urban areas. Ecosocial epidemiology demands that we critically examine the efficacy of traditional indicators that measure morbidity and mortality, since they tend to place responsibility for improving health either on the medical and public health communities alone or on vaguely identified institutions such as the economy, education, or the built environment. The result is an overemphasis on medical and public health solutions while failing to articulate the specific agents, institutions, and policies that might need to change to promote greater urban health equity.

FRAMEWORK 4: SCIENCE AND TECHNOLOGY STUDIES FOR THE CITY

Scholars of science and technology studies (STS), among others, have emphasized that science is now pursued less in centralized research institutions and is much more dispersed, context-dependent, and problem-oriented. That community members are monitoring the toxins they are exposed to in their homes and streets in partnership with community-based organizations and academics is just one example of this new model of science. Gibbons and colleagues have called this "Mode 2" science and described it as having the following characteristics:

> Knowledge is increasingly produced in contexts of application (i.e., all science is to some extent "applied" science).
>
> Science is increasingly transdisciplinary—that is, it draws upon and integrates empirical and theoretical elements from a variety of fields.
>
> Knowledge is generated in a wider variety of sites than ever before, not just in universities and industry, but also in other sorts of research centres, consultancies, and think-tanks.
>
> Participants in science have grown more aware of the social implications of their work (i.e., more "reflexive"), just as publics have become more conscious of the ways in which science and technology affect their interests and values.[28]

Ensuring the public accountability of Mode 2 science is difficult since typical methods of internal legitimacy, such as peer review, rarely if ever consider the social value of the work as a criterion. Further, who the peers are, how they are selected, and what standards they use for publicly accountable reviews are equally challenging questions.

Dissatisfied with the one-size-fits-all approach to peer review, Funtowicz and Ravetz proposed to divide the world of policy-relevant science into three nested domains each with its own quality controls.[29] First, they identify normal science (borrowing from Thomas Kuhn's well-known articulation)[30] as ordinary, or what we might call basic, scientific research. A second modality for Funtowicz and Ravetz is consultancy science, which is the application of science to well-defined problems. In both basic and consultancy science, traditional peer review might be effective in ensuring credibility. Finally, there is post-normal science, which they describe as situations with highly uncertain and contested knowledge claims but where decisions need to be made in a timely way, such as those over health and safety regulations. For Funtowicz and Ravetz, post-normal science demands what they call an "extended peer review community," involving not only scientists but also the stakeholders affected by the issue. The aim of extended peer review is to ensure public accountability and quality control for science policy decisions.

The implication is that science that continues to derive legitimacy solely from a socially detached position is too frail to meet the pressures placed on it by contemporary problems, such as climate change, sustainability, and healthy cities. Science must begin to focus more on gaining robustness from being embedded in, not increasingly detached from, society. However, as Jasanoff notes, this imperative raises a serious challenge regarding how to institutionalize polycentric, interactive, and multipartite processes of knowledge making within institutions that have worked for decades at keeping expert knowledge away from the vagaries of populism and politics.[31] The question confronting the governance of science is how to bring knowledgeable publics into the front end of scientific and technological production—a place from which they have historically been strictly excluded.

The explicit recognition of both professional information and local knowledge—and acknowledgment that neither can ultimately put to rest the uncertainty of slum health challenges—can encourage decision makers to acknowledge the necessity of renewal, flexibility, and adjustment as key elements of decision-making success. Instead of portraying themselves as the "source of certainty," professional decision makers can highlight the necessity for contingent decisions that must be open to renegotiation as new information becomes available. This means that the professional's role must be reconceptualized from a "guarantor of safety" to a "guarantor of recognition"—of new knowledge, new voices, new ideas, new possibilities, and new directions for intervention.

Robert Reich gives an eloquent account of how this practice of public deliberation can spur civic discovery. He suggests that professionals seize the opportunity for the public to deliberate over what it wants by

> convening of various forums . . . where citizens are to discuss whether there is a problem and, if so, what it is and what should be done about it. The public manager does not specifically define the problem or set an objective at the start. . . . Nor does he take formal control of the discussions or determine who should speak for whom. . . . In short, he wants the community to use this as an occasion to debate its future.
>
> Several different kinds of civic discovery may ensue. . . . The problem and its solutions may be redefined. . . . Voluntary action may be generated. . . . Preferences may be legitimized. . . . Individual preferences may be influenced

> by considerations of what is good for society. . . . Deeper conflicts may be discovered. . . . Deliberation does not automatically generate these public ideas, of course; it simply allows them to arise. Policy making based on interest group intermediation or net benefit maximization, by contrast, offers no such opportunity.[32]

Reich's vision and the process articulated by Funtowicz and Ravetz help us envision what the coproduction process might look like in practice.

However, if coproduction requires negotiation between experts and local people, slum residents should enter into this process with caution. As Arnstein's 1969 classic essay on the "ladder of citizen participation" highlighted, public participation can often backfire when the professionals controlling such processes do little to understand the residents of disenfranchised, low-income communities and do even less to meaningfully listen to and include them in decisions.[33] Arnstein discerned "a critical difference between going through the empty ritual of participation and having the real power needed to affect the outcome of the process."

Yet deliberative forums, especially those involving medical and public health decisions, have rarely found a way to avoid granting science and technical expertise a privileged position in the discourse. Technical language and disciplinary "standing" remain prerequisites for most slum health deliberative forums, often creating an intimidating and "disciplining" barrier for slum dwellers seeking to express their disagreements in the language of everyday life.[34] Speaking the language of science, as well as the jargon of a particular policy community, remains an essential, but often tacit credential for participation in slum health decision making.[35] These challenges raise the need for the final conceptual frame for slum health, adaptive ecosystem management.

FRAMEWORK 5: ADAPTIVE ECOSYSTEM MANAGEMENT

Adaptive ecosystem management and the related concept of sustainability science act as the fifth concept for moving action-research toward slum health. Sustainability science is one application or discipline that emerged in part as a response to the Mode 2 claims in STS.[36] It aims to reframe science around interactions between science and society, around a focus on problems rather than disciplinary methods and on coproducing knowledge for action. Adaptive ecosystem management is a subfield within sustainability science.[37]

Adaptive ecosystem management was designed with insights from complex adaptive systems research and ecological management. Adaptive management acknowledges the failures of linear processes in which narrow-disciplinary scientists have aimed to develop complex models, predict long-term outcomes, and suggest one-time policy standards. Instead, adaptive management begins with an acknowledgement of the inherent complexity and uncertainty within systems and recognition that this complexity demands an iterative, ongoing learning process among a range of expert stakeholders and that policy interventions must be adjusted to reflect newly acquired knowledge.[38] Another difference between adaptive management and conventional science policy is that adaptive management does not postpone actions until definitive causality is known about a system, but rather emphasizes the importance of action in the face of uncertain science and couples these decisions tightly to rigorous monitoring. The US National Research Council has characterized adaptive management as an iterative process with the following characteristics:

1. Management objectives that are regularly revisited and revised
2. A baseline model of change described for the system(s) being managed
3. A range of management choices
4. Monitoring and evaluation of choices
5. Mechanisms for incorporating learning into future decisions
6. A collaborative structure for stakeholder participation and learning[39]

The process of adaptive management is one in which a broad group of stakeholders, from scientists to policymakers to users of a resource, work together to generate evidence, make decisions, monitor the progress of those decisions, and make ongoing adjustments to decisions as new information emerges from monitoring.

The following five frameworks do not reflect a hard-and-fast theory of achieving slum health, but rather offer an approach for interdisciplinary action research.

Coproduction

Scientists and nonprofessionals with different areas of expertise contribute to research design and analyses, and interventions are implemented and managed by the local people most impacted.

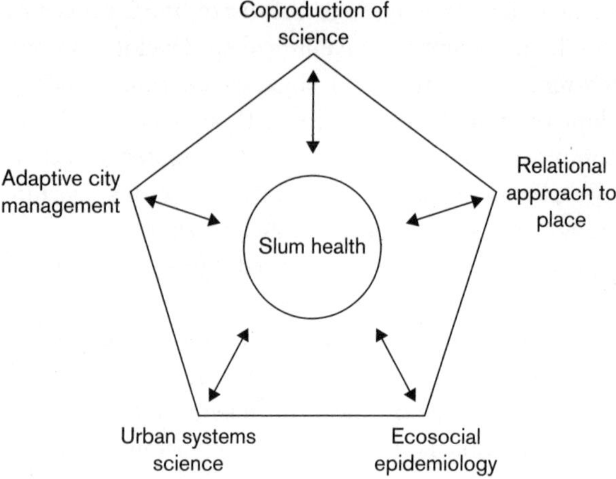

FIGURE 3.2. Slum health model.

Relational View of Place

This framework approaches urban places as being made by people, institutions, and policies, not just static built-environment features; places also shape people, such as by constraining or offering opportunities for physical and social interactions; endogenous and exogenous processes must be considered in terms of how they influence the slum determinants of health, including attention to a variety of spatial and political scales, not just the neighborhood and municipal government, over multiple time periods.

Ecosocial Epidemiology

A focus on understanding the distribution of disease among populations and places involves emphasizing that living environments and social status are biologically embodied, that populations are susceptible to multiple, hazardous exposures across the life course, not just at one point in time, and that specific institutions and decisions, in both the public and the private sectors, are responsible and accountable for hazardous exposures, and these need to be made explicit to reverse health inequities.

Urban Systems Science

This holistic approach to cities, slums, and the urban poor requires interdisciplinary methods that understand existing conditions, the dynamic behavior of these interactions, and the inherent uncertainty of these complex dynamics.

Adaptive City Management

This decision-making and monitoring approach recognizes uncertainty, organizes a multiplicity of stakeholders, including residents, to collaboratively make management decisions, designs into the process ongoing monitoring and evaluation of choices, and includes feedback loops that incorporate learning into future decisions.

TOWARD GREATER SLUM HEALTH EQUITY

This chapter outlines some of the guiding frameworks for moving action-research toward greater slum health equity. Each framework overlaps with and has similar characteristics with the others. Coproduction of knowledge is a central concept in science and technology studies and is consistent with the adaptive management approach to complex problem solving. Much like coproduction, a relational view of place also requires multiple kinds of expertise and inputs and overlaps with the concept of embodiment, or how the features of a place get into our bodies to influence health and well-being. Ecosocial epidemiology integrates a nuanced view of place and the science-and-society interactions articulated in coproduction and STS. In short, there is no one sufficient framework for moving toward greater health equity, but those offered here help articulate the components of a new, interdisciplinary field committed to collaboration, health equity, and embracing complex systems.

NOTES

1. Jasanoff, S. (2004). States of knowledge: The co-production of science and the social order. London: Routledge.

2. Ostrom, E. (1996). Crossing the great divide: Coproduction, synergy, and development. *World Development* 24:1073–87.

3. Jasanoff (2004).

4. Hacking, I. (1999). *The social construction of what?* Cambridge, MA: Harvard University Press.

5. Keller, E.F. (1985). *Reflections on gender and science.* New Haven: Yale University Press.

6. Corburn, J. (2005). *Street science: Community knowledge and environmental health justice.* Cambridge, MA: MIT Press.

7. Jasanoff (2004).

8. Davis, M. (2006). *Planet of slums.* London: Verso Press, p. 19.

9. Neuwirth, R. (2005). *Shadow cities: A billion squatters, a new urban world.* New York: Routledge.

10. Escobar, A. (2001). Culture sits in places: Reflections on globalism and subaltern strategies of localization. *Political Geography* 20:139–74.

11. Emirbayer, M. (1997). Manifesto for a relational sociology. *American Journal of Sociology* 103:281–317.

12. Macintyre, S., Maciver, S., & Sooman, A. (1993). Area, class and health: Should we be focusing on places or people? *Journal of Social Policy* 22: 213–34.

13. Krieger, N. (2011). *Epidemiology and the people's health.* New York: Oxford University Press.

14. Ibid.

15. Ibid.

16. Bourdieu, P. (1990). *The logic of practice.* Cambridge: Polity Press.

17. Krieger (2011).

18. Powell (2007).

19. Benson, L., & Yuen, L. (2014). "Structural racism" blamed for some of state's severe health disparities. Minnesota Public Radio. January 30. http://www.mprnews.org/story/2014/01/29/structural-racism-blamed-for-states-health-disparities. Accessed 22 November 2015.

20. Becker, M.H. (1986). The tyranny of health promotion. *Public Health Review* 14(1):15–23.

21. Darity W., Dietrich, J., & Guilkey, D.K. (2003). Persistent advantage or disadvantage? Evidence in support of the intergenerational drag hypothesis. *American Journal of Economics and Sociology* 60(2):435–70.

22. Krieger (2011).

23. Center on the Developing Child. (2014). "Toxic Stress." http://developingchild.harvard.edu/index.php/key_concepts/toxic_stress_response/. Accessed 22 November 2015.

24. Geronimus, A.T., Hicken, M., Keene, D., & Bound, J. (2006). "Weathering" and age patterns of allostatic load scores among Blacks and Whites in the United States. *American J Public Health* 96:826–33.

25. McEwen, B. (1998). Stress, adaptation, and disease: Allostasis and allostatic load. *Ann NY Acad Sci* 840:33–44.

26. Krieger (2011), 222–23.

27. Commission on Social Determinants of Health. (2008). Evidence on social determinants of health. World Health Organization. http://www.who.int/social_determinants/themes/en/. Accessed 22 November 2015.

28. Gibbons, M., Limoges, C., Nowotny, H., Schwartzman, S., Scott, P., & Trow, M. (1994). *The new production of knowledge: The dynamics of science and research in contemporary societies.* London: Sage.

29. Funtowicz, S.O., & Ravetz, J.R. (1993). Science for the Post-Normal Age. *Futures* 25(7):739–55.

30. Kuhn, T. (1970). *The structure of scientific revolutions.* Chicago: University of Chicago Press.

31. Jasanoff (2004).

32. Reich, R. (1990). *Power of public ideas.* Cambridge, MA: Harvard University Press, 144–46.

33. Arnstein, S.R. (1969). A ladder of citizen participation. *JAIP* 35(4):216–24.

34. Simon, A. (2008). The politics of the possible: Making urban life in Phnom Penh. *Singapore Journal of Tropical Geography* 29:186–204.

35. Mitlin, D., & Satterthwaite, D. (Eds.). (2004). *Empowering squatter citizen: Local government, civil society and urban poverty reduction.* London: Earthscan.

36. Clark, W.C., & Dickson, N.M. (2003). Sustainability science: The emerging research program. *PNAS* (*Proceedings of the National Academy of Science*) 100(14). http://www.pnas.org/content/100/14/8059.full.pdf. Accessed 22 November 2015.

37. Norton, B. (2005). *A philosophy of adaptive ecosystem management.* Chicago: University of Chicago Press.

38. Lee, K.N. (1993). *Compass and gyroscope: Integrating science and politics for the environment.* Washington, DC: Island Press.

39. National Research Council Board on Sustainable Development. (1999). *Our common journey: A transition toward sustainability.* Washington, DC: National Academy Press, 23–27.

CHAPTER 4

Urban Poverty

An Urgent Public Health Issue

SUSAN MERCADO, KIRSTEN HAVEMANN,
MOJGAN SAMI, AND HIROSHI UEDA

The World Health Organization (WHO) Commission on Social Determinants of Health (CSDH) has posed a provocative question for public health: "Why do we keep treating people for illnesses only to send them back to the conditions that created illness in the first place?"[1] For the WHO Centre for Health Development (WHO Kobe Centre), hub of the CSDH's Knowledge Network on Urban Settings (KNUS), this question represents a challenge to the public health sector not only to acknowledge the pervasiveness of urban poverty as a critical pathway to ill health and health inequities, but also to address the problem as an urgent public health issue affecting a billion people living in informal settlements, or "slums."[2]

People who live in informal settlements are often systematically excluded from opportunities, decent employment, security, capacity, and empowerment that would enable them to gain better control over their health and lives.[3] As noted in the interim report of the Millennium Development Goals (MDG) Task Force, which focuses on improving the lives of urban slum dwellers: "Much of urban poverty is not because of distance from infrastructure and services but from exclusion. They [slum dwellers] are excluded from the attributes of urban life that remain a monopoly of a privileged minority—political voice, secure good-quality housing, safety and the rule of law, good education, health services, decent transport, adequate incomes, access to goods and services, credit—in short, the attributes of full citizenship."[4] The issue of urban poverty is not new, but it is often narrowly viewed as an economic issue best addressed by economic policies and interventions. Urban poverty today, as driven by globalization and rapid uncontrolled urbanization, also needs to be recognized as a social, political, and cultural process that has profound impacts on public health. Exclusion of the urban poor from the benefits of urban life fosters discontent and political unrest. Within the broader context of health and human development, rapid urbanization of poverty and ill health has been characterized as a new human security threat.[5]

Rapid uncontrolled urbanization results from the interaction between global and local forces. The interconnectedness of cities through trade, business, industry, tourism, international travel, information technology, and media is reshaping social determinants of health that are manifest at the city level. On the other hand, local and national governance capacity in relation to health systems, housing, transport, property rights, migration, land use policy, working conditions, and employment may be unable to cope with the speed of change brought about by global economic restructuring. Both inequity in cities that leads to urban poverty and poor health, therefore, are also products of global and local forces in the urban setting. Public health can play an important role in ameliorating urban poverty through social processes (participation, social capital, social accountability, and social inclusion) that influence urban governance at multiple nodes of power.[6] Addressing urban poverty as an urgent public health issue opens a policy space for fairer health opportunities and healthier and more equitable cities.

IMAGINE THE WORLD AS A GROWING CITY

Today, for the first time in history, half of the world's population lives in cities. The United Nations estimates that the number of urban residents will increase by more than 2 billion people by 2030, whereas the rural population will decline by about 20 million.[7] Of the many risks to health that are linked to rapid urbanization, none is more compelling than the rise of urban poverty, manifested by the growth of informal settlements. Whereas rising urban poverty is evident in the developed world, this trend is more pronounced in developing countries.

UN-Habitat states that the global urban slum population is expected to double from 1 billion (estimated in 2002) to nearly 2 billion by 2030 (from 32 percent to 41 percent of the world's urban population), and to approximately 3 billion by 2050.[8] Among the 1 billion people who live in informal settlements today, one-third of households are headed by women. Hundreds of millions of children and youth live and work in deprived conditions in urban areas.[9] According to the latest *Global Report on Human Settlements,* 43 percent of the urban population in developing regions lives in slums. In the least developed countries, 78 percent are slum dwellers.[10] The scale and speed of this phenomenon pose serious and compelling risks and challenges to health—in sum, it is a crisis of unprecedented magnitude.

When disaggregated into the regions of the World Health Organization, the largest numbers of impoverished people living in poor conditions in urban settings are found in the Western Pacific Region (around 233 million), followed by the Southeast Asian Region (217 million) and the African Region (156 million).[11] Whereas the Western Pacific Region has the highest number of urban slum dwellers, they represent a relatively low one-third of the total urban population of approximately 700 million, on a par with the developing countries of the Americas Region.[12] The rapid expansion of urban areas in South and East Asia is creating megacities of unprecedented size and complexity that present new challenges to providing a decent environment for the poor: the urban slums of the South-East Asia and Eastern Mediterranean Regions account for almost half of urban populations there. Worst affected is the (largely sub-Saharan) African Region, where two-thirds of its urban inhabitants live in informal settlements. It is also experiencing the world's fastest rates of urbanization. Northern Africa is the only developing region where the quality of urban life is improving: here, the proportion of city dwellers living in slums has decreased by 0.15 percent annually (see box 1.1).[13]

The urban setting in a globalized world is increasingly exposed to unhealthy environments, disasters, climate change, violence and injuries, tobacco and other drugs, and epidemics including HIV-AIDS. Without access to adequate shelter, health care, and resources, the urban poor face the greatest threat. If current demographic trends continue, the majority of all urban inhabitants in years to come will suffer disproportionate exposure to the triple burden of ill health: injuries, communicable diseases, and noncommunicable diseases.[14]

UNDERSTANDING THE ROLE OF PUBLIC HEALTH IN AN URBANIZING WORLD

Between 2005 and 2006 the Knowledge Network on Urban Settings (KNUS) worked with researchers, local communities, academia, development organizations, donors, and practitioners from local, national, regional, and global organizations to distill what was known about social determinants of health and health inequities in urban settings.[15] While KNUS research is ongoing, the following findings are of particular relevance to public health:

> The urban poor do not "wait" for governments or organizations to act on their behalf. They have the desire and resourcefulness to find ways to improve their shelters, access running water, produce food, organize child care, educate themselves and their children, and protect each other amid extreme poverty.[16]
>
> While poor communities are severely affected by violence, it is important to recognize the wealth of untapped social resources within informal settlements. One case study from the favelas of Brazil notes the presence of "social networks, trust, solidarity and mutual support, celebration, cultural life, local businesses, informal activities on education, recreation, sports, religion, politics, and much more."[17]
>
> Uncontrolled, rapid urbanization and the unraveling of the traditional social fabric deepen inequity and give rise to alternative governance structures such as gangs (which target impoverished youth) and paramilitary organizations (known to recruit children for warfare).[18] People who live in informal settlements are at higher risk of exposure to crime and violence.[19]
>
> Since 2000, the world's fastest-growing urban areas are also those where there are increasing concentrations of informal settlements. This has profound consequences for public health strategies to control communicable (HIV-AIDS, TB, H5N1 virus, dengue, and other vector-borne diseases) as well as noncommunicable diseases (obesity, diabetes, cancer, chronic heart disease, stroke, hypertension)[20] and mental health and physical conditions associated with urban life (road traffic injuries, urban violence, obesity, unsafe settlements).
>
> Urban poverty has been narrowly framed as an economic development issue. Unless a broader development perspective is used, policies, programs, measurements, evaluations, and strategies—as well as the "actors" and "stakeholders" who are expected to take action—will fail to fully engage the social, cultural, environmental, and health dimensions of urbanization and urban poverty.
>
> Improving local urban governance as a strategy for alleviating urban poverty (as exemplified by the work of UN-Habitat[21]) has created a

new policy space for linking development to health and vice-versa, but the public health sector has not effectively used this space as a means of shaping healthier public policy in the majority of cities.

Given the high concentration of national resources in cities, it is often assumed that city dwellers have better access to services including health care, and that poor people in urban settings are therefore better off than their rural counterparts.[22] This is where the issue of equity emerges as crucial for the urban poor, who, in fact, grapple with complex and debilitating challenges: inability to pay for goods and services, lack of social support systems,[23] unhealthy and unsafe living and working conditions,[24] exposure to crime and violence,[25] limited food choices,[26] discrimination, isolation,[27] and powerlessness.[28]

Despite the obvious linkage between urban poverty and ill health and the potential impact on the rest of the population, the health sector in many countries continues to narrowly define its role as that of finding ways to improve access to services and improve the financing of health care services for the poor. Although important, this effort is far from sufficient.[29]

PUBLIC HEALTH: A RALLYING POINT FOR EQUITY IN CITIES

The need for intersectoral action and policy to address social determinants of health is not a new concept. The challenges and difficulties of mobilizing intersectoral support for policy and resources are known. In its review of eighty case studies, KNUS discovered that "health" can unite individuals, communities, institutions, leaders, donors, and politicians from divergent sectors, even in complex and hostile contexts where structural determinants of health are deep and divisive. Some of the case studies are highlighted below.

Whether it is mobilizing the members of a local community to design a health plan for themselves (e.g., Dar es Salaam, Tanzania's Healthy City Programme[30]), enabling citizens to vote for priorities in local resource allocations for health (participatory budgeting in Porto Alegre, Brazil[31]), decreasing dengue incidence (Marikina Healthy Cities Programme, The Philippines[32]), or involving the entire community in designing shared spaces that encourage walking and cycling (Healthy by Design, Victoria, Australia[33]), public health is an effective rallying point for achieving greater health equity in the urban setting.

While debate and discourse inevitably arise over methods, terminology, resources, and priorities for achieving better health, invoking health as a social goal and the imperative for "fairer health opportunities for all" has been a powerful lever for addressing social determinants of health in urban settings. The research and analysis also point to the critical importance of social processes in achieving more equitable health outcomes. Preliminary findings from KNUS thematic papers suggest that:[34]

> Integrated interventions that support community action through participation and empowerment (such as urban primary health care,[35] healthy cities,[36] community-based initiatives,[37] sustainable cities,[38] local agenda sites,[39, 40] "cities without slums,"[41] and many other integrated approaches) have been shown to reduce health risks, improve health outcomes, and promote better quality of life.
>
> Where integrated interventions are further linked to better urban governance (local government accountability, local capacity building in support of decentralization, land use policy, participatory budgeting, urban planning and design, sustainable food systems), a healthier social environment is possible.
>
> Where "change agents," "catalysts," and "facilitators" have stepped in to mobilize communities toward public health action and ultimately to influence intersectoral policy and mobilize resources for health equity (as in national urban renewal programs, agricultural policy, national housing policy linked to urban development), bringing interventions to scale is more likely.
>
> Networked governance,[42] whereby urban poor communities and other organized groups (e.g., Shack/Slum Dwellers International[43]) work with local or national government agencies—such as the Community Organizations Development Institute of Thailand[44] and the Committee of Resource Organizations of Mumbai, India[45]—and with international alliances or organizations—such as the Alliance of Healthy Cities,[46] European Healthy Cities Network,[47] Network of Healthy Municipalities,[48] Cities Alliance,[49] UN-Habitat, and WHO—demonstrates the power of harnessing social processes created by the interconnectedness of cities. Taking the principles of empowerment and participation a step further through city-to-city learning is a means of transforming global power relations and overcoming the structures that perpetuate urban poverty.[50]

SHARPENING THE FOCUS ON SOCIAL PROCESSES

Primary health care and its emphasis on community action and social process in the urban setting constitute a key strategy in achieving health equity for the urban poor.[51] Sharpening the focus on social processes throughout the entire public health arena paves the way for scaling up interventions that work.

The case studies of KNUS describe a range of actions that contribute to strengthening and supporting the role of public health:

1. Engaging in political processes (including budget hearings, elections, lobbying, and campaigns) that impact social determinants such as violence prevention, employment, child development, and gender equity
2. Strengthening "bonding" and "bridging" social capital by facilitating dialogue among stakeholders across sectors and within hierarchies
3. Using a "healthy settings approach"[52]
4. Engaging communities through participation and use of empowering processes
5. Engaging in intersectoral policy debates on non–health equity drivers (e.g., transportation, land use policy, land tenure, human rights)
6. Using existing networks to advance policy issues (local, national, regional, international)
7. Advocating social and financial accountability at all levels
8. Recognizing the links between mental health and well-being and public places, community spaces, parks, and gardens where social cohesion and the expression of diversity are simultaneously nurtured through cultural activities, art, recreation, sports and play
9. Using local data (intraurban health differentials) and local situations to forge the links between health and other sectors such as transportation, housing, and public services that impact social determinants
10. Supporting regulations that protect people, especially vulnerable or exposed groups, from threats and hazards (in workplaces, communities, schools)

USING SOCIAL CAPITAL TO INFLUENCE URBAN GOVERNANCE

How can we do a better job of linking disadvantaged people living in cities to the human and financial resources, policies, programs, and actions that would enable them to gain control over their health and their lives? How can we mobilize the resources to enable this process to happen at a scale that will make a difference for the world's urban poor? What is the link between social processes and urban governance?

Social capital, as part of social processes, is a critical means of changing power relations in cities. Public health can provide the glue to link, network, and bind the growing groups of poor and marginalized populations to nodes of power.

The urban setting is in itself a social determinant of health. Public health gains in disease prevention and control in our cities can easily unravel with the growth of physical and social environments of extreme deprivation. In an interconnected world, our cities can continue to be "engines of economic growth"[53] and "centres of culture."[54] The question is whether public health can use the interconnectedness of cities as a positive pathway to enhancing equity in health between and among cities and nations.

NOTES

1. Marmot, M. (2006). Social determinants of health. First Meeting of the Social Determinants of Health for the Asia Network. Tokyo: Asia Network.

2. UN-Habitat Features (2003). *What are slums and why do they exist?* United Nations Human Settlements Programme.

3. Kawachi, I., & Wamala, S.P. (2006). Poverty and inequalities in a globalized world. In Kawachi I. & Wamala S.P., eds. *Globalization and Health*, 122–37. New York: Oxford University Press.

4. Garau, P., & Sclar, E.D. (2004). Interim report of the Millennium Development Goal Task Force 8 on Improving the Lives of Slum Dwellers. New York: United Nations.

5. IDEA (2006). Democracy and human security. In *Democracy, conflict and human security: Further reading*. Stockholm: International Institute for Democracy and Electorate Assistance, 22.

6. Burris, S., Hancock, T., Herzog, A., & Lin, V. (2007). *Emerging strategies for healthy urban governance. J Urban Health.* DOI 10.1007/s11524-007-9174-6.

7. United Nations Population Fund. Urbanization: A majority in cities. http://www.unfpa.org/pds/urbanization.htm. Accessed 15 February 2007.

8. UN-Habitat (2005a). Urbanization, urban population and urban slum dwellers. In *Financing urban shelter: Global Report on Human Settlements, 2005*. London: Earthscan.

9. Bartlett, S., UN Children's Fund, Hart, R., Satterthwaite, D., de la Barra, X., & Missair, A. (1999). *Cities for children: Children's rights, poverty and urban management*. London: Earthscan.

10. UN-Habitat. (2005b). *Financing urban shelter: Global Report on Human Settlements*. London: Earthscan.

11. UN-Habitat (2005a).

12. UN-Habitat Features (2003).

13. UN-Habitat (2005a).

14. UN-Habitat (2003). *The challenge of slums: Global Report on Human Settlements.* London: Earthscan.

15. Kawachi & Wamala (2006).

16. Chitekwe, B., & Mitlin, D. (2001). The urban poor under threat and in struggle: Options for urban development in Zimbabwe, 1995–2000. *Environ Urban,* 13(85):85–101.

17. Becker, D. (2006). *Network of Healthy Communities of Rio de Janeiro, Brazil.* Rio de Janeiro: Network of Healthy Communities.

18. Rodgers, D. (2005). Youth gangs and perverse livelihood strategies in Nicaragua: Challenging certain preconceptions and shifting the focus of analysis. In *New Frontiers of Social Policy: Development in a Globalized World.* Arusha, Tanzania: World Bank.

19. Pangaea. Street children—Community children: Worldwide Resource Library. http://pangaea.org/street_children/kids.htm. Accessed 15 February 2007.

20. WHO (2005). *Preventing chronic diseases: A vital investment.* Geneva: World Health Organization.

21. UN-Habitat (2002). The Global Campaign on Urban Governance. 2nd ed. Nairobi, Kenya. http://unhabitat.org/books/global-campaign-on-urban-governance-the/. Accessed 13 February 2016.

22. Waelkens, M.P., & Greindl, I. (2001). *Urban health: Particularities, challenges, experiences and lessons learned.* A Literature Review. Eschborn, Germany: Deutsche Gesellschaft fur Technische Zusammenarbeit (GTZ).

23. Pridmore, P., Havemann, K., Sapag, J., Thomas, L., & Wood, L. (2007). Social capital and healthy urbanization in a globalized world. *J Urban Health.* DOI 10.1007/s11524-007-9172-8.

24. Kjellstrom, T., Friel, S., Dixon, J., et al. (2007). Urban environmental health hazards and health equity. *J Urban Health.* DOI 10.1007/s11524-007-9171-9.

25. Campbell, T., & Campbell, A. (2007). *Emerging disease burdens and the poor in cities of the developing world.* J Urban Health. DOI 10.1007/s11524-007-9181-7.

26. Dixon, J., Friel, S., Omwega, A., Donati, K., Burns, C., & Carlisle, R. (2007). *The health equity dimensions of urban food systems.* J Urban Health. DOI 10.1007/s11524-007-9176-4.

27. Pridmore et al. (2007).

28. Burris et al. (2007).

29. Marmot, M. (2005). *Status syndrome: How your social standing directly affects your health and life expectancy.* London: Bloomsbury.

30. Sheuya, S., Patel, S., & Howden-Chapman, P. (2007). Improving health and building human capital through an effective primary care system and healthy setting approach. *J Urban Health* 84(Suppl 1). DOI 10.1007/s11524-007-9175-5.

31. Wechtler, M. (2006). *Participatory budgeting in Porto Alegre.* Philadelphia: Temple University.

32. David, A. (2006). Marikina City, Guam.

33. Dixon, J. (2006). *Healthy by design: A planners guide to environments for active living*. Victoria, Australia: VicHealth and the Planning Institute.

34. Garau & Sclar (2004).

35. Regional Committee for the Western Pacific, WHO (1985). Urban primary health care. http://www.wpro.who.int/rcm/en/archives/rc36/wpr_rc36_r19.htm. Accessed 17 February 2007.

36. WHO. Healthy Cities and Urban Governance. http://www.euro.who.int/healthy-cities. Accessed 17 February 2007.

37. WHO. Community Based Initiatives. Available at: http://www.emro.who.int/cbi/. Accessed 17 February 2007.

38. WHO (1997). City planning for health and sustainable development. Geneva: World Health Organization.

39. Rodgers (2005).

40. United Nations (1992). *Agenda 21*. United Nations Conference on Environment and Development, Rio de Janeiro, Brazil, 3–14 June. UN Division for Sustainable Development. https://sustainabledevelopment.un.org/milestones/unced/agenda21. Accessed 23 November 2015.

41. Cities Alliance (1999). Cities without slums action plan. World Bank; UN-Habitat. http://www.citiesalliance.org/cws-action-plan. Accessed 24 November 2015.

42. Burris et al. (2007).

43. Slum/Shack Dwellers International. The challenge of engagement. http://www.sdinet.org/bulletins/b17.htm. Accessed 17 February 2007.

44. Community Organization Development Institute. http://www.codi.or.th/index.php?option=com_content&task=section&id=9&Itemid=52. Accessed 17 February 2007.

45. Palnitker, S. (1988). New culture of urban sanitation, Mumbai (CORO). Available at: http://www.archidev.org/article.php3?id_article=391. Accessed 24 November 2015.

46. AFHC. Healthy cities lead the way. Alliance for Healthy Cities. http://www.alliance-healthycities.com/. Accessed 17 February 2007.

47. Regional Committee for the Western Pacific, WHO (1985).

48. Panamerican Health Organization. BVSDE: Healthy Municipalities. http://www.bvsde.ops-oms.org/sde/ops-sde/ingles/municipios-acerca.html. Accessed 24 November 2015.

49. Cities Alliance (1999).

50. Campbell & Campbell (2007).

51. Lee, A., Kiyu, A., Molina, H., & Jimenez de la Jara, J. (2007). Improving health and building human capital through effective primary care system and healthy setting approach. *J Urban Health*.

52. WHO. Healthy Settings. World Health Organization. http://www.who.int/healthy_settings/en/. Accessed 24 November 2015.

53. Li, H. (2003). Management of coastal mega-cities—a new challenge in the 21st century. *Marine Policy* 27:333–337.

54. Rees, W.E. The conundrum of urban sustainability. http://www.earthscape.org/r3/ES14446/devuyst_introb.pdf. Accessed 17 February 2007.

CHAPTER 5

Urban Informal Settlement Upgrading and Health Equity

JASON CORBURN AND ALICE SVERDLIK

Few other measures have greater potential to transform the well-being of the urban poor than participatory, integrated slum-upgrading programs and policies. However, as we show in this chapter, the health equity benefits of slum upgrading are rarely acknowledged, explicitly designed into projects, or analyzed as part of project and policy impact evaluations. Informal settlements ("slums") are usually characterized by poverty, tenure insecurity, overcrowded dwellings, and inadequate infrastructure and services, as well as elevated rates of infectious and noncommunicable disease. Multiple environmental health hazards are concentrated in informal settlements, and residents often face sociospatial, political, and economic exclusion as compared to wealthier city dwellers.[1] We suggest in this chapter that urban health inequalities can be reduced by responsive governance and multisectoral initiatives that include participatory and integrated slum upgrading. While there is no one definition of slum upgrading, it has come to entail program and policy interventions spanning the delivery of land rights, infrastructure, and social programs that also include enhancements to community participation and political recognition.[2, 3] These claims alone suggest that slum upgrading has the potential to simultaneously improve living conditions and key social determinants of health.

In this chapter, we suggest that a multidimensional and relational approach to evaluating slum-upgrading projects can better capture whether and how upgrading can address the social determinants of health. Emerging processes in the field of public health, such as Health Impact Assessment, may offer methodologies for capturing the broad determinants of health that slum upgrading can influence, methodologies more robust than narrowly designed impact evaluations. We first suggest that while slum upgrading initiatives are increasingly salient as urbanization proceeds apace in cities of the global South, the health implications of upgrading are often overlooked. We argue that slum upgrading can address some aspects of deprivation faced by large sections of low-income urban populations, but they are no panacea. We next point out that urbanization can facilitate major advances in health, but these benefits are not reaching all city dwellers, especially those living in slums. Urban slum dwellers increasingly face a "triple threat" of infectious diseases, noncommunicable conditions (including diabetes, cardiovascular disease, and mental illness), and injuries due to violence or road traffic. After discussing the possible pathways between slum upgrading and health equity, we critically review existing literature on published evaluations of slum upgrading. We found that there are very few evaluations of urban slum-upgrading projects. Of the slum-upgrading evaluations we found and could review for whether and how they measured health impacts, most measured a single disease outcome, mortality, or behavioral change. Very few documented changes in health status, as defined by residents, explored the gender-health impacts of built-environment improvements or measured how community participation itself may have led to improved health among slum dwellers.[4] We conclude by suggesting how our relational framework might offer a more integrated and accurate portrait of the health equity impacts of slum upgrading. In this approach, mixed methods are used to evaluate how upgrading projects can influence health by incorporating residents' narratives, systematic observation, spatial mapping, and measures the effect of health services' locations and accessibility.[5] We argue that nuanced, comprehensive analyses of slum upgrading may reveal ways to achieve global health equity, especially as greater numbers of people are living in urban areas and slums around the world.

WHAT IS SLUM UPGRADING AND WHAT IS ITS RELATION TO HEALTH?

Complex slum environments and populations defy easy generalizations and measurement. Informal settlements are heterogeneous in terms of housing type, tenure security, levels of infrastructure service provision,

TABLE 5.1 DEFINING INFORMAL SETTLEMENTS ("SLUMS") AND ASSOCIATED HEALTH RISKS

UN-Habitat (2003) physical dimensions	Definition and indicators	Individual health risks	Community health risks
Overcrowding	> 2 persons/room or < 5 m^2 per person	Indoor air pollution and respiratory illness, exacerbated by minimal ventilation	TB, influenza, meningitis, and other respiratory diseases
Low-quality housing structure	Inferior building materials and substandard construction	Vectors or parasites from unprotected floors or roofs Burns, falls, or other unintentional injuries	Vulnerability to floods and extreme weather events (with health burdens and income losses)
Hazardous housing sites	Geological and site hazards (e.g., industrial wastes, power lines)	Children especially at risk from exposure to unsafe sites and contaminants	As above, with risks exacerbated by minimal infrastructure
Inadequate water access	< 50% of households have piped water, public standpipe, or rainwater collection	Diarrhea, typhus, cholera, hepatitis, scabies, bacterial skin or eye infections	Malaria, dengue, or enteric diseases from standing or contaminated water
Inadequate sanitation access	< 50% of households with sewer, septic tank, pour-flush or ventilated improved latrine	As above, with particular impacts on women's safety and well-being; maternal health complications	Fecal-oral diseases, hookworm, roundworm, etc. due to poor excreta disposal
Limited services and infrastructure	Inadequate health care, drainage, roads, transport, schools, and/or refuse collection	Vaccine-preventable diseases; fires, electrocution, and accidents; lower educational outcomes	Poor emergency provision; heightened flooding; disease transmission due to poor refuse collection
Socioeconomic dimensions	**Definition and indicators**	**Individual health risks**	**Community health risks**
Tenure insecurity	Lack of formal title deeds to land and/or structure	Heightened stress; reduced ability to advocate for oneself	Reduced housing investment, lower community participation

Poverty and informal livelihoods	Low incomes, few assets, and limited access to credit; safety standards lacking; lack of social protection	Low educational outcomes; food insecurity linked to undernutrition or mental deficiencies; solid fuels linked to respiratory illness	Lower community pride; increased occupational hazards (affecting households and communities)
Violence and insecurity	Elevated crime, including gender-based violence	Mental illness and stress; injuries and mortality due to violence	Decrease in trust, social capital, and investment or job opportunities
Political disempowerment	Low governmental responsiveness; inequalities in voice and political power	Reduced self-esteem (with impacts on health-seeking behaviors)	Social exclusion, diminished participation and collective efficacy

poverty, environmental hazards, and scales of violence, among other issues—all of which have important implications for the health and well-being of slum dwellers.[6] Slum-upgrading projects differ across regions of the world, and the definition of upgrading has changed over time. Beginning in 1972, the World Bank launched urban upgrading projects to improve services, infrastructure, and housing in hopes of reducing poverty and meeting basic needs.[7] Yet governments often persisted in slum clearance, while upgrading projects often failed to scale up across cities, struggled with cost recovery, and neglected infrastructure maintenance.[8, 9] With neoliberal ideologies ascendant in the 1980s and 1990s, government was increasingly viewed as an "enabler," and upgrading was sidelined in favor of supporting housing finance, land markets, and local governance.[10]

Today, many African upgrading projects still utilize top-down approaches, usually focusing on single sectors of infrastructure or providing tenure security.[11] In contrast, some Latin American and Asian cities have begun adopting participatory, integrated upgrading strategies.[12] Residents increasingly participate in design and implementation; upgrading is incorporated into land policies, economic development planning, and social policies.[13] Some national governments have embraced upgrading, as in the case of Mexico's Habitat Program and Thailand's Baan Mankong.[14, 15] Several Latin American upgrading initiatives have offered health facilities, cultural centers, and vocational training and have sought to reduce insecurity and crime.[16] Still, achieving citywide scale remains a fundamental challenge, and most successful projects "remain very local."[17]

In general, "slum upgrading" is the term given to measures designed to improve the quality of housing and the provision of housing-related infrastructure and services (including water and sanitation) to settlements considered to be (or officially designated as) slums.[18] The scope of the upgrading varies from some minor improvements—for instance, some communal water taps, paved roads, and street lighting—to comprehensive improvements to each house, as well as good-quality infrastructure (piped water and sewers to each house) and services (including schools and health care centers). The provision of legal land and housing tenure to slum residents may or may not be part of an upgrading program. Granting of tenure may be avoided because of associated costs and complications in negotiating with existing "structure owners" and slum landlords. Importantly, slum upgrading implies an acceptance by governments that the settlement to be "upgraded" is legitimate and

Slum Upgrading and Its Impact on the Social Determinants of Health

- The Commission on the Social Determinants of Health (CDSH) recommends slum upgrading, "including, as a priority, provision of water and sanitation, electricity, and paved streets for all households regardless of ability to pay. . . . Enabling slum upgrading will require the political recognition of informal settlements, supported by regularization of tenure [and provision of] infrastructure and services. . . . Such action will help to empower women and improve their health by increasing access to basic resources such as water and sanitation."[1]
- "In recent decades, there has been a shift toward a more integrated and participatory approach to slum upgrading programs. An integrated approach to upgrading informal settlements incorporates a range of complementary interventions that address physical, social, and economic development needs. [These] typically include the provision of flexible and secure forms of land tenure, [providing] basic infrastructure and facilities in ways that minimize the need for relocations, and appropriate support for residents to upgrade their dwellings."[2]
- Upgrading projects "provide infrastructure and public spaces and physically integrate the neighborhood. . . . They increase [settlers'] physical assets and enhance their market value through the regularization of tenure. They contribute to the development of human capital by [providing] access to better health, education, and recreation services. They enlarge social capital by creating community organizations and promoting settlers' involvement."[3]
- "[Slum] upgrading changes urban poor groups' relationships with city authorities and other city actors. . . . It is about urban poor groups becoming organized, and developing the confidence to make demands (and to negotiate solutions that suit them) . . . and about city authorities encouraging them to do so."[4]

1. Commission on Social Determinants of Health. (2008) *Closing the gap in a generation.* Geneva: World Health Organization.
2. Smit, W., et al. (2011). Toward a research and action agenda on urban planning/design and health equity in cities in low and middle-income countries. *Journal of Urban Health* 88(5):886–96.
3. Rojas (2010). *Building cities: Neighborhood upgrading and urban quality of life.* Washington, DC: Inter-American Development Bank; Cambridge, MA: David Rockefeller Center for Latin American Studies, 16–17.
4. Arif Hasan, Sheela Patel and David Satterthwaite (2005). How to meet the Millennium Development Goals (MDGs) in urban areas. *Environment & Urbanization* 17(1):3–19.

that the inhabitants have a right to live there. This "right to remain" and the legitimacy of slums and slum dwellers—rather than their illegality—in the eyes of governments represents an important shift that may, in itself, offer some health protections.

We reviewed a wide-ranging set of slum-upgrading evaluations in hopes of better understanding how health impacts were described and measured, if at all (table 5.2). We focused on slum-upgrading projects self-described as "integrated" and multisectoral, since our hypothesis was that these, as opposed to more narrowly defined projects, would result in the greatest health benefits for the urban poor. However, we also reviewed evaluations of single-sector projects (i.e., those focused on clean water, housing, or sanitation alone), to explore whether these employed multiple indicators of well-being in their evaluations.[19, 20] Focusing on self-described "integrated" initiatives and "multidimensional" evaluations distinguishes our analyses from other recent reviews in that we were able to include more studies.[21] R. Turley and colleagues' 2013 review, for instance, limited its analyses of slum upgrading to projects that included a case-control and/or randomized design.[22]

We summarize our findings in table 5.2. We narrowed our results to eighteen slum-upgrading projects and policies. We included projects from Latin American, African, and Asian cities and a range of approaches to project design and financing, with some emerging from and funded by national governments and international organizations like the World Bank, and others primarily conceived and financed by local NGOs. We briefly describe the economic and physical impacts of each project, since all projects aimed to change these conditions to some extent. Finally, we note where the evaluation documents explicitly include mention of human health impacts or if they make no mention at all of health effects.

HOW CAN SLUM UPGRADING INFLUENCE HEALTH EQUITY?

Of the eighteen studies we reviewed in depth, only ten explicitly mentioned health impacts. Of those ten, only two measured specific diseases. Of all the evaluations that mentioned health, only self-reported data were gathered, missing the opportunity to combine these reports with clinical and biological measures that are increasingly more affordable to assess. Surprisingly, none of the evaluations asked slum dwellers to "self-rate" their health, even though the basic question "How would you rate your health?" is a globally recognized indicator of overall

TABLE 5.2 SLUM-UPGRADING PROJECTS AND SOCIAL DETERMINANTS OF HEALTH

Project name and location	NGO participation?	Source(s) of financing	Sectoral focus	Economic and/or physical impacts	Health and well-being impacts (if measured)	Key source(s)
Visakhaptnam, Indore, and Vijaywada Upgrading, India	Yes	Department of International Development (DFID)	Roads, water, lighting, social services, loans	Reduced flooding and improved employment opportunities	Safety and reduction in women's time burdens	Amis (2001)
Slum Networking Project (SNP), Ahmedabad, India	Yes	Municipal, private-sector, community, and USAID	Electricity, water, sanitation, roads, garbage	100,000 households electrified	18% reduction in slum dwellers' annual insurance claims due to waterborne illness	Das and Takahashi (2009); Butala et al. (2010)
Toilet Blocks, Mumbai and Pune, India	Yes	State subsidies and user fees	Water and sanitation	Low-cost, replicable toilet blocks	None explicitly measured	Burra et al. (2003)
Baan Mankong, Thailand	Yes	Community Organizations Development Institute (CODI)	Housing, tenure, infrastructure, day care, activities for elderly	Improved tenure security and housing	None explicitly measured	Boonyaban-cha (2009); Archer (2012)
Kampong Improvement Project (KIP), Indonesia	Limited	World Bank and national funding	Roads, drainage, garbage, water, housing	Improved housing and piped water; reduced flood risk	None explicitly measured	Das and Takahashi (2009); World Bank (2007)
Zonal Improvement Program (ZIP), Manila, The Philippines	No	World Bank	Water, roads, housing, land, electricity	Improved housing and infrastructure	Reduced incidence of diarrhea	Aiga and Umenai (2002); Aiga et al. (1999)

(continued)

TABLE 5.2 *(continued)*

Project name and location	NGO participation?	Source(s) of financing	Sectoral focus	Economic and/or physical impacts	Health and well-being impacts (if measured)	Key source(s)
Neighborhood Upgrading and Shelter, Indonesia	No	Asian Development Bank (ADB)	Roads, electricity, water, sanitation, solid waste	2,600 public toilets, 600 km of roads, 16,000 streetlights	Avoided health costs for 3 million beneficiaries = $11.0 million/year	ADB (2012); Chomistriana (2011)
Orangi Pilot Project (OPP), Karachi, Pakistan	Yes	Government (trunk infrastructure only)	Water, sanitation, capacity building and mapping	In-home sanitation	Infant mortality rate reduced from 128 to 37/1000 over 9 years	Pervaiz et al. (2008)
PRIMED, Medellin, Colombia	Yes	German, national, and local funds	Tenure, infrastructure, housing	Reduced travel times, enhanced public spaces	Improved safety perceptions, reduced disaster risks	Betancur (2007)
Favela Bairro, Rio de Janeiro, Brazil	Yes	IDB, municipal funding	Infrastructure, housing, social programs	Infrastructure, public spaces, and community facilities	None explicitly measured	Soares and Soares (2005)
Bairro Legal, São Paulo, Brazil	Yes	IDB, USAID, Cities Alliance, and municipal funds	Roads, electricity, housing, social programs	Support for businesses; youth leadership	Parasópolis's electricity-related emergencies reduced; flood control	UN-Habitat (2009); USAID (2009)
Ribeira Azul and Technical and Social Support Project, Salvador, Brazil	Yes	World Bank, IDB, Cities Alliance	Housing, social programs, water, sanitation, solid waste, roads	Training sessions, cooperatives; 50 social and environmental projects	Self-reported reduction in disease (unspecified) and crime	Baker (2006); Cities Alliance (2008)

Piso Firme, Mexico	No—except for community labor	Municipal and state resources for cement	Housing	34,000 cement floors	Reductions in children's parasitic infestations, diarrhea, and anemia; reduction in mothers' stress and depression	Cattaneo et al. (2009)
PRODEL, Nicaragua	Yes	Swedish International Development Cooperation Agency (SIDA) and matching funds from municipality	Housing, infrastructure, microloans, savings	Reduced earth floors and pit latrines	None explicitly measured	Stein and Vance (2008)
citizen security initiatives in Cali, Bogotá, Medellín, Colombia	Yes	IDB, national, and municipal funds	Violence prevention	Crime reduction and increased use of dispute resolution	None explicitly measured	IDB (2010a, 2010b)
Huruma Community-Led Upgrading, Nairobi, Kenya	Yes	Resident savings and NGO loans	Infrastructure, housing	New housing and communal land tenure	None explicitly measured	Weru 2004
Imizamo Yethu upgrading, Cape Town, South Africa	Yes	National subsidies and NGO loans	Housing, sanitation, water, electricity	Increased access to piped water and flush toilets	None explicitly measured	Shortt and Hammett 2013

(continued)

TABLE 5.2 *(continued)*

Project name and location	NGO participation?	Source(s) of financing	Sectoral focus	Economic and/or physical impacts	Health and well-being impacts (if measured)	Key source(s)
Hanna Nassif Upgrading, Dar es Salaam, Tanzania	Yes	Donors and UN agencies	Water, transport, solid waste, tenure security	Waste and water kiosks managed by residents; enhanced tenure security	Reduced waterborne diseases (unspecified)	Sheuya 2008

SOURCES

ADB (Asian Development Bank) (2011). *Indonesia: Neighborhood Upgrading and Shelter Sector Project.* PCR Project 35143.

Aiga, H., & Umenai, T. (2002). Impact of improvement of water supply on household economy in a squatter area of Manila. *Social science & medicine*, 55(4), 627–641.

Aiga, H., Arai, Y., Marui, E., & Umenai, T. (1999). Impact of improvement of water supply on reduction of diarrheal incidence in a squatter area of Manila. *Environmental Health and Preventive Medicine* 4(3):111–16.

Archer, D. (2012). Baan Mankong participatory slum upgrading in Bangkok, Thailand: Community perceptions of outcomes and security of tenure. *Habitat International* 36(1):178–84.

Baker, J.L. (2006). *Integrated urban upgrading for the poor: The experience of Ribeira Azul, Salvador, Brazil.* World Bank Policy Research Working Paper 3861.

Betancur, J.J. (2007). Approaches to the regularization of informal settlements: A case of PRIMED in Medellín, Colombia. *Global Urban Development* 3(1).

Boonyaban-cha, S. (2009). Land for housing the poor—by the poor: Experiences from the Baan Mankong nationwide slum upgrading programme in Thailand. *Environment and Urbanization* 21(2):309–29.

Burra, S., Patel, S., & Kerr, T. (2003). Community-designed, built and managed toilet blocks in Indian cities. *Environment and Urbanization* 15(2):11–32.

Butala, N.M., VanRooyen, M.J., & Patel, R.B. (2010). Improved health outcomes in urban slums through infrastructure upgrading. *Social science and medicine* 71(5):935–40.

Cattaneo, M.D., Galiani, S., Gertler, P.J., Martinez, S., & Titiunik, R. (2009). Housing, health, and happiness. *American Economic Journal: Economic Policy* 1(1):75–105.

Chomistriana, D. (2011). Indonesia: Neighborhood Upgrading and Shelter Sector Project—Toward cities without slums. In *Inclusive Cities*, ed. F. Steinberg and M. Lindfield, 47–63. Manila, Philippines: Asian Development Bank.

Cities Alliance (2008). *The story of integrated slum upgrading in Salvador (Bahia), Brazil.* Washington, DC: Cities Alliance.

Das, A.K., & Takahashi, L.M. (2009). Evolving institutional arrangements, scaling up, and sustainability: Emerging issues in participatory slum upgrading in Ahmedabad, India. *Journal of Planning Education and Research* 29(2):213–32.

IDB (Inter-American Development Bank) (2010a). *An evaluation of the support for peaceful coexistence and citizen security: Bogota and Medellin.* Discussion Paper OVE/TDP-02/10.

IDB (Inter-American Development Bank) (2010b). *An evaluation of the support for peaceful coexistence and citizen security: Cali.* Discussion Paper OVE/TDP-03/10.

Pervaiz, A., Rahman, P., & Hasan, A. (2008). *Lessons from Karachi: The role of demonstration, documentation, mapping and relationship building in advocacy for improved urban sanitation and water services.* Human Settlements Working Paper, Vol. 6. London: IIED.

Sheuya, S.A. (2008). Improving the health and lives of people living in slums. *Annals of the New York Academy of Sciences* 1136(1):298–306.

Shortt, N.K., & Hammett, D. (2013). Housing and health in an informal settlement upgrade in Cape Town, South Africa. *Journal of Housing and the Built Environment* 28(4):615–27.

Soares, F., & Soares, Y. (2005). *The socio-economic impact of Favela-Bairro: What do the data say?* Working Paper WP-08. Washington, DC: Inter-American Development Bank.

Stein, A., & Vance, I. (2008). The role of housing finance in addressing the needs of the urban poor: Lessons from Central America. *Environment and Urbanization* 20(1):13–30.

USAID (2009). *Transforming electricity consumers into customers: Case study of a slum electrification and loss reduction project in São Paulo, Brazil.* Washington DC: USAID.

Weru, J. (2004). Community federations and city upgrading: The work of Pamoja Trust and Muungano in Kenya. *Environment and Urbanization* 16(1):47–62.

well-being, associated with premature mortality and health equity.[23, 24] Yet thirteen of the evaluations directly mentioned potential social determinants of health, such as reduced water collection times, sense of pride and happiness, and increased empowerment of women, though none of the reports explicitly framed these issues as important influencers of population health. Overall, our reviews of eighteen slum-upgrading project evaluations reflected the following challenges for understanding health equity:

Measures of health were very limited and tended to focus on childhood mortality or morbidity (particularly due to diarrheal or other communicable illnesses).

Economic impacts and financial status of populations dominated the discussion, but few attempted to evaluate how poverty or income influenced the health status of slum dwellers.

Infrastructure improvements were measured through such variables as the number of new access points and costs per unit, but rarely by assessing how infrastructure improvements changed pathogenic exposures, safety, or gender equity.

Infrastructure and health evaluation focused largely on the water sector.

Resident participation was often mentioned as a positive impact in evaluations, but the reports did not link participation, empowerment, or self-efficacy to population health.

All reports faced serious methodological challenges, including limited reliable baseline data and limited qualitative or participatory research, and follow-up times to measure impacts were often extremely short, averaging about six months.

In the following section we detail some of the key findings of the evaluation reports that did discuss social determinants of health and highlight these as examples of what is possible in slum-upgrading evaluations.

Health Indicators. Health indicators are often limited to changes in waterborne disease, a narrow focus that overlooks the broader potential of upgrading initiatives to support well-being and gender equality. Adequate water can improve household incomes by curtailing health expenditures or increasing productivity; enhance educational outcomes by reducing sick days or providing sanitation at school; and promote gender equity if women and girls' time collecting water is reduced.[25] However, evaluations of upgrading projects are usually limited to measuring changes in diarrhea or other communicable conditions.[26] In one exception, a study in Dar es Salaam found that after improving water, roads, and solid waste management in Hanna Nassif, cases of waterborne illness fell from 4,137 in 1994 to 2,520 in 1998.[27] In addition, the project helped reduce flooding, enhanced tenure security, and encouraged participation via community-managed water and solid waste projects.[28] Yet it is rare for upgrading assessments to consider such intangible, long-term changes as improvements in participation, empowerment, or gender equality.

Avoided Health Care Costs. While changes in household finances as a result of slum-upgrading projects are frequently measured, we found that evaluations of avoided health care costs were the exception. Only three evaluations considered the time savings, avoided health care costs, or health benefits of income generation linked to upgrading. In one project, Manila slum dwellers were provided with piped water under the Zonal Improvement Program (ZIP). Household water expenditures were reduced and three to four hours per day of waiting time for water was eliminated. The evaluation revealed that 72 percent of beneficiaries reallocated their time to income-generating activities.[29] Another integrated project focused on improving slum water and sanitation in Indonesia benefited nearly 3 million people and resulted in avoided health care costs of $11 million annually.[30] In Ahmedabad, Butala and colleagues found an 18 percent decrease in the fraction of slum-dwellers' insurance claims due to waterborne illness in an average year.[31]

Social Capital and Mental Health. Improvements in social capital are recognized as an important social determinant of health since social relations can reduce depression, isolation, and loneliness; improve information about accessing services; and prolong happiness. Fear of eviction or violent crime may exact a toll on residents' mental health, while upgrading may generate "changes in the psychological burden of stress, hostility, and depression."[32] The World Bank and International Development Bank's (IDB's) "citizen security initiatives" seek to prevent violence by upgrading public spaces, improving lighting, and organizing community policing activities. Evaluations in Cali, Bogotá, and Medellín, Colombia, all found some changes in residents' attitudes toward the police and improved perceptions of safety, but these same studies did not attempt to measure population stress, depression, or anxiety.[33] Residents of Salvador's favelas perceived a decline in crime after housing and roads were upgraded,[34] but these perceptions were not explored in greater detail or verified by police reporting. While reducing crime and insecurity is a complex, lengthy process, careful qualitative research can illuminate ongoing shifts in mental illness, social cohesion, and perceptions of a slum's safety.

Social Inclusion. Slum upgrading has the potential to reduce segregation and the exclusion of the urban poor from the benefits of city life, thereby improving health. For example, an evaluation of slum upgrading in São Paulo, Brazil, demonstrated that integrated infrastructure improvements can promote health and well-being by reducing the incidence of fires and enhancing citizenship rights and residents' access to credit. The Favela Real project provided public lighting, garbage collection, and improved roads and water service to the urban poor.[35] Only the electrification component was evaluated in Paraisópolis for its impacts on community well-being, and the report found a reduction in the frequency of fires, with residents reporting improved safety and pride in their place after tangled wires were removed. Importantly, São Paulo's housing authority generated multidimensional indices that reflect complex health and socioeconomic vulnerabilities. In particular, a health index was created that encompassed housing and infrastructure quality, fire risk, and social vulnerability.[36] Slum dwellers in São Paulo also noted that the project allowed them to gain an address and establish a history of paying electricity bills, both of which helped them get access to credit and other public benefits.[37] These details suggest that long-term changes in governance and social inclusion may unfold as more favela residents access credit, entitlements, and state recognition as citizens.

Gender and Health. Slum upgrading may disproportionately improve the lives and health of women since they are often more burdened than men with daily chores and taking care of the sick and are more exposed to pollution and pathogens in slums. In one slum-upgrading evaluation from India, we found reports of multiple benefits of infrastructure improvements focused on gender equity and community pride. To evaluate the Department of International Development's (DFID's) upgrading project in Visakhaptnam, Indore, and Vijaywada, Amis conducted research in four slums in each city that received roads, water, sanitation, electricity, childcare centers, and other social services.[38] Amis surveyed 550 households and included focus groups, interviews, and community dialogues. The evaluation noted that economic activity increased thanks to electrification and improved public spaces, which helped extend the workday. More than 80 percent of surveyed households reported an improved "image" of their settlements. Women noted enhanced security and safety at night, along with improved water service and lighting. The

Slum Networking Project in Ahmedabad, later renamed Parivartan, combined infrastructure with community development projects and strong NGO participation.[39] Surveys of more than 150 households found that 70 to 90 percent rated infrastructure, including drainage, roads, and household water connections, as "good" or "excellent."[40] An evaluation of Ahmedabad's electrification found improved quality of life and a 200 percent increase in daily electricity consumption, though no health impacts were given.[41]

These examples from slum-upgrading evaluations suggest that projects often fail to capture the broad health impacts of their work. Evaluations could be improved by attempting to measure the direct and indirect influences of projects and policies on improving the place-based physical, social, and political determinants of health. In the following section, we offer a model for why and how these relational evaluations might be integrated into slum-upgrading project design and health impact analyses.

TOWARD INTEGRATED, RELATIONAL EVALUATIONS OF SLUM-UPGRADING PROJECTS

Our review of published slum-upgrading evaluations suggests that upgrading can enhance health equity and address the social determinants of health, but this impact is rarely measured. The upgrading projects that seemed to have the greatest influence on population health were those that were integrated into local and national governments' ongoing urban investments, such as Baan Mankong, Thailand, and Favela Bairro in Rio de Janeiro, Brazil. Similarly, slum upgrading in which community organizations were leaders, rather than just partners, seemed to generate the most lasting improvements in the social determinants of health. For example, in the case of the Pakistani Orangi Pilot Project (OPP) in Karachi, households worked together to plan, finance, and implement sanitary toilets in their own houses, construct underground sewers, and link these to neighborhood trunk sewers constructed by the government.

Our review also revealed that it is difficult to measure whether upgrading initiated and driven by households and residents (e.g., in Huruma, Nairobi) versus upgrading conceived and promoted by external organizations, such as the World Bank and national governments (e.g., in Favela Bairro) has a greater health impact. Clearly, more research into these and other questions is needed. As we explore in greater depth in the following chapters of this book, using a more expansive definition of health impacts in evaluations and taking a relational approach may more accurately capture the health effects of slum upgrading.

Health impact assessment (HIA) is one approach that slum-upgrading evaluations might incorporate into pre- and postproject evaluations. HIA is often defined as a combination of procedures, methods, and tools that systematically judge the potential, sometimes unintended effects of a policy, plan, program, or project on the health of a population and the distribution of those effects within that population. HIA is as much a process as it is a method of analysis. It aims for transparent decision making, integrating multiple determinants of health and assessing short- and long-term human health impacts among specific population groups and the general population. HIA has emerged from a history of policy analysis and impact assessments, such as environmental and social impact assessment, and should be viewed as part of these literatures. Since the early 1990s, the practice of HIA has taken hold in Australia and Europe and more recently in North America and Asia. Local and national government agencies, as well as nongovernmental organizations, private consultants, and international organizations such as the World Health Organization (WHO) and the International Finance Corporation (IFC), have all produced guides for conducting HIAs. While the practice is still emerging and rarely if ever applied to slum upgrading, case studies and evaluations of practice exist within the peer-reviewed literature. Some local and national governments have formally institutionalized HIA as a distinct practice in public health and other agencies, while other governments integrate HIA within existing health analyses and public decision-making assessments. HIA is also increasingly linked to and part of other emerging public health paradigms, including social determinants of health and sustainability and health. HIA is also a strategy for implementing "health in all policies" (HiAP), a second integrated approach that holds promise for slum upgrading.[42] HiAP is an approach to decision making that recognizes that most public policies have the potential to influence health and health equity, either positively or negatively, but that policy makers outside the health sector may not be routinely considering the health consequences of their choices and thereby missing opportunities to advance health and prevention.

Both HIA and HiAP are rooted in relational analyses of place and population health, and slum upgrading ought to consider how such a relational approach might enhance evaluation. What we mean by a relational approach to place and health equity is that health promotion strategies avoid traditional interventions focused on a single exposure, disease, or risk factor. Instead, relational health analyses seek to understand how physical and social place-based characteristics interact with one another and how political and cultural norms and institutions might shape these interactions. For example, in relational analyses, "distance" would encompass physical and social relations, as populations and places are embedded in multiple networks that can be harnessed to achieve far-reaching health gains. In the Pakistani and Thai slum-upgrading initiatives reviewed above, the interventions integrated community, municipal, and national scales.

A relational approach to slum upgrading might also include oral histories that capture local meanings and "sense of place" and discover how projects shape the places and different populations. We found oral histories and resident narratives about how upgrading projects influenced perceptions of their place in the evaluations from Salvador, Brazil, but in few other projects. In other words, participatory slum upgrading—in which local knowledge is valued—could more explicitly capture the voices of those experiencing projects as a way to measure key social determinants of health (SDOH).

A relational approach would also pay attention to the shifts, if any, in governance practices—or the rules, norms, laws, and institutional procedures that often create urban slums in the first place and that can stymie opportunities for the urban poor to make healthy decisions. In short, a relational approach would pay particular attention to changes, if any, in power between slum dwellers and other institutions, particularly the state. Few of the projects we reviewed explored these social determinants of health, though those in Brazil, Colombia, and Thailand did discuss changes in state-community relations.

SLUM UPGRADING AS GLOBAL HEALTH PROMOTION

This brief review offers a summary of select urban slum-upgrading projects and describes how these projects were evaluated using an SDOH lens. We found that most slum-upgrading projects were not framed or evaluated for their broad health equity–promoting potential. We find this to be a missed opportunity, since integrated or holistic slum-upgrading projects often have multiple positive influences on the urban SDOH and can be an important contributor to global health promotion. From our review, we found that slum upgrading is largely evaluated based on impacts on shelter and infrastructure and that health "co-benefits" are rarely acknowledged. We suggest that the design and evaluation of slum upgrading can benefit from such practices and analytic processes as HIA and HiAP, and ultimately more relational and integrated approaches are necessary.

Clearly, our relational framework still faces practical and methodological challenges, and more work is necessary to explore this idea in greater depth. We also acknowledge that slum-upgrading evaluations (and projects for that matter) may be narrowly designed to respond to financing and/or donor requirements and objectives. Development agencies and foundations that typically finance slum upgrading in the global South increasingly require quantifiable outputs and may measure a narrow set of human health outcomes, rather than the subtler, often qualitative and hard-to-measure social determinants of health. Methods such as in-depth interviews, open-ended focus groups, spatial mapping before and after, and longitudinal cohort surveys could all add to the collection of SDOH data from slum-upgrading projects. While more work needs to be done on these and other methods for evaluation, urban slum upgrading remains an important health promotion strategy and one in need of greater input from public health practitioners.

NOTES

1. De Snyder, S., Nelly, V., et al. (2011). Social conditions and urban health inequities: Realities, challenges and opportunities to transform the urban landscape through research and action. *Journal of Urban Health* 88(6):1183–93.

2. Greene, M. (2010). Main policy and programmatic approaches for slum upgrading. World Bank. http://preview.tinyurl.com/q5ahpnx. Last accessed November 27, 2015.

3. Imparato, I., & Ruster, J. (2003). *Summary of slum upgrading and participation: Lessons from Latin America.* Washington, D.C.: World Bank.

4. Turley, R., Saith, R., Bhan, N., Doyle, J., Jones, K., & Waters, E. (2013). Slum upgrading review: Methodological challenges that arise in systematic reviews of complex interventions. *J Public Health* 35(1):171–75. doi: 10.1093/pubmed/fdt008.

5. Woolcock et al. (2010) and Bamberger & White (2008) also argue for mixed-methods evaluations of development projects, although without a focus on upgrading or urban health. Woolcock, M., Bamberger, M., & Rao, V. (2010). *Using mixed methods in monitoring and evaluation: Experiences from International Development.* Washington, DC: World Bank. Bamberger, M. (2009). Strengthening the evaluation of program effectiveness through reconstructing baseline data. *Journal of Development Effectiveness* 1(1):37–59.

6. Haines, A., Bruce, N., Cairncross, S., et al. (2013). Promoting health and advancing development through improved housing in low-income settings. *Journal of Urban Health* 90(5):810–31.

7. Buckley, R.M., & Kalarickal, J. (Eds.). (2006). *Thirty years of World Bank shelter lending: What have we learned?* Washington, DC: World Bank.

8. Werlin, H. (1999). The slum upgrading myth. *Urban Studies* 36(9):1523–34.

9. Pugh, C. (2001), "The theory and practice of housing sector development for developing countries, 1950–99." *Housing Studies* 16(4):399–423.

10. Buckley & Kalarickal (2006).

11. Gulyani, S., & Bassett, E. (2007). Retrieving the baby from the bathwater: Slum upgrading in sub-Saharan Africa. *Environment and Planning C* 25:486–515.

12. Das, A.K., & Takahashi, L.M. (2009). Evolving institutional arrangements, scaling up, and sustainability: Emerging issues in participatory slum upgrading in Ahmedabad, India. *Journal of Planning Education and Research* 29(2):213–32.

13. Imparato, I., & Ruster, J. (2003). *Slum upgrading and participation: Lessons from Latin America.* Washington, DC: World Bank.

14. Rojas, E. (2010). *Building cities: Neighborhood upgrading and urban quality of life.* Washington, DC: Inter-American Development Bank; Cambridge, MA: David Rockefeller Center for Latin American Studies.

15. Boonyabancha, S. (2009). Land for housing the poor—by the poor: Experiences from the Baan Mankong nationwide slum upgrading programme in Thailand. *Environment and Urbanization* 21(2):309–29.

16. Rojas (2010).

17. Das & Takahashi (2009), 216.

18. Satterthwaite, D. (2010). Upgrading slums: With and for slum-dwellers. *Economic and Political Weekly* 45(10):12–16.

19. Cattaneo, M.D., Galiani, S., Gertler, P.J., Martinez, S., & Titiunik, R. (2009). Housing, health, and happiness. *American Economic Journal: Economic Policy* 1(1):75–105.

20. Aiga, H., & Umenai, T. (2002). Impact of improvement of water supply on household economy in a squatter area of Manila. *Social Science and Medicine* 55(4):627–41.

21. Turley, R., et al. (2013). Slum upgrading strategies involving physical environment and infrastructure interventions and their effects on health and socio-economic outcomes. *Cochrane Database Syst Rev* 1.

22. Ibid.

23. Idler, E.L., & Benyamini, Y. (1997). Self-rated health and mortality: A review of twenty-seven community studies. *J Health Social Behavior* 38:21–37.

24. *PLoS One* (2014). 9(1):e84933. Quesnel-Vallée, A. (2007). Self-rated health: Caught in the crossfire of the quest for "true" health? *Int J Epidemiol* 36:1161–64.

25. Waddington, H., et al. (2009), *Water, sanitation and hygiene interventions to combat childhood diarrhoea in developing countries.* Vol. 31. International Initiative for Impact Evaluation, http://www.3ieimpact.org/media/filer_public/2012/05/07/17-2.pdf (accessed February 13, 2016).

26. Turley et al. (2013).

27. Sheuya, S.A. (2008). Improving the health and lives of people living in slums. *Annals of the New York Academy of Sciences* 1136:298–306.

28. Ibid.

29. Aiga and Umenai (2002).

30. ADB (Asian Development Bank) (2012). Project completion report: Neighborhood upgrading and shelter sector project, Indonesia.

31. Butala, N.M., VanRooyen, M.J., & Patel, R.B. (2010). Improved health outcomes in urban slums through infrastructure upgrading. *Social Science and Medicine* 71(5):935–40.

32. Field, E., & M. Kremer. (2006). *Impact evaluation for slum upgrading interventions.* Doing Impact Evaluation Series, No. 3. Washington, D.C.: World Bank.

33. IDB (2012). Citizen security: Conceptual framework and empirical evidence. Discussion Paper IDB-DP-232. Washington, DC: Inter-American Development Bank. https://publications.iadb.org/bitstream/handle/11319/5684/Citizen%20Security-Conceptual%20Framework-Final.pdf?sequence=1 (accessed February 13, 2016).

34. Baker, J.L. (2006). *Integrated urban upgrading for the poor: The experience of Ribeira Azul, Brazil.* World Bank Policy Research Working Paper, No. 3861. Washington D.C.: World Bank

35. USAID (2009). *Innovative approaches to slum electrification.* Washington D.C.

36. UN-Habitat & WHO (2009). *Hidden cities: Unmasking and overcoming health inequities in urban settings.* Geneva: World Health Organization and United Nations Human Settlement Programme.

37. USAID (2009).

38. Amis, P. (2001). Rethinking UK aid in urban India: Reflections on an impact assessment study of slum improvement projects. *Environment & Urbanization* 13(1):101–13.

39. Das and Takahashi (2009).

40. Ibid., 45.

41. USAID (2009), 33.

42. World Health Organization (WHO) (2014). Health in all policies: Training manual. http://who.int/social_determinants/publications/health-policies-manual/en/ (accessed February 13, 2016).

PART II

From the Cell to the Street

Slum Health in Brazil

Brazil is the largest country in Latin America, with an estimated population in 2013 of 199 million. Urbanization in Brazil evolved rapidly. In 1950, 36 percent of the Brazilian population lived in urban areas (in contrast to only 15% of the population in Africa and 17% in Asia).[1] By 2000, more than 80 percent of Brazilians resided in cities.[2] The rapid population increase in Brazil started a few years before the official abolition of slavery in 1888, when a shift to waged and salaried labor, filled largely by European immigrants, began. About 4 million immigrants are estimated to have entered Brazil between 1880 and 1930, many of whom came to work on rural coffee plantations.[3] Many freed slaves, unemployed and displaced by new paid workers flocked to cities. The Grande Seca (Great Drought) of the Northeast in 1877–79 devastated rural agriculture and caused massive internal migration into Brazil's coastal cities.[4] Then the stock market crash of 1929 caused coffee prices to plummet, which caused yet another large migration of rural workers into cities. Rural-to-city migration accelerated in the 1940s during the Second World War. Between 1940 and 1950 an estimated 3 million people moved into cities from rural areas. When the military took over the country in 1964, it instituted development programs that emphasized centrally planned technological improvement in agricultural and industrial production. While these programs greatly accelerated Brazilian output, the government-subsidized credit to support these programs favored large farmers and land speculators.[5] Between 1920 and 1965, the majority of the agricultural producers in Brazil consisted of small farm owners, squatters, sharecroppers, and tenant farmers. After the mid-1960s, as the proportion of large farms increased, small farmers and their workers were forced off their land, which led to another mass population movement into cities.

Between 1940 and 1980, an estimated 41 million migrants—representing 27 percent of the rural population during these forty years—left the rural areas to live in cities. In less than two decades (1960–80), Brazil evolved from a predominantly rural to a predominantly urban nation. The cities were not prepared to assimilate these large numbers of migrants so rapidly, and the inevitable consequence of these intense migrations was the expansion of urban informal settlements that came to be known as favelas.

The word "favela" comes from the favela tree or shrub, which belongs to the family Euphorbiaceae. In 1897, after their final victory in the Canudos War in the state of Bahia (1895–96),[6] a group of Republican government soldiers settled on top of one of the hills in Rio de Janeiro to await payment for their services. They named the hill "Morro da Favela" after the favela shrubs found at the location of their victory in Bahia. The soldiers waited but never got paid, and they never left the hill. This settlement became the first favela.

Today, the population of Brazilian slum communities continues to increase, not because of rural-urban migration, but mostly because of new births and internal urban migration. These communities have thus come to be entrenched as part of the Brazilian urban landscape. While officials may describe them as "informal" or as "*aglomerados subnormais*" (subnormal agglomeration) they have been in existence for many decades, through several generations of residents, and are indeed distinct permanent communities in themselves. In 2009, 45 million people, or about 30 percent of Brazil's urban population, resided in slum communities.[7]

Part II describes slum health of one such community in the city of Salvador in Bahia, Brazil, the third-largest city and the first colonial capital of Brazil. The community is called Pau da Lima, which until the 1970s was sparsely populated Atlantic forestland, mostly comprising hills and valleys located at the periphery of Salvador. With internal migration that began in the 1970s, the area rapidly transformed into a crowded settlement that now includes both formal and informal neighborhoods located next to each other. The estimated population of the slum neighborhood in Pau da Lima is 50,000.

In the mid-1990s, Pau da Lima became the site of a community-based research project initiated by a group of researchers from the Gonçalo Moniz Research Center of the Oswaldo Cruz Foundation in Salvador and from Cornell University Medical College (now Weill Cornell Medical College) in New York, in collaboration with the Urban Health Council and community leaders and residents of Pau da Lima. Initially, the project investigated the natural history and epidemiology of leptospirosis, an infectious disease caused by the spirochete bacterium Leptospira, transmitted by rat urine.[8] Pau da Lima was selected for this investigation because this community was found to have one of the highest incidences of severe leptospirosis in the city. Chapter 6 outlines the history of and lessons learned from this collaboration.

The project continues to this day and continues to generate new knowledge regarding the coproduction approach to understanding slum health. Chapter 7 (reprinted from *PLoS Neglected Diseases,* 2008) describes a study that examined environmental and social determinants of disease transmission at the population level in a slum community. The project involved microbiology researchers, epidemiologists, veterinarians, physicians, mapping experts, demographers, statisticians, sociologists, economists, and community organizers. It serves as an example of slum health research that examines the interaction of an infectious agent (cell) and individual hosts with the physical, structural, and social factors (street), interaction that determines the outcome of a disease that occurs almost exclusively in a slum community.

Chapter 8 discusses another infectious disease, Group A streptococcal pharyngitis, associated with yet another common disease in urban slums—rheumatic heart disease (RHD), a chronic heart disease. A molecular biology method was applied to genotype Group A streptococcal organisms (cell) isolated in children with sore throat residing in slum versus nonslum communities in Salvador (street). The researchers genetically analyzed the bacterial organisms to develop a hypothesis to explain why the prevalence of RHD is so much higher in slum communities in Salvador and in urban centers all over the world.[9]

The chapters and research described in part II reflect some of the components of our slum health framework, described previously: coproduction, a relational approach to slum health, and urban systems science, but not necessarily ecosocial epidemiology or adaptive management. Researchers and residents in Pau da Lima worked together to identify the drivers of infectious disease, and narrow exposures were related to issues of poverty and social exclusion. The project has integrated insights

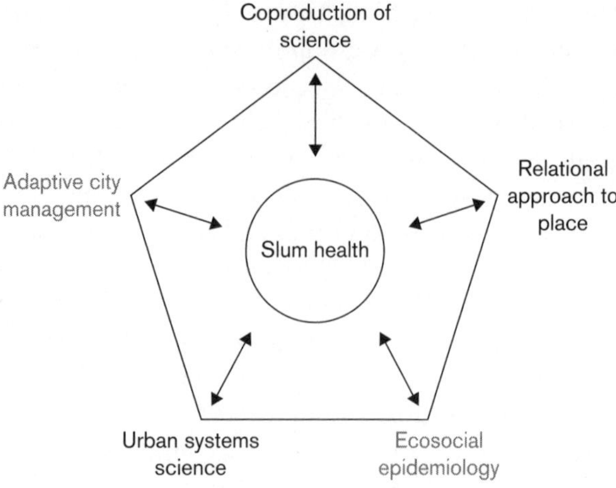

Dimensions of slum health explored in the case of Pau da Lima, Salvador, Bahia, Brazil.

from the cell to the street, as clinicians and laboratory science combined knowledge and expertise from local residents, community-based organizations, and local and national government institutions.

NOTES

1. United Nations (2007). *World urbanization prospects.* New York.
2. IBGE Brasil (2007). *Perfil dos Municípios Brasileiros, 2006.* Rio de Janeiro.
3. Merrick, T., & Douglas, G. (1979). *Population and economic development in Brazil, 1800 to the present.* Baltimore: Johns Hopkins University Press.
4. Greenfield, G.M. (1986). *Migrant behavior and elite attitudes: Brazil's Great Drought, 1877–1879.* Philadelphia: Academy of American Franciscan History.
5. Martine, G., & McGranahan, G. (2010). *Brazil's early urban transition: What can it teach urbanizing countries?* London: Human Settlements Group, International Institute for Environment and Development.
6. Madden, L. (1993). *The Canudos War in history.* Madison: University of Wisconsin Press.
7. United Nations (2013). *Slum population in urban areas.* New York.
8. Ko, A.I., Reis, M.G., Dourado, C.M.R., Johnson, W.D., & Riley, L.W. (1999). Salvador Leptospirosis Study Group: Urban epidemic of severe leptospirosis in Brazil. *Lancet* 354:820–25.
9. The impact on the community of RHD, and the importance of understanding the biology—the proximal cause—of a disease together with social determinants of disease, is discussed in chapter 1 of this book.

CHAPTER 6

Favela Health in Pau da Lima, Salvador, Brazil

ALON UNGER, ALBERT KO, GUILLERMO DOUGLASS-JAIME

I think that the science has a role in what is important. Our health resources are very scarce so it is important to maximize them as much as possible to give as much benefit to the community as possible. But there is a need to make the science serve the community. This is what this project has done. It has given us so much.

—A resident of Pau da Lima, Salvador

This chapter offers the voices of slum dwellers and scientists as they work on slum health in the Pau da Lima favela in Salvador, Brazil. The chapter is based on more than three hundred hours of interviews with project leaders, scientists, community residents, government officials, and others involved in and making observations of the health work in this slum. As we recount here, this project started with a discovery in a local hospital that a disproportionate number of people with leptospirosis seemed to be coming from Pau da Lima, and it evolved into an action-research project that aimed to combine laboratory and clinical research with community-based interventions. What follows is our summary of what we heard in our interviews.*

Pau da Lima is an informal settlement on the periphery of Salvador, the capital of the state of Bahia in northeastern Brazil and the country's third-largest city. Nearly two-thirds of the city's inhabitants, like

* This chapter is based on the authors' interviews and observations.

30 percent of the Brazilian population, live in places like Pau da Lima, also called slums, or *favelas* in Portuguese. This project began as research into the causes of leptospirosis, a rat-borne, life-threatening infectious disease, in Pau da Lima, a population at the time of roughly 50,000 people. The project grew into an ongoing collaboration between academic universities in the United States, the research branch of the Brazilian Ministry of Health (FIOCRUZ), and local community groups and leaders investigating other infectious and chronic illness. Since 1997 the project has evolved from investigating outbreaks of severe leptospirosis in one community to the study of the epidemiology of leptospirosis, rat populations, and social and environmental determinants of disease transmission, immunology, and new rapid test and vaccine development—or what we are calling the coproduction of slum health. Brazilian and US researchers have described the model used by this initiative as moving *from the cell to the street,* since biometric data were combined with social and environmental data to inform new research and development of novel diagnostics, treatment protocols, and preventative strategies.

More important, the project was based on the paradigm that the most effective solutions for addressing emerging slum health problems necessitate providing residents the capacity to solve their own problems through research and production of evidence, in addition to advocacy and implementation and monitoring of interventions. The major thrust of this Pau da Lima initiative and the coalition of community associations, researchers, multidisciplinary experts, and local government has been capacity building and training of residents through high school head start and college work-study programs and graduate education. These programs, supported by the Brazilian Ministries of Science and Technology and the US National Institutes of Health, created the leadership and capacity required to obtain evidence and convert that evidence into action and community-based intervention.

The slum health work in Pau da Lima has had multiple returns for both residents and researchers beyond revealing the epidemiology of leptospirosis. For instance, findings about risk factors for leptospirosis have contributed to reduced exposures to other disease-causing pathogens, especially those that cause waterborne diseases. The research has also uncovered new hypotheses and led to research and interventions that may prove crucial for improving slum health. For example, the study found a high prevalence of rheumatic heart disease among the slum population and provided new opportunities to study noncommu-

PHOTO 6.1. Pau da Lima community, Salvador, Brazil.

nicable diseases including diabetes and cardiovascular disease outcomes in the community.

LEPTOSPIROSIS, RESEARCH, AND COMMUNITY

The action-oriented research in Pau da Lima was spearheaded by Albert Ko, a fellow in infectious diseases at Cornell University, who went to the coastal city of Salvador in 1995 to study tuberculosis in that city's favelas. Ko's mentors, Lee Riley and Warren Johnson Jr. had collaborated with researchers at the Federal University of Bahia (UFBA) since 1964, and together they had worked in the countryside of Bahia on devastating rural-based, poverty-promoting diseases such as cutaneous leishmaniasis, Chagas disease, and other parasitic infections. Their research had been supported by such entities as the Commonwealth Fund, the Rockefeller Foundation, and the US National Institutes of Health. Another key actor in this initiative was Mitermayer Galvão dos Reis, who, as director of the Fundação Oswaldo Cruz (FIOCruz), recognized the rural-to-urban shift of the disease burden and the future impact that processes of rapid urban growth and urbanization of poverty would have on Brazilian health. As a team, Doctors Ko, Reis, Riley, and Johnson mobilized the support necessary to establish a research and training program on urban health and social equity in Salvador.

Ko and Reis's first step was to establish the program at the Hospital Couto Maia, a 120-bed state infectious-disease hospital that served the rapidly growing population of slum residents in Salvador. Built in 1853 as the Hospital de Isolamento de Mont Serrat, the facility had historically treated sailors and merchants arriving in Bahia with yellow fever. It played an important role in treating patients of many urban epidemics, such as cholera, bubonic plague, the "Spanish flu," and typhoid fever.

Shortly after arriving and attending on the wards in Hospital Couto Maia (HCM), Dr. Ko noticed a large number of patients brought into the emergency room nearly unconscious with fever, jaundice, and kidney failure. These cases were diagnosed as a severe form of leptospirosis called Weil's disease. Leptospirosis is caused by a spirochete, predominantly *Leptospira interrogans* in Bahia, which may also cause nonspecific symptoms such as fevers, chills, headache, and myalgia. In 5 to 15 percent of cases it causes multisystem disease, including liver failure and jaundice, renal insufficiency, and bleeding diatheses. The disease follows a seasonal pattern and is closely associated with the rainy season. Because of its relatively nonspecific presentation in mild cases, it was often confused with dengue fever, which also occurs during the rainy season. Dr. Ko and his colleagues at HCM found that most of his patients were coming from poor urban areas of Salvador, with the highest number of cases from the Pau da Lima community.

At HCM, Dr. Ko and his team began tracking the cases of leptospirosis and identified 326 cases of severe leptospirosis in 1996. They found that the highest risk for severe leptospirosis was among those who lived in poor urban areas on the periphery of the city. These areas constituted fifteen districts, almost all favelas, where 47 percent of the housing structures had open sewers, as compared to 29 percent in other parts of the city. Most of the leptospirosis cases were male, 69 percent recalled having had contact with flood or sewage water within the previous four weeks, and 77 percent reported seeing rodents in the home or workplace. These pivotal findings not only showed that the epidemiology of this once rural disease was changing but also strongly endorsed the research team's opinion that the social and physical characteristics of favelas were likely playing an important role in disease transmission. According to Dr. Ko, the demographic and living-condition findings about patients began to alter the medical team's focus:

> We shifted gears and worked on leptospirosis. This was a large epidemic of a life-threatening disease, whose case fatality was as high as many of the deadliest infectious diseases. However this disease remained off the radar screen of the government officials and the general public since it occurred amongst the marginalized and most vulnerable segments of society. Most of our initial work was really very much based on trying to identify the burden of disease for this neglected disease . . . this is a disease that attacks the same slum community during the rain season, not only in the city of Salvador, but throughout Brazil.

By 1996, Dr. Ko and his colleagues had a great deal of experience studying specific infectious diseases such as leptospirosis, meningitis, and pneumococcal disease. Most of this work was done after diagnosis of the disease through case studies, outbreak investigations, and prevalence studies, and the results continued to indicate that the slum environment was making an indelible contribution to the epidemiology of these diseases. The research team, including US and local counterparts, began to refocus from the disease to the community. Dr. Ko recalled:

> Our initial work between 1996 until about 2000 was really very much based on doing basic public health, to define the epidemiology, to do outbreak investigations, case control investigation, to understand how people in slum communities were being exposed to leptospirosis [in order to] identify the barriers in appropriately addressing this disease. . . . It became clear to us during these investigations that the real answers need to be focused first on intervention and, second, working in the community because of the issue of marginalization in the urban slum communities. . . . By around 2001 the idea was to work intensively in the community with resident associations and leaders.

A key challenge for the medical team was selecting a specific community in which to address leptospirosis and initiate the action-oriented research. Like other parts of Brazil, Salvador had undergone an important demographic transition over the prior fifty years with rural-to-urban migration and the growth of slums. At this time in Salvador, nearly 67 percent of the 2 million residents of the city lived in favelas. In fact, during the 1996 epidemic of severe leptospirosis, many poor urban areas in Salvador saw a high incidence of leptospirosis. The team came to choose one community in particular, Pau da Lima (PdL), due to its location and the high incidence of the disease. Moreover, this community was selected as the site for the research and training program because of the strong grassroots network of residents associations that, despite little or no financial support, had a long track record in mobilizing the community and effecting social change through advocacy. In addition, Pau da Lima was the former home of Dr. Reis, who had migrated there from the countryside as an impoverished teenager before becoming a successful physician and researcher and director of a premier research institution in Brazil.

PAU DA LIMA: COMMUNITY-ENGAGED RESEARCH

Many of the public health colleagues who were initially part of the new, place-based research project were involved in the community association Associacão de Moradores do Pau da Lima (AMPLI), which was already deeply engaged in social projects in the community. AMPLI and other community groups were eager to create a partnership with the medical team, because they recognized the burden disease was having on society, the economy, and that quality of life in Pau da Lima. The team also chose PdL because there was medical infrastructure in the community, including an ambulatory and urgent care clinic run by a nearby charitable hospital, Hospital São Rafael. The aim was to extend the work to include disease prevention but not lose the clinical and lab-based aspects of the science. As one of the project initiators described the challenge of expanding the research enterprise:

> There were two driving motivations and both were kind of personal. The first one was that it was very obvious to us early on, that even if we had the best diagnostic test, the most effective solutions were going to be prevention, . . . and when we were there in the community, it was obvious that many of the problems related to leptospirosis were issues of infrastructure deficiency, neglect, and marginalization. So the best solutions had to come from the community in terms of prevention. . . . The second is that urban Brazil at that time was not that different from many of the poorest urban slums in many of the poorest regions of the world. . . . [We] always had the perspective that the work could speak to similar issues for other places that look like the slums in Brazil.

WORKING WITH PAU DA LIMA: PATHOGENESIS AND COMMUNITY INVOLVEMENT

The team's early hypotheses suggested that rats were the main reservoir for leptospirosis in the favelas of Salvador, including PdL. Thus, one of the first collaborations between community residents and medical researchers was the development of a lab-based hamster model. The medical team wanted to understand the pathogenesis of the disease, or why some infected people developed life-threatening complications; the role of the inoculum of the pathogen during exposure to the contaminated environment; and how the bacteria's virulence influenced transmission and disease progression. This work led to substantive collaboration in the laboratory and the beginnings of work on rapid diagnostics and even vaccine development.

However, as the research began, the primary Brazilian project leader, Mitermayer Reis, recognized the importance of enlisting the assistance of state and municipal health officials, including zoonotic control centers, and community residents, in order to capture rats and understand exposures in PdL. What the researchers soon discovered when partnering with the local public health agencies was that "many rodent control efforts were not placed in areas of [greatest] need with the highest incidence of leptospirosis, but there were some city councilmen calling them up saying they need to control rats in this beach or in this privileged community, and we thought this was a very good example of injustice in terms of resource allocation."

A first task of the team, in partnership with the PdL community, was to directly address this key element of marginalization and barrier to effective health responses by mapping the distribution of leptospirosis cases in Salvador. This work also included local public health officials and aimed to create a risk map that could be shown to the health authorities to highlight neighborhoods and communities where interventions at the local level should be prioritized. The environmental mapping was a digression from the biomedical-oriented pathogenesis work of the medical team, but soon became a central theme of the project.

The project researchers also focused on developing a rapid test for leptospirosis, which did not exist at that time. The lack of an effective diagnostic test hampered recognition of the public health impact of the disease and, moreover, prevented timely clinical intervention against this highly fatal disease. According to one community health worker:

> Leptospirosis requires early intervention. If you don't start right away, it is too late. . . . When people develop mild symptoms of leptospirosis, they just think it is dengue or something else, so they may not come into the clinic and get helped. A rapid test might be helpful, but another approach is a vaccine. If you could also close up the sewers and get rid of the rat population you could be just as effective. Do you allow the conditions to exist but give a vaccine so they don't develop lepto, or put resources [toward] improv[ing] infrastructure?

After receiving a number of external grants for the clinical work, the researchers expanded their partnership with the community. Residents were recruited to participate in the project's work, including mapping and data collection. One of the first steps was to hold meetings with community leaders and the AMPLI. One resident noted: "From the way I saw it, one of the innovative approaches was to incorporate some of the residents of the community into the research team, not just in the community doing research, but also the people living in these favelas coming to FIOCruz to analyze the data. They were really part of the research team." The relationship with community leaders and AMPLI and daily contact with residents were seen as critical to the work and integral parts of the project. Another community activist noted that the research partnership "was really important in terms of the community mobilization . . . that went a long way in terms of doing the research."

This early relationship with the community and the community's own grassroots organizing led to an interested and mobilized group of leaders who supported the work of the project. Practically, this allowed the researchers to move in and out of the community, to enlist residents to assist with mapping, and to ensure general cooperation from the community when visited by the research team. Also not to be underestimated was that the research teams were composed of medical and other students and young people who were not from the favela, and there was a certain amount of protection and safety from potential violence. The project also invested in training local residents and employing them within the project. In particular, the research team worked with community leaders to address the community's own concerns and problems:

1. Creating an urban health council among grassroots organizations
2. Having the residents' associations identify young students with potential for leadership
3. Placing these young students in high school head start programs
4. Building the pipeline with a college work study program supported by the Fogarty International Center as well as FIOCruz (students went to school at night and engaged in research for pay during the day)
5. Providing higher-level training for a cohort of students who pursued master's and doctoral degrees

Lastly, the project initiators were also clinicians, and on more than one occasion, the community recognized that the project was able to provide a certain amount of medical care for the community. According to one project leader:

> We helped empower the community. When they see you there and they know that you are someone that is representing the city, they ask you to generate information to give to the government to make improvement in the community. . . . I think it was a really good decision to include the community also to get trust from them and to get access of information that you couldn't have gotten without involvement of the community. I had the impression that when they see someone from the community involved in the project, they see them as being represented.

Community engagement expanded the range of health issues that the research team considered. As one clinical researcher noted: "When we first started that project, our team members that included medical students visited every single household, all three or four thousand households . . . when we asked people what were the problems, they told me 'leptospirosis is an important problem, but hypertension, diabetes, tuberculosis,' those are just as important. These were issues we knew about but just weren't working on." The team already had local community health workers who were performing the leptospirosis work, so, following the community's recommendations, it extended the project to investigate hypertension, heart disease, and stroke. Survey data the group and community researchers collected revealed that of the 14,867 adults over the age of 18 sampled, approximately 21 percent had hypertension, but only 66 percent already knew about their diagnosis and only half of those were taking medication. This work expanded the project to include noncommunicable diseases.

COMMUNITY COLLABORATION

Dr. Reis, the Brazilian project leader, was the director of the Oswaldo Cruz Foundation in Salvador, a research arm of the Brazilian Ministry of Health. This connection ensured the project access to national sources of funding. Yet Dr. Reis also noted that the team's constitution made a difference in the project's effectiveness and sustainability:

> I realized that in order to do science, we need to have a multidisciplinary team. Also we should have a big view. I think the manifestation of diseases depends on many factors: not just the agent, but also the environment, the agent, and the individual in the community. . . . This perception came from my real life. I was someone who was born in a small town. I knew that when someone had a disease, the situation was worse for those who had a lower social position, or less money available. . . . In this case, we recognized a multidisciplinary team was necessary to understand the social and ecological determinants of disease.

Over the years, the work has expanded from leptospirosis to many other infectious diseases, and now there is a focus on noncommunicable diseases. The work continues to address issues of inequality, as evidenced by an increasing concentration on the impact in disease transmission of the environment and of social gradients. The team has also begun to explore new metrics for assessing the burden of both communicable and noncommunicable diseases in slums. There has also been a large commitment to community involvement, particularly through place-based mapping of exposures and disease, and this has influenced community development and other non–medical care issues.

The community partnership with slum dwellers developed over time and has influenced both the science and community-based organizations. According to many residents, the community was highly fragmented politically at the time the research started. There were many political parties and the community was divided. According to one activist: "The resident associations were aligned with political parties. We started to discuss what was important for everyone, not just the politics. The problems were identified together. We discussed a lot. The researchers and the community first started with health fairs that educated and offered medical services. We worked closely with Raymunda [a worker in the research team], who was there as a co-coordinator."

As the partnership developed, community associations were enrolled to perform vital research tasks. As one community activist noted: "The parts of the community that were selected for mapping and research came about through discussions with residents. FIOCruz dialogued with us to find out what was the best area for the study. The area we helped them select had the worst conditions in Pau da Lima, and it was a place where there were many open sewers; it had problems of accessibility and [was] a favorable environment for leptospirosis." According to another community member, the mapping was a useful way to build the researcher-community collaborations:

> The mapping doesn't just identify the risk areas of the disease, but also includes extra information on where we can build and what infrastructure is needed to avoid disease exposures. It has also been an opportunity to train the community, and employ them, in computer mapping. When mapping identified that the disease comes about during the rainy season, we used the data from FIOCruz to push for the government to cover up the sewers so that we could minimize the problems to the community.

A number of community residents were trained as part of the project, and some eventually were employed as full-time researchers. One Pau

PHOTO 6.2. Project team mapping in Pau da Lima.

da Lima resident who is now a working on the project developing maps of exposure and disease locations noted:

> Since I am from that community, I can tell when an address is bad. If we can't find the house from the address, we go to the field and ask around for the house. Many residents now ask to work with me because they know me. They recognize that we are here to stay and improve the place. People from the community like me who worked with the researchers continued to study and get degrees and improve their quality of life. The work continues. It is a good experience to work with people from the community and outside the community.

Another community resident explained how, as she learned more about research processes, such as taking biological measures, she began to raise ideas about additional studies. Community-trained researchers helped convince the medical team to pay attention to new health issues beyond just infectious diseases. She noted: "When I started in FIOCruz, I learned how to take blood pressure measurements. I was very concerned with the high rates of hypertension. The team was responsive to my concerns and we took blood pressure measurements from the people. We discussed a study of hypertension, and eventually this was successful because people were very responsive and there was a lot of follow-up."

The project is an example of the interaction between the lab and the street, as one Brazilian researcher noted:

> The uniqueness of the whole project is because of the use of the lab to understand what is going on in the community, and the community to make more

> sense of lab findings. Most projects tend to be either fieldwork or lab work . . . one field observation was a number of pulmonary hemorrhages, which had not been seen at all in Salvador before this project. So this informed new lab work, a sequencing project. This is an example of the back-and-forth between the lab and the community.

Moving *from the lab to the street* in this project is also made possible because the team members are committed to social justice. According to one clinical scholar, the work in Pau da Lima is as much political as technical:

> I quickly learned that the major issue here was social justice. It is something that I had been wanting to do since I started in medicine. I think that the reason that I was interested in Pau da Lima is because we had *companheiros* who would want to work on those issues together. The science alone doesn't change things. Only when it is used to help mobilize and empower the community. Working with communities like Pau da Lima brings people from different social classes together. This is a valuable experience, as many people who are privileged don't have exposure to the problems of poor communities; this can lead to people changing perceptions and ideas.

The partnership has also provided benefits to the community beyond the hospital and medical treatment. For example, community members who were trained to do exposure mapping are now acting as teachers as new scientists from the United States, Asia, and Europe come to Brazil to learn from and with them. These are opportunities that would not have been available to community residents without the presence of this project. As one community resident reflected:

> The people working on this project are special people, not just doing this to make money, but [who] also care about the community. Because of the work in our community, we have gotten more attention, and other people start to get curious. Other people who never would have taken a look at this community start getting interested. It brings people from different social classes together. This is a valuable experience, as many people who are privileged don't have exposure to the problems of poor communities. This can lead to people changing perceptions and ideas. It has also inspired other researchers to start similar projects, like one on TB.

However, there are still challenges that remain for improving health in Pau da Lima. Community residents and researchers acknowledge that many of the benefits have gone to a small number of people and not to the broader community. Much of the research funding has targeted individual and biological interventions, but not the physical and social determinants of health in the community.

CONCLUSIONS

The collaborative action-oriented science in Pau da Lima is an example of how a project can move from the cell to the street and back again to address infectious and chronic diseases faced in urban slums. The project has many important elements that demonstrate how high-quality science can be combined with a commitment to community-based participation can improve health and living conditions for the urban poor.

First, clinical care was combined with laboratory research and community-based action. In slums around the world, too often only one of these elements is present; the focus is often on immediate care needs, but not on asking why this disease occurs in this place and what social conditions might also be influencing susceptibility. Second, spatial mapping and analyses were combined with laboratory and clinical insights. Again, many slum health projects tend to focus either on environmental place-based conditions or population-based research and interventions, but rarely both places and people. Third, community residents were trained as researchers and eventually became trainers themselves. The idea was that the sustainability and social justice aspects of the project required that residents become leaders, not just employees, of the project. Finally, there were multiple avenues for intervention, treatment regimes, infrastructure improvements, community mobilization and organizing, and additional research. Some of these efforts were made possible by the success and publication of the clinical research (and the grant funding it attracted), but some was also made possible through the ongoing governmental investment in Pau da Lima by FIOCruz.

Slum health challenges such as those found in Pau da Lima demand long-term, sustained commitment to research and action. As this case study shows, short-term, single disease–focused projects will not address the multiple exposures, lack of services, and living-condition issues faced by slum dwellers. The Pau da Lima case is not complete; the work continues and residents remain beneficiaries of research, development projects, and the building of community knowledge and power that has resulted from this partnership. While more work needs to be done, much can be gained from a detailed review of the Pau da Lima case. In the following two chapters, we offer more details on research methods, findings, and interventions in Pau da Lima that together have worked to promote and coproduce slum health.

CHAPTER 7

Impact of Environment and Social Gradient on Leptospira Infection in Urban Slums

RENATO B. REIS, GUILHERME S. RIBEIRO, RIDALVA D. M. FELZEMBURGH, FRANCISCO S. SANTANA, SHARIF MOHR, ASTRID X. T. O. MELENDEZ, ADRIANO QUEIROZ, ANDRE´ IA C. SANTOS, ROMY R. RAVINES, WAGNER S. TASSINARI, MARILIA S. CARVALHO, MITERMAYER G. REIS, AND ALBERT I. KO

At the beginning of the 2000s, one billion of the world's population resided in slum settlements.[1] This number was expected to double in twenty-five years.[2] The growth of large urban populations marginalized from basic services has created a new set of global health challenges[3, 4]. As part of the Millennium Development Goals,[5] a major priority has been to address the underlying poor sanitation and environmental degradation in slum communities, conditions that in turn cause a spectrum of neglected diseases that affect these populations.[6, 7, 8].

Leptospirosis is a paradigm for an urban health problem that has emerged due to the recent growth of slums.[9, 10] The disease, caused by the *Leptospira* spirochete, produces life-threatening manifestations, such as Weil's disease and severe pulmonary hemorrhage syndrome, for which fatality is more than 10 percent and 50 percent, respectively.[11, 12. 13] Leptospirosis is transmitted during direct contact with animal reservoirs or with water and soil contaminated with their urine.[14, 15] Changes in the urban environment associated with expanding slum communities has produced conditions for rodent-borne transmission.[16, 17] Urban epidemics of leptospirosis now occur in cities throughout the developing world during seasonal heavy rainfall and flooding.[18, 19, 20, 21, 22, 23, 24, 25, 26]

There is scarce data on the burden of specific diseases that affect slum populations;[27] however, leptospirosis appears to have become a major infectious disease problem in this population. In Brazil alone, more than 10,000 cases of severe leptospirosis are reported each year due to outbreaks in urban centers,[28] whereas roughly 3,000, 8,000 and 1,500 cases are reported annually for meningococcal disease, visceral leishmaniasis, and dengue hemorrhagic fever, respectively, which are other infectious disease associated with urban poverty.[29, 30, 31] Case fatality from leptospirosis (10%)[32] is comparable to that observed for meningococcal disease (20%), visceral leishmaniasis (8%), and dengue hemorrhagic fever (10%) in this setting.[33, 34, 35] Furthermore, leptospirosis is associated with extreme weather events, as exemplified by the El Nino–associated outbreak in Guayaquil in 1998.[36] Leptospirosis is therefore expected to become an increasingly important slum health problem as predicted global climate change[37, 38] and growth of the world's slum population evolves.[39]

Urban leptospirosis is a disease of poor environments since it disproportionately affects communities that lack adequate sewage systems and refuse collection services.[40, 41, 42] In this setting, outbreaks are often due to transmission of a single serovar, *L. interrogans* serovar Copenhageni, which is associated with the *Rattus norvegicus* reservoir.[43, 44, 45, 46] Elucidation of the specific determinants of poverty that have led to the emergence of urban leptospirosis is essential in guiding organizers of community-based interventions, who, to date, have been uniformly unsuccessful. Herein, we report the findings of a large seroprevalence survey performed in a Brazilian slum community (favela). Geographic information system (GIS) methods were used to identify sources for *Leptospira* transmission in the slum environment. Furthermore, we evaluated whether relative differences in socioeconomic status among slum residents, in addition to the attributes of the environment in which they reside, contributed to the risk of *Leptospira* infection.

METHODS

Study Site and Population

The study was conducted in the Pau da Lima community, situated in the periphery of Salvador, a city of 2,443,107 inhabitants in northeast Brazil.[47] Pau da Lima lies in a region of hills and valleys that was a sparsely inhabited area of Atlantic rain forest in the 1970s and was subsequently transformed into a densely populated slum settlement by in-migration of squatters. In total, 67 percent of the population of Salvador and 37 percent of the urban population in Brazil reside in slum communities with levels of poverty equal to or greater than that found in Pau da Lima.[48, 49]

A study site was established that comprised of four valleys in an area of 0.46 km^2. Active, hospital-based surveillance found that between 1996 and 2001 the mean annual incidence of severe leptospirosis was 57.8 cases per 100,000 population at the study site. The study team conducted a census during visits to 3,689 households within the site in 2003 and identified 14,122 inhabitants. Households were assigned sequential numbers. A computer-based random number generator was used to select a list of 1,079 sample households from a database of all enumerated households. Eligible subjects who resided in sample households and were five years of age or older were invited to be study participants. Subjects were enrolled in the study between April 2003 and May 2004 according to a written informed consent approved by the institutional review boards of the Oswaldo Cruz Foundation, Brazilian National Commission for Ethics in Research, and Weill Medical College of Cornell University.

Household Survey

The study team of community health workers, nurses, and physicians conducted interviews during house visits and administered a standardized questionnaire to obtain information on demographic and socioeconomic indicators, employment, and occupation and on exposures to sources of environmental contamination and potential reservoirs in the household and workplace. Responses reported by subjects were used to obtain information on race. The study team evaluated literacy according to the ability to read standardized sentences and interpret their meaning. Informal work was defined as work-related activities for which the subject did not have legal working documents. The head of household, defined as the member who earned the highest monthly income, was interviewed to determine sources and amounts of income for the household. Subjects were asked to report the highest number of rats sighted within the household property in the previous week and the site of work-related activities. The study team surveyed the area within the household property to determine the presence of dogs, cats, and chickens.

Geographic Information System (GIS) Survey

An ArcView version 8.3 software system (Environmental Systems Research Institute) database was constructed with georeferenced aerial photographs and topographic maps provided by the Company for Urban Development of the State of Bahia (CONDER). Photographs of the study site, which had a scale of 1:2,000 and spatial resolution of 16 cm, were taken in 2002. During the census, the study team identified households within the study site and marked their positions on hard-copy 1:1,500 scale maps, which were then entered into the ArcView database. A survey was conducted during the seasonal period of heavy rainfall between April and August 2003 to geocodify the location of open sewage and rainwater drainage systems. At three points within this period, the study team mapped the sites of open accumulated refuse and measured the area of these deposits. Mean values for areas of refuse deposits were calculated and used for the analyses.

Serological Analysis

Sera were processed from blood samples collected from subjects during house visits. The microscopic agglutination test (MAT) was performed to evaluate for serologic evidence of a prior *Leptospira* infection.[50] A panel of five reference strains (WHO Collaborative Laboratory for Leptospirosis, Royal Tropical Institute, Holland) and two clinical isolates were used that included *L. interrogans* serovars Autumnalis, Canicola, and Copenhageni; *L. borgspetersenii* serovar Ballum, and *L. kirschneri* serovar Grippotyphosa.[51] The use of this panel had the same performance in identifying MAT-confirmed cases of leptospirosis during surveillance in Salvador[52, 53] as did the WHO recommended battery of nineteen reference serovars.[54] Screening was performed with serum dilutions of 1:25, 1:50, and 1:100. When agglutination was observed at a dilution of 1:100, the sample was titrated to determine the highest titer.

Statistical Methods

Information for subjects was double-entered into an EpiInfo version 3.3.2 software system (Centers for Diseases Control and Prevention) database. Chi-square and Wilcoxon rank sum tests were used to compare categorical and continuous data, respectively, for eligible subjects who were and were not enrolled in the study. A P value of 0.05 in two-sided testing was used as the criterion for a significant difference. Preliminary analyses evaluated a range of MAT titers as criteria for prior *Leptospira* infection and found that the use of different cutoff values (1:25–1:100) identified similar associations with respect to the spatial distribution of seropositive subjects and risk factors for acquiring *Leptospira* antibodies. A titer greater or equal to 1:25 was therefore used to define the presence of *Leptospira* antibodies in the final analyses. The presumptive infecting serovar was defined as the serovar against which the highest agglutination titer was directed.[55] Crude prevalence rates were reported since age and gender-adjusted values did not differ significantly from crude values. Ninety-five percent confidence intervals (CIs) were adjusted for the cluster sampling of households.

Kernel density estimation analysis was performed with a range of bandwidths (10–120 meters) to evaluate smoothed spatial distributions of subjects with *Leptospira* antibodies and all subjects. The R version 2.4.1 statistical package (R Foundation for Statistical Computing) was used to obtain estimates that were adjusted for boundary effects. The ratio of the Kernel density estimators for subjects with *Leptospira* antibodies to that of all subjects was measured to determine the smoothed population-adjusted risk distribution. A digital terrain model of topographic data (ArcGIS 3D Analyst Extension software) was used to obtain continuous estimates of altitude for the study area. The distances, calculated in three-dimensional space, of households to nearest open drainage systems and refuse deposits were evaluated as proxies of exposure to these sources of environmental attributes. Elevation of households with respect to the lowest point in the valley in which they were situated was used as a surrogate for flood risk. Generalized additive models (GAMs) were used to evaluate the functional form of the association between continuous variables and the risk of acquiring *Leptospira* antibodies.[56] When indicated, continuous variables were categorized in multivariate analyses according to the x-intercept value observed in the plots of fitted smoothed values.

We used Poisson regression (PR) to estimate the effect of demographic, socioeconomic, household-, and workplace-related factors on the prevalence of *Leptospira* antibodies.[57] A Bayesian inference approach was used that incorporated two random effects in order to account for overdispersion and cluster sampling within households. This approach has been used to estimate parameters in complex models[58] and is less sensitive to sparse data.[59] Standard noninformative prior distributions were used in models fitted with WinBUGS version 1.4.2 (MRC Biostatistics Unit). In multivariate analysis, all variables that had a P value below 0.10 in univariate analyses were included in the initial model. To address colinearity among variables, we identified sets of covariates with high Spearman correlation coefficients (>0.3 or <–0.3). Highly correlated variables were aggregated in a single variable when indicated, and were evaluated in the model. The final model obtained used backward variable selection with an inclusion rule of P value <0.05.

RESULTS

Among 3,797 eligible residents from the slum community site, 3,171 (84%) were enrolled in the study. Study subjects had a higher proportion of females (56% of 3,171 subjects versus 37% of 626 subjects, respectively; P<0.05) and a younger mean age (25.8±15.2 versus 28.1±14.6 years, respectively; P<0.05) than eligible residents who did not participate in the study. The Kernel distribution of enrolled subjects according to place of residence was similar on visual inspection to that of residents who did not participate (data not shown). The majority (85%) of subjects were squatters who did not have legal title to their domiciles. Subjects belonged to mostly mixed (*pardo,* 66%) or black (28%) racial groups. Median household per capita income for study subjects was US$1.30 per day. Among the subjects, 76 percent had not completed elementary school education, and 23 percent were illiterate. Among 2,077 subjects 18 years of age and older, 77 percent did not have formal employment and 35 percent engaged in informal work.

Among the 3,171 subjects, 489 had *Leptospira* agglutinating antibodies, as determined by the presence of MAT titer 1:25. Highest titers were directed against *L. interrogans* serovar Copenhageni in 436 (89.2%) of the 489 subjects with *Leptospira* antibodies. For the 22 subjects (4.5%) who had the highest titers against two or more serovars, agglutination reactions recognized Copenhageni as one of the serovars. Copenhageni was the predominant serovar (88–100%) recognized for the range of highest reciprocal titers (figure 7.2).

The overall prevalence of *Leptospira* antibodies was 15.4 percent (95% CI 14.0–16.8). The crude prevalence among enrolled subjects was not significantly different from the prevalence (15.9%, 95% CI 14.6–17.1), which was adjusted for the age and gender distribution of eligible subjects in the study population. Prevalence was highest among adolescents and adults (16.2% and 21.2% for age groups 15–24 and

>44 years, respectively). However, 8.3 percent (95% CI 6.2–10.5) of children 5–14 years of age had evidence of prior exposure to *Leptospira*. The prevalence was higher in males than in females (17.8% versus 13.6%, respectively; PR 1.32, 95% CI 1.10–1.57). Similar associations with age and gender were observed when MAT titers of 1:50 and 1:100 were used to define subjects with *Leptospira* antibodies.

The population-adjusted distribution showed that risk of acquiring *Leptospira* antibodies clustered in areas occupied by squatters at the bottom of valleys. Similar spatial distributions were observed in analyses that used higher titer values to define subjects with *Leptospira* antibodies.

Univariate analysis found the risk of acquiring *Leptospira* antibodies to be associated with increasing age, male gender, indicators of low socioeconomic level, occupations that entail contact with contaminated environments, informal work, time of residence in the study household, and environmental attributes and the presence of reservoirs in the household. Significant risk associations were not found for formal employment or for reported sighting of rats in the workplace environment. Open rainwater drainage structures and refuse deposits were distributed throughout the site; yet open sewers were more frequently encountered at the bottom of valleys. The distance from the household to the nearest open sewer was a risk factor, whereas a significant association was not observed for distance to an open rainwater drainage system.

GAM analysis showed that the risk of acquiring *Leptospira* antibodies had an inverse linear association with the distance from the subject's household to an open sewer and with the household's elevation from the lowest point in the valley, a proxy for flood risk. Increased risk was observed among subjects who resided within a threshold distance of 20 meters from these attributes. The risk of acquiring *Leptospira* antibodies had an inverse nonlinear association with distance of the subject's household to an open refuse deposit. We explored a range of dichotomization criteria and found significant risk associations when subjects resided less than 20 meters from an open refuse deposit. This association was not influenced by the size of the refuse deposit. Subjects who reported sighting two or more rats in the household environment had increased risk of acquiring *Leptospira* antibodies. Household per capita income had an inverse linear association with the presence of *Leptospira* antibodies. Of note, the distance of the household from an open sewer was highly correlated (Spearmen correlation coefficient = 0.71) with household elevation since open sewers drain into the bottom of valleys. An aggregate variable, distance of household located less than

20 meters from an open sewer and the lowest point in a valley, was therefore used to examine the association between open sewer and flood-related exposure and infection risk. In contrast, household per capita income was not highly correlated (Spearmen correlation coefficient = 0.16) with the household's elevation.

Multivariate analyses found that the risk of acquiring *Leptospira* antibodies was associated with exposures in the household environment and not in the workplace setting. Subjects who resided less than 20 meters from an open sewer and the lowest point in the valley had a 1.42 times (95% CI 1.14–1.75) increased risk for acquiring *Leptospira* antibodies than those who lived 20 meters or more from these attributes. Residence less than 20 meters from accumulated refuse was associated with a 1.43 times (95% CI 1.04–1.88) increased risk. Sighting of two or more rats and presence of chickens—a marker for rat infestation—in the household were significant reservoir-associated risk factors. After controlling for age, gender, and significant environmental exposures, indicators of low socioeconomic level, household per capita income (PR 0.89 for an increase of US$1.00 per day, 95% CI 0.82–0.95), and black race (PR 1.25, 95% CI 1.03–1.50) were risk factors for acquiring *Leptospira* antibodies.

DISCUSSION

Efforts to identify interventions for urban leptospirosis have been hampered by the lack of population-based information on transmission determinants. In this large community-based survey of a slum settlement in Brazil, we found that 15 percent of the residents had serologic evidence for a prior *Leptospira* infection. The prevalence rate of *Leptospira* antibodies in the study slum community was similar to that (12%) found in a citywide survey performed in Salvador.[60] Risk factors for acquiring *Leptospira* antibodies were associated with exposures in the household environment. Interventions therefore need to target the environmental sources of transmission—open sewers, flooding, open refuse deposits, and animal reservoirs—in the places where slum inhabitants reside. After controlling for the influence of poor environment, indicators of low socioeconomic status were found to be independently associated with the risk of acquiring *Leptospira* antibodies. This finding suggests that in slum communities with overall high levels of absolute poverty, relative differences in socioeconomic level contribute to unequal outcomes for leptospirosis.

Leptospirosis has traditionally been considered an occupational disease, since work-related activities are frequently identified as risk exposures.[61] However, slum inhabitants reside in close proximity to animal reservoirs and environmental surface waters that contain *Leptospira*.[62] We previously found that *Leptospira* infection clusters within households in slum communities in Salvador.[63] In this study, we found that after controlling for confounding, significant risk exposures were those associated with the household environment rather than the workplace. As a caveat, interview-elicited responses were used to evaluate work-related exposures, since GIS surveys were not performed at the sites where subjects worked. It is possible that slum residents may have had work-related risk exposures not detected by our survey. Nevertheless, our findings support the conclusion that the slum household is an important site for *Leptospira* transmission and provides the rationale for interventions that target risk exposures in this environment.

The study's findings indicate that the domestic rat was the principal reservoir for *Leptospira* transmission in the study community. Highest agglutination titers among 89 percent of the subjects were directed against *L. interrogans* serovar Copenhageni, the serovar associated with the *R. norvegicus* reservoir. Reported sighting of rats is considered to be an unreliable marker of rat infestation. However, we found that the number of rats sighted by residents was correlated with their risk of acquiring *Leptospira* antibodies, indicating that rat sightings may be a useful marker of infection risk in slum communities where inhabitants are accustomed to the presence of rats. Although dogs were not found to be a risk factor, detailed investigations of *Leptospira* carriage in urban reservoirs need to be performed. Of note, the presence of chickens in households was a risk factor, though they themselves are not reservoirs. This association may reflect a rat-related exposure not accounted for by reported sightings, since rats are attracted to chicken feed and waste. Raising chickens is a widespread practice in slum communities; 48 percent (519) of the 1,079 study households raised chickens. Control of rodent reservoir populations may therefore need to incorporate measures that directly address this practice.

Our findings confirm hypotheses raised by previous ecologic studies that infrastructure deficiencies related to open sewers, flooding, and open refuse deposits are transmission sources for leptospirosis in the slum environment.[64, 65, 66] Furthermore, defined areas of risk appear to be associated with open sewers and refuse deposits, which serve as habitats and sources of food for rats. Home range radius of the domestic rat varies from 30 to

150 meters,[67, 68] but home range use decreases from the center to the edge. GAM analysis demonstrated that slum residents had a positive risk for acquiring *Leptospira* antibodies when households were situated within 20 meters from open sewers and refuse deposits. In addition, infection risk increased as distances from an open sewer or refuse deposit decreased, suggesting that households situated closer to these foci have a higher degree of environmental contamination with *Leptospira* and that inhabitants of these households are exposed to higher inoculum doses during infection. Molecular approaches to quantify *Leptospira* in environmental samples[69] will be useful in answering this question and guiding recommendations for environmental decontamination and barrier control measures that can be implemented in slum communities.

In addition, GAM analysis found that residents had a positive risk for *Leptospira* infection when their households were situated within 20 meters from the lowest point in the valley. In Salvador[70, 71, 72, 73] and other urban centers,[74, 75, 76, 77, 78] outbreaks of leptospirosis occur during heavy rainfall and flooding events. Slum communities are built on poor-quality land and often in areas susceptible to frequent flooding. At the study site and other slum settlements in Salvador, the water table rises up to 1 meter during flooding events because of inadequate rainwater drainage and blockage of drainage systems with silt and refuse. The finding that subjects had increased infection risk when their households were located within 20 meters from the lowest point in the valley suggests that this distance was a proxy for the degree of contact that residents encounter through flood-related exposures in the peridomiciliary environment.

We found that in addition to attributes of the environment where slum inhabitants reside, low per capita household income and black race, an indicator of health inequality in Brazil,[79, 80] were independent risk factors for *Leptospira* infection. The social gradient in health is a widespread phenomenon.[81, 82] Our findings, though not unexpected, are noteworthy since they suggest that differences in status contribute to unequal health outcomes in a slum community where the household per capita income was less than US$1 per day for 44 percent of the inhabitants. Although errors in the measurement of risk exposures and residual confounding were a possibility, the strength of the association indicates a role for social determinants in *Leptospira* transmission. These factors may relate to risky behaviors, such as cleaning open sewers after flooding events, or limited use of protective clothing that reduce the risk of abrasions that facilitate entry of the *Leptospira* spirochete.[83] Low social status and lack of access to amenities and social support are features of disadvantaged communities that conceivably influence risk behaviors for leptospirosis.[84] Further research is needed to evaluate the role of social factors such that effective interventions, including health education, can be implemented at the community level.

A limitation of our study was its cross-sectional design, which used serologic evidence for a prior *Leptospira* infection as the outcome. The MAT is the standard assay used in prevalence surveys,[85] yet there is not an established titer criterion for defining seropositive reactions. We previously found that a MAT titer of >1:25 was a specific marker for prior *Leptospira* infection among slum residents from Salvador and, when applied, identified household clustering of infection risk.[86] In this study, cutoff titers of 1:25 and above identified similar risk associations. In Salvador, leptospirosis is due to transmission of a single agent, *L. interrogans* serovar Copenhageni.[87, 88] Titers of 1:25, as well as higher titers, were directed against this serovar, indicating that this cutoff was a specific and more sensitive criterion for identifying prior infections in a region where a single serovar agent is circulating. In the study, there were more men and younger subjects among nonparticipating subjects than among participating subjects. Crude prevalence was not different from the prevalence of *Leptospira* antibodies adjusted by the age and gender distribution of the overall study population, indicating that differences between participating and nonparticipating subjects may not have introduced a significant bias in the estimates. Infections may have occurred up to five years prior to the survey since agglutinating antibodies may persist for this period.[89, 90] Although major interventions to improve basic sanitation were not implemented in the study community, the possibility that environmental exposures were modified over time cannot be excluded. Migration may have affected our ability to estimate prevalence and risk associations. An ongoing cohort investigation of subjects enrolled in this study found that the annual out-migration rate is approximately 12 percent. The study's findings therefore need to be confirmed in prospective studies.

We found that *Leptospira* transmission was due to the interaction of factors associated with climate, geography, and urban poverty. Since the study was performed in a single community in Salvador, Brazil, our findings may not be generalizable to other slum settings. However, a large proportion of the world's slum population resides in tropical climates similar to that in Salvador. Moreover, conditions of poverty and environmental degradation similar to those encountered in the study site are found in many slum settlements. In Brazil, 37 percent of the urban population resides in slums with levels of poverty equal to or greater than that found in the study community.[91] Our findings may therefore be relevant to other slum communities where leptospirosis is endemic and have increasing significance as global climate change[92, 93] and the growth of the world's slum population occur in the future.[94, 95]

The infrastructure deficiencies found to be transmission factors for *Leptospira* in this study can readily be addressed by improving sanitation in slum communities. Investment in sanitation is a cost-effective health intervention.[96, 97] In Salvador, a citywide sanitation program (Bahia Azul) was recently shown to have a major beneficial impact for diarrheal disease.[98] However, as frequently encountered with large-scale sanitation projects, the Bahia Azul program did not provide coverage to the study community or many of the slum settlements in the city's periphery. Equitable access to improved sanitation is therefore essential in reducing the burden of the large number of environmentally transmitted infectious diseases, including leptospirosis, that affects slum populations. Furthermore, the finding that the social gradient within slum communities, in addition to the unhealthy environment, contributes to the risk of *Leptospira* infection suggests that prevention of urban leptospirosis will need to combine approaches for improving sanitation with approaches that identify and address the social determinants that produce unequal health outcomes.

NOTES

1. United Nations Human Settlements Programme. (2003). *The challenge of slums: Global report on human settlements.* London: Earthscan.

2. United Nations Human Settlements Programme (2003).

3. Riley, L.W., Ko, A.I., Unger, A., & Reis, M.G. (2007). Slum health: Diseases of neglected populations. *BMC Int Health Hum Rights* 7:2.

4. Sclar, E.D., Garau, P., & Carolini, G. (2005). The 21st century health challenge of slums and cities. *Lancet* 365:901–3.

5. The General Assembly of the United Nations (2000). United Nations Millennium Declaration. http://www.un.org/millennium/. Accessed 11 March 2008.

6. Riley et al. (2007).

7. Sclar et al. (2005).

8. Bartram, J., Lewis, K., Lenton, R., & Wright, A. (2005). Focusing on improved water and sanitation for health. *Lancet* 365:810–12.

9. Ko, A.I., Reis, M.G., Ribeiro Dourado, C.M., Johnson, W.D. Jr., & Riley, L.W. (1999). Urban epidemic of severe leptospirosis in Brazil. Salvador Leptospirosis Study Group. *Lancet* 354:820–25.

10. McBride, A.J., Athanazio, D.A., Reis, M.G., & Ko, A.I. (2005). Leptospirosis. *Curr Opi Infect Dis* 18:376–86.

11. McBride et al. (2005).

12. Bharti, A.R., Nally, J.E., Ricaldi, J.N., Matthias, M.A., Diaz, M.M., et al. (2003). Leptospirosis: A zoonotic disease of global importance. *Lancet Infect Dis* 3:757–71.

13. Levett, P.N. (2001). Leptospirosis. *Clin Microbiol Rev* 14:296–326.

14. Bharti et al. (2003).

15. Levett (2001).

16. Ko et al. (1999).

17. Ganoza, C.A., Matthias, M.A., Collins-Richards, D., Brouwer, K.C., Cunningham, C.B., et al. (2006). Determining risk for severe leptospirosis by molecular analysis of environmental surface waters for pathogenic Leptospira. *PLoS Med* 3:e308. doi:10.1371/journal.pmed.0030308.

18. Ko et al. (1999).

19. Barcellos, C., & Sabroza, P.C. (2000). Socio-environmental determinants of the leptospirosis outbreak of 1996 in western Rio de Janeiro: A geographical approach. *Int J Environ Health Res* 10:301–13.

20. Caldas, E.M., & Sampaio, M.B. (1979). Leptospirosis in the city of Salvador, Bahia, Brazil: A case-control seroepidemiologic study. *Int J Zoonoses* 6:85–96.

21. Karande, S., Kulkarni, H., Kulkarni, M., De, A., & Varaiya, A. (2002). Leptospirosis in children in Mumbai slums. *Indian J Pediatr* 69:855–858.

22. LaRocque, R.C., Breiman, R.F., Ari, M.D., Morey, R.E., Janan, F.A., et al. (2005). Leptospirosis during dengue outbreak, Bangladesh. *Emerg Infect Dis* 11:766–69.

23. Romero, E.C., Bernardo, C.C., & Yasuda, P.H. (2003). Human leptospirosis: A twenty-nine-year serological study in Sao Paulo, Brazil. *Rev Inst Med Trop Sao Paulo* 45:245–48.

24. Sarkar, U., Nascimento, S.F., Barbosa, R., Martins, R., Nuevo, H., et al. (2002). Population-based case-control investigation of risk factors for leptospirosis during an urban epidemic. *Am J Trop Med Hyg* 66:605–10.

25. Tassinari, W. de S., Pellegrini, D. da C., Sabroza, P.C., & Carvalho, M.S. (2004). Spatial distribution of leptospirosis in the city of Rio de Janeiro, Brazil, 1996–1999. *Cad Saude Publica* 20:1721–29.

26. Kupek, E., de Sousa Santos Faversani, M.C., & de Souza Philippi, J.M. (2000). The relationship between rainfall and human leptospirosis in Florianopolis, Brazil, 1991–1996. *Braz J Infect Dis* 4:131–34.

27. Riley et al. (2007).

28. Health Surveillance Secretary, Brazilian Ministry of Health (2007a). [Leptospirosis case notification records, Brazil].

29. Health Surveillance Secretary, Brazilian Ministry of Health (2008). [Dengue epidemiological report, January–December 2007]. http://portal.saude.gov.br/portal/arquivos/pdf/boletim_dengue_010208.pdf. Accessed 11 March 2008.

30. Health Surveillance Secretary, Brazilian Ministry of Health (2007b). [Confirmed cases of meningococcal disease, Brazil, major regions and federal units,

1990–2006]. http://portal.saude.gov.br/portal/arquivos/pdf/tabela_meningites_brasil.pdf. Accessed 11 March 2008.

31. Health Surveillance Secretary, Brazilian Ministry of Health (2007c) [Visceral leishmaniasis case notification records, Brazil].

32. Health Surveillance Secretary, Brazilian Ministry of Health (2007a).

33. Health Surveillance Secretary, Brazilian Ministry of Health (2008).

34. Health Surveillance Secretary, Brazilian Ministry of Health (2007d) [Meningococcal disease deaths, Brazil, major regions and federal units, 1990–2006]. http://portal.saude.gov.br/portal/arquivos/pdf/tabela_obitos_dm_brasil.pdf. Accessed 11 March 2008.

35. Health Surveillance Secretary, Brazilian Ministry of Health (2007e). [Visceral leishmaniasis case fatality rate, Brazil, major regions and federal units, 2000–2006]. http://portal.saude.gov.br/portal/arquivos/pdf/tabela_lv_letalidade.pdf. Accessed 11 March 2008.

36. Ministerio de Salud Pública, Organización Panamericana de la Salud (1998). El fenómeno El Niño en Ecuador. In Organización Panamericana de la Salud, editor. *El Niño, 1997–1998*. Washington, D.C.: Organización Panamericana de la Salud. Pp. 175–230.

37. Epstein, P.R. (1999). Climate and health. *Science* 285:347–48.

38. Patz, J.A., Campbell-Lendrum, D., Holloway, T., & Foley, J.A. (2005). Impact of regional climate change on human health. *Nature* 438:310–17.

39. United Nations Human Settlements Programme (2003).

40. Ko et al. (1999).

41. Ganoza et al. (2006).

42. Barcellos & Sabroza (2000).

43. Ko et al. (1999).

44. Barocchi, M.A., Ko, A.I., Ferrer, S.R., Faria, M.T., Reis, M.G., et al. (2001). Identification of new repetitive element in *Leptospira interrogans* serovar Copenhageni and its application to PCR-based differentiation of *Leptospira* serogroups. *J Clin Microbiol* 39:191–95.

45. Pereira, M.M., Matsuo, M.G., Bauab, A.R., Vasconcelos, S.A., Moraes, Z.M., et al. (2000). A clonal subpopulation of *Leptospira interrogans sensu stricto* is the major cause of leptospirosis outbreaks in Brazil. *J Clin Microbiol* 38: 450–52.

46. Romero, E.C., & Yasuda, P.H. (2006). Molecular characterization of *Leptospira* sp. strains isolated from human subjects in Sao Paulo, Brazil using a polymerase chain reaction–based assay: A public health tool. *Mem Inst Oswaldo Cruz* 101:373–78.

47. Instituto Brasileiro de Geografia e Estatística (2002). *Censo demográfico 2000—resultados do universo*. Rio de Janeiro: Instituto Brasileiro de Geografia e Estatística.

48. Secretaria de Combate à Pobreza e às Desigualdades Sociais/SECOMP (2005). *Mapamento da pobreza em áreas urbanas do estado da Bahia*. 2005 (CD-ROM).

49. UN-Habitat (2003). *Slums of the world: The face of urban poverty in the new millennium?* Nairobi, Kenya: UN-Habitat.

50. World Health Organization (2003). *Human leptospirosis: Guidance for diagnosis, surveillance and control*. Malta: World Health Organization.

51. Ko et al. (1999).
52. Ibid.
53. Sarkar et al. (2002).
54. World Health Organization (2003).
55. Ibid.
56. Hin, L.Y., Lau, T.K., Rogers, M.S., & Chang, A.M. (1999). Dichotomization of continuous measurements using generalized additive modelling—Application in predicting intrapartum caesarean delivery. *Stat Med* 18: 1101–10.
57. Barros, A.J., & Hirakata, V.N. (2003). Alternatives for logistic regression in cross-sectional studies: An empirical comparison of models that directly estimate the prevalence ratio. *BMC Med Res Methodol* 3:21.
58. Ashby, D. (2006). Bayesian statistics in medicine: A 25 year review. *Stat Med* 25:3589–3631.
59. Greenland, S., Schwartzbaum, J.A., & Finkle, W.D. (2000). Problems due to small samples and sparse data in conditional logistic regression analysis. *Am J Epidemiol* 151:531–39.
60. Dias, J.P., Teixeira, M.G., Costa, M.C., Mendes, C.M., Guimaraes, P., et al. (2007). Factors associated with *Leptospira* sp infection in a large urban center in Northeastern Brazil. *Rev Soc Bras Med Trop* 40:499–504.
61. Levett (2001).
62. Ganoza et al. (2006).
63. Maciel, E.A.P., Carvalho, A.L.F., Nascimento, S.F., Matos, R.B., Gouveia, E.L., et al. (2008). Household transmission of *Leptospira* infection in urban slum communities. *PLoS Negl Trop Dis* 2:e154. doi:10.1371/journal.pntd.0000154.
64. Ko et al. (1999).
65. Ganoza et al. (2006).
66. Barcellos & Sabroza (2000).
67. Jackson, W.B. (1982). Norway rat and allies. In Chapman, J.A., & Feldhamer, G.A., editors. *Wild mammals of North America.* Baltimore: Johns Hopkins University Press. Pp. 1077–88.
68. Nowak, R.M. (1991). *Walker's mammals of the world.* Baltimore: John Hopkins University Press.
69. Ganoza et al. (2006).
70. Ko et al. (1999).
71. Caldas & Sampaio (1979).
72. Sarkar et al. (2002).
73. Maciel et al. (2008).
74. Barcellos & Sabroza (2000).
75. Karande et al. (2002).
76. Romero et al. (2003).
77. Tassinari et al. (2004).
78. Kupek et al. (2000).
79. Barros, F.C., Victora, C.G., & Horta, B.L. (2001). Ethnicity and infant health in Southern Brazil: A birth cohort study. *Int J Epidemiol* 30:1001–8.
80. Travassos, C., & Williams, D.R. (2004). The concept and measurement of race and their relationship to public health: A review focused on Brazil and the United States. *Cad Saude Publica* 20:660–78.

81. Marmot, M. (2001). Inequalities in health. *N Engl J Med* 345:134–36.

82. Marmot, M. (2005). Social determinants of health inequalities. *Lancet* 365:1099–1104.

83. Phraisuwan, P., Whitney, E.A., Tharmaphornpilas, P., Guharat, S., Thongkamsamut, S., et al. (2002). Leptospirosis: Skin wounds and control strategies, Thailand, 1999. *Emerg Infect Dis* 8:1455–59.

84. Marmot (2001).

85. Levett (2001).

86. Maciel et al. (2008)

87. Ko et al. (1999)

88. Barocchi et al. (2001).

89. Cumberland, P., Everard, C.O., Wheeler, J.G., & Levett, P.N. (2001). Persistence of anti-leptospiral IgM, IgG and agglutinating antibodies in patients presenting with acute febrile illness in Barbados, 1979–1989. *Eur J Epidemiol* 17:601–8.

90. Lupidi, R., Cinco, M., Balanzin, D., Delprete, E., & Varaldo, P.E. (1991). Serological follow-up of patients involved in a localized outbreak of leptospirosis. *J Clin Microbiol* 29:805–9.

91. UN-Habitat (2003).

92. Epstein (1999).

93. Patz et al. (2005).

94. United Nations Human Settlements Programme (2003).

95. UN-Habitat (2003).

96. Hutton, G., Haller, L., & Bartram, J. (2007). Global cost-benefit analysis of water supply and sanitation interventions. *J Water Health* 5:481–502.

97. Laxminarayan, R., Chow, J., Salles, S., & Maslen, P. (2006). Intervention cost-effectiveness: Overview of general messages. In Jamison, D.T., Breman, J.G., Measham, A.R., Alleyne, G., Claeson, M. et al., eds. *Disease control priorities in developing countries.* New York: Oxford University Press. Pp. 35–86.

98. Barreto, M.L., Genser, B., Strina, A., Teixeira, M.G., Assis, A.M., et al. (2007). Effect of city-wide sanitation programme on reduction in rate of childhood diarrhoea in northeast Brazil: Assessment by two cohort studies. *Lancet* 370:1622–28.

CHAPTER 8

Factors Associated with Group A *Streptococcus emm* Type Diversification in a Large Urban Setting in Brazil

A Cross-Sectional Study

SARA Y. TARTOF, JOICE N. REIS, AURELIO N. ANDRADE, REGINA T. RAMOS, MITERMAYER G. REIS, AND LEE W. RILEY

Group A *Streptococcus* (*Streptococcus pyogenes*; GAS) causes a wide spectrum of diseases, from pharyngitis and pyoderma to more severe diseases such as toxic shock syndrome, necrotizing fasciitis, glomerulonephritis, and rheumatic heart disease (RHD).[1] Children are the major reservoir of GAS.[2] The highest prevalence of GAS infections and their complications are found in developing countries.[3] GAS strain typing is frequently used to characterize the epidemiology and pathogenesis of GAS infections. The most common target of typing methods is the M protein, which is a cell surface virulence factor serving as a target of the immune response to GAS that confers type-specific resistance. A sequence-based typing system called *emm* sequence typing, based on the N-terminus hypervariable region (5′) of the M protein gene, is now widely used.[4] Many studies have been conducted using *emm* typing to show associations of specific strain types with disease outcomes.[5, 6, 7, 8, 9] Information about geographic *emm* type distribution can also be used to assess candidate vaccine coverage,[10, 11] including that of a 26-valent vaccine that has recently completed phase II trials.[12]

Reprinted, with permission, from *BMC Infectious Diseases* 10 (2010):327.

Epidemiologic studies have revealed that developing countries have high–*emm* type diversity,[13, 14] while high-income countries are more likely to have a limited number of *emm* types.[15, 16, 17, 18] This pattern was clearly demonstrated in a recent systematic review of 120 articles and reports on GAS *emm* types.[19] It found a higher diversity of *emm* types in Africa and the Pacific than in high-income countries, which may be related to differences in geographic, environmental, socioeconomic, or host factors. However, comparisons made across continents cannot evaluate the impact of local factors on genotype distribution. In this study, we compared the *emm* types of GAS isolates obtained from children in slum and wealthy neighborhoods in the same city, Salvador, Brazil, to examine the influence of urban environmental, demographic, and socioeconomic factors on diversification of GAS. Furthermore, we collected isolates from children with and without sore throat to identify associations of certain *emm* types with clinical outcome.

METHODS

Study Sites

This study was conducted at three pediatric outpatient emergency clinics (Clinics A, B, and C). Clinical services at Clinic A and Clinic B are offered free to patients through Brazil's publicly funded Unified Health System (SUS). These clinics serve primarily low-income patients. The socioeconomic status and demographic characteristics (household density, income, education level of mother and father) of patients seeking care at Clinics A and B are similar. Clinic C serves wealthier clientele and only those with private insurance. Clinic B is located 24 km from Clinic C, Clinic A is located 32 km from Clinic B, and Clinic A is located 11 km from Clinic C. The size of the patient population is comparable among the three clinics. Each clinic receives 5,000–6,000 children as outpatients each year.

Patient Recruitment

Patients aged 3–15 years were consecutively recruited from Clinics A, B, and C from April 17, 2008, to October 31, 2008. Recruitment occurred while patients waited for their medical evaluation, or immediately following their appointment. Parents/guardians of children were approached by a research team member for recruitment and consent to participate in the study. At this time, a brief description of the study and its risks, benefits, and issues of confidentiality were provided. Following consent from parents/guardians and verbal assent from minors, a trained member of the research team administered a standardized questionnaire and collected a throat swab sample of the study participant. All members of the research team were trained in standardized techniques for both procedures. Institutional review board (IRB) approval was obtained from all hospitals, the Comissão Nacional de Ética em Pesquisa (*Conep*; National Bioethics Commission of Brazil), the Comitê de Ética em Pesquisa–Centro de Pesquisa Gonçalo Moniz–Fiocruz (Ethics Committee for Research-Fiocruz), and the University of California, Berkeley, Committee for the Protection of Human Subjects.

Definitions

Slum communities were defined according to the United Nations Human Settlements Program as human settlement areas that have one or more of the following characteristics: (1) inadequate access to safe water, (2) inadequate access to sanitation and other infrastructure, (3) poor structural quality of housing, (4) overcrowding, and (5) insecure residential status.[20] In the neighborhoods served by Clinics A and B, these characteristics vary at the individual household level. However, what these slum settlements all have in common is that they were illegally built on land with unclear tenure status. The structural quality of housing also varies among residential units in these slums (ranging from redbrick houses with unfinished walls and tile roofs to shacks made of discarded lumber and corrugated tin roofs), but the common characteristics are that they were all built with no official permit.

Cases were defined as those children whose chief complaint was sore throat. GAS culture–positive sore throat was defined as a child with a sore throat in whom GAS was isolated from the throat swab. Controls were defined as those visiting the clinics for other reasons. Exclusion criteria included use of antibiotics in the previous two weeks, or any illness requiring inpatient hospitalization on the day of recruitment. Slum children were defined as those attending Clinics A and B, and nonslum children were those attending Clinic C.

Data Collection

The following variables were recorded: reason for visit to the hospital, date of birth of patient, sex of patient, household income, home address, whether in school and where, whether in day care and where, total number of people living in house, number of children 15 years or younger in household, whether study participant had sore throat in past six months, level of education of mother, level of education of father, and comorbidities.

Laboratory Sample Isolation and Identification

Swab cultures were obtained from the pharynx of the study children following a standard protocol. All study technicians were observed periodically at the clinic sites for proper and consistent swabbing technique. A sterile cotton swab tip was applied to the posterior pharynx and tonsils, as recommended by the Infectious Disease Society of America (IDSA).[21] The swabs were immediately placed in a Stuart transport medium, transported to the laboratory, and plated the same day of collection on 5% sheep blood agar. The plates were incubated at 37°C for 24–48 hours with 5% CO_2. Streptococci were phenotypically identified by beta-hemolysis, colony morphology, and the catalase test. Carbohydrate group identification (Groups A, B, C, F, G) was performed by positive latex agglutination (Remel PathoDx Strep Grouping Latex Test Kit, Remel, Lenexa, Kansas, USA). Pure culture samples were stored in 5% glycerol at –80°C until further use.

Emm Typing

Emm-typing of all isolates was performed as described by the Center for Disease Control and Prevention (CDC) protocol http://www2a.cdc.gov/ncidod/biotech/strepblast.asp.

Statistical Analysis

Analyses were conducted by STATA 11.0 (Stata Inc., College Station, Texas). Categorical variables were compared with the chi-square test. Student's t-test and ANOVA were used to compare means, and multivariable logistic regression was used to evaluate the association between specific *emm* types and case status while controlling for covariates. Models were restricted to those children with culture-positive GAS. Simpson's index of diversity was used to calculate the variation of the number of *emm* types of GAS isolates by clinic or by case status.[22] Higher index measures represent greater diversity of *emm* types, since the method calculates the probability that any two randomly selected isolates from the same population will be of different *emm* types. Confidence intervals (CIs, 95%) for the diversity index measures were calculated.[23]

RESULTS

Demographic and Clinical Characteristics

Between April 17, 2008, and October 31, 2008, 2,194 children aged 3–15 years who met the eligibility criteria were identified from the three study clinics (759 in Clinic A, 518 in Clinic B, 917 in Clinic C). Of 2,181 children with data on case status, 624 (28.6%) came with a complaint of sore throat (cases), and 1,557 (71.4%) came for other illnesses. The distribution of reasons for visiting among the controls was comparable across the three hospitals (data not shown).

The mean age of all the study children differed between slum (7.2 years) and nonslum residents (7.8 years) ($p < 0.001$; table 8.1). The sex distribution did not differ between slum and nonslum populations. One minimal monthly salary (MS) or less (equivalent to US$246.10 as of April 2008) was reported by 648 (53.8%) of 1,205 slum households, and 37 (4.3%) of 870 nonslum households ($p < 0.001$). Salary was positively correlated with level of education in this study. The mean number of members per household in the slum population (4.5) was greater than that in the nonslum population (4.0) ($p < 0.001$). The mean number of children under age 15 per household was greater in the slum population (2.0 persons) than in the nonslum population (1.6 persons) ($p < 0.001$).

The difference in mean age between cases (7.4 years) and controls (7.5 years) or between patients who tested positive for GAS (7.6 years) those who tested negative (7.5) was not significant, either in the total study population or when stratified by slum status.

Microbiological Studies

In total, 529 *Streptococcus* isolates (groups A–G) from 2,194 children were obtained. Of these, 254 (48%) were GAS (table 8.2). Of 253 GAS isolates (1 isolate-missing case per control status), 125 (8%) were from controls and 128 (20.5%) were obtained from cases ($p < 0.001$). The proportion of cases who tested culture positive for GAS differed by slum (23.1%) versus nonslum clinic subjects (17.4%), which approached statistical significance ($p = 0.08$). The proportion of controls that tested positive for GAS did not differ between slum and nonslum children (7.8% versus 8.2%).

TABLE 8.1 DEMOGRAPHIC CHARACTERISTICS AND STREPTOCOCCAL GROUP DISTRIBUTIONS OF CHILDREN ATTENDING SLUM AND NONSLUM CLINICS

	Total population (n = 2,194)	Nonslum[a] (n = 917)		Slum[b] (n = 1,277)		
		N		N		p value
Cases	624	915	287	1,266	337	
Controls	1557	915	628	1,266	929	
Mean age in years	7.5	917	7.8	1,277	7.2	<0.001
(95% CI)	(7.3–7.6)		(7.6–8.1)		(7.1–7.4)	
Sex						1
Female	1,060	917	443	1,277	617	
Male	1,134	917	474	1,277	660	
Monthly salary (US$)		870		1,205		<0.001
≤415	685		37		648	
416–830	550		161		389	
831–1,660	336		204		132	
1661–2,490	195		173		22	
≥2,491	309		295		14	
Mean no. of people/ house (95% CI)	4.3 (4.2–4.3)	917	4.0 (3.9–4.1)	1,275	4.5 (4.4–4.6)	<0.001
Mean no. of people/ house ≤15 yrs. old (95% CI)	1.8 (1.8–1.9)	917	1.6 (1.5–1.6)	1,276	2.0 (2.0–2.1)	<0.001
Group A	254	917	99	1,277	155	0.33
Group B	34	917	24	1,277	10	0.001
Group C	57	917	30	1,277	27	0.09
Group F	51	917	24	1,277	27	0.44
Group G	133	917	46	1,277	87	0.08

N = Total number with available response
[a]Includes all children from Clinic C
[b]Includes all children from Clinics A and B

Emm *Diversity*

Of 254 GAS isolates, 238 yielded interpretable *emm* sequences. These 238 isolates represented 61 unique *emm* types. In the nonslum population, 94 isolates comprised 36 distinct *emm* types (38.3%). In the slum population, 144 isolates comprised 53 distinct *emm* types (36.8%). Between these two groups, the proportion of unique *emm* types did not differ (p = 0.81). The proportion of unique *emm* types was higher for carriage isolates than for sore throat cases in the slum population, but this finding did not reach statistical significance (p = 0.11).

TABLE 8.2 DEMOGRAPHIC AND STREPTOCOCCAL GROUP DISTRIBUTIONS, BY SORE THROAT AND CARRIAGE IN SLUM VERSUS NONSLUM CHILDREN

	Nonslum (n = 915)[a]			Slum (n = 1,266)[b]		
	Case (%)	Control (%)[c]	p value	Case (%)	Control (%)	p value
	287 (31.4)	628 (68.6)		337 (26.6)	929 (73.4)	
Mean age (95% CI)	7.8 (7.3–8.2)	7.9 (7.6–8.1)	0.67	7.2 (6.8–7.5)	7.3 (7.1–7.5)	0.57
Male	139 (48.4)	335 (53.3)	0.17	146 (43.4)	508 (54.7)	<0.001
Monthly salary (US$)	N = 274	N = 594	0.02	N = 312	N = 882	0.75
≤415	11 (4.0)	26 (4.4)		178 (57.1)	468 (53.1)	
416–830	38 (13.9)	123 (20.7)		91 (29.2)	291 (33.0)	
831–1,660	58 (21.2)	145 (24.4)		34 (10.9)	96 (10.9)	
1,661–2,490	55 (20.1)	117 (19.7)		5 (1.6)	17 (1.9)	
≥2,491	112 (40.9)	183 (30.8)		4 (1.3)	10 (1.1)	
Mean no. of persons/household (95% CI)	4.0 (3.9–4.2)	4.0 (3.9–4.1)	0.96	4.5 (4.3–4.8)	4.4 (4.3–4.5)	0.27
Mean no. of persons <15 yrs. old/household (95% CI)	1.5 (1.5–1.6)	1.6 (1.6–1.7)	0.16	2.1 (2.0–2.3)	2.0 (1.9–2.1)	0.06
Group A	50 (17.4)	49 (7.8)	<0.001	78 (23.1)	76 (8.2)	<0.001
Group B	7 (2.4)	17 (2.7)	0.81	4 (1.1)	6 (0.6)	0.34
Group C	8 (2.8)	22 (3.5)	0.57	6 (1.8)	21 (2.3)	0.6
Group F	6 (2.1)	18 (2.9)	0.5	7 (2.1)	20 (2.2)	0.93
Group G	8 (2.8)	38 (6.1)	0.04	17 (5.0)	70 (7.5)	0.12
No isolate	208 (72.5)	475 (75.6)	0.17	225 (66.8)	736 (79.2)	<0.001

[a]Includes all patients from Clinic C. Case/control status missing for 2 study participants.
[b]Includes all patients from Clinics A and B. Case/control status missing for 11 study participants.
[c]Case = sore throat; control = carriage.

TABLE 8.3 DIVERSITY OF *EMM* TYPES IN NONSLUM VERSUS SLUM POPULATIONS

	Simpson's diversity index	CI	Number of unique *emm* types	Number of isolates	Proportion unique (%)
All	0.95	(0.94–0.97)	61	238	26.10
Nonslum	0.92	(0.89–0.96)	36	94	38.30
Case	0.9	(0.84–0.97)	24	49	49.00
Carriage	0.93	(0.88–0.97)	21	45	46.70
Slum	0.97	(0.96–0.98)	53	144	36.80
Case	0.96	(0.94–0.98)	34	74	45.90
Carriage	0.98	(0.97–0.99)	41	69	59.40

Simpson's diversity index for all the *emm* types was 96% (94–97%). The index was 92% (89–96%) for the nonslum GAS *emm* types, and 97% (96–98%) for slum *emm* types. The CIs for slum versus nonslum overlap only at the lower-bound estimate for slum, and the upper-bound estimate of nonslum. When the two slum communities were separated, the Simpson's diversity index was 96% (94–98%) for Clinic A and 97% (96–99%) for Clinic B. For both slum and nonslum populations, the diversity index was lower for cases than for controls (nonslum 90% versus 93%; slum 96% versus 98%].

In both slum and nonslum populations, *emm*12.0 was the predominant type, followed by *emm*1.0 (figure 8.1). However, in the nonslum population, 20 (21.3%) of 94 isolates were *emm*12.0, whereas in the slum population, 18 (12.5%) of 144 isolates were *emm*12.0 (p = 0.07). *Emm*1.0 was the second most prevalent *emm* type in both populations, and also constituted a larger proportion of nonslum isolates. In the nonslum population, 14 (14.9%) of 94 isolates were *emm*1.0, and in the slum population, *emm*1.0 constituted 9 (6.3%) of 144 isolates (p = 0.03). The three most predominant *emm* types constituted a much larger proportion of isolates in the nonslum population than in the slum population (41.5% versus 24.3%; p = 0.005), suggesting that GAS diversification was greater in the slum population.

Only 7 *emm* types—12.0 (n = 38), 1.0 (n = 23), st2904.1 (n = 13), 66.0 (n = 12), 87.0 (n = 9), 49.3 (n = 8), and 27G.0 (n = 8)—constituted 46.6% of the total. There were 22 *emm* types that were represented by only a single isolate. In total, 25 distinct *emm* types were detected in slum children alone, compared with only 8 *emm* types found only in nonslum children. *Emm* types represented by only one isolate were more likely to

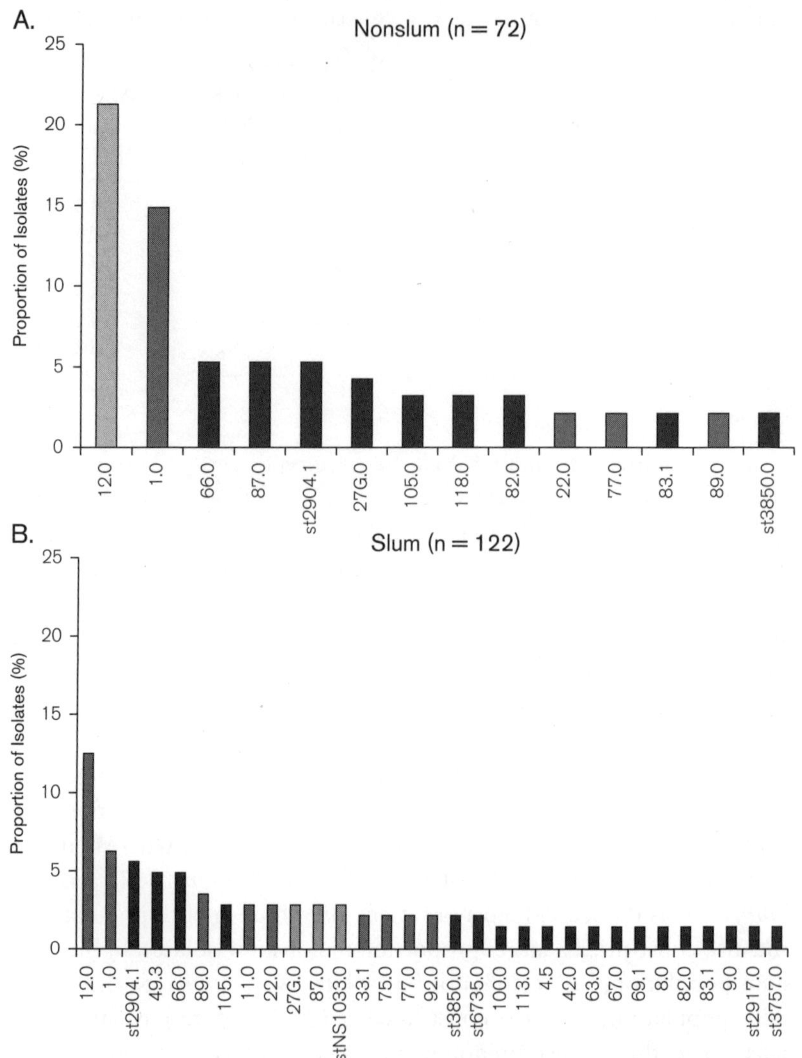

FIGURE 8.1. Proportion of the most common *emm* types in nonslum (A) and slum (B) populations. Only *emm* types represented by more than one isolate are included in the graphs. Lighter-shaded bars indicate *emm* types included in the 26-valent vaccine. Darker-shaded bars indicate *emm* types not included in the vaccine.

TABLE 8.4 COMMON *emm* TYPES, AND THEIR ASSOCIATION WITH SORE THROAT OR CARRIAGE, AMONG GAS CULTURE–POSITIVE PATIENTS (N = 253)

emm type	N (%)	Case (n = 128)	Control (n = 125)	Crude OR	p value	95% CI	OR[a]	p value	95% CI	Multivariable OR[b]	p value	95% CI
12.0	38 (15.0)	25	13	2.09	0.05	1.0–4.3	2.12	0.04	1.0–4.4	2.21	0.04	1.1–4.7
1.0	23 (9.1)	11	12	0.89	0.78	0.4–2.1	0.88	0.77	0.4–2.1	0.84	0.69	0.4–2.0
st2904.1	13 (5.1)	7	6	1.15	0.81	0.4–3.5	1.15	0.80	0.4–3.5	1.13	0.83	0.4–3.5
66.0	12 (4.7)	9	2	4.65	0.05	1.0–22.0	4.64	0.05	1.0–21.9	8.70	0.04	1.1–70.5
87.0	9 (3.6)	5	4	1.23	0.76	0.3–4.7	1.22	0.77	0.4–7.1	1.29	0.71	0.3–5.0
49.3	8 (3.2)	5	3	1.65	0.5	0.4–7.1	1.66	0.50	0.4–711	1.13	0.88	0.2–5.8
27G.0	8 (3.2)	1	7	0.13	0.06	0.0–1.1	0.13	0.06	0.0–1.1	0.14	0.07	0.0–1.1
Unique	22 (8.7)	10	12	0.80	0.61	0.3–1.9	0.79	0.61	0.3–1.9	0.65	0.39	0.3–1.7

[a]Adjusted for age
[b]Adjusted for age, income, number of persons <15 yrs. old in household

be found in children 10 years of age or older than in those 9 and younger, which approached statistical significance ($p = 0.08$).

Emm *Type and Case Status*

Three *emm* types were significantly associated, conferring either risk or protection, with sore throat. Of those who tested positive for GAS, those with *emm*12.0 ($n = 38$) had 2.2 times the odds of having sore throat compared with those with a different *emm* type ($p = 0.04$), after adjusting for age, income, and number of children less than 15 years of age in the household (table 8.4). For those patients with *emm*66.0 ($n = 12$), the odds of sore throat were 8.7 times that of sore throat with other *emm* types in the multivariable model ($p = 0.04$). Interestingly, an inverse relationship was seen for *emm*27G.0 ($n = 8$), where those with this *emm* type had 0.1 times the odds of sore throat compared with other *emm* types in the multivariable model ($p = 0.07$).

Vaccine Coverage

In this study, 100 (42.0%) of the 238 *emm*-typed isolates and 15 (24.6%) of the 61 *emm* types would be covered by the 26-valent M protein–based GAS vaccine, assuming cross-immunity between type 1.2 and subtype 1.25, between type 101 and subtype 101.1, and between type 33.0 and subtype 33.1.[24] Stratifying by populations, 45 (47.9%) of 94 isolates and 10 (27.8%) of 36 *emm* types from nonslum children would be covered by the vaccine. In the slum, the coverage for isolates would be 52 (36.1%) of 144 isolates, and 11 (20.8%) of 53 *emm* types.

In children presenting with sore throat, 55 (44.7%) of 123 *emm*-typed isolates, and 13 (30.2%) of 43 *emm* types would be covered by the current 26-valent M protein–based GAS vaccine. In the nonslum population, 25 (51.0%) of 49 *emm*-typed isolates and 8 (33.3%) of 24 *emm* types would be covered. In the slum population, 32 (43.2%) of 74 *emm*-typed isolates and 10 (29.4%) of 34 *emm* types would be covered by the vaccine.

DISCUSSION

In Salvador, Brazil, we found significant differences in *emm* type diversity among GAS isolates obtained from different populations in the same city. The diversity index was significantly higher among GAS isolates from children residing in slum communities (97%) than among those living in wealthier neighborhoods (92%). In fact, the diversity index of the nonslum GAS isolates was closer to that of *emm* types reported from high-income countries (92%) than to those found in the slum populations of the same city, Salvador. This study suggests that GAS strain diversification may be influenced by local factors. Such factors may include crowding, which is more prevalent in slum communities. Crowding may facilitate increased transmission opportunities and possible horizontal gene transfers that contribute to strain diversification. For socioeconomic reasons, slum residents are also less likely to undergo antibiotic treatment for sore throat. Our data found significant differences in household density, type of health insurance plan, and income between slum and nonslum communities.

In addition to *emm* type differences in GAS strains across high-income versus low-income populations in the same city, we found certain *emm* types to be over- or underrepresented among children with sore throat (*emm*66.0 [OR = 8.7], *emm*12.0 [OR = 2.2], *emm*27G.0 [OR = 0.1]). Furthermore, we were able to identify clinically relevant strains that comprised less than 5% (emm66.0) and less than 3% (emm27G.0) of the sample population. Further laboratory studies are warranted to determine why certain *emm* types predominate in clinical cases (emm66.0, emm12.0) or are inversely associated with sore throat (emm27G.0).

A vaccine against GAS would have substantial benefits worldwide. However, the impact on disease reduction could vary by region depending on the vaccine composition. Currently, the only vaccine to complete phase I and II trials is a 26-valent recombinant M protein vaccine.[25, 26] In our study, only 42% of the total isolates and 44.7% of isolates from cases would be covered by the 26-valent M protein–based GAS vaccine. Furthermore, the coverage of the 26-valent vaccine in all slum (36%) versus nonslum (48%) isolates would not be equal even within the same city.

CONCLUSIONS

This study suggests that local demographic and socioeconomic factors may contribute to the diversification of GAS *emm* types, and that distinct bacterial population distribution occurs between different neighborhoods separated by 11–32 km in the same city. This distinction might be particularly pronounced in cities with slums. We note that it is not simply poverty itself that determines this difference.[27, 28] As the world moves toward the projected population size of two billion slum residents in less than thirty years, it will be essential to better elucidate the structural dynamics in slums that contribute to major differences in disease outcomes and vaccine coverage.[29]

NOTES

1. Cunningham, MW: Pathogenesis of group A streptococcal infections. *Clin Microbiol Rev* 2000, 13(3):470–511.

2. Bisno AL: Streptococcus pyogenes. In *Principles and Practice of Infectious Diseases*. 3rd edition. Edited by Gerald L, Mandell GD, & John E Bennett. New York: Churchill Livingstone, 1990:1519–1528.

3. Carapetis JR, Steer AC, Mulholland EK, Weber M: The global burden of group A streptococcal diseases. *Lancet Infect Dis* 2005, 5(11):685–694.

4. Beall B, Facklam R, & Thompson T: Sequencing *emm*-specific PCR products for routine and accurate typing of group A streptococci. *J Clin Microbiol* 1996, 34(4):953–58.

5. Stollerman GH: The relative rheumatogenicity of strains of group A streptococci. *Mod Concepts Cardiovasc Dis* 1975, 44(7):35–40.

6. Veasy LG, Tani LY, Daly JA, Korgenski K, Miner L, Bale J, Kaplan EL, Musser JM, & Hill HR: Temporal association of the appearance of mucoid strains of *Streptococcus pyogenes* with a continuing high incidence of rheumatic fever in Utah. *Pediatrics* 2004, 113(3 Pt 1):e168–e172.

7. Miner LJ, Petheram SJ, Daly JA, Korgenski EK, Selin KS, Firth SD, Veasy LG, Hill HR, & Bale JF Jr: Molecular characterization of *Streptococcus pyogenes* isolates collected during periods of increased acute rheumatic fever activity in Utah. *Pediatr Infect Dis J* 2004, 23(1):56–61.

8. Kaplan EL, Johnson DR, & Cleary PP: Group A streptococcal serotypes isolated from patients and sibling contacts during the resurgence of rheumatic fever in the United States in the mid-1980s. *J Infect Dis* 1989, 159(1): 101–3.

9. O'Loughlin RE, Roberson A, Cieslak PR, Lynfield R, Gershman K, Craig A, Albanese BA, Farley MM, Barrett NL, Spina NL, et al.: The epidemiology of invasive group A streptococcal infection and potential vaccine implications: United States, 2000–2004. *Clin Infect Dis* 2007, 45(7):853–62.

10. Dale JB: Multivalent group A streptococcal vaccine designed to optimize the immunogenicity of six tandem M protein fragments. *Vaccine* 1999, 17(2):193–200.

11. Batzloff MRPM, Olive C, & Good MF: Advances in potential M-protein peptide-based vaccines for preventing rheumatic fever and rheumatic heart disease. *Immunol Res* 2006, 35(3):233–48.

12. McNeil SA, Halperin SA, Langley JM, Smith B, Warren A, Sharratt GP, Baxendale DM, Reddish MA, Hu MC, Stroop SD, et al.: Safety and immunogenicity of 26-valent group a *Streptococcus* vaccine in healthy adult volunteers. *Clin Infect Dis* 2005, 41(8):1114–22.

13. Abdissa A, Asrat D, Kronvall G, Shittu B, Achiko D, Zeidan M, Yamuah LK, & Aseffa A: High diversity of Group A streptococcal *emm* types among healthy schoolchildren in Ethiopia. *Clin Infect Dis* 2006, 42(10):1362–67.

14. Dey N, McMillan DJ, Yarwood PJ, Joshi RM, Kumar R, Good MF, Sriprakash KS, & Vohra H: High diversity of Group A Streptococcal *emm* types in an Indian community: The need to tailor multivalent vaccines. *Clin Infect Dis* 2005, 40(1):46–51.

15. Kim SJ, Kim EC, Cha SH, & Kaplan EL: Comparison of M-serotypes of *Streptococcus pyogenes* isolated from healthy elementary school children in two rural areas. *J Korean Med Sci* 1996, 11(2):133–36.

16. Tanaka D, Gyobu Y, Kodama H, Isobe J, Hosorogi S, Hiramoto Y, Karasawa T, & Nakamura S: *Emm* typing of Group A *Streptococcus* clinical isolates: Identification of dominant types for throat and skin isolates. *Microbiol Immunol* 2002, 46(7):419–23.

17. Johnson DR, Stevens DL, & Kaplan EL: Epidemiologic analysis of Group A streptococcal serotypes associated with severe systemic infections, rheumatic fever, or uncomplicated pharyngitis. *J Infect Dis* 1992, 166(2):374–82.

18. Smeesters PR, Vergison A, Campos D, de Aguiar E, Deyi VY, & Van Melderen L: Differences between Belgian and Brazilian Group A *Streptococcus* epidemiologic landscape. *PLoS ONE* 2006, 1:e10.

19. Steer AC, Law I, Matatolu L, Beall BW, & Carapetis JR: Global *emm* type distribution of Group A streptococci: Systematic review and implications for vaccine development. *Lancet Infect Dis* 2009, 9(10):611–16.

20. UN-Habitat: *The challenge of slums: global report on human settlements*. Nairobi, Kenya: UN-Habitat, 2003.

21. Bisno AL, Gerber MA, Gwaltney JM Jr, Kaplan EL, & Schwartz RH: Practice guidelines for the diagnosis and management of Group A streptococcal pharyngitis. Infectious Diseases Society of America. *Clin Infect Dis* 2002, 35(2):113–25.

22. Simpson E: Measurement of diversity. *Nature* 1949, 163:688.

23. Grundmann H, Hori S, & Tanner G: Determining confidence intervals when measuring genetic diversity and the discriminatory abilities of typing methods for microorganisms. *J Clin Microbiol* 2001, 39(11):4190–92.

24. McNeil et al. (2005).

25. Ibid.

26. Hu MC, Walls MA, Stroop SD, Reddish MA, Beall B, & Dale JB: Immunogenicity of a 26-valent Group A streptococcal vaccine. *Infect Immun* 2002, 70(4):2171–77.

27. Kyobutungi C, Ziraba AK, Ezeh A, & Ye Y: The burden of disease profile of residents of Nairobi's slums: Results from a demographic surveillance system. *Popul Health Metr* 2008, 6:1.

28. Madise NJ, Banda EM, & Benaya KW: Infant mortality in Zambia: Socioeconomic and demographic correlates. *Soc Biol* 2003, 50(1–2):148–66. PubMed Abstract OpenURL

29. UN-Habitat (2003).

PART III

Urban Upgrading and Health in Nairobi, Kenya

In part III we follow slum upgrading in the Mathare informal settlement in Nairobi, Kenya, work led largely by Muungano wa Wanavijiji, the federation of the urban poor in Kenya. This civil society organization is part of the global network Shack/Slum Dwellers International (SDI). As the following chapters show, health in the slums of Nairobi is about building power, advocating for rights and services, and changing the landscape of power. This fight does not come easy or without strategic partnerships. We reveal how slum dwellers built a partnership with university researchers to survey, map, and analyze local living conditions and turn these data into action plans for health and equity. The group accomplished some significant improvements for health, including a new piped water supply. Just as important, however, is the establishment of long-term advocacy processes so that slum dwellers can continue to demand and receive improvements to their economic, social, and physical living conditions, improvements that can in turn improve human health. In chapter 10, we highlight the voices of slum-dwelling women working to decouple their health from inadequate sanitation. The unfortunate reality is that women in Mathare are disproportionately burdened by a lack of safe, clean, and dignified toilets. We suggest that slum health must, at its foundation, provide for this human right and ensure dignity for women.

Part III also details how the Muungano microsavings groups in Mathare act to protect and improve health. Across Kenya, at least

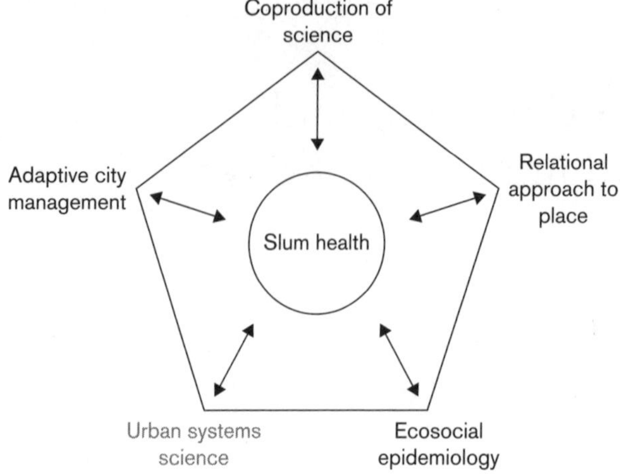

Dimensions of slum health explored in the case of Mathare, Nairobi, Kenya.

60,000 urban slum dwellers participate in the Muungano savings group network. Groups from slums in different cities build network power to sometimes negotiate with, and at other times demand, government to provide the physical improvements and social services that urban citizenship requires. Microsavings differs from microcredit in that the latter aims primarily to use fiscal discipline to organize previously unorganized resident interests into a viable social movement. Savings groups organize residents and assist with vital local knowledge in the abovementioned research and advocacy processes. However, the savings groups do much more: they offer a fiscal safety net for families, promote women as leaders, and build advocacy networks across the complex social dynamics of the urban slum. We describe the myriad ways four different microsavings groups in Mathare are promoting health and well-being, using a social-determinants-of-health framework. Ultimately, we show that there is no one path to slum health in Nairobi; rather, slum health is an ongoing process of action-research, community-based organizing, negotiating with state service providers, implementing community-based projects and learning by doing.

Chapters 9–11 further elaborate the processes of coproduction, a relational view of place, and adaptive management. Slum dwellers and Muungano work with researchers to make their living conditions and health burdens visible to outsiders. Yet they go beyond visibility to negotiate interventions and participate in the construction and management of these interventions, often in collaboration with state institutions. While emphasizing infrastructure, the projects also engage with the multiplicity of related health issues in slums, from housing and rights to safety and dignity, and reflect how these influence the economic and social determinants of health. Thus, in the spirit of ecosocial epidemiology, multiple and cumulative exposures were considered, as well as some of the institutions responsible for them and the complex ways slum dwellers build resilience, survive, and thrive in their harsh conditions. The interventions in this case are small-scale, such as the water supply project, but have built-in malleability, such as altering the financing scheme to ensure more residents can access in-home water meters, and managing public kiosks to ensure even the poorest of the poor could benefit. Importantly, the interventions informed larger-scale policy making, offering an example of policy learning by doing.

CHAPTER 9

Coproducing Slum Health in Nairobi, Kenya

JASON CORBURN AND JACK MAKAU

In Nairobi, Kenya, close to 65 percent of the population lives in informal settlements, or slums, on about 10 percent of the city's land area. Children under five living in Nairobi's slums are almost three times as likely to die than their counterparts in the rest of the city. Women in Nairobi's slums experience disproportionate health burdens compared to men. For example, over a quarter of all women and girls in Nairobi's slums reported an episode of diarrhea in the past month, compared to about a fifth for all Kenyans. Over 36 percent of slum-dwelling women report being physically forced to have sex, and over one-third report being sexually abused.

Mathare is an informal settlement located about 6 kilometers from the city center and comprises thirteen villages: Gitathuru, Kiamutisya, Kosovo, Kwa Kariuki, Mabatini, Mashimoni, and Villages 2, 3A, 3B, 3C, 4A, 4B, and 10. Mathare sits in a river valley, near a former quarry, and its steep slopes and river frontage present a host of environmental risks to today's residents. Disease and death for Mathare's residents by some measures are worse than for other Kenyans (figure 9.1). A third of Mathare residents are estimated to be infected with HIV/AIDS, compared to only 7 percent of the Kenyan population; the number of people in Mathare suffering from a parasitic infection is almost twice that in the Kenyan population; and over one-quarter of the population reported suffering from diarrhea in the past month, compared to 17 percent of the Kenyan population.[1]

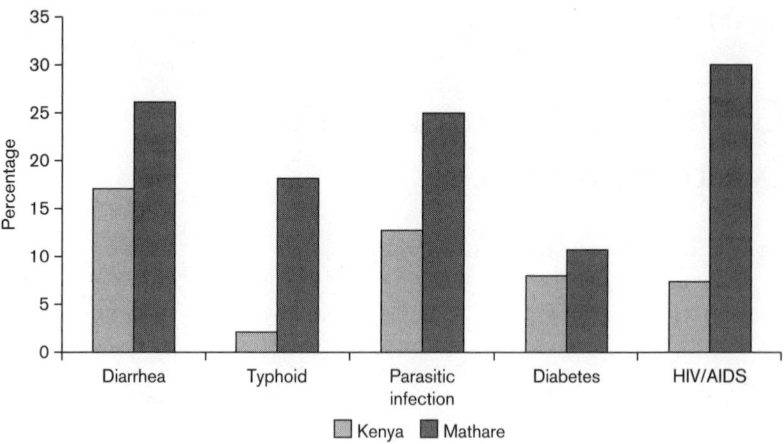

FIGURE 9.1. Incidence of diseases in Kenya and Mathare, Nairobi, in 2010. Sources: Ayah, R., Joshi, M.D., Wanjiru, R., Njau, E.K., Otieno, C.F., Njeru, E.K., & Mutai, K.K. (2013). A population-based survey of prevalence of diabetes and correlates in an urban slum community in Nairobi, Kenya. *BMC Public Health* 13:371. Madise, N.J. et al. (2012). Are slum dwellers at heightened risk of HIV infection than other urban residents? *Health & Place* 18(5):1144–52.

Many of these poor health outcomes are due to a combination of a dangerous physical environment (i.e., crowded housing, pathogens in open sewerage, indoor air pollution from lack of electricity); social inequalities (discrimination in the workplace; disproportionately high costs for food, water, and toilets; insecure housing and threats of eviction); and structural violence (lack of health care services, rampant sexual violence against women, government divestment in security and basic infrastructure). These related health determinants contributed to a slum-dweller response that aimed to coproduce health improvements by negotiating with the state for immediate needs, partnering with outsiders to develop long-term improvement strategies, and working to redefine relationships between the urban poor and development institutions that have for too long viewed slums and their residents as in need of only treatment and professional care.

This chapter explores the factors that contributed to inequitable health burdens that Nairobi's slum dwellers face and how partnerships among residents, nongovernmental organizations, and academic entities are working to coproduce greater health equity in Mathare. We start with a history of Nairobi's development from the colonial period through independence and up to the contemporary period. We show that colonial powers used health justifications to segregate the African population, deny them services, and construct a city devoted to extracting resources, not serving the local population. The human health legacy of these colonial decisions are reflected in Nairobi's slums today.

We then detail some of the history and living conditions in Mathare. Mathare has a history of resident organizing and activism, as some of its Kikuyu residents were active in the struggle for independence and later, in the 1970s and 1980s, formed cooperatives to buy land and build housing. However, ethnic tensions and state neglect, along with an influx of new residents, divided residents and contributed to widespread violence in the 1990s and control of much of the local economy by the Mungiki gang in the early 2000s. Postelection violence erupted in Mathare in 2007, and civil society organizations have played a role in reestablishing peace, organizing residents, and helping them advocate for essential, life-promoting basic services.

In the third section of this chapter, we detail the coproduction planning process and how it addresses social and biologic determinants of health. We explore the tensions and challenges that arise in community-based health planning; how housing, safety, and infrastructure issues are framed as public health concerns; and the responses (and lack thereof) of the state and other global institutions (such as the World Bank and donors) to the on-the-ground work in Mathare. We argue that local health equity planning in Mathare has delivered some immediate health benefits, but also supported the community and civil society actors to more effectively advocate for long-term policy changes that have even greater potential to improve health and equity for all of Nairobi's slum dwellers.

COLONIAL NAIROBI: DISCRIMINATION AND HEALTH INEQUITIES

In the late nineteenth century, the British settled an area on the African coast of the Indian Ocean elevated from the heat of the savanna and the humidity of the port city of Mombasa. For centuries, the Athi, Kikuyus, Kambas, and Maasai, among other tribes, moved their caravans through this area and often stopped to replenish food supplies, graze their cattle, and trade.

The location was also strategic for expanding the railway that the British imperialists had built on the backs of imported Indian laborers. The British Uganda Railway Committee decided in 1895 to build a line connecting the heart of East Africa at Lake Victoria—a major source of the White Nile River—to the Indian Ocean coast at Mombasa. The British plan was to extract natural resources from the region and transport them to the port. The resources would fuel the expansion of the British Empire. In 1895 the British declared control over this area, called the East African Protectorate, which stretched from the Indian Ocean across the African continent to the far western edge of the Rift Valley. The Maasai called the managing town Enkare Nyrobi, or "the place of cold waters."[2]

European housing was built on the highest elevations in town. The colonists drew on their experiences in India, where camps built on higher elevations were thought to have fewer pests carrying tropical diseases.[3] Racially segregated planning in Nairobi was soon adopted and linked to medical beliefs of the day. As Curtain notes, the medical advisory committee of the Colonial Office for Tropical Africa declared in 1911: "It has been proved that the separation of Europeans from natives is one of the most efficient means of protection against disease endemic amongst native races. Even partial separation, such as sleeping outside the native quarter at night time, affords a very considerable degree of security."[4]

After a case of the bubonic plague in 1897 and another in 1902, British colonial leaders sought to identify the cause and act to prevent future deaths. Sir Charles Eliot, colonial administrator and commissioner of British East Africa from 1900 to 1904, blamed the Indian settlements: "The Indians had built their houses so close together that they neutralized the natural advantages of air and light and then allowed the most disgusting filth to accumulate on a small area."[5] The Indian Bazaar, Nairobi's hub of residential and economic activity for non-Europeans, was ultimately blamed for disease and was burned to the ground and relocated away from European settlements. According to medical officers in Nairobi in 1902 and 1904, in the Indian Bazaar, "damp, dark, unventilated, overcrowded dwellings on filth-soaked and rubbish-bestrewn ground housed hundreds . . . tin sheds [were] used indiscriminately as dwelling houses, shops, stores, laundries, wash houses, opium dens, bakeries, brothels, butchers' shops, etc., etc. . . . rats abounded and the general conditions of life of the 1,500–2,000 inhabitants were miserable and filthy in the extreme."[6]

W. J. Simpson of the London School of Hygiene and Tropical Medicine was enlisted to study the problem and devise a solution for the health of the white colonialists. Simpson's 1913 report, known as the

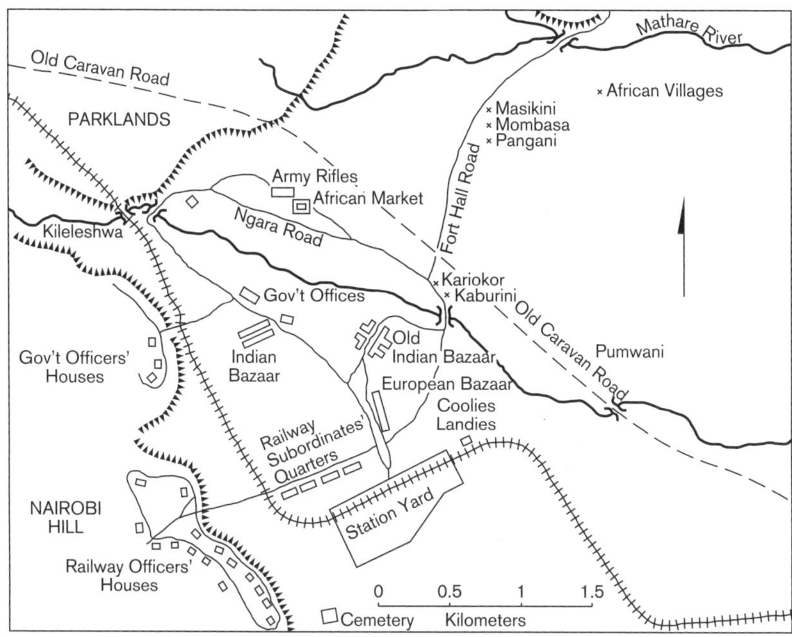

MAP 9.1. Nairobi, 1910s.

Simpson Plan, declared land use control the central issue for colonial rule. A layout was needed that demarcated land for specific uses and designated areas where Europeans, Indians, and Africans would be allowed to live separately. Maps were drawn (see map 9.2) demarcating boundaries and spatial control. Simpson's report declare, "The haphazard growth of the town which is being permitted, have [*sic*] brought about such a condition of insanitation that Nairobi, although scarcely 14 years old, and aspiring to be a European town, is in its commercial area one of the most insanitary I have seen."[7] In addition to the removal of the Indian Bazaar, Simpson recommended the separation of functions and ethnic groups and justified this undertaking on public health grounds:

> In towns where the nationality is of the same, town planning resolves itself into arranging for residential, commercial and manufacturing areas, which are further governed in character by rental and class, and in such a way as to secure convenience, good transit, pleasing amenities and permanent healthiness for all. Something more than this is required in towns, such as those in East Africa, where nationalities are diverse and their customs and habits different from one another. Though the same objects have to be aimed at, it has

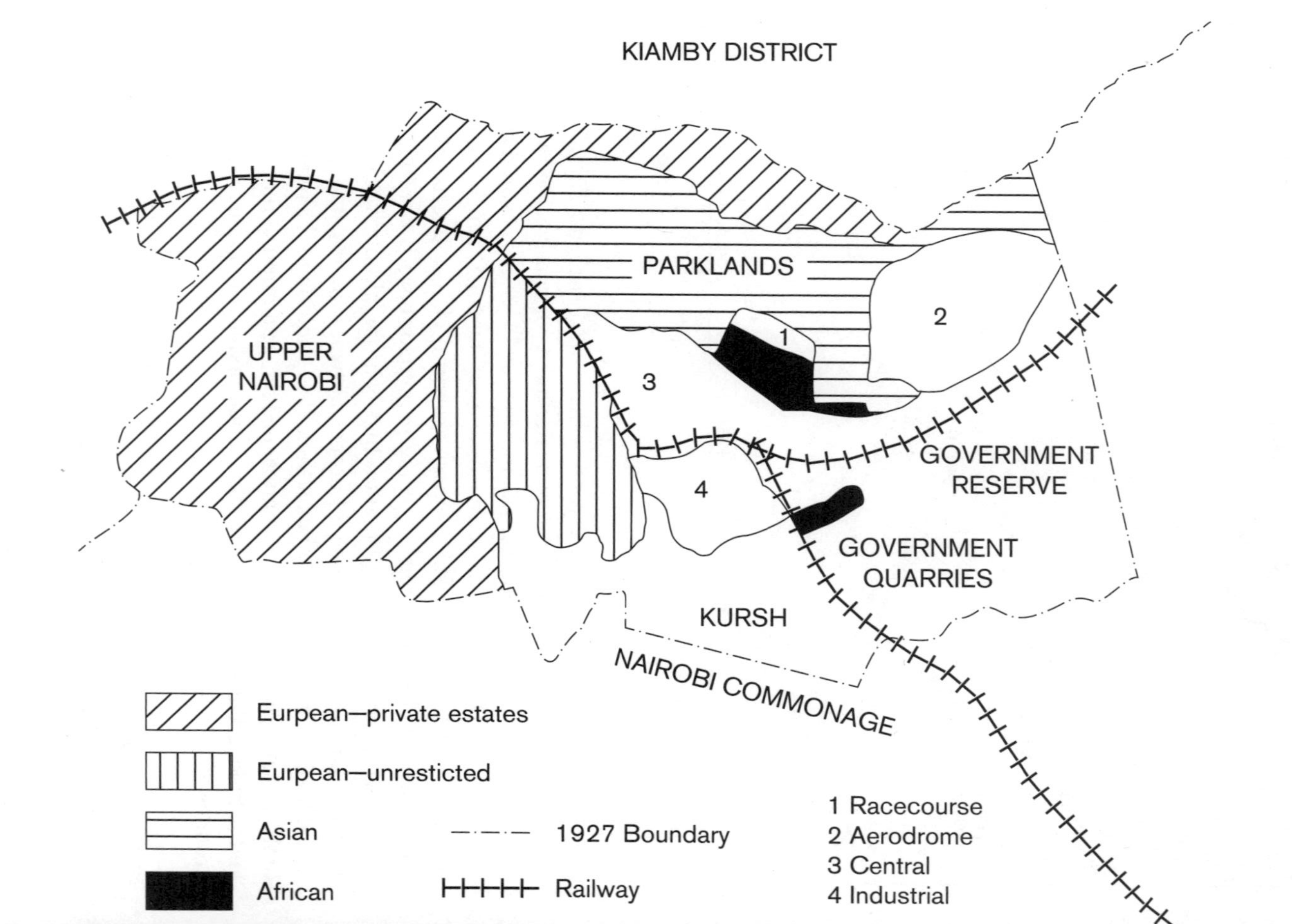
KIAMBY DISTRICT
PARKLANDS
UPPER NAIROBI
1
2
3
4
GOVERNMENT RESERVE
GOVERNMENT QUARRIES
KURSH
NAIROBI COMMONAGE
Eurpean—private estates
Eurpean—unresticted
Asian
African
1927 Boundary
Railway
1 Racecourse
2 Aerodrome
3 Central
4 Industrial

> to be recognized that the standard and mode of life of the Asiatic, except in the highest class, do not consort with those of European . . . and that the customs of the primitive African, unfamiliar with and not adapted to the new conditions of town life, will not blend in with either. In the interest of each community and of the healthiness of the locality and country, it is absolutely essential that in every town and trade centre the town planning should provide well-defined and separate quarters for European, Asiatic and African.

Simpson's racist recommendations were grounded in the dominant colonial medical belief that the African city was like a sick patient in need of curing. The planner's solution, much like that of the physician at the time, was immunization and separation: either treat malaria with quinine or isolate the sick from the healthy. The result in 1913 was a segregation plan organized by ethnicity and functions titled "Nairobi: Sketch-Map of Segregation Proposals." The plan was signed and endorsed by A.M. Jeevanjee, one of two Asian members of Nairobi's Municipal Committee, and included six zones: European residential; high-class commercial; Asiatic residential; middle-class commercial and swamp; African and protective zones. The land area demarcated for Europeans and "high-class" activities was more than double that for Asians and more than ten times the area for Africans.[8] Racial residential and economic segregation took hold in Nairobi, justified in part by prominent public health and medical scientists.

INSTITUTIONALIZING SPATIAL SEGREGATION OF AFRICANS

Kenya became an official British colony in 1920, the same year the Native Pass Law and Vagrancy Ordinance was adopted. This law restricted residence in Nairobi to only those employed by Europeans or Indians.[9] The profits of colonialist farms depended on cheap African labor, and the British were intent on keeping Africans away from the growing city. Yet, by 1923, official policy justifying racial segregation on sanitary grounds shifted. White, Silberman, and Anderson described the new policy:

> Following up on Professor Simpson's report, a policy of segregation was adopted in principle, and it was proposed by Lord Milner to retain this policy both on sanitary and social grounds. So far as commercial segregation is concerned, it has already been generally agreed that this should be discontinued. . . . It is now the view of the competent medical authorities that, as a sanitation measure, segregation of Europeans and Asiatics is not absolutely

> essential for the preservation of the health of the community; the rigid enforcement of sanitary, police and building regulations without any racial discrimination, by the Colonial and municipal authorities will suffice. It may well prove that in practice the different races will, by natural affinity, keep together in separate quarters, but to effect such separation by legislative enactment except on the strongest sanitary grounds would not, in the opinion of Her Majesty's Government, be justifiable.[10]

Enforcement of this directive was nonexistent since it rested in the hands of a newly created town council in Nairobi that included nine elected European councilors, seven Indians (elected but nominated by the British governor), two government-nominated members, and one administrative officer intended to represent or "safeguard native interests." It wasn't until 1946 that Africans had two directly elected representatives on the town council.[11]

The health of Africans living in Nairobi remained an issue for Europeans who depended on their cheap labor. Waterborne diseases continued unabated because the British-dominated council refused to allocate the financial resources to build a drainage and water delivery system recommended by engineers in the 1910s.[12] By 1923, disparities in crude death rates were increasingly apparent and documented by the annual reports of the medical officer of health: 8.4 per 1,000 for Europeans, 16.5 per 1,000 for Asians, and 33.5 per 1,000 for Africans.[13] Rising mortality rates and the rapid expansion of unplanned African villages throughout Nairobi lead the colonialists to build the first housing for Africans.

A planned community called Pumwani (meaning "resting place") was constructed in 1922 and was the first area in Nairobi that the British planned and built specifically for Africans. Roads, latrines, and ablution blocks were constructed along with housing plots in a rectangular grid.[14] Pumwani was intended to be the one official place where all Africans living in Nairobi would stay.[15] The location was specifically selected to decrease the distance of the African labor force from the industrial area while increasing the distance between African and European settlements.[16] Pumwani was physically separated from the rest of Nairobi by a river and the Old Caravan Road, a major commercial route. The Europeans hoped that the settlement's rational plan and sanitary services (along with a 10 PM–5 AM curfew) would quell increasing African demands for political participation and curb depravity, particularly prostitution and sexual relations.[17] Africans were forcibly relocated from other squatter areas to Pumwani. While residents were responsible for building their own homes, they were required to follow newly created

British building and planning rules for the area that defined house size and forbade subletting. Nevertheless, most Africans built as they wished, subletting was common because of the transient nature of work, and social bonds within the African community increased.

HEALTH INEQUITIES IN COLONIAL NAIROBI

By 1929 Nairobi had its own Public Health Committee and a municipal Public Health Department under the direction of the National Ministry of Health. Each Public Health Committee section was headed by a European officer and a mostly Indian technical staff. The Public Health Department oversaw the municipality's health care institutions, communicable and noncommunicable disease, urban sanitation and housing, and hygiene investigation. The department's responsibilities would expand to include many urban planning functions, such as the siting and regulation of municipal markets, dispensaries and health centers, day nurseries, funerals, ambulance service, and others.[18] In one dispute between the Public Health Department and the city council, the department demanded that the council allocate resources to address the ongoing unsanitary conditions in the Indian Bazaar and other African living areas. Specifically, the department wanted the council to replace mud-and-wattle housing with structures made of permanent materials. The council refused, claiming the health department's request was financially impractical.[19]

A report in 1933 by the chief medical officer in Nairobi, R.A. Paterson, emphasized the importance of community-based prevention and service delivery:

> Of even greater importance than the relief of sickness is its prevention, and with the latter object in view both doctors and nurses, and midwives, as well as health visitors and sanitary inspectors, must come into the most intimate contact with the people in their own homes from day to day; and if the behests of these workers are to carry weight . . . so medical workers must live among the people in all quarters of the area to be served; and they must be sufficient in number, and so posted that there is intimate and easy contact between the whole of the personnel of the medical service and the folk of the countryside. Facilities for treatments must, therefore, be brought almost to their doors, while teaching must be taken actually over their doorsteps. For these purposes the primary health centers have been established.[20]

In the 1950s a postwar colonial policy, based on a similar UK model, was adopted to train and hire African women to bring their own "healthy living knowledge" to positions as "Health Visitors."[21, 22, 23]

THE 1948 COLONIAL MASTER PLAN

Rapid urban population growth and a desire for modernization led the mayor of Nairobi to invite a South African team of architects to generate a new master plan for the city. The plan, published in 1948 as the "Nairobi Master Plan for a Colonial Capital," called on the city to "develop naturally out of the present land usage and particularly the present land values."[24] In reality, the plan imposed a Eurocentric City Beautiful and Garden City model on the growing capital. At the heart of the plan was a civic center modeled after those in other capital cities that the architects revered, such as Canberra and Paris, and reflecting the modernism of popular designers of the day such as Le Corbusier. The architects' enthusiasm for simple, geometric design, repetition, and uniformity reflected their faith that a modern civic design would modernize the people of Nairobi. Using Paris as a model, the architects proposed a Kenya Centre and Parkway, both with grand parallel boulevards, uniform monument buildings, and height restrictions to ensure that the government buildings were the tallest in the city. The 1948 planners defined their task as purely technocratic:

> The Master Plan . . . is able to be completely neutral on the subject of racial segregation by being confined to the principles of planning which take their measure on the human and technical needs. It is concerned with the satisfaction of the wants which all men require such as privacy, open space, education, protection from through-traffic, water supplies, etc. The more attention that can be devoted to what is common to man the more likely are we to concentrate on what can to-day be planned in the light of reason while leaving to political and educational action and to the individual to sort out the rest. If the Plan has a bias it is this humanistic one.[25]

Yet, by defining planning as pure reason separate from politics, the 1948 plan left unchanged and unchallenged colonial racial segregation. The idea that Africans had been planning their own functional communities within Nairobi for decades, surviving in the face of widespread racial discrimination and physical isolation, went unnoticed by the 1948 planners.[26] Planning was couched as a science (however imperfect) realized through neutral technology.

MATHARE, 1970–1999: FROM COOPERATIVES TO CONFLICT

The Mathare settlement grew alongside a rock quarry along the banks of the Mathare and Gitathuru Rivers. While informal settlements—or villages, as they are often referred to in Nairobi—have been present in the Mathare Valley since at least the 1920s, the settlement had a population explosion beginning in 1969, doubling in just over sixteen months.[27] This was due in part to Africans returning to Mathare after the Emergency (aka the Mau Mau Uprising), but many others were forced to relocate in Mathare after being moved from Eastleigh Section VII to allow for the expansion of Pumwani and after the Nairobi City Council ordered the Kaburini settlement burned down.[28] To the surprise of many urban squatters in Nairobi, the new Kenyan government followed the colonial practices of demolition and eviction of their communities.[29] Nairobi's population and the proportion thereof who were squatters grew rapidly during the 1960s, with the overall population increasing from about 267,000 in 1963 to over 500,000 by 1969, and Mathare's population reaching over 34,000 across nine distinct villages by 1969.[30, 31]

The households in Mathare organized into cooperative organizations to purchase the land they occupied with the hope of protecting themselves from future evictions. This was an innovative strategy for urban squatters. With the original intent of securing land tenure for all squatters, the cooperatives allowed members to purchase shares.[32] However, all but one of the cooperatives became companies and began building rental housing units to satisfy the rapidly increasing demand.

The housing built by all the companies was haphazard but dense. According to Etherton and colleagues, "the objective of all the companies seems to have been to concentrate as many lettable rooms as possible on the site."[33] This was accomplished by building long structures divided into four to eight -3-by-3-meter rooms. Very few of the companies provided for adequate public services. Four provided no water, but six provided and paid for water for residents. The average number of residents per water tap in 1970 Mathare was 870, while the average number of people per pit latrine was 136, but ranged across villages from 22 to 3,555 per latrine.[34] In short, the companies built housing in Mathare, 83 percent of which was filled by noncompany renters, and provided very few services.

A health survey of Mathare residents visiting a local clinic and analysis of stool samples taken from primary school children provided an overview of the health status of residents. The stool sample analysis found that 81 percent of children had roundworm and 62 percent bilharzia, or schistosomiasis. These are both parasitic diseases linked to poor sanitation and, while rarely fatal, can impair children's growth and cognitive development. The Mathare clinic staff reported that the most pressing health issue for children was malnutrition and that they most frequently distributed vitamins and milk to visiting patients. Over 55 percent of children visiting the clinic suffered from a chronic cough, and over 43 percent stomach ailment or diarrhea, or both.[35]

Kenya's National Development Plan in the mid-1970s halted slum demolitions.[36] The World Bank began a "sites and services" loan program to Kenya that required housing and utility services to be coupled in development projects.[37] Under this scheme, the Nairobi City Council would retain control of the squatter land, and after the World Bank–financed services and housing were built, new residents (former squatters) were expected to pay rent to the city to "pay back" the loan. Some slum upgrading resulted in tenement housing being built by the National Housing Corporation in the 1980s, but the limited housing supply failed to meet the growing need.[38] By the 1990, slum demolitions were common again, displacing an estimated 30,000 residents in 1991 alone.[39]

In Mathare 4A, one village in the larger settlement, the German Development Bank financed a pilot upgrading project in 1992. The project was overseen by the Catholic Church, which was granted the land in Mathare 4A by the Kenyan government. The Church commonly filled a vacuum left by an absent state by providing a range of services from health care to education, and this gave it legitimacy in the eyes of both the government and international donors. To ensure local participation, a project management organization called the Amani Housing Trust was created to run the day-to-day implementation and steward the new housing. The project's initial phase replaced temporary structures with over 1,400 more permanent units with access to water and sanitary infrastructure.[40] In a second phase, the absentee landlords who were renting most of the structures in Mathare 4A were to be expropriated and compensated between 4,000 and 12,000 Kenyan shillings (KSh) per structure. In exchange, the structure owners were required to sign away sale of their property to the Church as well as any future claims to land in 4A.[41]

Father Klaus Braunreute was in charge of St. Benedictine Church, just across Thika Road from Mathare 4A, and was the leader of the project. Using its stature as a service provider, its relationship with the German embassy, and support from Zacharia Maina, a Kenya African National Union (KANU) member of parliament who represented Mathare 4a, the Catholic Church secured the funds to implement the project. As the group began the project in 1993, one challenge was persuading existing residents to leave their homes so the new construction could begin.

Youth gangs were enrolled to forcibly remove reluctant families.[42] Displaced residents were temporarily resettled in another area, but had to pay rent to St. Benedictine Church for their new accommodations. The displaced residents protested, as did the landlords, who did not like that they were being forced to give up their lucrative business.[43]

Opposition to the project continued after the first set of new houses were built. Rents rose to 800 KSh per month, more than double what residents had been paying before the upgrading. The Church allocated a number of new units to workers and others who were not living in Mathare 4A before the project began. This stoked more opposition and resentment.[44]

As protest against and resistance to the church-led project increased, some residents accused Father Klaus, a white priest, of using colonial tactics and political favors to his financial advantage.[45] Litigation ensued, as residents and former landlords formed an unlikely alliance against the Church and demanded a return of their land. After six months of hearings, the Makadara court rejected the requests of the residents and landlords. More protests followed and project employees were attacked. By 1998 150 new houses had been built with access to a toilet, shower, and electricity. A new dispensary, two day-care centers, and thirty business kiosks were also constructed. However, police were deployed to the area as gangs fought over the project and on January 27, 1999, the Nairobi City Council and the Ministry of Public Works ordered the suspension of the project.[46, 47]

Many saw the outcome of the Mathare 4A project as symptomatic of a larger political challenge in Kenya: under the Moi presidency and thereafter, land was increasingly used for political favors and patronage.[48] In a series of corruption scandals, government officials were accused of allocating public land to their supporters that was already occupied by informal settlements.[49] The state, in many cases the Nairobi City Council, and the police were used to forcibly evict residents from their homes and trading places, despite slum dwellers fighting the evictions with the assistance of the Legal Advice Center, or Kituo cha Sheria.[50, 51] The lack of transparency and the accusations of patronage in the Mathare 4A project reflected a larger frustration with corruption in politics related to land among the urban poor and Kenyans more generally. Slum dwellers were seeking an alternative model wherein they would be active shapers and direct beneficiaries of planning and improvement schemes that went beyond "boutique" projects and instead instituted lasting improvements for the millions of slum dwellers now living in Nairobi's informal settlements.

MUUNGANO WA WANAVIJIJI IN MATHARE: MICROSAVINGS AND POLITICAL POWER

By 2010, over 65 percent of Nairobi's estimated 3.5 million people were living in the city's informal settlements. Seeking to ensure slum dwellers were leading, not just responding to, government and international organization projects, Shack/Slum Dwellers International (SDI) helped create Muungano wa Wanavijiji. The slum-dweller federation was supported by the NGO Pamoja Trust, founded in 2000 by human rights lawyer Jane Weru, but is now supported by the NGO Muungano Support Trust (MuST). Founded to help the urban poor oppose demolitions, Pamoja Trust quickly evolved into generating alternative solutions to the related challenges of housing, services, human rights, and health. According to Weru:

> Stopping evictions was critical but it was only a small part of the change that was necessary. The laws and policies were broken. We needed to also be clear about what was causing the evictions and lack of services. Namely, lack of policies, planning and investment in the urban poor, you see. We began enumerating and mapping the settlements to document the extent of the challenge. The federation was organized to build local accountable institutions that built power for social change.[52]

The structure of Muungano helped move the work from protest to short- and longer-term solutions. Muungano's core function is organizing daily savings groups. Joining a group is voluntary. Members are required to deposit a small amount of money each day into their own account, held by the group, and attend weekly meetings to keep track of community savings. Resources are pooled to provide a financial safety net for members, such as when an emergency medical expense occurs. According to Jack Makau, an SDI director working to coordinate networks across Africa:

> The savings group strategy says slum dwellers have some resources that, if pooled together, can leverage other assets and begin to finance their own projects. It rejects the notion that the poor have to wait for someone else's handout. It wasn't that we didn't want government and donor support, but money, or at least helps get you a better seat at the table. So the savings groups are a community organizing strategy to build power, with the added benefit of building financial capital for slum dwellers.

The savings act as an entry point for building relationships between individuals and groups; they express an organizational commitment to a public, not just individual, good and highlight the role of women as prime savers among the urban poor. The combination of the political and financial capital is one of the innovations of savings groups as defined by Muungano and SDI, compared to more popular microcredit schemes. Microcredit has had mixed results in building a lasting community base of accountable institutions and in providing financial resources for a range of communities beyond the microenterprise.

The Muungano savings groups in each village support members in saving small amounts of money each day and then organize these savers into groups, often led by women, that meet weekly to discuss progress and build trust. Everyone in a village is invited to participate and the organization usually builds slowly. According to Joseph Kimani, a community organizer with MuST—the technical support NGO for the Muungano network—word of mouth and small projects build interest:

> When we start, people are rightly skeptical. Why should I give money to this group? Will they steal it? What are they doing? Transparency, accountability and trust are at the heart of the organization for these reasons. Community members are leaders, manage the accounts, and keep one another accountable. We discuss community priorities and what we can do in the short term. Of course, many issues come up for people struggling in the slums, so these discussions about priorities and sharing of stories build trust and community.

Within each savings group, at least six teams execute the core functions of Muungano's mission: surveying and mapping; welfare; savings and loans; land and housing; advocacy; and auditing. The surveying and mapping team organizes members, as David Mathenge of MuST explains, to "make the invisible visible." With the support of MuST, this team trains members to conduct house-to-house enumerations, collecting detailed information on each household and compiling these data for community "ground truthing." The data are crucial for documenting which people live in the informal settlements and detailing the living conditions they face. According to Mathenge:

> The enumerations go to every household and we return to validate the data. Then we post the findings in the community. This is real peer review. We not only need to know how many people live where, but to also know who would benefit as projects and planning occur. We put this demographic information into maps of every [square] meter of the village. We do what the census and planners in NCC [Nairobi City Council] have avoided or just do not have the will to do.

The data and maps are used in various ways, sometimes to resist evictions and state-sponsored relocations, in other cases to speak back to government in its own language, challenge official statistics, and negotiate with government agencies for land tenure and basic services. Surveys, data, and maps are technologies regularly used by the state to "discipline" or order society. Yet, when slum dwellers engage in these practices, they not only see themselves in the data but also have greater power to resist how these technologies are used.

The other teams within each Muungano savings group are equally important to the organizing and social change mission. The welfare team discusses how the group should spend resources to support members that need assistance, such as payment for an emergency hospitalization, a funeral, or food assistance. The savings and loans team keeps track of savings issues and reviews requests for individual loans and repayment. The auditing team reviews finances and works with Muungano's fiscal agent, Akiba Mashinani Trust (AMT), which supports the village-level groups and networks of savings groups by providing professional financial services.

The land and housing team focuses on tenant and structure owner issues and disputes, while building a negotiated agreement among members of the entire community for securing tenure and land rights. The idea is that each village has its own land use and allocation histories involving a range of stakeholders, from tribal chiefs to religious institutions to political parties. Land rights and control issues are intimately wrapped into this politics, and Muungano recognizes that no one model of securing land tenure and housing security will apply in every informal settlement or village within a settlement. All the teams coordinate with one another to develop advocacy strategies but focus on building coordinated campaigns across the entire network. The Muungano network structure appears as figure 9.2.

MUUNGANO AND SHACK/SLUM DWELLERS INTERNATIONAL

The Muungano advocacy work builds on SDI's model of network power. According to Jack Makau, the approach for Muungano and its sister supportive organization MuST reflects SDI's core social change model:

> The SDI model is fluid but built on the idea that international development as defined by donors and other professionals tends to fragment what must be

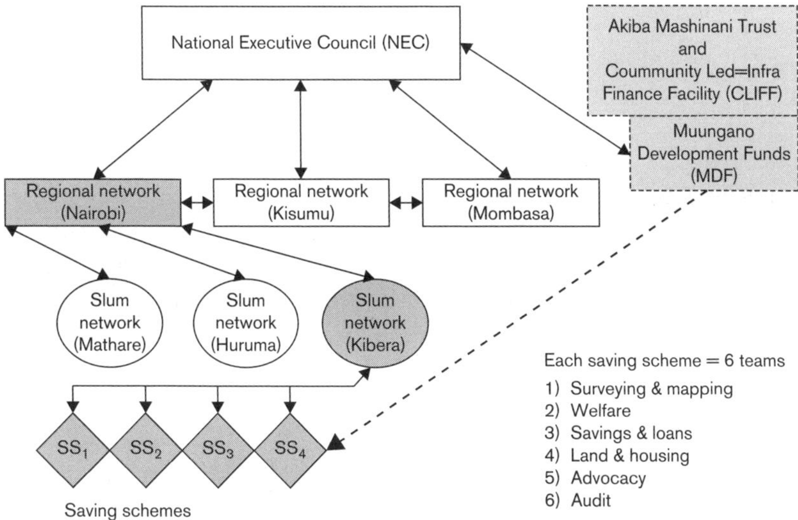

FIGURE 9.2. Muungano wa Wanavijiji microsavings network model, example schematic.

> brought together. For SDI, organizing is the base. Organizing allows for the human technology—counting, mapping, planning, house modeling—that delivers short-term improvements. Planning is about negotiating a different future. Partnerships are woven into all this, since we recognize communities can't do this alone. Government needs to be a partner since they are the ones with the resources and responsibility to bring our innovations to scale. Our networks of slum dwellers have exchanges, or content-focused visits. This is often where innovations come. It's incremental. It builds power. It leads to real change.[53]

The exchanges Makau mentions form a crucial component of the SDI model and something the organization calls horizontal exchanges. These exchanges include trips on which small groups of slum dwellers travel to other slums, often in another country, to learn from and among other slum dwellers about what is possible in their own place. In this way, the local struggle in one community becomes "translocal" and relational as knowledge and innovations from multiple sites around the world are shared and emerge into a network of strategies and ongoing knowledge creation.

In Mumbai, India, a powerful network of SDI affiliates also learn from one another about their different strategies for improving slum dwellers' lives and conditions. The National Slum Dwellers Federation, a rights-based group; Mahila Milan ("Women Together"), a microsavings group focused on housing and infrastructure; and the Society for Promotion of Area Resources Centers (SPARC), a broader-based NGO, have come together. They share a resource center in Byculla, in central Mumbai, where the constant flow of people and phone calls ensures that the groups exchange information about breaking crises, policy initiatives, and what is happening with other SDI networks around the world.[54] With the long-standing experiences and range of local expertise, the Mumbai alliance acts as one hub for information sharing across the global network of SDI.

PREVENTING EVICTIONS AND PLANNING FOR HOUSING AND INFRASTRUCTURE

In 2008 residents in Mathare were once again facing eviction. This time, a United Nations Environment Programme (UNEP) and Kenyan National Environment Ministry project aimed at cleaning up the Nairobi River was to blame. One of the first places to be "cleaned" was along the Mathare and Gitathuru Rivers, tributaries of the Nairobi River. The Kenyan government called for a standard 30-meter riparian buffer to be cleared on each side of all rivers, an environmental requirement left over from the British administration. The evictions would displace tens of thousands of Mathare residents with no place to go. Muungano and Pamoja Trust were already organizing residents when the river cleanup project was announced, and they mobilized to stop the slum clearance.

Mathare was just emerging from some of its worst violence since the Emergency. Postelection conflicts flared across Kenya in 2007–8 after a disputed presidential election, and Kikuyus and Luos fought and killed hundreds. In Nairobi, Mathare was ground zero for the ethnic violence. As the *New York Times* reported in 2007:

> The bloodshed began with a bootlegging dispute, but it has been fueled by ethnic rivalry. The epicenter is Mathare, a cluster of slums with approximately 500,000 people, crammed between downtown Nairobi and an affluent neighborhood where many ambassadors live. Mathare is a landscape of rust—thousands of shacks squeezed together with rusted metal roofs and rusted metal sides, and the occasional rusted metal bridge between. Even the mud here, where not a blade of grass grows, is rust red. The area is notorious

> as a pocket of anarchy in a relatively orderly city, a place where street gangs levy taxes and teenage boys with machetes and dreadlocks shake down people at checkpoints. Most days, the police are nowhere to be found. Residents say it has been like this for years.[55]

Mathare residents were also blamed for stealing water, and the Nairobi Water and Sewer Company (NWSC) responded by closing the water main that supplied Mathare with its drinking water. Within a day children were sick and diarrheal disease spiked. Dehydration and hospitalizations followed. Mathare residents took to the streets to demand the water be turned back on. They closed Thika Road, a major thoroughfare adjacent to the settlement, causing traffic in the city to come to a standstill. According to Jane Weru, Pamoja Trust executive director at the time, "More violence and a major crisis was looming. We had to intervene and called a meeting with the City and water company. We marched to City Council and demanded the meeting."

DESIGNING A HEALTHY COMMUNITY PLANNING PROCESS

Pamoja Trust (PT) was a respected advocate for slum-dweller rights, and Weru was a trained lawyer who negotiated for squatter rights for most of her career. The meeting at the city council was tense as the streets were still occupied. According to Jack Makau, PT communication director at the time: "Fires were literally still burning. The memory of the postelection and more recent violence was fresh in everyone's mind. Mathare was capable of blowing up. We demanded that the water be turned back on immediately and for a halt to the riparian evictions. They [the Nairobi City Council] had almost had no option but to engage and meet our demands. We also had residents waiting outside." The meeting was a success. Pamoja Trust and Muungano got the NWSC to turn the water back on. In exchange for a halt to the evictions, the groups agreed to work with residents to draft an upgrading plan for Mathare that would be presented to the council for formal approval.

The groups left the council meeting intent on building upon their successful planning and upgrading project in a neighboring informal settlement called Kambi Moto, Huruma. In Kambi Moto, Muungano organized residents to save enough money for down payments on new housing and to negotiate with structure owners on the allocation of new plots. The city council owned the land and agreed to construct sanitary

Kambi Moto, Huruma: Community-Led Healthy Slum Upgrading

Kambi Moto, a village in the Huruma informal settlement of Nairobi, has undergone a radical transformation through community-led upgrading.[1, 2] The process has improved the physical characteristics of the community but, just as important, has also enhanced the social status of women, decreased childhood illnesses, and improved incomes and the overall economic status of participants. While an imperfect model, the Kambi Moto, Huruma, upgrading project is an example of how slum dwellers can come together to save money, build trust and an accountable local institution, connect with national and international partners for additional financial and technical support, and use all these resources to coproduce improved housing, land rights, services, and health.

Kambi Moto, which means "fire camp" in Kiswahili, was known for its regular fires and displacement of families in the 1990s and early 2000s. By 2003, Kambi Moto's approximately 6,500 residents occupied a mere 0.4 hectares, lived on about 5,000 KSh per month, and shared six city council–built public toilets and nine water taps. Muungano leaders organized Kambi Moto residents, and upon joining, members were expected to save daily to help finance construction. Members in this savings scheme were also required to attend weekly meetings convened by a seven-member elected executive committee and volunteer for one of the saving scheme teams, such as auditing, loaning, and project planning. The savings group also surveyed the existing community to count who lived where and agreed that existing residents could be allocated one new plot to purchase. The group also mapped the community to begin the urban design and housing-layout process.

At the same time, residents and Muungano leaders began negotiating with the Nairobi City Council (NCC) for access to Kambi Moto's land, since it was government owned, and the NGO Pamoja Trust secured the land for residents through a memorandum of understanding with the NCC in 2003. The MOU stipulated that the land could be upgraded and the city would provide trunk water, sewer connections, and electricity. The MOU also specified that both structure owners and existing tenants could benefit from the upgrading—a key source of community controversy—and that building standards would be relaxed to allow low-cost construction. Participatory design, utilizing architects from the University of Nairobi, resulted in a model house that could be affordably built incrementally; tenants could live on the first floor as additional walls were built upward to three stories. Each house was designed with a small kitchen, indoor water connection (with a storage tank on the roof to ensure access to water even in times of poor provision by the state-run water company), a shower and toilet connected to the main sewer, and formal electricity, all regulated by proper utility-installed meters. The designs included a central courtyard with a gate to the street, allowing children to play safely.

Eventually 270 ten-by-ten-meter plots were created to form the new community. The construction proceeded incrementally; once a family had 10 percent of the cost of the housing for a down payment, the local Muungano savings group provided another 10 percent, and the groups' national financial management arm, Akiba Mashinani Trust (AMT), provided a loan for the remaining 80 percent. At this point the beneficiaries' shack was removed. A grant from the Italian organization Cooperazione Internazionale (COOPI) provided additional resources as necessary to secure construction materials. Construction proceeded with twenty to thirty units at time, so there was minimal displacement of existing residents. Sweat equity was required, as residents were to work at least one day every week on their house and for the entire community in producing metal doors and Ladhis, or precast-concrete floor and roofing slabs. The latter were also sold to other construction contractors to raise extra capital for the local group. Housing costs varied as the project proceeded in multiple phases over about eight years. The early-phase homes cost about 160,000 KSh, but by 2013, the cost had increased to about 450,000 KSh (US$1,800–5,300).

As of 2014, some 120 of the originally planned homes were completed. While planning began in 2000, the US$2.1 million project was significantly delayed by postelection violence in the area in 2008 and 2009. However, water, sewer, electricity, drainage, and road-paving improvements are complete and reach everyone in the community, whether living in a newly constructed home or an older shack. The community has seen additional health benefits, though on a small scale. According to our focus groups and interviews, women are now a majority of community leaders, and fewer are struggling to get out of poverty. One woman told our team that she could now rent a room in her home to supplement her income as a street food vendor. Another woman mentioned that she saved enough to pay for all her children's education and one is now in university.[6]

1. Selva, M. (2004). Kenyans buy into slum plan. *Christan Science Monitor.* May 26. http://www.csmonitor.com/2004/0526/p07s01-woaf.html (accessed 19 December 2015).
2. Muiruri, P. (2011). Innovative building for slum dwellers. *Standard Digital.* November 3. http://www.standardmedia.co.ke/article/2000046044/innovative-building-for-slum-dwellers?categoryID=0 (accessed 19 December 2015).
3. Kenya: "A dream come true" for many slum residents. (2010). IRIN. February 23. http://www.irinnews.org/report/88211/kenya-a-dream-come-true-for-many-slum-residents (accessed 19 December 2015).

infrastructure if the residents could agree on a new housing layout. Pamoja Trust organized a planning process that included enumerating households to determine the current housing need and a design-visioning process for creating the new layout. An economic development plan was devised whereby residents would start a business making cement blocks to be used for constructing their own homes. To raise additional capital, the building materials would also be sold in the general market. The Kambi Moto, Huruma, project was successful and a new improved community exists today.[56, 57, 58]

VILLAGE-SCALE INFRASTRUCTURE PLANNING

The planning process that began in Mathare in 2008 focused on four of the villages on government land: Kosovo, 4B, Mashimoni, and Mabatini. The Muungano savings group in these communities spent most of 2008 and the beginning of 2009 organizing and training residents for household enumerations. The initial plan was to build upon the Kambi Moto, Huruma, model and focus on housing upgrading. By May 2009, more than 12,000 households had been surveyed and the community mapped electronically and entered into a geographic information system (GIS). A partnership among the University of Nairobi Department of Urban and Regional Panning, Pamoja Trust, Muungano, and SDI was expanded to include the Department of City and Regional Planning of the University of California, Berkeley. The universities were enlisted to help analyze the data and draft integrated upgrading proposals that included housing, infrastructure, community facilities, open space, and environmental issues.

Planning meetings were held weekly among residents. The NGO-university team reported findings from the enumerations and drafted proposals that reflected community-negotiated standards. A decision was made to focus on Kosovo initially and then the other three villages. Four key objectives for the improvement plan emerged from the community planning meetings. First, the new project should cause no or very limited displacement. This meant that all those who currently lived in Mathare, 95 percent of whom were renters, would be offered somewhere to live in the newly designed community. Second, infrastructure was to be designed for in-home water and sewer connections. Third, a land tenure process should be drafted; and fourth, an alternative to the 30-meter riparian reserve should be explored. After over a year of meetings and draft proposals, three community workshops in July and August 2009 were scheduled to move toward community approval of a final plan.

More than one hundred residents attended the first workshop, and almost immediately the tension between structure owners and residents surfaced. Owners wanted to know how many units and structures they were going to be given, while tenants wanted to know who was going to get ground-floor apartments and who would be living in a multistory structure. The land issues were proving a challenge. According to community organizer Joseph Kimani: "Even before the meeting ended, the structure owners wanted to meet separately with us [the planning team]. They were concerned with their investment and we knew from past experiences that this would be the case. But we had strong agreement that everyone, the structure owners and tenants, wanted improved infrastructure and some agreement that a road that was encroached on should be opened back up." The planning team and Muungano members discussed the dynamics of the meeting and decided to focus the next meeting on infrastructure and not attempt to sort out the housing and land tenure issue until the community moved toward agreement on infrastructure.

At the second community workshop, organizers focused on the infrastructure improvement proposals, discussing roads, drainage, sanitation, and water service. The proposals integrated water, sewerage, drainage, and roads into a comprehensive plan. The water service proposal included a design for in-home water taps and a series of new public kiosks managed by community members. Residents were tapping water "illegally" from pipes running adjacent to the village, had intermittent and sometimes contaminated water, and regularly faced long walks, high costs, and extortion from water vendors. The prospect of new water service with in-home taps—the first slum in Nairobi to propose such a model—galvanized the community planning process. Members of the Athi Water Trust Fund, a capital improvement entity associated with the Nairobi Water and Sewer Company, proclaimed that if the community could agree to a management and payment scheme, they would initiate and finance the construction with a combination of company and local labor.

The third community meeting was held at St. Theresa's church in Mathare. A series of before-and-after sketches were presented showing potential improvements to the community as a result of water supply system upgrades, and these images were then shared widely among residents. A final plan was developed out of that meeting and, as mentioned earlier, the city council endorsed the draft plan.

The Kosovo plans and workshops turned into the Kosovo Water Project. According to Kosovo resident and Muungano secretary, Jason Waweru, the plan opened up a dialogue that was challenging for

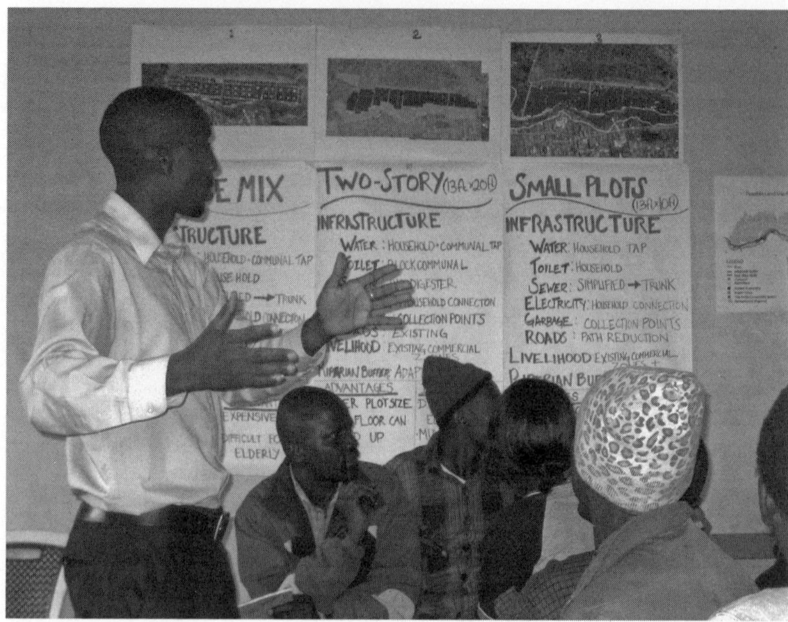

PHOTO 9.1. Community planning workshop, Kosovo village, Mathare, Nairobi, 2009.

participants but eventually yielded consensus. The influence of gangs wanting to control water service was ever present, but the new model put community residents in control of water management. According to Weweru: "The 'delegated management model' meant that the community in Kosovo would control all the issues surrounding distribution of the water, including communal collection of fees. Everyone was scared. If we approved the delegated management model, would it just allow more militias and gangs to step in?" The interim solution specified that Muungano and the water company would first build a pilot kiosk in one area of Kosovo and would implement the community construction and management model. A distribution kiosk was built, and each household was required to give a small deposit as a down payment for an in-home water meter. Community residents hired by the water company dug trenches and helped lay pipe. The pilot project was a success, as Muungano took the lead in organizing the community management plan and collecting down payments for the water meters. Those who could not afford a meter could collect water at the new community-operated public kiosk. By June 2011, six additional kiosks had been constructed and the informal water network was removed.

WATER AND HEALTH IN MATHARE

According to Jason Waweru, the new water kiosk in the community acts as a planning center:

> People come asking how they can get a meter and water in their homes. The youth gang members even want to learn what is happening. The discussion almost always moves to some other need, such as food, electricity, or safety or schools. We direct them to services or an upcoming meeting on the subject. This is how we negotiated with the power company for more regular electricity after they were arresting people with illegal wires to the power poles. Having this place here is more than managing water. It is a place for answering questions, learning about issues, and solving problems together.

As Weweru describes it, the water kiosk acts like a community resource center—referring people to services but also collecting knowledge about and experience with issues and mobilizing residents to seek solutions. He also mentioned that it has become a site recognized for helping keep the peace, since gangs and others were ready to react with violence after the police came into Kosovo in the middle of the night and arrested people with illegal electricity connections. The regular day-to-day presence of Muungano members ready to answer questions and address issues is, according to Weweru, equally important: "It's not just a structure, but a place with people who live here and have the interests of the community at heart."

Mati and Macharia evaluated the pilot phase of the water project in Kosovo.[59] Using quantitative survey data and focus group discussions with residents, the evaluation found that the reliance on informal vendors had decreased by 50 percent. The primary source of water for Kosovo residents had changed significantly from vendors and unmetered taps to metered water in homes and new water kiosks. The percentage of residents with in-home metered water service increased from 7.5 percent before the pilot project to 35.6 percent after; over 34 percent relied on water vendors before the project, while 17 percent used vendors after and over 20 percent used the new kiosk as their primary water source. Before the project, residents paid 2.5 KSh per 20-liter jerrican of water. After the project residents using water vendors reported paying less than 2 KSh per jerrican. The in-home water service has reduced the distance to the nearest water source and the time spent gathering water for 92 percent of residents. While only 36 percent of respondents reported that their health improved after the water project, 70 percent reported that their life had improved since the pilot project was completed.[60]

THE MATHARE VALLEY ZONAL PLAN

While the Kosovo water project was moving forward, other villages wanted to benefit from the Muungano-led planning process and infrastructure upgrading. Muungano and MuST, with support from SDI and the university teams, recognized that a village-by-village approach would be too slow and miss the economies of scale, particularly for infrastructure, that would come from investments in the entire community. According to Irene Karanja, the leader of MuST: "We collectively decided that a plan for the entire of Mathare—the zonal plan—was the only way forward to achieve the 'scale' results we focus on. SDI helped share the work in Mumbai by SPARC in Dharavi. We visited there and learned from slum dwellers that this could be done in a complex and contested environment such as Mathare. We established a new, Mathare Valley planning process."

MuST organized village-scale planning teams, and a Mathare Zonal Planning Team was established with at least two representatives from the village teams. A coalition of community-based organizations was organized, and a Mathare Planning Network was proposed. Additional data were gathered on each village, and comparisons were made between Mathare, Kibera, and Mukuru, the three largest informal settlements in Nairobi. Maps and results were shared with residents as the planning process moved forward. The data yielded some surprise findings that helped frame the planning process. For example, water costs per month and monthly rents were higher in Mathare than in the other informal settlements. Infant mortality in Mathare was also greatest in Mathare. In some cases, hundreds of people were sharing one toilet, often a pit latrine, while the Sphere International Humanitarian standard was no more than twenty people per toilet (figure 9.3). These new data helped further mobilize the broader community around the urgency of and the need for healthy planning.

GOING TO SCALE WITH HEALTHY COMMUNITY PLANNING

The first Draft Mathare Valley Zonal Plan included a detailed set of infrastructure improvement proposals focused on roads, drainage, water, sanitation, and electricity.[61] A plan for managing the river and the riparian area was also included. The plan included two strategies for ongoing monitoring, recognizing that the complexity of the place could not be

MAP 9.3. Mathare distribution of toilets.

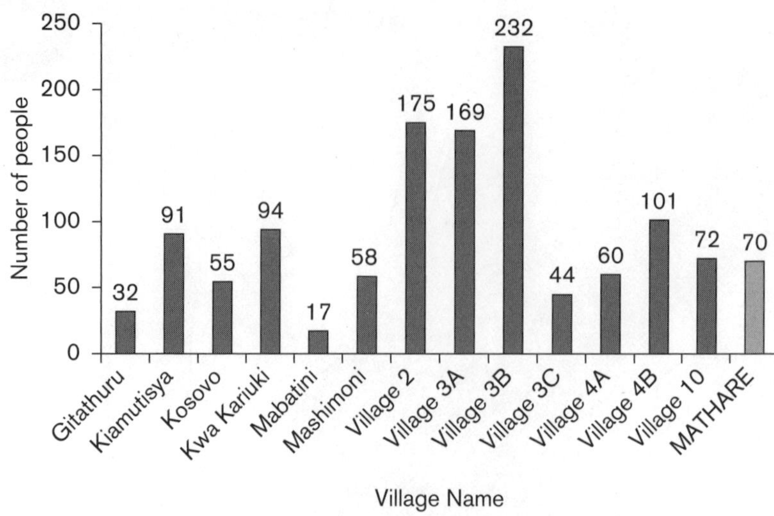

FIGURE 9.3. Number of people per functioning community toilet in Mathare, 2014.

addressed in a single plan at one point in time. First, a new coalition-building process was proposed that identified many of the key stakeholders who needed either to participate in the process or to approve some aspect of it. A long-range work plan was developed for this process focused on short-, medium-, and long-term implementation projects.

Second, a set of monitoring indicators were drafted in the plan to track progress on a number of issues identified by slum dwellers as priority issues. The indicators were grouped into three equity categories, living conditions, economics and services and political power/outcomes. Under each category specific indicators and measures were included. The aim was to have a plan for tracking change and a way for residents to track the suite of measures that together contribute to greater equity in Mathare (table 9.1).

FROM PLANS TO HEALTHY SLUM POLICY

The Mathare Zonal Plan was presented to the Kenyan Ministry of Lands and Housing and the newly created Nairobi metropolitan, or county, government in 2012 and 2013. The ministry adopted the plan and the metropolitan government agreed to use it, the first of its kind in any Kenyan city, as a model for area upgrading and improvement plans across Nairobi. The Mathare Zonal Plan helped communicate to deci-

TABLE 9.1 EXAMPLE INDICATORS FOR HEALTHY SLUM UPGRADING, MATHARE, NAIROBI, KENYA

Equity category	Indicators	Measures for Mathare Zonal Plan
Living conditions	Housing	Percentage of residents in savings program for housing
		Ratio of structure owners to tenants
	Water, sanitation, and food	Self-reports of food insecurity
		Percent of households with in-home water and toilet service
		Number of new electricity connections installed by utility company
	Environment	Number of infrastructure projects launched to secure housing on steep slopes and in flood areas
		Number of non-charcoal-burning cookstoves sold at subsidized cost
	Safety	Self-reports from women of safety and violence
	Transportation	Public spending on transportation
Economics and services	Primary health care	Percent of free clinics offering maternal and childhood care using in-home community health workers
	Mental/substance abuse care	Percent of international health research budgets spent on mental health services/ interventions
	Education	Percent of families receiving free day care
	Employment	Percent of local residents hired to work on government and internationally funded contracts in past year
	Wealth access	Ratio of slum-dweller new bank accounts to all new accounts by local banks in past year
Political power and outcomes	Community participation	Percent of residents participating in a community-based organization
	Government responsiveness	Number of meetings held in community by Nairobi City Council, Water and Power Company, addressing ongoing infrastructure, housing, and health issues
	Recognition of minority rights (women)	Number of women given land rights/housing tenure by city council
	Health status	Self-rated health
	Art/cultural expression	Percent of youth and adults participating in cultural programs

sion makers that slum dwellers and their partner organizations were more than capable of producing new knowledge and analyses to support slum health and upgrading. The partnership of Muungano, SDI, University of Nairobi, and UC Berkeley used their new evidence and local expertise to influence Kenya's two slum improvement policies: the Kenyan Slum Upgrading Program (KENSUP) and the Kenya Informal Settlements Improvement Program (KISIP). Muungano, slum-dweller civil society organizations and the universities were also invited in 2013 to participate in the drafting committee for Kenya's first Slum Upgrading and Prevention Policy.

KENSUP is a UN-Habitat–sponsored program focused on building infrastructure and housing in slums across Kenya, with an initial focus on Kibera in Nairobi. A national Slum Upgrading Department within the Ministry of Housing was created to manage KENSUP. To complete housing upgrading in Kibera, the government built a decanting site where slum residents displaced because of new construction would be housed until their permanent structures were completed. The Ministry of Housing was using KENSUP resources to reconstruct and tarmac a 4-kilometer spine road within Kibera and to build more than 600 housing units in an area called Soweto East.[61] KISIP is a World Bank–financed program (with Agence Française de Dévelopement and the Swedish International Development Agency contributing resources and providing management assistance), also channeled through the Kenyan Ministry of Housing. KISIP focuses on both improving urban governance and building new infrastructure but not housing. KISIP was launched in 2011 and was slated to be a five-year, $155 million–dollar initiative targeting fifteen Kenyan municipalities.

From 2009 through 2013, the Muungano, University of Nairobi, and UC Berkeley partners met with government officials to design and implement both KENSUP and KISIP. Presentations were made to the World Bank to highlight the findings of the Mathare Zonal Plan and the importance of civil society leadership in any government-sponsored slum-upgrading programs. By 2013, the World Bank decided to use the Mathare Zonal Plan as its guide for upgrading the municipal trunk sewer within and through Mathare. UN-Habitat also adopted the zonal plan and launched a project to build playground and recreation space based on the plan's analyses of the limited open space for children and youth.

The drafting committee for the Kenya National Slum Upgrading and Prevention Policy (NSUPP) began in 2012 and had seven thematic groups, each co-led by a representative from a civil society group working with slum dwellers. At the request of slum dwellers, and reflecting their knowledge of global slum-upgrading activities, the policy committees reviewed upgrading policies around the world from Brazil to India to Ethiopia. The Muungano representatives offered their experiences from processes like the one in Mathare in order to emphasize an integrated slum-upgrading approach be adopted as part of the policy. The final draft of the NSUPP, issued in January 2014, did not demonize slum dwellers: "The residents of these [Kenyan] slums and informal settlements contribute immensely to the urban economy and are a true reflection of social, cultural, political diversity and dynamism to their city. They are homes to highly talented young men and women in the field of arts, technical innovations and sports. These talents can be tapped and nurtured to provide homegrown solutions to slums questions. However, slums and informal settlements have never been officially recognized by the government." The policy continued by articulating a set of goals and "inclusive city" objectives, many put forward by slum-dweller civil society organizations themselves:

> The National Slum Upgrading and Prevention Policy is intended to promote, secure and protect lives and livelihoods of the urban poor and people living and working in slums and informal settlements by strategically integrating them into a social, political and economic agenda in line with the Constitution of Kenya 2010.
>
> The objectives of the policy are:
>
> Recognition and integration of slums and informal settlements into the urban fabric which guarantees access to adequate housing.
>
> Provide a legal, regulatory and institutional framework and projects to guide coordinated and accountable implementation of Slum Upgrading and Prevention at national and county level[s].
>
> To encourage, facilitate and secure community and stakeholder participation, transparency and accountability in Slum Upgrading, rehabilitation, redevelopment and slum improvement programmes.
>
> Mainstream Slum Upgrading and Prevention programs and projects at Counties and other units of Devolution.
>
> To create linkages, strengthen and enhance capacity for research, planning, monitoring and Evaluation.
>
> Provide for direct Government's intervention in provision of social housing for the urban poor.
>
> Provision of urban land for private sector led development in low cost housing, slum rehabilitation and improvement.
>
> Promote National and County integrated financial planning and budgeting and advocate for creation of amalgamated Fund for Slum Upgrading and Prevention.[62]

The policy also included a detailed monitoring and evaluation plan, drawing heavily from ideas in the Mathare Zonal Plan.

PLANNING AS PROPHYLAXIS

This chapter reviews how urban policy and planning can both be detrimental to slum health and act to prevent disease and reduce health and safety risks. Innovations in Nairobi's Mathare slum offer public health and urban policy officials a framework for improving community health in a manner consistent with democracy, transparency, and addressing the broad social determinants of health. No single intervention and no focus on one disease will improve slum health in places like Mathare. These complex communities require complex, negotiated solutions that are flexible and adapt to community needs. We cannot treat or immunize our way out of slum health issues.

This chapter emphasizes the coproduction of slum health solutions. Residents in Mathare were able to define what issues mattered most to them and worked with partners to research these issues and devise solutions. The immediacy of basic sanitation, safety, and general living conditions suggested important health-promoting interventions. Yet the work in Mathare also recognized that boutique, one-off interventions were like treating a disease and sending the patient back into the living conditions that contributed to the illness in the first place. Scaling-up slum health means coproducing short-term immediate needs while also working on longer-term changes to institutions and policies so they are more responsive to the needs of the urban poor. While still ongoing, the slum health work in Mathare takes an incremental, evolutionary, social-learning approach to shifting actions and the state to secure improvements.

There are some important considerations and potential challenges for this type of slum health work. First, the coproduction of partners in Mathare tends to work outside and sometimes against established rules and procedures. The challenge is for coproduction actors and institutions to simultaneously work outside development and health procedures that often fail to meet their needs, while working to renegotiate those same rules and procedures to better serve the urban poor. Second, the work in Mathare highlights the fact that community members can coproduce not just plans but also the delivery of basic services, and that they can and should be paid and entrusted to do these tasks. Yet, as the Mathare Kosovo water project revealed, this can again create tension with the state and private sectors, which often see their role as delivering and managing urban services. Third, and related to the previous challenge, when delivering services, slum dwellers are likely to be less concerned with "cost effectiveness" and "cost-recovery" than their institutional partners. Rather, slum dwellers are more apt to value health and safety improvements, employment and empowerment, and increased power and representation in ongoing decisions about resource allocation. The enumerations and mapping done by slum dwellers is one example of how slum dwellers seek to reclaim power over the interpretation of data that shapes decisions from state and international development institutions that have worked for decades to exclude and marginalize what they know. In short, power is recognized as a health-promoting or -damaging resource, depending on who holds it and how it is exerted, and Mathare's slum dwellers explicitly aim to gain power while establishing and improving services. While the Mathare health-planning processes may not have changed the economic system that helps produce their poverty and poor health outcomes, they are working to challenge the distribution of political power that supports and perpetuates their marginalization at the city and national scale. While an unfinished symphony, the work of Mathare slum dwellers is part of the ongoing struggle for power, recognition, and health by the urban poor across the Global South.

NOTES

1. Ayah, R., Joshi, M.D., Wanjiru, R., Njau, E.K., Otieno, C.F., Njeru, E.K., & Mutai, K.K. (2013). A population-based survey of prevalence of diabetes and correlates in an urban slum community in Nairobi, Kenya. *BMC Public Health* 13:371.

2. Morgan, W.T.W. (1976). *Nairobi: City and region.* Nairobi. Oxford: Oxford University Press.

3. Curtain, P.D. (1985). Medical knowledge and urban planning in tropical Africa. *American Historical Review* 90(3):594–613.

4. Ibid.

5. Eliot quoted in Hill, M.F. (1949). *Permanent way*, Vol. 1: *The Story of the Kenya and Uganda Railway.* Nairobi, Kenya: East African Literature Bureau.

6. White, L.W.T., Silberman, L., & Anderson, P.R. (1948). *Nairobi: Master plan for a colonial capital.* London: HMSO.

7. Ibid.

8. Barnow, N.F., Wittus Hansen, N., Johnsen, M., Poulsen, A., Rønnow, V., & Sølvsten, K. (1983). *Urban development in Kenya: The growth of Nairobi, 1900–1970.* Copenhagen: Kunstakademiets Arkitektskole, 300.

9. Morgan (1976).

10. White et al. (1948), 15.

11. Achola, M.A. (2001). Colonial policy and urban health: The case of colonial Nairobi. *Azania: Archaeological Research in Africa* 36–37(1):119–37.

12. Leys, N. (1973). *Kenya.* London: Frank Cass.

13. Ibid.

14. McVicar, K.G. (1968). Twilight of an African slum: Pumwani and the evolution of African settlement in Nairobi. PhD thesis, University of California, Los Angeles.

15. White, L. (1990). *The comforts of home: Prostitution in colonial Nairobi.* Chicago: University of Chicago Press.

16. McVicar (1968).

17. White (1990).

18. Leys (1973).

19. Curtain (1985).

20. Chaiken, M.S. (1998). Primary health care initiatives in colonial Kenya. *World Development* 26(9):1701–17.

21. Porter, D. (1999). *Health, civilization and the state: A history of public health from ancient to modern times.* London: Routledge.

22. Moradi, A. (1998). Confronting colonial legacies: Lessons from human development in Ghana and Kenya, 1880–2000. *Journal of International Development* 20:1107–21.

23. Mudhune, S.A., Okiro, E.A., Noor, A.M., Zurovac, D., Juma, E., Ochola, S.A., & Snow, R.W. (2011). The clinical burden of malaria in Nairobi: A historical review and contemporary audit. *Malaria Journal* 10(138).

24. White et al. (1948).

25. White et al. (1948).

26. Hake, A. (1977). *African metropolis: Nairobi's self-help city.* New York: St. Martin's Press.

27. Etherton, D., Jorgensen, N., Steele, R., & Mulili, M. (1971). *Mathare Valley: A case of uncontrolled settlement in Nairobi.* Housing Research and Development Unit, University of Nairobi.

28. Ibid.

29. Obudho, R.A., & Aduwo, G.O. (1992). The nature of the urbanization process and urbanism in the city of Nairobi, Kenya. *African Urban Quarterly* 7(1–2):50–62.

30. Obudho, R.A. (1997). Nairobi: National capital and regional hub. In Rakodi, C. (ed.). *The urban challenge in Africa.* Tokyo: UN University Press, 292–334.

31. Etherton (1971).

32. Ibid.

33. Ibid.

34. Ibid.

35. Ibid., 41.

36. Huchzermeyer, M. (2011). *Tenement cities: From 19th century Berlin to 21st century Nairobi.* Trenton, NJ: Africa World Press.

37. Bassette, E.M. (2003). *Informal settlement upgrading in sub-Saharan Africa: Retrospective and lessons learned.* Washington, DC: World Bank. http://

people.virginia.edu/~emb7d/docs/wblitreview-Jan03_web.pdf (accessed 19 December 2015).

38. Huchzermeyer (2011).

39. Weru, J. (2004). Community federations and city upgrading: The work of Pamoja Trust and Muungano in Kenya. *Environment and Urbanization* 16(1):47–62.

40. Kamau, H.W., & Ngari, J. (2002). Integrated urban housing development: Assessment of the Mathare 4A development programme against the sustainable livelihoods approach. Working Paper 4. https://practicalaction.org/docs/shelter/iuhd_wp4_mathare_4a_assessment.pdf (accessed 19 December 2015).

41. Rodriguez-Torres, D. (2010). Public authorities and urban upgrading policies in Eastlands: The example of Mathare 4A slum upgrading project. In Charton-Bigot, H., and Rodriguez-Torres, D. (eds.). *Nairobi today: The paradox of a fragmented city*. Dar es Salaam, Tanzania: Mkuki Na Nyota, 61–94.

42. Lamba, A. (2005). Land tenure management systems in informal settlements: A case of Nairobi. Master's thesis, Delft University of Technology.

43. Kamau & Ngari (2002).

44. Huchzermeyer (2011).

45. Rodriguez-Torres (2010).

46. Weru (2004).

47. Rodriguez-Torres (2010).

48. Wrong, M. (2009). *It's our turn to eat: The story of a Kenyan whistle-blower.* New York: Harper.

49. Chege, M. (1981). A tale of two slums: electoral politics in Mathare and Dagoretti. *Review of African Political Economy* 20:74–88.

50. Weru (2004)

51. Wrong (2009)

52. This and all following quotations, unless otherwise documented, are from in-person interviews conducted between June 2012 and January 2013. Notes were taken, but the interviews were not audio-recorded.

53. Jack Makau, personal communication with author, 2011.

54. Chege (1981).

55. Appadurai, A. (2002). Deep democracy: Urban governmentality and the horizon of politics. *Public Culture* 14:21–47.

56. Selva, M. (2004). Kenyans buy into slum plan. *Christian Science Monitor.* May 26. http://www.csmonitor.com/2004/0526/p07s01-woaf.html (accessed December 22, 2015).

57. Muiruri, P. (2011). Innovative building for slum dwellers. *Standard Digital.* November 3. http://www.standardmedia.co.ke/article/2000046044/innovative-building-for-slum-dwellers?categoryID=0 (accessed December 22, 2015).

58. Kenya: "A dream come true" for many slum residents. (2010). IRIN. February 23. http://www.irinnews.org/report/88211/kenya-a-dream-come-true-for-many-slum-residents (accessed 19 December 2015).

59. Mati, E., & Macharia, D. (2011). *Influence of water supply on quality of life for urban slum dwellers: The case of Kosovo-Mathare pilot water project in Nairobi, Kenya.* Saarbrucken: Lambert Academic Publishing.

60. Ibid., 56.

61. Corburn, J. & Shack/Slum Dwellers International (SDI) (2012). Mathare Zonal Plan, Nairobi, Kenya: Collaborative plan for informal settlement Upgrading. July. http://sdinet.org/wp-content/uploads/2015/04/Mathare_Zonal_Plan_25_06_2012_low_res-2.pdf (accessed 27 December 2015).

62. Kenya Slum Upgrading Programme (KENSUP), http://www.housing.go.ke/?cat=18; Kenya Slum Upgrading Programme (KENSUP) http://unhabitat.org/books/un-habitat-and-kenya-slum-upgrading-programme-kensup/ (accessed February 3, 2016).

63. Ministry of Housing, Republic of Kenya (2013). Background document: The National Slum Upgrading and Prevention Policy. Nairobi, Kenya. http://healthycities.berkeley.edu/uploads/1/2/6/1/12619988/kenya_slum_upgrade prevent_policy_may_2013.pdf (accessed February 4, 2016).

CHAPTER 10

Sanitation and Women's Health in Nairobi's Slums

JASON CORBURN AND IRENE KARANJA

Global urbanization and a lack of political response from national or municipal governments are contributing to the persistence of urban poverty, slums or informal settlements, and health inequities in cites of the global South.[1] Worldwide, an estimated 828 million people currently live in slum conditions (about 45% of the global South's population), and the number is expected to reach over 2 billion by 2020, with close to 85 percent of slum settlements in cities of the global South.[2] Among cities in sub-Saharan Africa with a million or more population, between 50 and 80 percent of the urban population lives in informal settlements.[3] In other words, informal settlements are the norm, not the exception, in large portions of the global South. While urbanization can be beneficial for health, the increase in the number and size of urban informal settlements represents a significant challenge for promoting healthier cities in the global South, since informal settlements are also the location of persistent health inequities.

We acknowledge that there is no one definition of urban informal settlement and in particular that "slum" is not only an absolute term measuring human deprivation but also a relative concept that differs from city to city according to social class and culture and often changes over time. UN-Habitat has defined an informal settlement as an area with "inadequate access to safe water, inadequate access to sanitation and other infrastructure, poor structural quality of housing, overcrowding, and insecure residential status." The UN also defines a slum as a household or group of individuals in an urban area that lacks the following:

Durable housing of a permanent nature that protects against extreme climate conditions

Sufficient living space, which means not more than three people sharing the same room

Easy access to safe water in sufficient amounts at an affordable price

Access to adequate sanitation in the form of a private or public toilet shared by a reasonable number of people

Security of tenure that prevents forced evictions[4]

This chapter focuses on informal settlements and health in Nairobi, Kenya. We acknowledge that the 2014 Kenyan National Slum Upgrading and Prevention Policy defines a slum as "a human settlement characterized by dilapidated housing structures, overcrowding, abject poverty and unemployment, high insecurity incidences, insecure land tenure, exclusion of physical development, inadequate infrastructural services and often located in unsustainable environment."[5]

The challenge of urban slums is particularly acute in Kenya and its capital city, Nairobi, where more than 65 percent of the capital's almost 3.2 million people live in informal settlements occupying less than 10 percent of the land area.[6, 7] According to the African Population and Health Research Center (APHRC) report "Population and Health Dynamics in Nairobi's Informal Settlements" (2012), infant mortality, under-five mortality, and low birth rates were all significantly higher in Nairobi's informal settlements than the rest of the city, the country and is rural areas.[8] The prevalence of childhood diarrhea with blood was higher in the slums in 2012 (8.0 percent) than in Nairobi (0.6 percent) or in the country as a whole (3.3 percent).[9] Fewer households in slums than in Nairobi more generally in 2012 had access to electricity, clean water, or flush toilets (19.5% versus 88.6%; 27.6% versus 78.2%; and 46% versus 83%, respectively).[10] Yet most of these analyses focus on only one disease, risk factor, or treatment regime and fail to account for the multiple and related environmental, social, and political forces that influence health in these communities.[11]

In this chapter, we use a range of data collected by and with slum dwellers in the Mathare informal settlement of Nairobi to highlight the importance of a relational approach to health equity analyses and intervention design. By "a relational approach," we mean that rather than focusing just on static variables of people or places, we aim to highlight how the characteristics in places interact with one another, how political and cultural institutions shape these interactions, and what role local people and their knowledge can play in defining and interpreting action-oriented place-based research.[12] We explore the relational idea in more detail below. Our process and findings are important because slum dwellers, nongovernmental organizations, global health practitioners, and others grapple with ways to promote healthy and equitable cities in the global South that recognize and value the often contested, gendered, and variegated characteristics of urban informal settlements.

A RELATIONAL VIEW OF SLUM HEALTH

As an alternative to the static, narrowly constructed variable view of place offered by some slum health research, we employ a relational view of slum health in this study. In the relational view, place is understood as having physical and social characteristics, but these characteristics are shaped by and given meaning through their interactions with politics and institutions, with one another and, most important, with the people living in a place. The relational interplay between place characteristics and their meaning-making for health is often contingent and contested, particularly in informal settlements, as new groups with new cultural orientations move into a place. The relational view of place is crucial for promoting health equity because social processes, such as power, inequality, and collective action, are often revealed through the construction and reconstruction of the material forms and social meanings of places.[13]

A relational view of place and health demands research and analysis that combine multiple ways of characterizing and understanding places, including resident narratives, systematic observation, spatial mapping, and quantitative and qualitative measures of the location and accessibility of resources. For health promotion this means documenting not just whether a health-promoting resource exists but also the opportunities and barriers different population groups might face in accessing that resource. In the relational view, geographic scales must explore the interactions between local and global decisions, not just static administrative boundaries. Too often in public health, such as in neighborhood effects research, the most proximate scale is used because easily accessible data are available.[14] However, forces outside the neighborhood or local place, such as national and international policies, can influence local access to a health-promoting good, such as affordable food. Distance under the relational view ought to include physical and social relations and should view populations and places as embedded within networks. This concept of distance is important for health promotion because the poor might not use a resource, such as health care, even though it is physically close to them, if they perceive the service as not being culturally appropriate or affordable, or if traveling far away from one's home might reduce the chances of being stigmatized for being treated for a particular disease in one's community.[15]

In a relational view of place, population groups are not treated as static, but rather as dynamic and heterogeneous. Intersectionality is a central feature whereby, for instance, the male slum dweller in Nairobi's Kibera settlement is not assumed to be afflicted by the same health stressors as his neighbor in an adjacent village or a young female slum dweller in the Mathare settlement on the other side of town. The biographies of people and the histories of places matter, in the relational view, for understanding and acting to improve health. Governance and political power are essential features that are investigated, analyzed, and incorporated in the relational approach, not "controlled for" as confounding or ignored, in urban health research and practice. What all this means is that urban health promotion is not simply a matter of making the right interventions or even of having necessary resources in places. Rather, how distributive decisions are made and by whom also matter. This is what we mean by the term "governance"; governance influences the social structures that can sort people into unequal health outcomes by upholding existing distributions of resources such as power, money, and knowledge. Thus, participation in place-based governance should be understood as a positive social determinant of health.[16] However, a major challenge to employing this relational approach to health and place is the lack of local data, particularly in urban slums.

METHODS AND DATA

In this chapter, we focus on the Mathare in Nairobi, Kenya, an informal settlement located about 6 kilometers from the city center and comprising thirteen villages: Gitathuru, Kiamutisya, Kosovo, Kwa Kariuki, Mabatini, Mashimoni, and villages 2, 3A, 3B, 3C, 4A, 4B, and 10. All data are the result of collaboration between the nongovernmental organizations Muungano wa Wanavijiji (Muungano) and Muungano Support Trust (MuST), the University of California, Berkeley, and the University of Nairobi. Muungano is an organization of more than 60,000 slum dwellers across Kenya that supports community organizing and microsavings and advocates for slum upgrading and human rights.[17] Daily meetings of microsavings groups serve as the primary means of organizing slum residents for Muungano, and these groups provide a social and financial safety net for slum dwellers. The savings groups surveyed themselves, called for enumerations, and mapped the entire community of Mathare. MuST provided technical, surveying, planning, and mapping support for the local savings groups.[18] Both Muungano and MuST are members of Shack/Slum Dwellers International (SDI), the international network that works in more than thirty-three countries in Africa, Asia, and Latin America to promote community-driven, inclusive urban development.[19] The University of California, Berkeley, and the University of Nairobi were invited to partner with Muungano and MuST to support the data-gathering, analytical, and planning processes described here.

We report multiple results from data gathered in Mathare from 2009 through 2012. First, we report on a survey of more than 650 households randomly stratified across all thirteen villages in Mathare in August 2011. We also present spatial data gathered by residents and MuST from 2009 to 2011 for a project in which every village and structure was mapped along with water access points, toilets, lighting, roads, drainage, commercial activity, and environmental hazards such as garbage dumps. Survey and environmental mapping data were reviewed, discussed, and validated with residents using unstructured interviews.

We acted as participants and observers while Muungano leaders facilitated more than twenty-two community planning meetings and focus groups with Mathare residents between 2010 and 2012. We include selected narratives from these meetings, which discussed such health-related topics as land tenure, housing construction, women's access to safe toilets, water and electricity access, childcare, food access, economic opportunities, and general security and safety. In the food security focus group, we asked participants the nine specific questions from Version 3 of the Household Food Insecurity Access Scale (HFIAS), developed by USAID's Food and Nutrition Technical Assistance (FANTA) project.[20]* The Institutional Review Board for the Protection

* Each question of this instrument first produces a "yes/no" response. If the response is "no," the score is 0 and the interviewer moves on to the next question. If the response is "yes," the interview then asks, "How often did this happen?" with scores of 1, 2, and 3 corresponding to responses of "rarely" (once or twice in the past four weeks), "sometimes" (three to ten times in the past four weeks), and "often" (more than ten times in the past four weeks), respectively. Scores from the nine questions are tallied for each respondent to produce a total score along a 0–27 scale, with 0 representing the most food secure (access) and 27 representing the most severely food insecure (access).

of Human Subjects at UC Berkeley approved our survey questions and focus group protocols, as well as our data-sharing processes.

A RELATIONAL PROFILE OF HEALTH IN AN INFORMAL SETTLEMENT

History and Context of Kenyan Slums

A first step in taking a relational approach to slum health is to understand the history of the place and the biographies of the people who live there. As Fox has noted, living conditions—and, we suggest, health conditions—in Nairobi's slums today cannot be separated from colonial-era planning and policy decisions and post-independence governance.[21] For example, British colonial policies racially segregated Africans and Indians living in Nairobi to the most marginal, riskiest land to the east and south of the city center, a practice often justified as protecting Europeans from exposure to "native diseases."[22] The few African settlements that were allowed within Nairobi were designed for a fixed number of sojourners and did not accommodate population growth.[23] The British also refused to finance basic services such as water and sanitation to reach the areas where Africans lived, and instead infrastructure was built for resource and commodities extraction, not intracity services or mobility.[24, 25]

The independent Kenyan government continued colonial policies of removing shacks, displacing more than 50,000 people in 1971.[26] To protect themselves from future evictions, the households in Mathare organized into cooperatives to purchase the land they occupied.[27] However, all but one of the cooperatives became companies by 1969 that began building 3-by-3-meter shacks to let. By 1970 in Mathare, the population had tripled in less than ten years, the average number of residents per water tap was 870, and an average of 136 people were using a single pit latrine.[28]

Postcolonial Kenya adopted a centralized governance system that left the Nairobi City Council virtually powerless in relation to the central government. Until the 2010 Kenyan Constitution instituted a decentralized system of governance, the central government used its authority over urban land, taxation, and infrastructure development for political patronage.[29] Further, Nairobi's slums offered lucrative business opportunities for government officials and others who controlled land, collected rents, and received payments from cartels that provided informal services such as water in the state's absence.[30]

Findings: Infrastructure, Gender, and Health

Using our relational framework, we offer examples of how place-based living conditions can be understood using a range of data to best inform health equity–promoting interventions. We focus on sanitation and highlight how this seemingly technical and physical characteristic can be understood and analyzed in a relational way. We reveal the intersecting social, economic, and dignity dimensions of sanitation in the Mathare informal settlement and suggest how this approach can highlight often overlooked gendered health impacts in urban informal settlements.

The Spatial Distribution of Safe Sanitation

In Mathare, more than half of the residents live in a structure with a dirt floor, and 80 percent of these structures do not have permanent walls. More than 83 percent of residents rely on a shared toilet, and most pay 5 KSh per use, which can present a significant economic burden on the poor. We found that more than two-thirds of our respondents continue to use flying toilets† or practice open defecation, or both, due to the cost and limited availability of more dignified sanitation options (table 10.1).

We mapped community toilet blocks across Mathare and found that almost none were connected to the municipal trunk sewer. Human waste is often concentrated around the communal toilets and drains openly into streets, pathways, and frequently, homes. We compared our findings of access to toilets to the Sphere Humanitarian Standards, one of the most widely known and internationally recognized sets of common principles and universal minimum standards in life-saving areas of humanitarian response. Given the lack of universally accepted indicators for comparing slum conditions, we referenced the Sphere Standards to put our findings in Mathare in a broader, comparative context. For instance, Sphere suggests a maximum of 20 people per latrine, but in Mathare we found everyday chronic conditions across the villages of between 17 people per toilet (Mabatini) and 232 per toilet (Village 3B).

Our mapping of public sanitary or ablution blocks, where groups of usually three to six toilets are located, revealed that more than 71 percent of Mathare residents had to walk more than 50 meters to reach a toilet. The spatial distribution is especially problematic at night since few toilets have adequate lighting. As we explain in greater detail below,

† One uses a "flying toilet" when one defecates into a plastic bag and throws the bag into a waste dump.

TABLE 10.1 DEMOGRAPHY OF AND SANITATION ACCESS IN MATHARE, NAIROBI

Mathare village	Population (2009 Kenyan census)	Tenants or renters (%)	Monthly income >10,000 KSh (% yes)	Avg. monthly expenses (KSh)	Avg. no. of households per shared toilet	Avg. no. of people sharing toilet	% of HHs within 50 m of functioning toilet
Gitathuru	3,737	90	55	14,762	11	32	36
Kiamutisya	5,825	90	20	12,250	37	91	34
Kosovo	8,085	74	56	11,933	19	55	41
Kwa Kariuki	9,024	89	29	13,833	29	94	50
Mabatini	1,160	80	40	17,364	6	17	24
Mashimoni	5,153	85	48	13,447	22	58	33
Village 2	7,875	82	34	12,220	63	175	8
Village 3A	4,059	85	39	13,104	64	169	15
Village 3B	7,433	92	48	16,112	84	232	20
Village 3C	5,316	94	27	13,564	16	44	46
Village 4A	18,776	71	39	11,795	18	60	32
Village 4B	5,681	88	50	12,665	32	101	23
Village 10	2,594	82	87	14,206	28	72	10
All Mathare	8,4718	85	42	13,635	24	70	29

the distribution of and general lack of sanitary infrastructure in Mathare disproportionately impacts the physical, social, and cultural determinants of health for women.[31]

Inadequate Sanitation and Disease

Inadequate sanitation in Mathare contributes to a disproportionate burden of infectious and chronic diseases among the population, but particularly for women and girls. According to Cheng and colleagues, close to 90 percent of diarrhea in urban slums is from fecal contamination in drinking water and food.[32] Our survey found that more than 26 percent of women and girls reported an episode of diarrhea in the past month, compared to about 13 percent for all Nairobi and 17 percent for all Kenya, as reported in the Kenyan Demographic and Health Survey.[33] Our focus groups also revealed the pathways between inadequate toilets and exposure to pathogens that contribute to diarrhea. One women noted:

> The children are often playing in the streets where the waste [human] drains from toilets. There is no sewer here that works. There is no place for hand washing and clean water is another cost. The cost of each toilet use [about 5 KSh] means our children cannot use them. I have four children and I can't pay for each to use a flash toilet a few times a day. They come home and touch food and me and I worry this is spreading disease.

Diarrheal diseases caused by inadequate sanitation puts children at multiple risks, leading to vitamin and mineral deficiencies, malnutrition, and stunting of growth. Sustained or long-term exposure to excreta-related pathogens—including helminths or worms—in early life limits cognitive or brain development and lowers long-term disease immunity. As inadequate slum sanitation contributes to the cascading impacts on children of waterborne illness, malnutrition, and, in turn, stunting, it can result in poorer cognitive development and performance in school for young people in Mathare.[34]

Restricted toilet access for women have shown to increase the chance of urinary tract infections (UTIs) and chronic constipation by 80 percent.[35] According to our focus group, women face challenges during menstruation from a lack of a private and hygienic toilet. As one women recalled:

> During my monthly period I can't urinate in the tin, so I have to wait until morning. Sometimes some drops of blood can remain in the tin and everyone

> uses the tin, so it's embarrassing. The Always sanitary pad makes some crackly noise when changing, so when I have a visitor, I feel embarrassed to remove it. I therefore have to wait until morning to change. If I had a private toilet, I would have been able to change the pad anytime.

The lack of adequate toilets also disproportionately impacts women living with HIV. Madise and colleagues have shown that women in Nairobi's slums had 38 percent higher HIV prevalence than men.[36] People living with HIV/AIDS are particularly vulnerable to intestinal parasites, since they tend to suffer from more frequent diarrheal episodes than those with stronger immune systems. When frequent diarrhea leads to insufficient nutrient absorption and weight loss, intestinal parasites can be lethal for people living with HIV.[37] Frequent diarrhea can reduce the efficacy of antiretroviral (ARV) drugs that otherwise can reduce mortality from HIV. According to our focus groups in Mathare, women with HIV faced interrelated health stressors of accessing medication, preventing exposure to disease, and affording food. One woman noted:

> I don't have any childcare or work, so food is hard for me and my baby. I skip meals every day and many in a week to feed him [the baby]. I can't buy cooking fuel, so I get some credit with vendors for prepared foods. When credit runs out, I am forced to be with men. My child was hungry for two days, so this man came with 200 bob [KSh], and I couldn't tell him no because I needed that 200 bob to eat. When I told him to use a CD [condom], he said no and I had no choice. My boy was hungry. I know I'm HIV positive and can get medicines from the clinic, but without food I can't take them. I can sell the pills for food sometimes. This is what I must do now to survive.

Inadequate Sanitation, Girls' Education, and Economic Burdens

As noted above, a Mathare resident typically spends about 5 KSh per toilet use, or 3–7 percent of their total monthly expenditures, according to our survey data. The high cost often means fewer visits to a toilet and being forced to use a flying toilet, defecate in the open, or use a can inside one's structure. In our focus groups, we heard more details about the economic and social costs related to inadequate and costly toilets and the prevalence of diarrhea. We frequently heard that girls were more likely than boys to miss school due to sanitation-related illness and lack of safe, private, and hygienic toilets at their school. A lack of adequate toilets in schools decreases girls' attendance especially during their menstrual cycle. One schoolgirl told us:

> As girls, when we don't have a toilet in school, we are forced to stay with one pad for a whole day. I know many girls who just do not come to school during those days. Even if we have a toilet at school and we have to share them with boys, girls will avoid them and stay home. We do not have a bath place, so I know when you have your period, you do not want to smell in school, so us girls avoid it.

Freeman and colleagues found that improving sanitation for the poor in Kenya resulted in a 58 percent reduction in the odds of a two-week absence from school for girls.[38]

During focus group discussions about the burdens from diarrheal disease, women described the extra costs for transportation to a clinic and for oral rehydration therapy and other medications. Avoidance costs for diarrhea included paying extra for additional water and toilet use, bathing facilities, and fuel to boil water. Women also described being forced to take time away from jobs and home chores when either caring for an ill child or being sick themselves.

Using our interview and focus group data, we generated estimates of the economic costs from sanitation-related diarrheal disease for a typical household in Mathare. We estimated direct medical care costs, avoidance costs, lost family wages, and, after monetizing the value of household chores, homemaker productivity costs for a typical 4–10–day diarrheal episode. To ensure that only chores that were foregone are included, women were asked to report if these chores were actually not carried out, were completed with free help from another person, or were simply delayed in the day or week. The opportunity cost was, then, the product of the forgone number of chores and the cost to hire a person to complete that chore using the hypothetical maid and urban replacement cost. We used the conservative estimate that each Mathare household would experience six diarrhea episodes in one year (e.g., at least one household member experiences sanitation-related diarrhea six times in a year). Our results, displayed in table 10.2, suggest the relational impacts of inadequate sanitation on household economic status.

We estimate that each diarrhea episode costs a household about 1,150 KSh and 6,900 KSh per year, given that the typical episode frequency, we heard, was every other month. With the average Mathare household having a monthly income between 10,000 and 13,000 KSh, diarrhea alone can account for 9.5–11.5 percent of monthly expenditures. Combined with the 3–7 percent of monthly household expenditures devoted to toilet access, inadequate sanitation can represent a

TABLE 10.2 ESTIMATED ECONOMIC BURDENS FROM DIARRHEA IN MATHARE, NAIROBI

	Household cost per episode
Direct costs (oral rehydration; medication; transport to clinic; clinic fees)	KSh 300
Avoidance costs (extra water; more toilet visits; additional fuel to heat water/cook)	KSh 130
Lost wages (from missed work outside home)	KSh 600
Homemaker productivity loss (forgone chores, monetized)	KSh 120
Total estimated household cost per episode	KSh 1,150

significant economic burden on slum households and contributes to keeping slum dwellers in poverty.

One HIV-positive woman described how disease vulnerability relates to her economic status: "People around here know of my HIV-positive status and this impacts my informal business selling *sukuma wiki* [kale]. I frequently get diarrhea because I am more vulnerable to contaminated water and food. When I am sick, I either can't sell or, if I do, people will say to my face they won't buy from me because they think my food will make them sick too."

Sanitation and Dignity

We also heard from Mathare women in focus groups about the indignity they endure from a lack of private, safe, well-lit, nearby toilets. One woman noted:

> Past eight, we can't go out to use the toilet. There is no lighting and the men drinking Chang'aa [local alcohol] on that side, get violent with us, even girls. We are forced to use a bucket . . . a bucket in one room in front of your children, fathers, and brothers. Can you imagine? Sometimes we use the "flying toilets" at night, but your neighbors don't like this. Without any garbage collection, I wake up at dawn and sneak away to empty the bucket or dispose the bag. There is no dignity in our toilet situation.

Another woman remembered: "The toilet I used to go to was made out of wood planks. I could see someone from inside and the person outside could also see me. It was really stressful going for a short or long call, as I would feel eyes watching me. Once I was raped there, but I couldn't tell anyone. The police don't do anything about this and you are just ashamed in your own community."

According to a recent study in Nairobi's Kibera slum and the Kenyan Demographic and Health Survey, more than 36 percent of slum-dwelling women report being physically forced to have sex, while 14 percent of all Kenyan women reported the same.[39] Also in Kibera, more than 30 percent of women reported being forced to perform other sexual acts, as compared to 4.3 percent of all Kenyan women reporting the same experience. Thus, building more communal toilets without attention to women's security and dignity is not an adequate health promotion strategy in Mathare and other informal settlements in Nairobi. For women in Mathare, toilets are an issue of adequate infrastructure, safety, economic opportunity, stigma avoidance, dignity, and human health.

FROM RESEARCH TO ACTION

Our findings on the relational aspects of toilet infrastructure and health have contributed to a number of actions in Mathare since 2010. First, our coalition of residents, the Muungano NGO, and academics worked together to draft an infrastructure-upgrading plan for the villages of Kosovo, 4B, Mabatini, and Mashimoni. These four villages were targeted since they are on government-owned land and our coalition learned through meetings with the Nairobi City Council that the local government would support improvements on its land if a plan was developed and endorsed by residents. After completion of this plan, the Athi Water Board and the Nairobi Water and Sewer Company adopted our proposal for piped water service, financed the project, and began construction in Kosovo, Mathare. The Kosovo Water Project now provides more than 20,000 slum dwellers with piped water, and for the first time in a Nairobi informal settlement, residents can get a household water connection with a meter. This means that Mathare residents do not have to walk to community water taps and gangs are less likely to control water access in Mathare.[40]

A study sponsored by the University of Nairobi found that the Kosovo Water Project helped reduce self-reports of water-related diseases in the community from 67 percent to 26 percent. The same study noted a 36 percent increase in the number of Kosovo, Mathare, residents reporting having access to a private toilet after the water project, and 62 percent of these toilets were flash or nonpit latrines.[41] This improvement was due, at least in part, to the increase of in-home water connections and the ability of households to invest in private in-home toilets now that they had a reliable water source for removing waste.

Another action resulting from the Mathare research was the drafting of the Mathare Zonal Plan, an integrated upgrading plan for the entire informal settlement.[42] The Mathare Zonal Plan documented living conditions and proposed improvements to water, sanitation, electricity, transportation, and health infrastructures, as well as addressing land use, open space, housing, and land rights issues. The first such protocol for an entire informal settlement in Nairobi, the Mathare Zonal Plan was adopted by the Nairobi City Council in 2012. The World Bank is also using the analyses in and recommendations of the Mathare Zonal Plan to upgrade and build a new municipal sewer that serves the entire settlement under the bank's Kenya Informal Settlement Improvement Project (KISIP). UN-Habitat has also adopted the Mathare Zonal Plan for its 2014 project that will develop new recreation and play spaces for youth in Mathare.

CONCLUSIONS

Taken together, our survey, narrative, and spatial mapping results help suggest a method for constructing a relational view of health with residents of informal settlements. Clearly, this is still an incomplete picture, and additional data over time and space would help to more accurately capture physical and social exposures. Additional disease outcome data for specific populations in Mathare could also help clarify who is suffering from which communicable and noncommunicable diseases. However, most of our survey findings on disease burdens and risk factors in Mathare are consistent with those from other studies in Nairobi's informal settlements[43, 44, 45]

Perhaps most important, our findings suggest the need for more complex and multisectoral approaches to urban informal settlement health planning, informed by residents' local knowledge and taking account of interactions between multiple types of services and living conditions. Our Mathare Zonal Plan is one example of this type of integrated improvement strategy for promoting well-being in urban informal settlements. Our relational approach highlights the potential limits of intervention strategies and slum upgrading focused on one service, disease, or behavioral risk factor at a time. As we have shown, participatory research approaches are essential for generating accurate data for healthy informal settlement planning and development, yet slum residents are too often ignored or seen as passive recipients in urban public health and planning initiatives.[46] These strategies might encourage planners and health promoters in the global South to move from a "health in cities" approach (i.e., intervening to address one disease or risk at a time) to a more holistic, healthy cities approach.[47, 48]

As we have emphasized, inadequate slum sanitation has a disproportionate impact on women and girls, and the gender inequality dimensions of our findings are of particular urgency for health promotion. Improvements in urban sanitation in Kenya have consistently been shown to improve child and maternal health by enhancing nutrition, reducing morbidity, and curtailing fatal diarrheal outbreaks.[49] As this study and others have shown, improved sanitation is also fundamental for what ought to be a human right to privacy, dignity, and hygienic conditions for menstruating women and girls.[50] Our work is also consistent with that of others from Kenya revealing that improving water and sanitation for the urban poor significantly reduces girls' school absenteeism.[51] Last but surely not least, adequate and dignified sanitation is vital for women with HIV/AIDS, who are especially susceptible to diarrhea and opportunistic infections and who bear the added burdens of caring for those with HIV/AIDS.[52]

Kenya's national policies now recognize that safe, hygienic, and dignified sanitation is a right for all. Kenya's 2010 constitution protects the inherent dignity of every person in Article 28; Article 43(1)(b) grants every person the right to accessible and adequate housing and to reasonable standards of sanitation; Article 56(e) imposes an obligation on the state to formulate affirmative action programs to ensure access to water, health services, and infrastructure for marginalized communities.[53] Kenya's National Slum Upgrading and Prevention Policy enumerates the policy's core aims: "to provide an integrated framework for slum upgrading & prevention [in order] to meet the standard of adequate housing, reasonable levels of sanitation and other relevant rights provided for in the Constitution."[54] Kenya's National Water Services Strategy (NWSS) for 2007–2015 states as a guiding principle that "sustainable access to safe water and basic sanitation is a human right"; and Kenya's National Environmental Sanitation and Hygiene Policy states that "all Kenyans should enjoy a quality of life with dignity in a hygienic and sanitary environment and be free from suffering any ill health caused by poor sanitation."[55] As we have shown, an integrated approach to health promotion is necessary to fulfill the commitments to slum dwellers made in these and other Kenyan policies.

Ultimately, more work needs to be done to clarify the data collection, reporting, and translation that characterize the relational approach to promoting health in urban informal settlements. We hope our work in Mathare inspires others to build trusting partnerships with communities to more accurately capture their circumstances and inform more integrated and effective actions for health equity.

NOTES

1. Unger, A., & Riley, L. (2007). Slum health: From understanding to action. *PlosMedicine* 4(10):e295. doi:10.1371/journal.pmed.0040295 (accessed 3 December 2013).

2. WHO and United Nations Human Settlements Programme (UN-Habitat) (2010). Hidden cities: Unmasking and overcoming health inequities in urban settings. http://www.who.int/kobe_centre/publications/hidden_cities2010/en / (accessed 26 December 2015).

3. UN-Habitat. (2014). *State of African cities, 2014: Re-imagining sustainable urban transitions.* http://unhabitat.org/books/state-of-african-cities-2014-re-imagining-sustainable-urban-transitions/ (accessed 4 February 2016).

4. UN-Habitat (n.d.). Housing and slum upgrading. http://unhabitat.org /urban-themes/housing-slum-upgrading/ (accessed 4 February 2016).

5. Kenya, Government of (2014). National Slum Upgrading and Prevention Policy (KNSUPP). Nairobi, Kenya: Ministry of Land, Housing and Urban Development. 29 January.

6. Cities Alliance and Shack/Slum Dwellers International (2010). *Nairobi Slum Inventory.* http://citiesalliance.org/node/430 (accessed 3 Janaury 2014).

7. Obeng-Odoom, F. (2010) *The state of African cities 2010. Governance, inequality, and urban land markets.* United Nations Human Settlement Program. http://www.unhabitat.org/content.asp?cid=9141&catid=7&typeid=46 (accessed 20 December 2013).

8. African Population and Health Research Center. (2014). *Population and health dynamics in Nairobi's informal settlements: Report of the Nairobi Cross-Sectional Slums Survey (NCSS), 2012.* Nairobi, Kenya: APHRC.

9. Ibid.

10. Ibid.

11. Amendah, D.D., Buigut, S., & Mohamed, S. (2014). Coping strategies among urban poor: Evidence from Nairobi, Kenya. *PLoS One* 9(1):e83428. doi:10.1371/journal.pone.0083428.

12. Cummins, S., Curtis, S., Diez-Roux, A., & Macintyre, S. (2007). Understanding and representing "place" in health research: A relational approach. *Social Science and Medicine* 65(9):1825–38.

13. Corburn, J. (2009). *Toward the healthy city: People, places, and the politics of urban planning.* Cambridge, MA: MIT Press.

14. Macintyre, S., Ellaway, A., & Cummins, S. (2002). Place effects on health: How can we conceptualise, operationalise and measure them? *Social Science and Medicine* 55:125–39.

15. Agarwal, S. Satyavada, A. Patra, P., & Kumar, R. (2008). Strengthening functional community–provider linkages: Lessons from the Indore urban health programme. *Global Public Health: An International Journal for Research, Policy and Practice* 3(3):308–25. DOI: 10.1080/17441690701592957.

16. Burris, S., Hancock, T., Lin, V., & Herzog, A. (2007). Emerging strategies for healthy urban governance. *Journal of Urban Health* 84(1):154–63.

17. Weru, J. (2004). Community federations and city upgrading: The work of Pamoja Trust and Muungano in Kenya. *Environment and Urbanization* 16(1):47–62.

18. Muungano Support Trust (MuST) (2014). Investing in slum dwellers to tailor own solutions. https://muunganosupporttrust.wordpress.com (accessed 1 August 2015).

19. Shack/Slum Dwellers International (SDI). (2015). Kenyan SDI Alliance ramps up activities. http://sdinet.org/2015/11/the-kenya-sdi-alliance-ramps-up-activities/ (accessed 11 November 2015).

20. Coates, J., Swindale, A., & Bilinsky, P. (2007). Household Food Insecurity Access Scale (HFIAS) for measurement of food access: Indicator guide. http://www.fantaproject.org/monitoring-and-evaluation/household-food-insecurity-access-scale-hfias (accessed 29 June 2013).

21. Fox, S. (2013). The political economy of slums: Theory and evidence from Sub Saharan Africa. *World Development* 54:191-203.

22. K'Akumu, O.A., & Olima, W.H.A. (2007) The dynamics and implications of residential segregation in Nairobi. *Habitat International* 31(1):87–99.

23. Home, R. (1997). *Of planting and planning: The making of British colonial cities.* London: E. & F.N. Spon.

24. Achola, M.A. (2001). Colonial policy and urban health: The case of colonial Nairobi. *Azania: Archaeological Research in Africa* 36–37(1):119–37.

25. Obudho, R.A. (1997). Nairobi: National capital and regional hub. In Rakodi, C. (ed.). *The urban challenge in Africa.* Tokyo: UN University Press, 292–334.

26. Hake, A. (1977). *African metropolis: Nairobi's self-help city.* New York: St. Martin's Press.

27. Etherton, D., Jorgensen, N., Steele, R., & Mulili, M. (1971). *Mathare Valley: A case of uncontrolled settlement in Nairobi.* Housing Research and Development Unit, University of Nairobi.

28. Etherton et al. (1971), 49.

29. Wrong, M. (2009). It's our turn to eat: The story of a Kenyan whistle-blower. New York: Harper.

30. Syagga, P., Mitullah, W., & Karirah-Gitau, S. (2002). *A rapid economic appraisal of rents in slums and informal settlements.* Prepared for Government of Kenya and UN-Habitat Collaborative Nairobi Slum Upgrading Initiative.

31. Amnesty International. (2010). *Kenya: Insecurity and Indignity; Women's Experiences in the Slums of Nairobi, Kenya.* London: Amnesty International Publications. https://www.amnesty.org/en/documents/afr32/002/2010/en/ (last accessed 27 December 2015).

32. Cheng, J.J., Schuster-Wallace, C.J., Watt, S., Newbold, B.K., & Mente, A. (2012). An ecological quantification of the relationships between water,

sanitation and infant, child, and maternal mortality. *Environmental Health* 11(4). doi:10.1186/1476-069X-11-4.

33. Kenya National Bureau of Statistics (2010). *Kenya Demographic and Health Survey, 2008–09: Final Report.* http://www.measuredhs.com/pubs/pdf/FR229/FR229.pdf (accessed 22 May 2014).

34. Niehaus, M., Moore, S., Patrick, P., et al. (2002). Early childhood diarrhoea is associated with diminished cognitive function 4 to 7 years later in children in a northeast Brazilian shantytown. *American Journal of Tropical Hygiene and Medicine* 66:590–93.

35. Cheng et al. (2012).

36. Madise, N.J., et al. (2012). Are slum dwellers at heightened risk of HIV infection than other urban residents? *Health and Place* 18:1144–52.

37. West, B.S., Hirsch, J.S., & El-Sadr, W. (2012). HIV and H_2o: Tracing the connections between gender, water and HIV. *AIDS Behavior* 17:1675–82.

38. Freeman, M.C., Greene, L.E., Dreibelbis, R., Saboori, S., Muga, R., Brumback, B., & Rheingans, R. (2012). Assessing the impact of a school-based water treatment, hygiene and sanitation programme on pupil absence in Nyanza Province, Kenya: A cluster-randomized trial. *Tropical Medicine and International Health* 17:380–91.

39. Swart, E. (2012). Gender-based violence in a Kenyan slum: Creating local, woman-centered interventions. *Journal of Social Service Research* 38(4):427–38.

40. Water Services Trust Fund (WSTF). (2010). *Formalising water supply through partnerships: The Mathare-Kosovo model.* Nairobi, Kenya.

41. Munyao, T.M. (2013). *Implications of water supply and sanitation projects on the livelihoods of slum dwellers in Kenya: A case of Kosovo Village in Mathare Constituency, Nairobi County.* University of Nairobi, Nairobi, Kenya.

42. MuST and Shack/Slum Dwellers International (SDI) (2012). Mathare Zonal Plan, Nairobi, Kenya: Collaborative plan for informal settlement Upgrading. July. http://sdinet.org/wp-content/uploads/2015/04/Mathare_Zonal_Plan_25_06_2012_low_res-2.pdf (accessed 27 December 2015).

43. Amendah et al. (2014).

44. Emina et al. (2011).

45. Sheuya, S. (2008). Improving the health and lives of people living in slums. *Annals of the New York Academy of Sciences* 1136:298–306.

46. Harpham, T. (2009). Urban health in developing countries: What do we know and where do we go? *Health and Place* 15:107–16.

47. De Leeuw, E. (2011). Do healthy cities work? A logic of method for assessing impact and outcome of healthy cities. *Journal of Urban Health* 89:217–31 (226).

48. Lawrence, R. (2005). Building healthy cities: The World Health Organization perspective. In Galea, S., & Vlahov, D. (eds.). *Handbook of urban health: Populations, methods and practice.* New York: Springer, 479–501.

49. Rheingans, R., et al. (2012). *Estimating inequities in sanitation-related disease burden and estimating the potential impacts of pro-poor targeting.* London: SHARE. http://www.shareresearch.org/research/estimating-inequities-

sanitation-related-disease-burden-and-estimating-potential-impacts (accessed 27 December 2015).

50. Sommer, M., Kjellén, M., & Pensulo, C. (2013). Girls' and women's unmet needs for menstrual hygiene management (MHM): The interactions between MHM and sanitation systems in low-income countries. *Journal of Water, Sanitation and Hygiene for Development* 3(3):283–97. doi: 10.2166/washdev.2013.101.

51. Freeman, M.C., Greene, L.E., Dreibelbis, R., Saboori, S., Muga, R., Brumback, B., & Rheingans, R. (2012). Assessing the impact of a school-based water treatment, hygiene and sanitation programme on pupil absence in Nyanza Province, Kenya: A cluster-randomized trial. *Tropical Medicine and International Health* 17:380–91.

52. Madise et al. (2012).

53. Kenya, Government of (2010). The Constitution of Kenya. National Council for Law Reporting. https://www.kenyaembassy.com/pdfs/The%20Constitution%20of%20Kenya.pdf (last accessed 3 March 2014).

54. Kenya, Government of (2014), 15.

55. Kenya, Government of (2007). National environmental sanitation and hygiene policy. Nairobi, Kenya: Ministry of Healthhttp://www.waterfund.go.ke/sanitation/Downloads/2.%20National%20Environmental%20Sanitation%20Hygiene%20Policy.pdf (accessed 29 June 2015).

CHAPTER 11

Microsavings and Well-Being in a Nairobi Informal Settlement

JASON CORBURN, JANE WAIRUTU, JOSEPH KIMANI, BENSON OSUMBA, AND HEENA SHAH

In the slums of Nairobi, residents are saving small amounts of money every day to build both financial and social capital and improve their personal, family, and community health and well-being. Slum savings groups allow individuals a safe and secure way to save money when, as often happens, the poor are denied access to the formal banking system. Microsavings groups also act as a source of credit and loans for slum dwellers, providing an emergency safety net and allowing residents to plan for place-based improvements, including upgrading their housing, infrastructure, and economic and educational services. Savings groups organize the urban poor into a powerful social movement that delivers life-supporting physical and social infrastructure and also negotiates with the state to deliver the essential rights, services, and social programs that act as building blocks for a healthy community.

In this chapter, we explore how the savings groups affiliated with Muungano wa Wanavijiji, the federation of the urban poor in Kenya, might promote health among slum dwellers.[1] Muungano was founded in 1997 as an alliance of slum dwellers with support from Shack/Slum Dwellers International (SDI). An NGO, SDI is a global network of community-based organizations of the urban poor that originated in India but that now has a presence in thirty-three countries in Africa, Asia, and Latin America (see www.sdi.org). SDI comprises regional and national federations, or networks, of organizations led by the urban poor; these federations assist the national groups organize, survey, and map themselves, build place-based projects, and share experiences through international exchanges, all to improve living conditions and the social determinants of health.[2, 3]

Muungano is a movement of the urban poor formed by slum dwellers to address the challenges of forced eviction, with a keen interest in addressing tenure security and people's livelihoods in poor communities. The movement was and still is an avenue for resistance against the brutal evictions and land grabbing that were rampant from the mid-1990s to the early 2000s. In 2015, Muungano represented more than 64,200 slum dwellers in over three hundred informal settlements across Kenya.[4]

Muungano savings groups are networked into a national federation in which savings groups from different slums come together in settlement-wide, regional, and national coalitions to exchange experiences and strategies, engage in collective advocacy, and pool resources that provide collateral for loans from the formal banking system to buy land and secure land rights for the urban poor. In addition, the local and networked groups form partnerships with academics and NGOs to perform research and political work that can promote health, such as mapping community resources and hazards and using locally gathered data to negotiate with government and utility providers for improved services.[5] In contrast with more confrontational approaches, federations take negotiation and partnerships with state actors as their rallying strategy, using the to-scale "modeling" of community designs and "precedent setting" of pilot projects to highlight strategies created by local ingenuity. This practice of "coproduction" stems from the understanding that vulnerable groups are rarely effective when challenging state actors without also offering community-endorsed experimental solutions.[6] In addition, Muungano acknowledges that in most cases the organization is negotiating with a weak state that rarely has the capacity to innovate and propose solutions for slum dwellers. A key objective of savings groups is to pilot projects, show "proof of concept," and gain government support for a wider-scale implementation.[7]

Muungano facilitates health promotion in a number of ways. First, the group engages in everyday community organizing, primarily through the process of microsavings, and this builds a constituency for collective negotiations with the formal and informal providers of basic, life-supporting services such as water, sanitation, and electricity. A second entry point for health promotion in the work that savings groups such as Muungano do is mapping and documenting their living conditions, offering a more accurate contextual understanding of risks, hazards, and health-promoting opportunities in their communities. Third, the savings groups act as a collective, a network of urban poor across all of Kenya, that allows the community-level groups to combine voices with others and scale up their claims for health protection and human rights. This process is critical in health promotion since it can frame the health issues of the urban poor as part of the struggle for citizenship and governance—that is, the processes that determine which issues get on the political agenda, who participates in raising issues, what evidence is deemed credible, and who benefits from implemented decisions.[8] Yet, as we argue in this chapter, the processes through which slum dwellers' microsavings protect and promote health and well-being are not well documented. We offer detailed case studies from the villages of the Mathare slum in Nairobi, Kenya.

INVESTIGATING SAVINGS GROUPS IN MATHARE, NAIROBI

This chapter focuses on microsavings groups in the Mathare informal settlement of Nairobi, Kenya. It combines data from interviews with savings group participants and Muungano leaders, from focus group meetings in select villages, and from observations by outside researchers who attended village-scale meetings and selected regional and national Muungano network meetings between 2009 and 2013. The research protocol was approved by the University of California, Berkeley's institutional review board, and the names of all interviewees have been removed to protect their confidentiality. While the environmental, economic, and social dynamics in Mathare's thirteen villages differ, all the villages experience severely limited access to basic, life-supporting goods, such as clean drinking water, safe toilets, electricity, and secure housing (see previous chapters).

HOW MUUNGANO MICROSAVINGS GROUPS ARE ORGANIZED

Each Muungano savings group has six teams: advocacy, welfare, auditing, savings and loans, land and housing, and youth.[9] The Advocacy Team is responsible for mobilizing the broader community, conducting household enumerations (surveys of who lives in the community), and participating in negotiations with government and service providers. The Welfare Team is tasked with developing programs or projects that

TABLE 11.1 MATHARE SAVINGS GROUP VILLAGE PROFILES

	Bondeni (aka 3A)	Kiamutisya	Kosovo	Mabatini
Year est'd	2007	2007	2010	2007
No. of members (approx.)	100	200	100	260
% female active members	75	55	90	45
Women in leadership positions?	Yes	No	Yes	No
% of households using shared toilet	69	97	64	80
% reporting unreliable water	100	64	72	98
% unsatisfied with health care	87	44	41	77
% with monthly income <10,000 KSh	63	81	44	67
% report feeling insecure in village	86	67	70	75
% total population active in any community organization	36	65	72	82

support the well-being of members, such as providing insurance or funds for health emergencies. The Auditing Team is responsible for conducting training and reviewing all group records (minutes, accounts, etc.) at least once a month. The Savings and Loans Team collects daily savings, keeps records, and reviews and manages loans (applications, interests, payments). The Land and Housing Team facilitates the acquisition of land and seeks to secure tenure for members. The Youth Team organizes young people, develops their leadership skills, attaches them to elder mentor, and provides a forum for young people to share their concerns and obtain resources for projects such as recreation space and equipment for sports, music, and other activities.

HOW SLUM MICROSAVINGS CAN PROMOTE HEALTH

Microsavings members in Mathare shared many stories about how they had benefited from participation: receiving small loans for boosting their business, learning how to save, or gaining more information about community issues such as plans for evictions, pending developments, and the location of newly offered or better quality services. We divided the health-promoting benefits of savings group participation into five categories recognized as social determinants of health:

Economic security

Social capital

Gender empowerment

Neighborhood infrastructure (physical)

Political and legal recognition

ECONOMIC SECURITY

Income and financial security directly impact health by enabling individuals to access material resources necessary for survival. In slums such resources can include access to clean water and safe sanitation, adequate supply of nutritious food, and transportation to and from a job outside the community. Economic security can reduce stress, a known contributor to hypertension and related illnesses. Economic stability can have an indirect positive influence on health by allowing people to participate in social and cultural activities and to feel like they have greater control over their life circumstances, which can also reduce anxiety.

The Muungano savings structure provides guidelines for managing savings. Each group keeps strict records using daily savings books and retains a formal financial institution for auditing and accounting. At each meeting, the group's elected treasurer would update members as to the value of the account, deposits, and loans.

As savings groups discussed how to leverage their economic savings into land rights, housing improvements, and other life-supporting services, the conversations seemed to have a positive influence on some group members' health. According to one member: "Our planning for cooperative housing has me seeing a brighter future. I'm not worried as much about possible evictions or some land grab. We have hired architects, and students from the university are helping with legal issues. I am confident that this will be a safe and secure community soon."

In another savings group, women were using its financial capital to secure loans to pay their children's school fees and build a microenterprise. According to one woman in the savings group: "I took the loan for school fees when things were not so good. The good thing about Muungano is unlike a bank, this is your money, and they don't pressure you to pay back. My children are safe in school and now I do not worry about them having to miss days." Another woman noted, in a focus group conversation:

> I have a small market. For kale, by the second day they are turning yellow, so you get rid of those. For tomatoes, there are rats in my store. That is stress. I cannot refuse credits to my friends. So I have to get loans. These are my customers; I must adjust to their needs, 'cause I know eventually they will

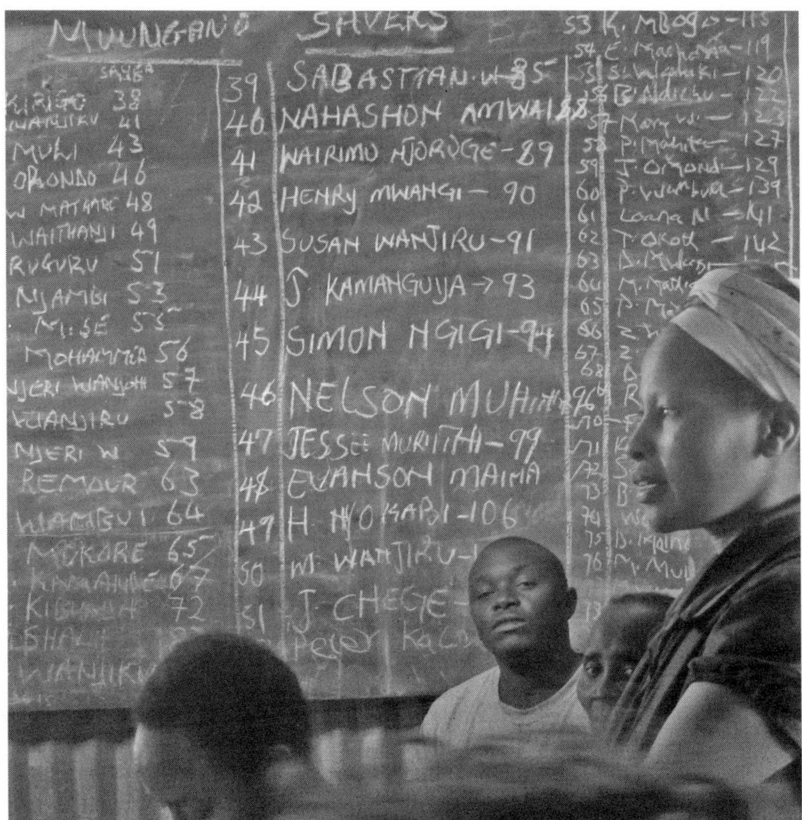

PHOTO 11.1. Woman leading savings group discussion. Savings are posted on the wall.

> pay. That is stress. Also, at the end of the month, there is house rent and school fees. By the 20th, you know, ulcers and stress are not friends. Sometimes I close shop for a week when the ulcers wake up. . . . When you don't have money, you cannot have good health. . . . When I have money, it's easier. When I needed 100 bob [KSh], Muungano was there. I buy more kale, spinach, carrots and sell hot food and make 1,000. Now I eat meat.

In all the groups, savings offered slum residents the security of knowing that there was always money available to meet essential needs, such as food, rent, or a health care bill. One woman recalled: "They wouldn't let me out of the hospital with my baby. I couldn't pay the fees. Can you imagine not being allowed to see your child, nurse your child, love your child, because you cannot pay? This system is unfair to the poor. I did not choose to have a hospital birth. Muungano paid my fees. I got my baby back and I am forever grateful." Other members described a fund established by Muungano for hospitalizations and deaths. If a member was hospitalized for five or more days, she or he received 10,000 KSh. If a child died, the member parent received 5,000 KSh, and if an adult in the member's household died, the member received 10,000 KSh. If a member died, the family received 20,000 KSh.

Economic security also improved access to and consistency of primary health care and use of medication for Muungano members. Mathare residents are generally faced with three health care options: (1) private clinics characterized by little or no wait times and a convenient location, but higher prices and inconsistent (often poor-quality) care; (2) NGO-operated clinics with higher-quality care at lower cost but long queues and highly specialized services, often offering care only to those with HIV/AIDS, TB, or other infectious diseases; and (3) government-run clinics with adequately trained staff, but with frequent medication shortages and long wait times. Mathare residents tend to prefer the private clinics and chemists, and the additional economic resources from savings group participation allows some slum dwellers greater options for health care. One Muungano member told us: "Proper health facilities are not easily accessible. You have to go far to get treatment and you may not have the resources to do so. The government facilities may also lack medicine. You may be sent to buy the medicine from a chemist. Muungano savings help me have resources to travel where I need to take my family for care, not worry about missing work or paying the chemist." Another Muungano member described her experiences with local health care: "I wash clothes for others to make money. It is casual labor, so I can't miss a day. Before I joined Muungano, I would never go to the clinic for a well-women visit. Now I do not miss appointments. I also used to have to go to the clinics where some lady would be selling her powdered milk or medications. Now I can afford those things with the help of Muungano."

Yet participation in a savings groups can also have a negative influence on health and contribute to stress, particularly when a member cannot pay back a loan. During one Mathare network meeting we heard that members were stealing money or overstating the price of goods they were requesting for emergency funds. Accountability seems to be an ongoing challenge and was managed differently across the four groups we observed. Some groups publicly shamed those who did not pay back their loans by listing the amount they owed on a blackboard in a community center. Other groups asked that members provide more "sweat equity" by working for the organization.

SOCIAL CAPITAL

The Kiswahili Muungano slogans *Nguvu yetu* (Unity, our strength) and *Habari ni nguvu* (Information is power) are the two mantras that open and close every Muungano meeting. Information sharing and community building constituted the second health-supporting function we found among the processes of the savings groups. Weekly village-level meetings served as a venue for sharing information, and Muungano regularly organized information sessions on health risks and how to avoid these hazards in the community. For example, Muungano members learned about water contamination and practices for sanitizing water before drinking it or using it for cooking. Other seminars focused on healthy eating and cooking. A third seminar centered on newborn care, particularly for single mothers.

The building of social capital was apparent to us during a seminar that Muungano organized on the history of their community. In this seminar, elders and historians described how land had been acquired in the community over time. Adults and youth shared family narratives and personal histories. In another seminar organized by Akiba Mashinani Trust, the fiscal agent for the local Muungano savings groups, slum dwellers learned about the value of their informal economy. One statistic that resonated with many slum dwellers was that 65 percent of the Kenyan GDP was generated by the "informal labor sector," meaning that they were valuable contributors to the economic health of the entire country. These seminars instilled in residents a sense of collective pride and self-worth and built trust.

The importance of social capital was strikingly apparent when savings group members discussed their responses to a recent spate of fires in the community. The fires had burned more than sixty shacks in Bondeni village. The members discussed what Muungano could do, and after the meeting the entire group went to visit the site of the fires. The group sent members to the Red Cross to secure clothing to support those who needed help. One community resident reflected on what had happened only days before: "My house burned down and there is nothing left. Now, whenever I see smoke, I worry because it reminds me. . . . I was already feeling stressed, but since my house burned down, I have had very high blood pressure. I now have to take pills every day. I pay 600 shillings every month for them. Either I take pills or buy sheet metal for my house. I don't know what to do." The Muungano group decided to call its regional network partners and ask for funds to help all those who had lost a home in rebuilding, whether they were members or not. In this case, the savings group facilitated a commitment to collective efficacy, since the group came together to offer support and assistance to the entire community.

Of course, community networks can also link people to knowledge and action that do not support health and well-being. In one instance we heard of, the Muungano savings groups within the same network were not sharing resources or building financial or social capital together. One member noted in a meeting:

> We also need to have unity among the groups themselves so that the entire network can be strengthened. A while back you would easily know what project each group was undertaking, even though you were not a member. We had unity as members of the various groups under the network, and we had the interests of each other at heart. Today, we don't even know what each one is doing. Some of the group reports presented at the network meetings each week are also inaccurate as they do not truly reflect what is on the ground.

Thus, savings groups must be in constant conversation within themselves and with one another to ensure accountability, honesty, and legitimacy. However, that groups become more independent may also be interpreted as a sign of a maturing and growing network, since it may now be more difficult for larger groups and broader networks to stay in constant communication and hold one another accountable. While there are continual challenges of building and maintaining social capital among microsavings groups in urban slums, being part of the collective seems to provide numerous health-protective benefits.

GENDER

A key inequality among the urban poor, especially prevalent in Nairobi's slums, is that between men and women. Women face greater barriers to social mobility, access to infrastructure services, and financial stability, as well as risks of violence.[10, 11] There is often an institutionalized gender bias against the education of female children in urban slums. In Mathare, women bear the brunt of inadequate infrastructure provision as they have to spend time on water collection, waste disposal, and securing fuel for cooking. In Mathare, girls are expected to collect water even if it means missing school. A lack of adequate toilets at schools for girls contributes to their missing school days, especially during menstruation. These inequities early in life can create barriers for slum women to being healthy over their entire lifetimes.[12]

We found that savings groups did not eliminate gender inequities, but did mitigate some of them and reframe the role for women in the social hierarchy. Women formed a majority of savings group members in Muungano and often assumed leadership roles in the organization. As one woman from a savings group said: "In many families, the women suffer. But in the group, you learn 'Oh, so I can claim my rights, as a woman, my children's rights.' Before the group, I was just an ordinary woman. But now I know things can be done to move forward." Women in Muungano savings groups participated in the different teams, took leadership roles in community enumerations, and facilitated group meetings. As another woman recalled:

> Before Muungano my husband controlled all our money, and when he decided to drink it away, it was gone. I had no control. When I joined and we started to save, I kept track of things. He didn't take it too seriously. I learned to manage our money and had more confidence to make decisions. I started speaking out in meetings. I was unsure at first, but then I was asked to be a leader. Now we've saved enough to improve our structure and this wouldn't have happened if I didn't keep us involved.

She continued:

> I joined a march to support the Mabatini group to protect them against a land grabber. I was scared but found support from other women that joined. I stood there . . . I stood there wondering what to do next [laughs], but I found myself doing it and I was so happy. Later, I traveled to Tanzania to meet another slum savings group organized by SDI. Imagine, me traveling! I never thought anyone would value what I had to offer.

Muungano women also organized meetings that addressed their concerns. For example, when it became clear that many young women were doing sex work, one village's savings group organized meetings just for young women and single mothers. During a meeting facilitated by women leaders from Muungano, the group learned that child care was a significant issue for the single mothers and often forced them into sex work at night. As one woman from Muungano recalled: "During that meeting, we were surprised that child care was such a big issue. We though most women share this. Those young girls with small babies turned to sex work at night when their babies were asleep. This of course put them at risk for violence and disease, but they did what they had to feed their children." One outcome of this meeting was that Muungano used its resources and network to dedicate a structure in the community as a child care center and organize a child care cooperative in which women would share responsibilities. Payment for child care work was subsidized by the local Muungano savings group and national federation resources. The benefit of this project extended beyond just women with young children, as one non-savings-group resident noted: "Even though my children are not young enough so as to be under the day care center, they are still cared for well. It could be raining after school. They will not be left out in the rain. Or I may get back late. I will find them at the day care center that the group runs." Child care is critical for slum dwellers, since children of the urban poor have a higher risk of fatal disease than those who are not poor, and since slum children under one year of age with working mothers are twice as likely to get sick as those whose mothers do not work. In this case, child care can help protect the health of both mothers (by reducing the necessity for sex work at night) and children (by offering them consistent food and a safe play space).

During another women-only meeting organized by Muungano, community members shared their experiences with domestic violence, a subject that they rarely discussed openly.[13] Some women reported arguing with men they had seen beating their wives, but never reporting this to the police. As one woman noted, Muungano was playing an active role in reducing domestic violence:

> If you tell the police, they will just tell you to go home and sort it out. The members came together and discussed solutions, . . . encouraging men to get help for alcoholism, buying new locks for one's door, . . . but these were not enough. We learned about our rights and organizations that protected women. In Mathare, people don't know about rights; they take their chief like he's the end of the road. . . . [Y]ou know about the administration, how it works? . . . Now I know it's not a must [that] you use the chief for justice. You can go to the police station. You can go to the DO [district officer] if the chief cannot hear you, because sometimes they intimidate people.

Yet others noted that it wasn't easy to overcome entrenched accepted violence against women in the slums. One woman noted: "There are challenges to knowing your rights. You find some husbands—because we know the truth—you find some husbands beat their wives because they come to tell them about women's rights. You find that man says you don't deserve to tell me [about your rights]. So those challenges are there. And you find even the family you are married to doesn't understand or care."

Savings group participation has the potential to enhance women's standing and economic resources in slums. However, these health-promoting benefits do not come easily and may also exact a social cost for some women.

PHYSICAL ASSETS FOR COMMUNITY HEALTH

Perhaps the most tangible health benefits produced by the savings group are improved housing, water access, secure toilets, electricity connections, and other life-supporting infrastructure. In the absence of the state, civil society groups in Nairobi's slums are often empowered through financing from international organizations to design, build, and manage new physical infrastructure. The savings groups facilitate the complex processes of planning, negotiating, constructing, and managing this infrastructure.

We learned from one Muungano savings group that it had designed a water reticulation system with the help of local universities, and secured financing for this project from the local water utility.[14] The water project delivered clean piped water from a municipal trunk line to a number of public kiosks located strategically through the village and offered residents the opportunity to purchase a water meter that would connect water directly to their home. This was the first time a slum water project had delivered both public water and in-home water connections to a slum in Nairobi. The initiative, now known as the Kosovo-Mathare water project, was the result of the ingenuity of the Muungano savings group. As we heard from an NGO leader outside Mathare:

> The water project in Kosovo was something different. They designed that with the universities and used the design to get the Athi Water Board to pay for the project. That is where it would usually end. But Muungano negotiated a labor agreement to ensure local people—not just savings group members—but youth and others, got paid for the labor. They also insisted on the kiosks for everyone and the in-home connections.

The water had to be paid for and this is also where the savings group played an important role. According to one Muungano member:

> The savings group established a model where members would pay 10 percent of the initial cost of the water meter and Muungano would pay the water company the rest. The member would pay back the cost of the meter through small payments every month. This allowed hundreds of families to get a meter. Muungano also recognized that there are a lot of tenants here. They don't want to pay for anything permanent. So they also set up a system to subsidize payments for water collected at the kiosks. This helped the poorest and renters take advantage of the new water project.

PHOTO 11.2. A Muungano meeting devoted to planning a water project.

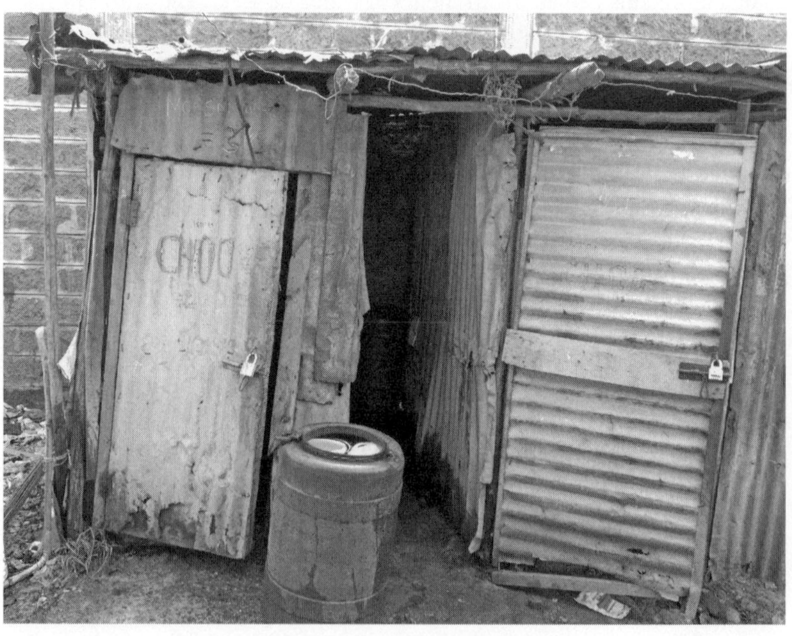

PHOTO 11.3. Typical toilet in Mathare before upgrading.

In another Mathare village, the Muungano group used collective savings to design and build a new public ablution block with a water tank. The savings group negotiated with the community and the Nairobi City Council to obtain a space on which to build the facility and raised the necessary capital. The new building was constructed using residents' labor, ensuring all community members were invested in its success. The facility has multiple toilets, washing stalls or showers, lights for twenty-four-hour use, locks on the doors, and a small space for growing vegetables in sacks. Like the water project in Kosovo, the toilet-shower block is managed and maintained by Muungano, which employs members to collect per-use fees from residents that go toward maintenance.

The members described how things had changed in Mabatini since the construction of the ablution block. One member recalled during a focus group:

> We say that in our area there weren't public toilets and also when people passed by, you found men urinating everywhere because they have no place to stand. Women used cans or dirty toilets where there was no privacy. I remember one night it was dark but only 7 P.M. when I had gotten to the latrine. A group of four young men confronted me. I recognized them but that didn't matter. They hit me. I tried to shout as they undressed me. One said I should not be out at that time. They raped me. No one could hear my shouting. I haven't used a latrine since. Now I feel safer with the new toilets.

The savings groups also regularly organized days for cleaning up trash and unclogging informal drains, practices that can have positive community health impacts by reducing exposure to disease-causing pathogens and by preventing injuries.

POLITICAL POWER

For Nairobi's slums dwellers, a persistent political question is why some instances of informality are designated as illegal by the government and slum dwellers criminalized while other land areas, service provision, and labor practices are protected and "formalized," meaning they enjoy state protection? We observed savings groups acting not only to negotiate with the state for services, as described above, but also to challenge the state when it denies them life-supporting services.

In the first case, the United Nations Environment Program (UNEP) was launching its Nairobi River cleanup project in 2008. Two tributaries of the Nairobi River, the Mathare and Gitathuru Rivers, run through Mathare. The UNEP plan, endorsed by the Kenyan National Environmental

Management Authority (NEMA), was to enforce a land use law that required a 30-meter riparian setback from all river banks in which no development could occur. The river cleanup project was slated to start in Nairobi's slums, and since every village in Mathare is adjacent to one of the two tributaries, many homes and business were going to be impacted by this riparian buffer. According to one Muungano researcher: "The slum dwellers were being blamed for pollution in the river and this arbitrary buffer 60 meters in total was the crass solution. We acquired aerial photos and digitized these maps. We put this into a geographic information system (GIS) to measure the 30 meters from each riverbank. Savings group members field-validated our maps with on-the-ground data checking. We described the uses of every structure in the village that would be impacted by the riparian buffer" (see map 11.1).

The Muungano researchers estimated that hundreds of homes and tens of businesses, schools, places of worship, community centers, and ablution blocks would be razed as part of the government-UNEP plan. They estimated that more than 50,000 people would be displaced. A Muungano member from Kosovo recalled: "We held emergency meetings to share the findings and maps. While everyone knew that living near the river was not as desirable as on the upper side, since it is prone to flood, we did not know how big an impact this would have."

As Muungano savings groups and others met to devise a strategy, the Nairobi Water Company shut off the main line serving all of the Mathare villages along Thika Highway. Tens of thousands of people were left without access to clean water. The results were tragic, according to a Muungano member: "Within a day of the water shutoff, people were getting sick. Going to hospital. Hundreds of people seemed to need medical attention. Can't remember anyone whose health wasn't quickly worsened."

Residents took to the streets and demanded the water be turned back on. They protested along Thika Highway, stopping traffic to gain media attention. The Muungano group met and decided to march their members to the Nairobi City Council and demand a meeting. They reached the city council with a few hundred Mathare residents, including both savings group members and other concerned residents. Jane Weru, the director of the NGO Pamoja Trust, which supported research and advocacy for the Muungano network, demanded and was allowed to meet with city council leaders. With savings group members by her side, she demanded that the water be turned back on and that the river project not displace hundreds of slum dwellers. According to Weru:

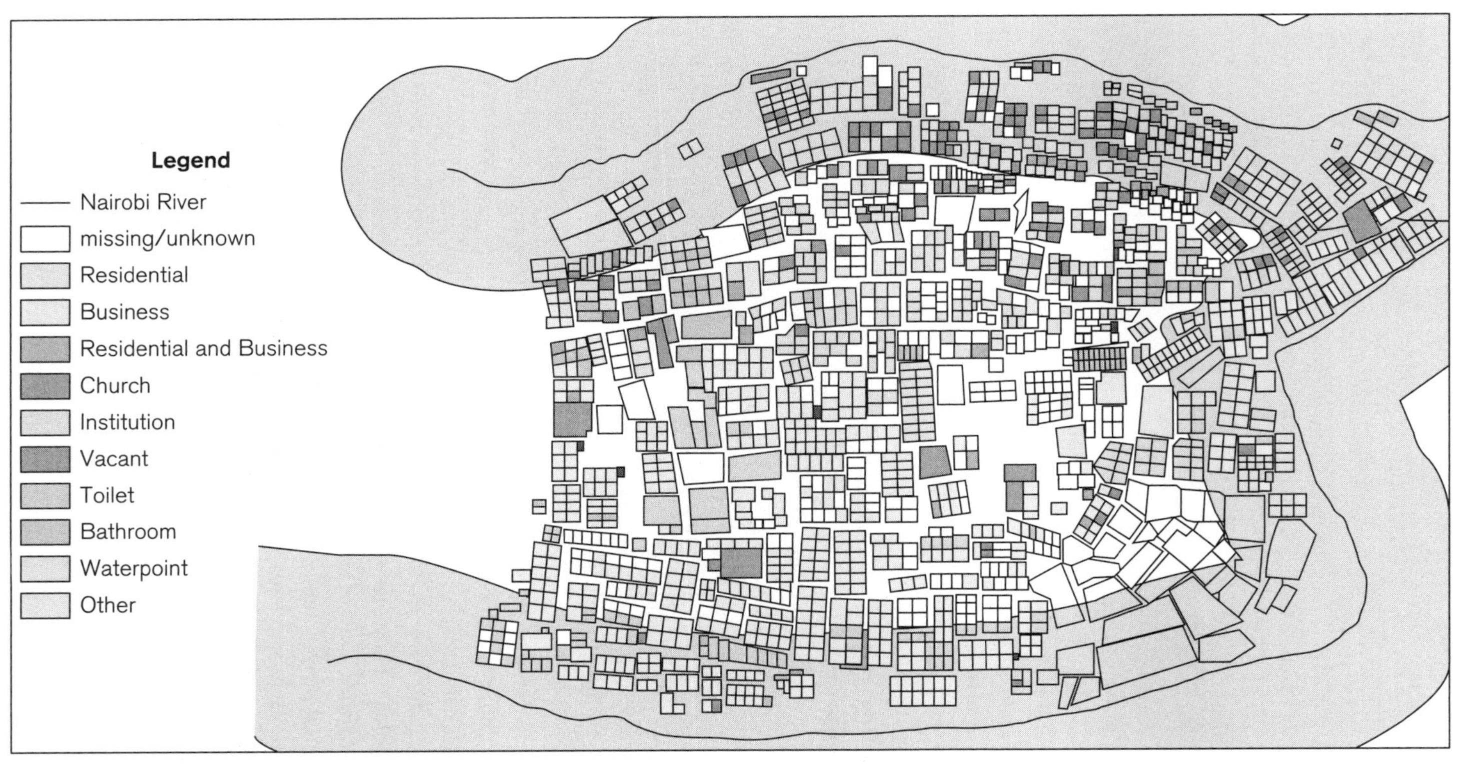

MAP 11.1. Structures in Mathare Village 4B impacted by proposed 30-meter riparian zone.

> We wanted the right to water and to remain. The council only agreed if we conceded to develop community-upgrading plans that would address the waste dumping into the river. Slum dwellers might have been dumping their waste into nearby rivers, but it was because of poverty and lack of infrastructure and rubbish collection. There were many other, larger polluters dumping into the river. We agreed to work on the plans so we could get the water turned back on.

The savings group acted to quickly mobilize residents and offered them negotiating power. In this case, the state recognized the slum dwellers' right to basic services and to remain in place. As of 2014, the riparian zone still had not been enforced in Mathare. However, Muungano had completed at least four village-scale upgrade plans and a settlement-wide improvement plan called the Mathare Zonal Plan.[15]

Many slum dwellers in Mathare are forced to splice into overhead electricity wires that run adjacent to the community and run their own wire from the pole to their home for power. These are generally called informal connections by slum dwellers and illegal connections by the power company. Many of these connections are controlled by gangs in Mathare that extort a high price for slum dwellers to have electricity in their homes. In 2011–12, the police started arriving in Mathare at night to arrest anyone who had a light on. According to one Kosovo resident: "It was easy for them to find us, but we were surprised by the violence. If you resisted, some were shot or beaten. Many were taken away . . . for having a light bulb. Can you imagine? You just didn't know if you would be next." After a few weeks of what some described as "living in fear of terror," the savings groups organized to discuss how they could respond. They contacted the Kenya Power and Lighting Company (KPLC) to ask the reason for the arrests, but they did not get an explanation. A Muungano member observed: "The company never comes in here without police. They say when we tap into the power lines, we overload the transformer. They blame slum dwellers for the fires that come from these informal power lines. They also blame their lost revenue on us."

The savings groups arranged to meet with the power company and a local gang. They assured the company that workers would be safe when they came into the community. They convinced the gang that the power company was intent on shutting off the electricity, so the gang's business was about to disappear. Muungano negotiated a master power meter system with the KPLC whereby select power poles throughout the community would receive new transformers. The master meters would have the capacity to allow individual households to safely connect an electric cable to their homes. The cables would be supplied by the company and installed by Muungano members trained by electricians. They would remain secured and high on the poles to prevent vandalism. Muungano negotiated a fixed payment per month for constant power to the master meters. After the weeks-long negotiation, the police stopped coming and arresting residents for using power. While gangs still control electricity for some slum dwellers, many others are benefiting from the master meter concept.

Microsavings have also supported groups fighting eviction and helped them secure the legal right to remain. Land titling in slums is notoriously complicated, with multiple individuals or groups coming forward to claim the same plot of land. In some cases, village chiefs "sell" to new residents land to which they have no rightful claim. The Muungano network and its resources provide support to local groups to fight eviction claims. We observed the Mabatini savings group using the Muungano network to arrange meetings with the Ministry of Lands, the Nairobi City Council, and various courts to prevent a land grab and eviction. While the case remains open, the seemingly powerless urban poor, organized through the savings group, gained a voice and access to those with power in government and the judicial system.

Securing services and land rights can benefit health. Whereas insecure tenure is associated with injuries, respiratory problems, infectious diseases, and mental health problems, secure tenure can pave the way for improved health. Those who own their own houses enjoy better health than those who do not. Secure tenure can promote a sense of security, control, continuity, and attachment. Preventing displacement also has positive health impacts as the poor can avoid economic hardships, utilize supportive social and other networks, and avoid homelessness.

SAVINGS GROUPS ARE NO PANACEA

As in any city where interest groups jockey for power, control, and money, the same happens in Mathare. When the savings groups and their members gain, Muungano is criticized by those who lose, including slum landlords, structure owners, and the gangs that tend to control most of the services in the community. One savings group member told us that after the water project in Kosovo, the "water vendors looked at us like the enemy." Other Muungano members admitted that others in the community, particularly new arrivals and the poorest of the poor, suspect that the group is there just to take people's land. One member noted: "We are all struggling, but some find the time to fight their neighbors. When we built

TABLE 11.2 SLUM MICROSAVINGS AND THE SOCIAL DETERMINANTS OF HEALTH

Social determinant of health	Role of microsavings groups
Economic	
Inadequate and unstable income	Accumulate savings and/or access loans
Nonexistent/limited livelihood opportunities	Create new employment opportunities and/or support existing businesses
Limited/nonexistent safety net	Provide safety net and emergency funds
Inadequate, unstable, or risky asset base	Help build up an asset base
Physical	
Poor quality and insecure, hazardous, and overcrowded housing	Designs and builds in situ housing
Inadequate infrastructure for basic services (sanitation pipes, roads, lights, footpaths, water points, toilets, etc.)	Carry out enumeration and mapping that make invisible suffering visible to all; quantify the extent of need and living conditions; help slum dwellers negotiate with state for services; pilot own infrastructure construction projects
Social	
Inadequate provision of social services (water, health clinics, policing, waste disposal, etc.)	Help urban poor negotiate with local authorities and engage in long-term processes to bring services into communities
Gender inequality	Majority of savers and leaders are women; projects improve social, economic, and safety conditions for girls and women.
Political	
Inadequate protection through law of poorer groups	Federation negotiates for better social protections through advocacy aimed at government policies
Lack of land tenure, threat of eviction	Equip groups with knowledge of rules of how to fight evictions
Poorer groups' voicelessness and powerlessness	Network of savings groups builds collective power, amplifies voice of the urban poor, and negotiates with government.

the toilets, some said, 'Next time you'll take our land.' They don't see it as a positive thing, but we struggle, we struggle. They know the importance of water. They are paid by the people who own those shacks, so they block you from building." Of course, the microsavings initiative itself is limited in its ability to raise significant amounts of capital that might radically transform urban slums. The strength of microsavings groups comes, instead, from organizing, collective priority setting, and leveraging small amounts of financial capital but large amounts of social capital to gain additional fiscal resources from external donors and political commitments from government agencies.

This chapter outlines the multiple and complex ways microsavings can support health and protect slum dwellers. While they are no panacea, we found savings groups to be an essential life-support system in Mathare.

NOTES

1. Weru J. (2004). Community federations and city upgrading: The work of Pamoja Trust and Muungano in Kenya. *Environ Urban* 16(1):47–62.

2. Shack/Slum Dwellers International (n.d.). SDI's practices for change. http://sdinet.org/about-us/sdis-practices-for-change/ (accessed February 4, 2015).

3. World Health Organization (n.d.). Social determinants of health. www.who.int/social_determinants/sdh_definition/en/ (accessed July 30, 2014).

4. Mitlin, D., Satterthwaite, D., & Bartlett, S. (2011). *Capital, capacities and collaboration : The multiple roles of community savings in addressing urban poverty*. Human Settlements Working Paper 34. London: International Institute of Environment and Development (IIED).

5. Karanja, I. (2010). An enumeration and mapping of informal settlements in Kisumu, Kenya, implemented by their inhabitants. *Environ Urban* 22(1):217–39.

6. Mitlin, D. (2008). With and beyond the state: Co-production as a route to political influence, power and transformation for grassroots organizations. *Environ Urban* 20(2):339–60. doi:10.1177/0956247808096117.

7. D'Cruz, C., & Mudimu, P. (2013). Community savings that mobilize federations, build women's leadership and support slum upgrading. *Environ Urban* 25(1):31–45. doi:10.1177/0956247812471616.

8. Barten, F., Akerman, M., Becker, D., Friel, S., Hancock, T., Mwatsama, M., Rice, M., Sheuya, S., & Stern, R. (2011). Rights, knowledge, and governance for improved health equity in urban settings. *Journal of Urban Health* 88(5). doi:10.1007/s11524-011-9608-z.

9. Muungano wa Wanavijiji. (2012). Constitution of the Federation of Slum Dwellers of Kenya. Nairobi, Kenya: Muungano Support Trust.

10. Women's UN Report Network (2008). Women, slums and urbanisation: Examining the causes and consequences. Geneva: Centre on Housing Rights and Evictions (COHRE).

11. McIlwaine, C. (2013). Urbanisation and gender-based violence: Exploring the paradoxes in the Global South. *Environ Urban,* 25(1):65–79.

12. Magadi, M. (2004). Maternal and child health among the urban poor in Nairobi, Kenya. *African Population Studies* 19(2):179–98.

13. Amnesty International (2010). *Insecurity and indignity: Women's experiences in the slums of Nairobi, Kenya*. London: Amnesty International.

14. Water Services Trust Fund (2010). Formalising water supply through partnerships: The Mathare-Kosovo water model. Nairobi, Kenya: Water Services Trust Fund.

15. Muungano Support Trust, Shack/Slum Dwellers International, & University of Nairobi, & University of California, Berkeley (2012). Mathare Zonal Plan: Collaborative Planning for Informal Settlement Upgrading. http://sdinet.org/wp-content/uploads/2015/04/Mathare_Zonal_Plan_25_06_2012_low_res-2.pdf (accessed December 28, 2015).

PART IV

Understanding Slum Health in Urban India

In part IV, we turn to India and the challenges faced in one of the world's largest and fastest-growing economies. India's 2010 census reported about 93 million slum dwellers, and about 21 percent of the total urban population in India lives in slums. A substantial proportion of the slum population consists of squatters, migrant colonies, pavement dwellers, families living on construction sites, street children, and other vulnerable populations. Chapter 12 highlights the health inequities experienced by the urban poor in India. Combining data on economic inequality, housing and living conditions, and food insecurity and from the National Family Health Survey (NFHS), this chapter offers an integrated and relational view of health determinants and outcomes facing the urban poor in India. While there are clear data gaps, this chapter sets the stage for understanding opportunities for intervention. It also discusses the ambitions of public policies such as the National Urban Health Mission and Rajiv Awas Yojana. These policies seek to improve the health of the urban poor by improving living conditions and improving access to health facilities while also strengthening the existing capacity of health services in urban poor areas.

Chapter 13 explores the specific impacts of infrastructure improvements on slum health. It examines how basic infrastructure improvement in water supply and sanitation in an urban slum in Ahmedabad, India, affected the incidence of waterborne illness. Using health insurance

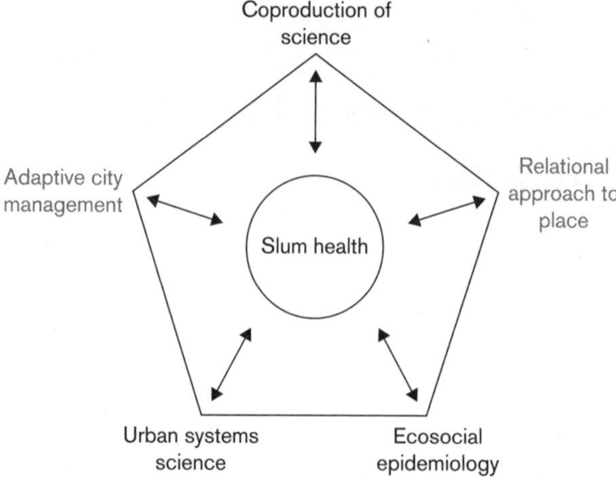

Dimensions of slum health explored in the case of Ahmedabad, India.

claims as a proxy for illness incidence, the authors discuss the strengths and weaknesses of this approach for studying slum health in India. Changes in the frequency of waterborne disease–related illness episodes relative to other illnesses are analyzed with respect to the slum-upgrading intervention. The results are impressive. The study found that slum upgrading reduced any particular resident's likelihood of claiming for waterborne illness from 32 percent to 14 percent and, mosquito-related illnesses are excluded, from 25 percent to 10 percent. This study shows that upgrades in slum household infrastructure can lead to improved health outcomes.

Equally important, chapter 13 also explores the coproduction processes of slum upgrading that contribute to health improvements. Slum upgrading in Ahmedabad is the result of a partnership involving target communities and their representative community-based organizations, the Ahmedabad Municipal Corporation, local partnering nongovernmental organizations, and participating private-sector organizations and charitable trusts. This complex mixture of expertise includes such groups as the Self-Employed Women's Association (SEWA), the Mahila SEWA Housing Trust, and SEWA's micro-insurance cooperative. As in Nairobi, Kenya, microsavings and financial institutions that serve the urban poor are critical aspects of slum health promotion in India.

Taken together, these two chapters offer detailed data on the challenges of slum health in urban India, specific strategies for improving slum health, and an evaluation of one infrastructure intervention on slum health. They reveal strategies for addressing the multiple dimensions of slum health.

CHAPTER 12

Health Disparities in Urban India

SIDDHARTH AGARWAL

Effective policies for poverty reduction clearly depend on the availability of good data on who is poor and the nature of their deprivation. The data must be collected and analyzed not only at the national level but also at the state and the local, rural or urban level.

Many comparisons of health-related deprivation are made between rural and urban areas, but far less attention has been given to identifying the range of deprivation related to health, nutrition, and well-being within urban populations. India's urban population in 2001 was 286 million (the second-largest national urban population in the world). In 2011, this number reached 377 million.[1] Between 1981 and 2001, the number of Indian cities with more than 1 million inhabitants grew from twelve to thirty-five; in 2009, this number was expected to reach fifty by 2015.[2] However, according to India's 2011 census data, there were already fifty-three cities that met the 1 million–inhabitant criteria.[3] The population growth rate for India between 2001 and 2011 was 17.64 percent, and while the rural population grew over the decade by 12.18 percent, the urban population grew by 31.8 percent. The year 2011 marked the first since Independence that total urban population grew more, in absolute numbers, than total rural population.[4] Unless there is an unexpected reversal of the urban growth the country is witnessing, India's urban population is estimated to be 442.75 million in 2016 (midway between the most recent and the following census), 508.39 million in 2021, and 685.38 million in 2031.[5] The United Nations estimates that 875 million people will live in Indian cities and towns by 2050.[6] The pace and scale of metamorphoses in human habitation is immense. This urban population increase and the increase in the number and population size of cities and towns is attributable to expansion of city limits, reclassification of erstwhile rural areas as urban, and movement of several million citizens to cities and towns. This scenario, the associated issues of equitable distribution of services in urban areas and the extent of deprived populations laboring at very low wages all contribute to the rich growing richer and present an ongoing, increasingly pressing crisis. Given the country's decades-old track record of slow, weak implementation, national, state, and city governments will have to develop policies capable of addressing the demographic and economic situation predicted for ten years in the future. Along with planning and formulating policies that can address likely future scenarios, there is a need for urgent and expeditious implementation.

The scale of urban deprivation in India can be estimated using a variety of data sets, four of which are analyzed below.

The first data set is based on average monthly per capita expenditure (MPCE), a metric that the Tendulkar Committee used for arriving at official poverty lines for the Planning Commission in 2009. The Tendulkar Committee's 2009 Report of the Expert Group to Review the Methodology for Estimation of Poverty used 2004–5 National Sample Survey (NSS) data to determine a poverty line of 578.8 Indian rupees (INR) MCPE in 2005. The Tendulkar Committee also used 1993–94 NSS data as a preliminary exercise to calculate poverty rates that could be compared to the 2005 numbers.[7] The Planning Commission's 2011–12 Press Note on Poverty Estimates calculated an updated poverty line of INR 1,000 MCPE using the detailed analysis and methodology outlined in the 2009 Tendulkar Committee report. Evaluated together, these reports illustrate a clear, unambiguous trend. The Tendulkar Committee's 2009 report revealed that in 1994, 31.8 percent of India's urban population was below the poverty line, amounting to 74.5 million urban poor residents, and in 2005, urban poverty was at 25.4 percent, amounting to 80.8 million urban poor residents. The Planning Commission's 2012 press note revealed an urban poverty rate of 13.7 percent, amounting to 53 million urban poor residents. Thus, it would appear that between 1994 and 2005, although urban poverty increased in absolute numbers, it decreased as a proportion of the urban population, and between 2005 and 2012, it decreased significantly, both absolutely and relatively, to below 1994 levels. These results allow a very clear conclusion to be drawn: urban poverty rates have not only been slowing down since 1994, they have in fact fallen drastically.

One fundamental concern with these urban poverty figures is that they are misleading because they adopt what C.P. Chandrasekhar calls a "minimalist notion of survival."[8] According to the World Bank, US$2/day represents the international median poverty line across developing nations, while US$1.25/day represents extreme poverty.[9] India's INR 1,000 MPCE poverty line converts roughly to US$0.57/day (INR 33/day), which, when crudely compared, is significantly lower than the World Bank's standard for extreme poverty. It is important to acknowledge that the World Bank's methodology is not strictly comparable to the MPCE used by the Planning Commission. Yet it is an international consensus method used to estimate poverty for global comparisons, and the stark contrast between India's poverty line and the World Bank's is notable. The World Bank estimated that in 2010, 57.59 percent of India's urban population was living below the US$2/day threshold, and 28.93 percent of the urban population was living below US$1.25/day.[10] If we compare these rates to the Planning Commission's 2012 numbers, we find that the World Bank's urban extreme poverty rate was more than double the government of India's below–poverty line rate. It is safe to say that India's incidence of urban poverty did not experience so significant a drop in merely two years, which suggests that the two estimations are irreconcilable. Illustratively, if we consider the Delhi National Capital Region, Greater Mumbai, Bangalore, the poverty line for daily per capita consumption expenditure of less than Rs 28 would not be sufficient to enable a person to use the public transport system from one end of the city to the other, let alone providing for food, shelter, clothing, health care, education of children, and all other necessary items of consumption. Thus, in adopting a "minimalist notion" of what it takes to survive, the Indian government has adopted a maximalist definition of poverty in the sense that in order to qualify as being poor in India, one must be in the furthest depths of poverty and vulnerability by most of the world's standards. This facilitates the "poor" in developing the capacity to survive despite sleeping hungry!

The UNDP's Multidimensional Poverty Index (MPI) also suggests that India's numbers are underestimates. The MPI takes into account several forms of deprivation, such as poor health, lack of education, inadequate living standard, lack of income (as one of several factors considered), social exclusion, disempowerment, poor quality of work, and lack of security from exploitation and violence. It assesses three vital dimensions of poverty—education, health, and living standard—through ten indicators and provides both the extent and nature of simultaneous deprivations people are facing. The latest MPI analysis put the multidimensional poverty at 53.7 percent in India—or more than 650 million poor people.

Another, more important concern is that the Tendulkar Committee's poverty line is only a one-dimensional analysis of deprivation and vulnerability in India as it only focuses on expenditures as a measure of poverty. This single-indicator approach excludes a number of additional factors influencing health, nutrition, well-being, and prosperity.

The second data set for measuring the scale of urban deprivation in India is based on housing conditions, specifically, the proportion of the population living versus not living in slums. This metric depends on accurate and complete surveys of all vulnerable populations within an urban area, as well as a comprehensive definition for what a slum is.

The Census of India defines a slum as "a compact settlement of at least 20 households with a collection of poorly built tenements, mostly of [a] temporary nature, crowded together usually with inadequate sanitary and drinking water facilities in unhygienic conditions." This definition excludes a number of smaller settlements that would otherwise be characterized as slums; the Pranab Sen committee has stated that the threshold should be 20 households.[11] But even using the census definition, official statistics on the proportion of the population living in slums are known to be inaccurate for many cities in India because they do not include unaccounted-for and unrecognized informal settlements and people residing in poor-quality housing in inner-city areas, on construction sites, in urban fringe areas, or on pavements.[12]

As reported by the *Times of India* of October 12, 2013, the 2011 census reported the presence of slums only in what it called "statutory towns," meaning towns governed by a municipal body.[13] Of the 7,933 towns included in the census, 4,041 were considered statutory, resulting in the exclusion of well more than 3,000 towns from slum assessment.[14] Furthermore, the census reported the presence of slums in only 63 percent of the statutory towns (2,543 towns), which itself suggests some significant errors in evaluating slum existence.[15]

Census 2001 estimated that 49 percent of Mumbai's population lived in slums.[16] In 2006, it was estimated that one hundred to three hundred new families come to Mumbai every day.[17] Most end up in slum colonies, where small rooms are erected to house them in often creative ways, or they find themselves in shanties along the nearest available footpath or next to a railway track if space is available. Furthermore, populations already living in the slums, on pavements, and in chawls of Mumbai have continued to increase because of natural growth. Nevertheless, Census 2011 reported that Greater Mumbai has a slum population of 5,206,473. This census data are inconsistent with other figures. According to Jan Nijman, in 2008 over 50 percent of Mumbai's 12 million people lived in slums.[18] The Municipal Corporation of Greater Mumbai released data that corroborates this figure, reporting that in 2011 Mumbai had a slum population of 6.5 million, or roughly 52 percent of the total population of about 12.5 million.[19] Given this apparent consensus, the Census 2011 slum population figure is very likely an underestimate.

The 2011 census estimated an urban slum population in Delhi of 1.79 million,[20] which is 10.7 percent of Delhi's 2011 census-reported population.[21] Meanwhile, the Office of the Registrar General and Census Commissioner reported that in 2011, 14.6 percent of Delhi households were located in slums.[22] However, in the 2005–6 Economic Survey of Delhi, what would normally be considered slums by Census of India standards were divided into a number of settlement categories including *jhuggijhopri* (JJ) clusters (squatter settlements),[23] designated slum areas, unauthorized colonies, and JJ resettlement colonies.[24] According to the Economic Survey of Delhi (published by the Delhi government's Planning Department), these settlements collectively accounted for 51.9 percent of Delhi's total estimated population.[25] The 2012–13 Economic Survey of Delhi, on the other hand, equated slums with *jhuggijhopri* clusters (see chapter 14, section 8.1), but did not feature a similar breakdown of housing settlements in Delhi; instead, it cited figures from the Delhi Urban Shelter Improvement Board estimating that in 2010, there were roughly 2 million slum dwellers in Delhi, amounting to roughly 12 percent of Delhi's 2011 census-reported population.[26] These discrepancies would suggest an almost 40 percent reduction in the slum population of Delhi within a span of seven years. Meanwhile in 2012, the *Times of India* reported, "In a note filed before the Supreme Court on management of municipal solid waste, the capital's civic bodies said, 'About 49 percent of the total population of Delhi lives in slum areas, unauthorized colonies and about 860 jhuggi-jhonpri clusters with 420,000 jhuggies.'"[27] These figures likely do not account for the additional 100,000 people who are homeless and reside on pavements, under bridges, and by the roadside, many of whom are rickshaw pullers and casual workers.[28]

Taking the Census of India's definition of a slum and lowering the bar to include clusters of 20–25 households (in line with the Pranab Sen committee's recommendations), based on field observations and community feedback, the Urban Health Resource Center (UHRC), an NGO based in a number of Indian cities, engaged in an effort to update slum population numbers in Indore, where it facilitates slum women's community group programs. Vulnerability criteria assessments, mapping, and field visits to communities were conducted through collaborations with Anganwadi workers of the Department of Women and Child Development and with Health Department outreach workers including Auxiliary Nurses and Midwives (ANMs) and Lady Health Visitors (LHVs), UHRC slum women's group members and the UHRC team in Indore.

A study in Indore showed that there were 438 officially recognized slums,[29] but a process of community mapping found an additional 101 slums in 2004. At the request of the District Health Department of Indore, UHRC updated the earlier slum list and population count in 2011–12. This exercise included group and individual interactions with Anganwadi workers, UHRC's women's groups, and the Health Department's outreach workers (ANMs and LHVs). The new numbers reveal a total count of 633 distinct slums in Indore, with an estimated population of 918,575, which is 47 percent of Indore's population according to Census 2011. According to 2011 census data, Indore's population in 2011 was 1,960,631,[30] and a total of 590,257 people lived in slums, accounting for around 30 percent of Indore's population identified a number of unlisted slums excluded from official government records.[31]

Thus, any statistic on slum population for a city or state has to be viewed with caution, as it generally includes only settlements that have been officially classified as "slums" or "notified slums." As a large proportion of low-income urban clusters are informal or "illegal," they are not part of official slum lists and hence are often not part of the public authorities' mandate to provide basic services such as drainage, water, sanitation, and health care. According to the National Sample Survey 65th Round (2008–9), 49 percent of slums were nonnotified.[32]

The third dataset is based on food insecurity. It is worth noting that according to India's National Food Security Act of 2013, 50 percent of India's urban population is designated as vulnerable and eligible for a minimum quantity of assured food grains per month at highly subsidized prices.[33] With India's urban population in 2016 estimated to be 442.74 million, this translates to approximately 221 million urban people officially designated as vulnerable. This would suggest that the Indian government views urban food insecurity as a much broader problem than urban poverty, given that the Rangarajan Committee reported a 13.7 percent urban poverty rate for all of India for 2011–12.

The fourth data set on urban deprivation in India is based on a wealth index constructed from data in the latest National Family Health Survey (NFHS), conducted in 2005–6. The NFHS is conducted by the International Institute for Population Sciences (IIPS) under the auspices of the government of India's Ministry of Health and Family Welfare (MOHFW).[34] It represents India's variation on the internationally recognized Demographic and Health Surveys (DHS) protocol funded by USAID. According to the DHS website, "Demographic and Health Surveys (DHS) are nationally-representative household surveys that provide data for a wide range of monitoring and impact evaluation indicators in the areas of population, health, and nutrition."[35] Standard DHS surveys are conducted in roughly five-year increments so that change over time can be analyzed, and they involve sample sizes ranging from 5,000 to 30,000 households.[36] The 2005–6 NFHS represents India's third iteration of the survey (NFHS-3).

Data from NFHS-3 serves as the backbone for a methodology of vulnerability assessment that I refer to as the "poorest quartile analysis." This method of deprivation and vulnerability assessment differs from those used in data sets described above. While poverty lines, discussed above, largely rely on single-number thresholds for assessing poverty, NFHS-3 uses a comprehensive wealth index that includes information on thirty-three household assets and housing characteristics.†* However, rather than relying solely on this wealth index or data concerning

† These include a range of housing characteristics (including electrification, type of windows, drinking water source, type of toilet facility, flooring, roofing and exterior walls materials, cooking fuel, house ownership) and a range of assets (including ownership of a mattress, chair, cot/bed, table, electric fan, radio, television, sewing machine, mobile or other phone, computer, refrigerator, watch or clock, bicycle or motorcycle).

* To assign economic status scores to the households, NFHS–3 used the wealth index (which combines data on a household's ownership of assets into an index using the factor analysis procedure) based on thirty-three assets. To arrive at health indicators for the urban poor that adequately capture the intraurban differences, I calculated the cut-offs based on the wealth index specifically for the urban sample population.

housing conditions or food insecurity the poorest-quartile analysis allows us to characterize deprivation in a region more holistically.

For the purposes of this chapter, NFHS-3 sample data were divided into quartiles using the wealth index, and the lowest quartile was taken as representative of the urban poverty in India in view of the Planning Commission's 2005–6 estimated urban poverty rate of 25 percent. As the rest of this chapter shows, using the survey data compiled in the NFHS-3 reports, I conducted an analysis of key health indicators in order to identify the health categories that revealed the largest disparities between the poorest quartile and the rest of the urban population.‡

This chapter presents data for child (under five) mortality and health, maternal health, health care, and environmental health for the poorest urban quartile versus the rest of the urban population of India as a whole and of eight states in India. It also includes data for particular cities.[37] For almost all indicators relating to health, health care, or key social or housing-related determinants of health, I found large, sometimes dramatic, differences between the poorest quartile and the rest of the urban population.

As Philip Amis discusses in his exploration of slum improvement projects in India, poverty is complex and multidimensional.[38] The analysis of poverty should reflect these same qualities. Thus, not only is the wealth index used by the NFHS-3 multidimensional, but so too are the indicators used to characterize deprivation that this chapter assesses.

The goal of the poorest-quartile analysis is not to show the proportion of the urban population facing deprivation, but rather to show how high a proportion of the poorest quartile (and the proportion of the rest of the urban population) faces deprivation with regard to health outcomes, poor housing conditions, or the availability of health services. This chapter seeks to show how the method of assessment explained above can be used to transcend the technocratic semantics of quantifying poverty and move us toward a more holistic understanding of what deprivation and vulnerability look like in different parts of the world. Because "NFHS" is the Indian name for the DHS, a widely used survey tool in the global community, the poorest-quartile analysis can be conducted in other developing nations as well. An understanding of the

‡ The analyses were prepared by the Urban Health Resource Center in New Delhi. The data tables and a range of city and state reports from which this report draws are available online at no charge (see http://www.uhrc.in/ for more details); they also cover many more indicators than are presented here.

social, health-related, and environmental indicators in which the poorest quartile of urban families are performing the lowest (at the national, state, or city level) can be used to guide the formation of more pragmatic, regionally specific policy concerning public health interventions for the poor. Such an understanding can also allow us to shift from words, such those in this chapter, to action.

CHILDREN'S HEALTH

In 2005–6, the under-five child mortality rate for all India was 73 per 1,000 live births in the poorest quartile and 42 per 1,000 live births in the rest of the urban population. Among the six states, the highest under-five mortality rate in the poorest quartile occurred in Uttar Pradesh, India's most populous state, which had 44.4 million urban dwellers in the 2011 census.[39]

Only 40 percent of children in 2005–6 were completely immunized in the poorest quartile, compared to 65 percent for the rest of the urban population. The percentage of children completely immunized was particularly low among the poorest quartile of the urban populations in Uttar Pradesh, Bihar, Rajasthan, and Jharkhand; it was also only 40 percent in Delhi. Even among the rest of the urban population, fewer than half the children were completely immunized in Rajasthan and Uttar Pradesh.

For India's urban population in 2005–6, 54 percent of children were stunted, and 47 percent underweight in the poorest urban quartile, compared to 33 percent and 26 percent, respectively, for the rest of the urban population. Even in the best-performing states close to half of the children under five were stunted among the poorest quartile, and in all states but West Bengal more than one-quarter of the children under five within the rest of the urban population were stunted. High levels of stunted growth and underweightness among the urban poor in India indicates not only high susceptibility to infections owing to a suboptimal physical environment, but also high levels of food insecurity among this segment of the population. A study carried out in the slums of Delhi showed that 51 percent of slum families were food insecure.[40] A large majority of these children will, in the next fifteen years, form the bulk of the urban informal-sector workforce of the world's second-fastest-growing economy. The urban contribution to India's GDP is estimated at 60 to 70 percent and is increasing steadily. If we were able to take better care of the nutrition and food security of this segment of the population, its members would be more able to make a more robust contribution to the country's economy.

MATERNAL HEALTH

Among India's urban population, a much lower proportion of mothers receives maternity care in the poorest quartile; only 54 percent of pregnant women had at least three antenatal-care visits, compared to 83 percent for the rest of the urban population. Less than a quarter of mothers within the poorest quartile are receiving adequate maternity care in Bihar and Uttar Pradesh, and less than half in Madhya Pradesh, Delhi, Rajasthan, and Jharkhand.

With regard to the attendance of health personnel at births, among the poorest quartile of India's urban population only half of all births were assisted by health personnel in 2005–6; among the rest of the urban population, 84 percent were assisted by health personnel. The percentage of births assisted by health personnel was particularly low among the poorest quartile of the urban populations in Uttar Pradesh, Delhi, Bihar, and Rajasthan.

HOUSING, PHYSICAL ENVIRONMENT, AND LIVING CONDITIONS

The percentages of households that have access to piped water at home and that use a flush or pit toilet for disposing of excreta are also important measures of poverty. Among the poorest quartile of India's urban population in 2005–6, 81.5 percent did not have access to piped water at home and 52.8 percent did not use a sanitary flush or pit toilet; among the rest of the urban population, 62 percent had access to piped water at home and 96 percent used a sanitary toilet.

Even in the best-performing states, only half the population in the poorest quartile had piped water in their homes; for all India the figure was less than 20 percent, and in Delhi, the capital and one of the wealthiest cities, it was only 30 percent. In Bihar, just 2 percent of the poorest quartile had access to a piped water supply at home; in Uttar Pradesh, the state with the largest urban population, it was just 12 percent. Also notable is that more than one-third of urban households in the rest of the urban population did not have a piped water supply to their home. Among India's urban population, just 2 percent of the poorest urban quartile in Bihar had access to a piped water supply at home, while in the rest of Maharashtra's urban population, more than 90 percent were so served.

With regard to sanitation, for all India less than half the poorest urban quartile had a flush toilet or pit latrine for disposing of excreta in 2005–6, whereas more than 95 percent of the rest of the urban population had this facility. This is quite low, as the percentage with flush toilets would be much lower since pit latrines are still so common in urban areas. In Bihar, Madhya Pradesh, and Jharkhand, more than two-thirds of the poorest quartile did not use a flush or pit toilet for disposing of excreta. In Delhi, one-third of the poorest quartile did not have access to a sanitary toilet.

One study analyzed evidence on the adverse economic impacts of inadequate sanitation, including costs associated with death and disease, accessing and treating water, and losses in education, productivity, time, and tourism.[41] Although the findings are based on 2006 figures, a similar magnitude of losses is likely to have persisted in the years since. The report indicates that, in monetary cost, premature mortality and other health-related impacts of inadequate sanitation were greatest, at US$38.5 billion (INR 1.75 trillion, or 71.6 percent of total impacts), followed by productive time lost to accessing sanitation facilities or sites for defecation, at US$10.7 billion (INR 487 billion, or 20 percent), and drinking water-related impacts at US$4.2 billion (INR 191 billion, or 7.8 percent). Inadequate sanitation causes India considerable economic losses, at US$53.8 billion (INR 2.4 trillion), the equivalent of 6.4 percent of India's GDP in 2006.

Among the poorest quartile in Maharashtra, fewer than half of households had access to piped water at home in 2005–6, and half did not use a sanitary toilet (among the rest of the urban households, 88 percent had piped water supplies and 95 percent had a flush or pit toilet for disposal of excreta). In Delhi, the national capital, 70 percent among the poorest quartile did not have access to piped water at home and 34 percent did not use a flush toilet or pit latrine. A large proportion of slums are located adjacent to large open drains, dumping grounds, or railway lines, and slum families have to live amid heaps of garbage, feces strewn in the lanes or around the slum, and clogged drains with stagnant slushy water. Women and girls are much worse off under such squalid conditions. Women in slums tend to eat less and drink much less water than they should, to reduce the frequency of micturition and defecation because of the indignities they are subjected to in the absence of proper facilities and privacy (this assertion is based on personal observations and interactions with community members during slum visits). These conditions may lead women to relieve themselves in the open. Such adversities in the physical environment lead to contamination of water and the proliferation of flies, rodents, and mosquitoes that carry various diseases. Consequently slum families are prone to health risks associated with open sewage such as diarrhea, typhoid, jaundice, and vector-related diseases such as dengue, chikungunya, and leptospirosis.

POVERTY, SLUMS, AND HEALTH

According to Census 2011, the proportion of India's urban population living below the poverty line and the proportion of India's urban population living in slums are similar, at 13.7 percent and 17.4 percent, respectively, as discussed above. This might suggest (though not necessarily) a large degree of overlap between India's slum-dwelling and below-poverty-line populations. Yet there are large differences in the statistics for particular states or cities. For instance, in Delhi, a relatively low proportion of the population was considered poor (12.9 percent of its urban population fell below the poverty line in 2004–5), but, as noted earlier, the proportion living in poor-quality housing in slums and informal settlements in Delhi is much higher. In Mumbai, Delhi, and many other cities, a high proportion of those living in slums have income levels above the poverty line, as evidenced by the huge discrepancy between large slum-dwelling populations and relatively small, below-poverty-line populations. This nation-state-city distinction raises the question of whether the poverty line applied in such cities is appropriate to the costs of basic needs there. Another important caveat is that many of those who would qualify as living below the poverty line may not actually live in recognized slums. For example, populations living on or near construction sites, pavement populations, brick and limestone kiln workers (living in periurban areas), sex worker ghetto populations, small clusters living behind large buildings, populations living in dry river basins, and many other similar clusters of families do not live in what most would think of as slums. These communities are generally highly vulnerable and live on extremely low incomes. However, due to the often informal nature of their settlements, and due to their fear of eviction, punishment, or penalization, many of these communities try to stay under the radar and out of sight of local government authorities.

Particularly for sex worker communities, there is a gendered dimension to this desire to stay hidden from municipal and police personnel, with girls and women fearing possible police threats, extortion, and assault. This emphasizes the need to pay attention to unrecognized areas in addition to slums when attempting to implement poverty and public health interventions.

However, with regard to the overlap between those in the poorest urban quartile and those living in slums, certainly a high proportion of the poorest urban quartile in India and in each state is likely to live in slums and unlisted poverty clusters, especially if attention is given to improving the accuracy and comprehensiveness of statistics on slum populations. Slums, including unlisted poverty clusters, have the highest concentration of poor people and often the worst living conditions—especially if efforts are made to include a more accurate count of slum dwellers. It is therefore important that programs aimed at addressing urban poverty and related issues facilitate periodic updating of official slum lists by city authorities. Such efforts, when they succeed, will enable more disadvantaged urban communities to become eligible for slum improvement programs such as the Basic Services for the Urban Poor (BSUP) and Rajiv Awas Yojana (RAY) components of the India government's flagship urban program, the Jawaharlal Nehru National Urban Renewal Mission (JNNURM). RAY's guidelines mandate that slum lists of "urban local bodies" (municipal bodies) be updated by inclusion of unlisted slums with the help of satellite image and "ground truthing" exercises with the help of NGO and CBO representatives. This promising policy mandate has the potential to include hitherto unlisted poverty clusters in cities.

DATA FROM THE EIGHT-CITY STUDY

NFHS-3 also provides data for eight cities that allow us to compare health and living conditions between segments of the populations in each city. Care is needed in interpreting these statistics because the proportion of a city's population within the poorest quartile of India's total urban population varies: it can be well below 25 percent (in Mumbai it is only 7.7 percent, in Indore 12 percent, in Delhi and Kolkata 14 percent) or well above 25 percent (though for the eight cities studied, it was always below 25 percent). Analysis of the data reveals some interesting results. For instance, for cities for which an under-five mortality rate could be calculated for the poorest, the rate was higher among the poorest than among slum dwellers in those cities. For instance, in Meerut, it was 118.7 per 1,000 live births for the poorest, 86.1 in census slums (settlements classified as slums in the 2001 census), and 69.4 in census nonslums. This would suggest that not all of the poorest in those cities live in slums.

In fact, in all eight cities, a considerable proportion of the poorest population did not live in census slums. In Indore, 84 percent of the 12 percent of its population that are the poorest did not live in census slums. In Hyderabad, 76 percent of the poorest population did not live in slums, and in Chennai, 63 percent. For the rest of the cities the figure varied between 47 percent (Nagpur) and 21 percent (Mumbai). Of course, part of this nonslum poverty can be explained by the undercounting of slums or poverty clusters noted above. But it is also a reminder that programs to reduce urban poverty by addressing the needs of the poorest groups (defined by the wealth index) need to identify and focus on disadvantaged urban populations outside slums.

The study of these eight cities looked at a range of general, maternal, care, and environmental health indicators comparable to those used for the states. Some are discussed here, but caution is required when comparing these with the previous figures, because the "poorest" population is not the poorest quartile in that city (according to the NFHS wealth index), but the population in that city that is within the poorest quartile of India's urban population.

With regard to child mortality, rates for infant and under-five mortality were higher among the urban poor than they were for those living in slums or nonslums; the especially high under-five mortality rate for the poorest in Meerut was noted earlier.

Regarding child immunization, in five of the eight cities, more than one-third of children living in slums had not received any basic vaccination. In Delhi, 13.5 percent of children in slums had received no vaccinations, and among the poorest in Delhi, 26 percent had received no vaccinations.

With regard to children who were undernourished, a high proportion of children were stunted (height for age) in all the cities (as was the case in the urban populations of the states, as discussed earlier). When considering total city populations, Chennai had the lowest percentage of children who were stunted (25.4 percent), while Mumbai had the highest (45.4 percent). The proportion stunted was always highest among the poorest population and also always higher in slum populations compared to nonslum populations. Among the poorest, the percentage of children who were stunted was more than 50 percent in Chennai, Hyderabad, and Delhi and 65 percent in Meerut. A significant proportion of children in nonslums were stunted; only in Hyderabad and Kolkata is the figure below 20 percent. A high level of stunting (a reflection of food insecurity among these families) points to the need to rapidly improve urban poor families' access to the government's food subsidy schemes.

With regard to antenatal health care, the percentage of mothers who received at least three antenatal care visits varied greatly by city. Among the eight cities, for the poorest, the figure varied from only 32 percent in Meerut and 41 percent in Delhi to 99 percent in Chennai. For the slum populations, it varied from 58 percent in Delhi to 99 percent in Chennai. However, the percentage of mothers who received all recommended types of antenatal care was much lower for all cities—for their total population, their slum population, and their poorest population (in Delhi and Meerut, less than 4 percent of mothers from the poorest households received any care; even in the best-performing cities, less than one-third of the poorest mothers received any care).[42] This points to the need for a more comprehensive focus on antenatal care in the training of health care workers and community volunteers, as well as during communication efforts aimed at changing behavior.

With the exception of Chennai, where virtually all births were assisted by health personnel, the percentage of births assisted by health personnel was always lower among the poorest when compared to the census slum and nonslum populations, and often much lower. In the poorest households, less than one-third of births were assisted by health personnel in Delhi, Meerut, and Indore.

For the eight cities, the data on drinking water reflected only whether households had water piped into the dwelling, yard, or plot or a public tap or standpipe; there was no disaggregation between the two. Yet in six of the eight cities, 15 percent or more of the population lacked such provisions (62.5 percent in Meerut). A higher proportion of the poorest lacked such provisions than in slums; in Meerut, 86 percent lacked such provision, while in Indore, Kolkata, and Nagpur the figure was between 30 and 36 percent of their poorest population.

What is perhaps most notable is that in 2005–6, not only did much of the slum population not have an improved toilet facility that is not shared (more than 70 percent in Delhi, Kolkata, Mumbai and Chennai) but a significant proportion of the nonslum population did not either; for instance, more than 30 percent of the nonslum population in Meerut, Kolkata, Indore, and Hyderabad and more than half the nonslum population in Mumbai and Chennai lacked a private toilet. Among the poorest, more than 90 percent lacked an improved, nonshared toilet facility in Delhi, Kolkata, Mumbai, and Chennai, and the figure was not much better in the other cities

In Delhi, Meerut, and Nagpur 10–20 percent of the slum population had no toilet facility. For Delhi, Meerut, Indore, and Nagpur this was the case for more than 30 percent of their poorest population. This limited access to piped water and household toilets highlights the need to strengthen implementation of government schemes and programs such as the BSUP component of JNNURM, which has a substantial financial investment in water, sanitation, and improved drainage in urban poor habitations.

RECENT POLICY PROGRESS

The National Population Policy (NPP, 2000), National Health Policy (NHP, 2002), Tenth Five-Year Plan (Planning Commission, 2002), and the second phase of the Reproductive and Child Health Programme (RCH II) have clearly recognized the shortcomings of the existing health delivery system in order to effectively address the health needs of the urban poor, particularly the vulnerable slum populations. With the strengthened focus on urban poor in RCH II, several state governments have started implementing programs for enhancing RCH services for slum and other vulnerable urban groups in cities with high slum populations.[43]

Other developments that promise to address the health inequalities in Indian cities include the following:

1. Report of the Task Force to Advise the National Rural Health Mission on "Strategies for Urban Health Care," May 2006[44]
2. National Urban Health Mission (NUHM), 2008–13[45]
3. Rajiv Awas Yojana (RAY), December 2010[46]
4. Amendments in the approach of Integrated Child Development Services (ICDS) to integrate deprived urban areas and shift some focus toward the urban poor[47]

5. The Indian Supreme Court's order that Anganwadis be "on demand" in slums and informal settlements
6. The continued discussions on incorporating an Urban Health Mission into the Tenth, Eleventh, and Twelfth Five-Year Plans have helped bring urban deprivation to light.

It is encouraging to see that direct policies and programs are now being focused on the disparities *within* urban society, in addition to those between rural and urban populations. Still, large-scale improvements are contingent upon setting appropriate and inclusive standards for evaluating who is eligible for these programs and upon making a conscientious effort to bring the already approved programs, such as NUHM, to those who need them.

CONCLUSIONS

These data highlight the large disparities in health, health care provision, and housing conditions between the poorest quartile and the rest of the population in urban areas in India and in a selection of states. Large disparities exist in eight cities between their poorest population (the city's population within the poorest quartile of India's total urban population) and the rest of their population. The poorest population in the cities is defined by a wealth index drawn from data in the National Family Health Survey, 2005–2006, which is based on housing conditions and ownership of assets.

In general, the urban poor in each state and city are in the most disadvantaged position regarding all the indicators presented in this chapter, and the scale of the differentials for many indicators is high. Some of the greatest differentials are apparent when comparing the poorest quartile to the rest of the urban population in the states regarding access to piped water supply in the home and to a flush or pit toilet for disposing excreta. Almost all of the urban population not within the poorest quartile has access to a flush or pit toilet for excreta disposal, but this is not the case for more than half the population in the poorest quartile for India and for Bihar, Madhya Pradesh, Jharkhand, Rajasthan, and Maharashtra.

For the eight cities, some of the largest differentials can also be found in access to a flush toilet or pit latrine for disposing of excreta, and in the percentage of houses made of poor-quality materials. However, what is also noticeable is the poor performance in many cities and states regarding the population not part of the poorest quartile. For instance, for the urban population that was not within the poorest quartile in 2005–6:

> Under-five mortality rates were more than 60 per 1,000 live births in Uttar Pradesh, Rajasthan, and Bihar.
>
> Fewer than half the children were fully immunized in Uttar Pradesh and Rajasthan.
>
> More than one-third of children were stunted in Uttar Pradesh, Maharashtra, Bihar, Delhi, and Madhya Pradesh.
>
> More than half of households in Bihar, Jharkhand, and Uttar Pradesh did not have access to a piped water supply at home.

Collectively, the states of Maharashtra, Uttar Pradesh, Madhya Pradesh, Bihar, and West Bengal constitute over half of India's urban vulnerable populations. Thus it is critical that national and local program efforts be implemented with a sense of urgency and that no city be left behind.

This chapter highlights the disparities in health, nutrition, access to health care services, housing, water, and sanitation in urban areas of India and selected states and cities in order to direct greater attention and committed effort by politicians, administrators, civil society agencies, and health and social development professionals to addressing the disparities suffered by the urban poor. The findings presented clearly point to a need to better assess the number and proportion of uncounted (and often considered illegal) disadvantaged city dwellers, and to more focused efforts to reach the large segment of the urban poor who suffer sharp disparities, despite living in cities increasingly becoming booming centers of economic prosperity in the world's second-fastest growing economy.

A WAY FORWARD

The poorest-quartile analysis clearly illustrates that there is an urgent need to address urban health in the country, given the rapid pace of urbanization, the growing numbers of the urban poor with inadequate access to health and sanitation infrastructure, and the inability of city health systems to cater to the very basic living needs of their populations. While programs like NUHM have been implemented to address urban health, we have yet to see the results of such initiatives. Below are a series of qualitative recommendations based on fieldwork conducted by the Urban Health Resource Center (UHRC).

Address social determinants of health through coordinated interventions

There are a number of different sectors and avenues through which strategic interventions can be used to positively influence the health of urban disadvantaged population: physical environmental and infrastructure services; health, nutrition, and food-subsidy services; poverty alleviation and livelihood improvement programs; addressing gender inequality, alcoholism, domestic violence, and other social ills; and building social capital among slum communities and associated governance improvement efforts. Interventions must be made in each of these sectors, and they must work in a coordinated manner in order to make meaningful change.

Generate community demand for health care and other government or municipal services

Health education and outreach programs are crucial in slum communities because they help to build demand for health care services. The more communities know about which health services are available and relevant to them, the more they will seek out these services. UHRC, through its women's group programs in cities such as Agra and Indore, has been attempting to cultivate this understanding among slum communities. UHRC also works to educate women's groups about existing government schemes and programs and about how to interface with municipal service providers to expand coverage of their communities. The function of this kind of demand generation is to make communities more inclined to search for entitlements that should be available to them. Other organizations such as Strihikarini (in Mumbai) and Suraksha (in Bangalore) have also been mobilizing slum communities to provide a link between the community and service providers and to generate awareness and demand for health services in underserved communities.

Establish public-private partnerships to coordinate efforts more effectively

Partnerships between government and the private sector and NGOs are emerging as an effective strategy in rapidly improving access to services for the vulnerable and neglected sections of the urban population. Private bodies such as corporate hospitals and NGOs such as Sumangli

Sevashram in Bangalore and ARPANA Trust in Delhi work in areas where the government is not able to provide health services. NGOs often play an important role in running urban health centers (UHCs) operating in partnership with municipal governments. The UHRC has focused much of its efforts on creating these kinds of partnerships between NGOs and government bodies, particularly in its flagship Indore and Agra programs.[48] These partnerships can and should be taken further. By engaging government officials, private-sector representatives (i.e., municipal service providers, private health care providers, etc.), and NGOs in stakeholder discussions of how to expand service coverage to underserved communities, resources can be pooled more effectively in a coordinated manner to achieve scale in outreach efforts.

Build the capacity of slum communities

While each of the recommendations above is important, this one touches on perhaps the most fundamental area in which improvements must be made. As David Satterthwaite, editor of *Environment & Urbanization,* explains, while income inequality appears to be the most obvious issue behind urban poverty, when you delve deeper, you find issues of inadequate infrastructure. Delve deeper yet, and you find a limited or absent safety net. But at the bottom of it all is the voicelessness of the urban poor.[49] This voicelessness can be attributed to a vicious cycle among four important social dynamics that often take hold in slum communities: a sense of resignation, weak demand for rights, weak social cohesion, and powerlessness. The UHRC has approached the issue of social cohesion by proposing the formation of women's groups in slum communities. If the idea takes root in a community, the UHRC provides peripheral support with group formation, then works to provide groups with technical skills and knowledge about public health outreach, interfacing with government officials and municipal service providers, creating collective emergency funds, surveying, and other critical tasks. At the heart of this approach is a belief that underneath the apparent fragmentation of poor communities, there lies an inherent, powerful capacity within these communities.

Based on the UHRC's successes in Indore and Agra, particularly with regard to the collective savings program and the use of trained slum-based health volunteers, the NUHM has called for the introduction of *mahila arogya samitis* (women's health groups)[50] with the support of urban accredited social health activists (urban ASHAs), similar to ASHAs of NRHM who work in villages. This is an important step. The NUHM Framework for Implementation, May 2013, emphasizes the role of NGOs, civil society organizations, and government partnerships with NGOs to coordinate the formation, capacity building, and mentoring of *mahila arogya samitis* and urban ASHAs. Government accountability is an important part of this picture, and when building capacity from the bottom, groups must be encouraged to use their collective rights to demand for corruption-free progress from government institutions and processes. The UHRC has held this principle as a central tenet of its operations by facilitating workshops with women's groups on writing slum community petitions, applications, and request letters to local civic authorities. This form of capacity building moves beyond simple demand generation and allows communities to actively reach up and engage with the government, other NGOs, and the private sector in pursuit of self-selected and -directed community initiatives to improve infrastructure, health, and the environment.

Translate words into expeditious action

The National Urban Health Mission and urban health in general have been discussed since 2005 and announced repeatedly. Now that the mission has already been accepted and is ready to be rolled out, greater emphasis should be placed on increasing the availability, access, and acceptability of public health services in urban areas. There is no need to reinvent the wheel. It is time to build on existing experiences and lessons to develop effective and efficient program processes that can set context-specific examples of what success and good practices look like in a wide variety of urban settings in India.

NOTES

1. Government of India, Ministry of Home Affairs (2011). Census 2011: Primary Census Data Highlights—India; Executive Summary. New Delhi: Office of the Registrar General & Census Commissioner. http://www.censusindia.gov.in/2011census/PCA/PCA_Highlights/pca_highlights_file/India/4Executive_Summary.pdf (accessed 30 December 2015).

2. Gupta, K., Arnold, F., & Lhungdim, H. (2009). Health and living conditions in eight Indian cities: National Family Health Survey (NFHS-3), India, 2005–2006; Mumbai: International Institute for Population Sciences; Calverton. Rockville, MD: ICF Macro.

3. Press Information Bureau, Government of India (2011). India Stats: Million plus cities in India as per Census 2011." Press Information Bureau, Mumbai. 31 October. http://pibmumbai.gov.in/scripts/detail.asp?releaseId=E2011IS3 (accessed 6 June 2014).

4. Office of the Registrar General and Census Commissioner, India (2011). Census of India: Rural urban distribution of population (provisional population totals). New Delhi: Ministry of Home Affairs. 15 July. http://censusindia.gov.in/2011-prov-results/paper2/data_files/india/Rural_Urban_2011.pdf (accessed 30 December 2015).

5. World Urbanization Prospects (2011). The 2011 Revision.

6. Government of India, Planning Commission. (2009). Report of the Expert Group to Review the Methodology for Estimation of Poverty. New Delhi: Planning Commission. http://planningcommission.nic.in/reports/genrep/rep_pov.pdf (accessed 30 December 2015).

7. Chandrasekhar, C.P. (2013). "The grime beneath the glitter." *Infochange*. August. http://infochangeindia.org/agenda/urbanisation/the-grime-beneath-the-glitter.html (accessed 4 June 2014).

8. World Bank (2012). Poverty and equality data FAQs. World Bank Group. 16 February. http://go.worldbank.org/PYLADRLUN0 (accessed 5 June 2014).

9. Birdsall, N., & Meyer, C.J. (2014). *The median is the message: A good-enough measure of material well-being and shared development progress*. Working Paper 351. Washington, DC: Center for Global Development, January. http://www.cgdev.org/sites/default/files/median-message-good-enough-measure-shared-development-progress_final_0.pdf (accessed 31 December 2015).

10. Chandramouli, C., Office of the Registrar General and Census Commissioner (2010). Census of India, 2011—Circular No. 8. 20 January. New Delhi: Government of India, Ministry of Home Affairs. http://censusindia.gov.in/2011-Circulars/Circulars/Circular-08.pdf (accessed 31 December 2015).

11. Government of India, Ministry of Housing and Urban Poverty. (2012). Definition of slum. New Delhi: Press Information Bureau, Government of India, 27 March. http://pib.nic.in/newsite/erelease.aspx?relid=81777 (accessed 6 June 2014).

12. Agarwal, S., & Sangar, K. (2005). Need for dedicated focus on urban health within national rural health mission. *Indian Journal of Public Health* 49(3):142–52.

13. Varma, S. (2013). Census 2011 missed 5 crore slum dwellers. *Times of India*. 12 October. http://timesofindia.indiatimes.com/india/Census-2011-missed-5-crore-slum-dwellers/articleshow/24001477.cms (accessed 31 December 2015).

14. Registrar General and Census Commissioner, India (2011). Census of India: Primary Census Abstract; Figures at a Glance India. New Delhi: Ministry of Home Affairs. http://www.censusindia.gov.in/2011census/PCA/PCA_Highlights/pca_highlights_file/India/5Figures_at_glance.pdf.

15. Chandramouli, C. (2011). Housing stock, amenities and assets in slums—Census 2011 (PowerPoint slides). New Delhi: Office of the Registrar General and Census Commissioner. http://censusindia.gov.in/2011-Documents/On_Slums-2011Final.ppt.

16. Office of the Registrar General & Census Commissioner (n.d.). Census of India 2001 (provisional) slum population in million plus cities (municipal corporations): Part A. New Delhi: Ministry of Home Affairs. http://censusindia.gov.in/Tables_Published/Admin_Units/Admin_links/slum1_m_plus.html (accessed 31 December 2015).

17. 54% of Mumbai lives in slums: World Bank (2006). Infochange (reprinted from www.mid-day.com). January 9. http://infochangeindia.org/poverty/news/54-of-mumbai-lives-in-slums-world-bank.html (accessed 2 January 2016).

18. Nijman, J. (2008). Against the odds: Slum rehabilitation in neoliberal Mumbai. *Cities* 25(2):73–85.

19. Bambale, R.B. (2012). "Water Reforms—Mumbai, Maharashtra." Municipal Corporation of Greater Mumbai. Indian Council for Research on International Economic Relations. http://www.icrier.org/pdf/Maharashtra_05nov12.pdf.

20. Office of the Registrar General and Census Commissioner (2013). Primary census abstract for slum. New Delhi: Ministry of Home Affairs, September 30. www.censusindia.gov.in/2011-Documents/Slum-26-09-13.pdf (accessed 31 December 2015).

21. Office of the Registrar General and Census Commissioner (2011). Census of India 2011 primary census abstract data highlights NCT of Delhi. New Delhi: Ministry of Home Affairs. http://www.censusindia.gov.in/2011census/PCA/PCA_Highlights/pca_highlights_file/Delhi/DATA_SHEET_PCA_DISTRICTS_NCT_OF_DELHI.pdf.

22. Chandramouli, C. (2011).

23. According to *Oxford Dictionaries Online,* a jhuggi is a "slum dwelling" (http://www.oxforddictionaries.com/definition/english/jhuggi).

24. Menon-Sen, K. & Bhan, G. (2008). *Swept off the map: Surviving eviction and resettlement in Delhi.* New Delhi: Yoda Press.

25. Government of National Capital, Territory of Delhi (2006). Economic survey of Delhi, 2005–2006. Planning Department, 364. See also Bhan, G. (2009). This is no longer the city I once knew: Evictions, the urban poor and the right to the city in Millennial Delhi. *Environment and Urbanization* 21(1): 127–42.

26. Government of National Capital, Territory of Delhi (2013). Housing and urban development, chapter 14 (pp. 193–201) in Economic survey of Delhi, 2012–2013. Planning Department. http://delhi.gov.in/DoIT/DoIT_Planning/ES2012-13/EN/ES_Chapter14.pdf (accessed 31 December 2015).

27. Mahapatra, D. (2012). Half of Delhi's population lives in slums. *Times of India.* 12 October. http://timesofindia.indiatimes.com/city/delhi/Half-of-Delhis-population-lives-in-slums/articleshow/16664224.cms (accessed 29 February 2016).

28. Agarwal, S., Srivastava, A., Choudhary, B., & Kaushik, S. (2007). State of urban health in Delhi. Delhi: Ministry of Health and Family Welfare, Government of India, and Urban Health Resource Centre, p. 14.

29. Taneja, S., & Agarwal, S. (2004). Situational analysis for guiding USAID/EHP India's technical assistance efforts in Indore, Madhya Pradesh, India. Environmental Health Project Activity Report 133.

30. Office of the Registrar General and Census Commissioner (2011). Indore City Census 2011 data. New Delhi: Ministry of Home Affairs. http://www.census2011.co.in/census/city/299-indore.html (accessed 31 December 2015).

31. Directorate of Census Operations (2013). Primary census abstract for slum population. Madhya Pradesh, Bhopal. http://censusmp.nic.in/censusmp/All-PDF/Slum-MP-1.pptx (accessed 31 December 2015). See also MP's 28% urban population lives in slums: Census. *Times of India*. 27 December. http://timesofindia.indiatimes.com/city/bhopal/MPs-28-urban-population-lives-in-slums-Census/articleshow/27986846.cms (accessed 4 June 2014).

32. National Statistical Organisation, National Sample Survey Organization (2010). National Sample Survey Report No. 534: Some characteristics of urban slums, 2008–9. Government of India, Ministry of Statistics and Programme Implementation. http://mospi.nic.in/Mospi_New/upload/534_final.pdf (accessed 31 December 2015).

33. Government of India, Ministry of Law and Justice (2013). The National Food Security Act, 2013. *Gazette of India*. 10 September. http://indiacode.nic.in/acts-in-pdf/202013.pdf (accessed 31 December 2015).

34. National Family Health Survey, India (2014). International Institute for Population Sciences. http://www.rchiips.org/nfhs/about.shtml (accessed 5 June 2014).

35. USAID (2014). "The DHS Program." Demographic and Health Survey (DHS). USAID, n.d. Web. 5 June 2014. http://dhsprogram.com/What-We-Do/Survey-Types/DHS.cfm.

36. Ibid.

37. Indira Gandhi Institute of Development Research. (2006). 2005–6 National Family Health Survey (NFHS-3): Key findings. IGIDR. http://www.igidr.ac.in/conf/ysp/KGU.ppt (accessed 2 January 2016). Statistics not otherwise documented in the following discussion come from this source, NFHS-3.

38. Amis, P. (2001). Rethinking UK aid in urban India: Reflections on an impact assessment study of slum improvement projects. *Environment and Urbanization* 13(1):101–13.

39. Agarwal, S., Kaushik, S., & Srivasatava, A. (2006). State of urban health in Uttar Pradesh. Delhi: Ministry of Health and Family Welfare, Government of India and Urban Health Resource Center. Office of the Registrar General and Census Commissioner (2011). Census of India 2011: Rural urban distribution of population (provisional population totals).

40. Agarwal, S., Sethi, V., Gupta, P., Jha, M., Agnihotri, A., & Nord, M. (2009). Experiential household food insecurity in an urban underserved slum of North India. *Food Security* 1(3):239–50.

41. Water and Sanitation Programme, World Bank (2010). The economic impacts of inadequate sanitation in India: Report for the Water and Sanitation Programme's (WSP) global Economics of Sanitation Initiative (ESI). Washington, DC: World Bank

42. Rajiv Awas Yojana (2010). Ministry of Housing and Urban Poverty Alleviation, Government of India.

43. Agarwal, S., Satyavada, A., Kaushik, S., Kumar, R. (2007). Urbanization, urban poverty and health of the urban poor: Status, challenges and the way forward. *Demography India* 36(1):121–34.

44. Government of India, Ministry of Health and Family Welfare (n.d.). National Rural Health Mission: Meeting people's health needs in rural areas; framework for implementation, 2005–2012. New Delhi. http://nrhm.gov.in/images/pdf/about-nrhm/nrhm-framework-implementation/nrhm-framework-latest.pdf (accessed 2 January 2016).

45. Government of India, Ministry of Housing and Urban Poverty Alleviation (date?). Rajiv Awas Yojana guidelines for slum-free city planning. http://mhupa.gov.in/w_new/RAY%20Guidelines-%20English.pdf.

46. Government of India, Ministry of Health and Family Welfare (2013). National Urban Health Mission: Framework for implementation. May. http://www.pbnrhm.org/docs/nuhm_framework_implementation.pdf (accessed 2 January 2016).

47. Government of India, Ministry of Women and Child Development (2013). ICDS Systems Strengthening and Nutrition Improvement Project (ISSNIP). Central Project Management Unit. http://wcd.nic.in/issnip/ISSNIP-Web-Contents/RIGHT%20SIDE%20TABS/9-Technical%20Assistence%20Agency/Terms%20of%20References%20for%20the%20TA%20Agency%20(22Nov13).pdf (accessed 2 January 2016). See also Government of India, Ministry of Women and Child Development. Integrated Child Development Services (ICDS) scheme. http://wcd.nic.in/icds.htm.

48. Kulkarni, N.K. (2012). Healthcare delivery for the urban poor. *Searchlight South Asia*. 20 July. 6 June 2014. http://urbanpoverty.intellecap.com/?p=576.

49. Satterthwaite, D. (2001). Reducing urban poverty: Constraints on the effectiveness of aid agencies and development banks and some suggestions for change. *Environment and Urbanization* 13(1):137–57.

50. Mahajan, S., & Chatterjee, M. (n.d.). Operational guidelines for mahila arogya samiti (MAS). Health of the Urban Poor Program, Population Foundation of India, and USAID. http://www.hupindia.org/files/19320138061932oMahila_Arogya_Samiti.pdf (accessed 2 January 2016).

CHAPTER 13

Improved Health Outcomes in Urban Slums through Infrastructure Upgrading

NEEL M. BUTALA, MICHAEL J. VAN ROOYEN, AND RONAK BHAILAL PATEL

The world is rapidly urbanizing, with 2007 marking the first point in human history that the majority of humans were living in urban areas.[1] The urban population is expected to grow to 4.9 billion by 2030, while the rural population will decrease by 28 million.[2] Much of this growth in cities is fueled by the growth in their respective urban slum populations, with almost half the residents of developing economies and up to 78 percent in the least-developed countries living in such areas.[3] Accordingly, the population of slum dwellers worldwide grew to 1.2 billion by 2008.[4] Living conditions for the vast majority of slum dwellers are deplorable, with high rates of malnutrition, communicable diseases, and exposure to violence. This accelerated urbanization and consequent deterioration of living conditions constitute a major challenge for local, national, and international organizations alike. The necessity to address living conditions in urban slums must be a major national and international developmental priority.

The Millennium Development Goals—in particular, MDG 7, Targets 10 and 11—directly address achieving a significant improvement in the lives of slum dwellers and increasing access to water and basic sanitation.[5] Based on estimates published in 2003, up to 50 percent of the urban population in Asia lacks adequate provision of water, and up to 60 percent lacks adequate sanitation.[6] There is a pressing need for interventions to address these targets as improvements in sanitation, potable water supply, and distribution systems in urban areas have failed to keep pace with population growth.[7]

Furthermore, achieving these goals is essential for progress on other MDGs, specifically health-related targets. Although rarely collected at the slum level, health indicators show that urban slums concentrate hazards and risks to health and in many cases increase the baseline rates of morbidity and mortality. High rates of diarrhea and malnutrition reveal the link between water, sanitation, and health in urban slums. A recent study in the slums of New Delhi found that the average child under five had 1.7 episodes of diarrhea per year.[8] Another found that diarrhea was responsible for 36 percent of infant mortality and 50 percent of mortality in children 1–6 years of age.[9] Malnutrition rates also reported in several studies of slums in India show that rates of underweight across various ages under 5 years range from 40 percent to 90 percent, stunting in the same age group ranges from 55 percent to 62.8 percent, and vitamin A and D deficiencies afflict almost a quarter of children in this age range.[10] Correspondingly, recent data from Kenya show that in rural areas infant and under-5 mortality rates (IMR and U5MR) are 76 and 113 per 1,000 live births respectively, compared with 94 and 151 per 1,000 births in urban slums, respectively.[11]

Despite the need and explicit call for urban environmental interventions, relatively little research has focused on health outcomes of infrastructure improvement in urban areas. Crowding and lack of hygiene have long been identified as contributors to the spread of infectious diseases such as tuberculosis and respiratory infection.[12] A lack of basic services such as access to safe drinking water, adequate sanitation, and solid waste management increase the risk of waterborne disease.[13] Improved hygiene and water quality at point of use have been shown to reduce waterborne disease.[14, 15] However, this clear causal link does not exist between improvements in household water supply or sanitation and waterborne disease reduction. In a review of interventions that have shown a reduction in diarrheal disease, Zwane and Kremer corroborate that many of the studies involving individual water supply and sanitation suffer from critical methodological problems, such as failure to randomize or account for clustered sampling.[16] The literature also conflicts on the role of infrastructure interventions. A recent review finds insufficient evidence to support the view that improved housing is a means to improved physical health.[17] While many studies describe the health problems associated with urban environments, policy makers have surprisingly little evidence on interventions to act upon.[18]

It is likely that such evidence does not exist for multiple reasons. One simple reason may be that other hazards specific to slums may undermine the benefits provided by household infrastructure improvements. More likely, though, studies assessing the benefits of household infrastructure improvements are difficult to conduct. Urban slums are such a complex environment that it is difficult to attribute outcomes to specific exposures or interventions. Additionally, their heterogeneity makes it difficult to compare outcomes across a population.[19] Urban health interventions are also difficult to evaluate given a lack of longitudinal health outcome data sets. This is especially true in developing countries, where measuring health outcomes in urban slums presents challenging logistical and ethical problems.

This chapter uses a novel empirical strategy to demonstrate a causal relationship between, on one hand, basic infrastructure improvement in water supply and sanitation in urban slums and, on the other, a reduction in incidence of waterborne illness and overcomes the dearth of health outcome data by using micro–health insurance claims as a proxy for illness incidence. Each individual claim represents an observation of an illness episode, and changes in frequency of waterborne disease–related illness episodes relative to other illnesses are analyzed with respect to the slum-upgrading intervention. Health insurance claims have been used in clinical research as a proxy for health outcomes, providing a practical complement to randomized controlled trials in nonexperimental settings.[20, 21, 22, 23] This study extends the methodology to the field of public health outcomes evaluation to measure the health impact of slum upgrading in Ahmedabad, India.

Previous work has shown that multiple socioeconomic variables such as parents' education and income are associated with child morbidity and mortality.[24] These variables undoubtedly form part of the multifactorial cause of waterborne illness in this population as well. However, they have not been shown to have a direct causal relationship, and standard measures to control these variables are used in population studies.[25] The study described in this chapter assumes an equal distribution of these variables between those participating and not participating in the slum upgrade. While this assumption is not ideal, the lack of adequate data sets for urban slum populations as described above precludes a stratified analysis. However, as a comparison of the two differences in outcome rates before and after the upgrade within intervention and nonintervention slums (a difference-in-difference analysis), these variables should not confound the results.

Slum upgrading, an intervention currently being implemented in several cities across India, entails basic infrastructure improvements for residents and guaranteed freedom from eviction for ten years. This urban improvement strategy provides a set of seven interventions: connections to a water supply for individual households; underground sewage for individual households; toilets for individual households; storm water drainage; stone paving of internal and approach roads; solid waste management; and street lighting. This strategy thus provides services at the household level, whereas many slum improvements in the past have provided such upgrades on a neighborhood level through shared facilities that often do not reduce transmission of communicable disease.[26]

This chapter examines slum upgrading in the context of Ahmedabad, a city of 3.9 million people, 40 percent of whom live in slums and informal tenements known as chawls.[27] Table 13.1 presents the aggregated results of a 2006 census of Ahmedabad slums that had not received the slum-upgrading intervention. While this table does not account for the great variability of households living in slums, it presents a snapshot of slum-dwelling households' infrastructure and socioeconomic status. Slum upgrading in Ahmedabad is a partnership involving target communities and their representative community-based organizations, the Ahmedabad Municipal Corporation (AMC), local partnering nongovernmental organizations (NGOs), and participating private-sector organizations and charitable trusts. The AMC is responsible for the entire cost of bringing basic infrastructure services to the entrance of the slums, and the remaining cost of providing these services within the slum is split evenly among all of the stakeholders. While individual households must pay 2,000 Rs (approximately US$40) for this intervention, a microcredit organization offers a microfinance program with a participation rate of approximately 70 percent. The Mahila Housing Trust (MHT), formerly the housing cooperative of the Self Employed Women's Association (SEWA), a large NGO based in the city, facilitates the implementation of this intervention. There are no data describing migration patterns out of the slum based on uptake or nonuptake of the upgrade intervention. Given the potential positive externalities of a neighbor's upgrade, however, those households that did not upgrade likely had an added incentive to stay. Thus, there is likely no health-selective migration to overestimate its effect.

Very little data exist on the health impact of slum upgrading, despite its implementation in many cities. One study, based on the implementation in Visakhapatnam, examined many dimensions of the impact of slum upgrading, but finds no health impact three years after implementation.[28]

TABLE 13.1 CHARACTERISTICS OF HOUSEHOLDS IN AHMEDABAD SLUMS

	All slum-dweller
Variable	**households**
Total number of households	12,459
Average number of household members	4.59
Average monthly household income (savings + expenditures, in rupees)	3105.2
Maximum years of education attained by a member of the household	7.94
Presence of intervention components	**% of households**
Individual water connection	65.16
Storm drain	82.73
Solid waste management	88.94
Individual toilet	71.17
Individual toilet connected to sewer	61.71

NOTES: No settlements included in census had received the slum-upgrading intervention. Response rate ranged from 96.9% to 99.5% of all households surveyed.

Another study, based on the interventions in Indore in the 1990s, anecdotally shows that poor implementation of upgrading increases waterborne illnesses, most likely because of choked sewage drains.[29] An initial impact assessment from a follow-up survey sixteen months after an MHT slum intervention in Ahmedabad showed that 97 percent of respondents self-reported an increase in mental and emotional well-being and that 87 percent self-reported improvements in their social status as a result of infrastructure improvement.[30] However, the potential for self-reporting bias was high, the sample size was very small, and the study suggests further research is needed to determine the full health impact.

This chapter evaluates the causal health impact of slum upgrading in Ahmedabad using micro–health insurance claims as a proxy for illness episodes. VimoSEWA, the micro-insurance cooperative of SEWA, provided the claims data for this study. VimoSEWA was originally founded as an adjunct to SEWA Bank, the microfinance branch of SEWA, to address some of the major causes of loan default. VimoSEWA has since become independent of SEWA Bank and has grown tremendously. VimoSEWA currently offers a package of life, health, asset, and accidental death insurance. Given that the micro-insurance was targeted to the very poor and that the entry-level scheme cost only 100 Rs (approximately US$2) per year, there was minimal chance that the most vulnerable were excluded from the analysis. Over 40 percent of urban members are drawn from households from the bottom third of socioeconomic status, and submission of claims is equitable in Ahmedabad city.[31] The appropriateness of using micro–health insurance claims as a proxy for health outcomes to measure the health impact of slum upgrading in this context was further examined using the 2006 cross-sectional Ahmedabad slum census data. The incidence of waterborne disease among households was not significantly associated with whether or not one has insurance. Furthermore, the association between the slum-upgrading intervention and waterborne disease incidence was not significantly altered by whether or not one has insurance. While there may have been a bias between those who participated in the health insurance and those who did not, this analysis evaluated the impact of the intervention only among those taking up the insurance, thus negating that potential bias.

This study employs a quasi-experimental method of external evaluation through passive surveillance by using a difference-in-difference technique, in which the change in a variable of interest between program and nonprogram regions is compared in order to control for bias. Given the increasing importance of slum-upgrading interventions in development, some experts recommend that quasi-experimental studies be implemented when the required assumptions can be plausibly satisfied.[32] The difference-in-difference approach is valid when one can argue that the outcome would not have had significantly different trends in program and nonprogram areas if the program had otherwise not been implemented. This chapter employs this approach by examining a time series of data before the program was implemented and finding that there were no significantly different trends in the data during this period. Compared to the self-reported survey data from prior impact evaluations for slum upgrading, this quasi-experimental approach provides a less biased measurement of health outcomes. In the context of slum upgrading in Ahmedabad, the quasi-experimental approach is particularly advantageous, given that implementation of randomized controlled trials is often impractical, expensive, and labor-intensive.

METHODS

A database of 32,826 health insurance claims from the micro-insurance provider VimoSEWA in the years 2001–2008 was analyzed. The city of Ahmedabad accounted for 20,029 of the claims. An MHT history file provided a list of seventeen slums in Ahmedabad that received the full set of seven basic infrastructure services in the upgrading intervention.

The health insurance claims database was examined both manually and using a search algorithm for claims from slums that received the intervention. The resulting sample of 466 potential claims from slums of interest was sent to VimoSEWA, where the research coordinator scrutinized the data to verify that these claims did indeed come from a slum that had the intervention, as different slums can often have similar names. This process identified a total of 151 claims from fourteen different slums that had the intervention. These 151 claims represent 127 individuals from 112 households.

Each of these 151 claims was coded as to whether the illness occurred before or after the intervention. This variable serves as the primary independent variable of interest in subsequent regression analysis. Variation in the rollout of the intervention in different slums at different times allowed identification of pre-intervention claims that could serve as control observations. These can be used to detect whether or not a differential time trend occurred as a result of the slum-upgrading intervention. MHT considers six months as the average time to fully construct the basic infrastructure components of this intervention, and 24 claims occurred six months prior to the completion date in intervention slums. Thus these 24 claims representing illness episodes that occurred during the implementation of the intervention were dropped because they were not clearly representative of either the intervention or the nonintervention period, resulting in a final sample of 127 claims. These 24 observations were later included in the intervention group in an alternate specification of this variable to verify robustness of results. Dropping observations from claimants during the time of intervention construction also reduced confounding from the effects of a behavior-change education program implemented by SEWA, as this was its most active period.

Due to the small sample size of only 127 claims from slums that had the intervention, variation in the rollout of the intervention in different slums at different times did not generate enough pretreatment observations to define a clear trend in overall claiming behavior. Thus, to increase statistical power, additional control claims were added in the following manner. Each of the claims from intervention slums was serviced by a specific VimoSEWA field-worker. These field-workers often served nonintervention slums in the same vicinity; nearby nonintervention slums serviced by the same worker served as "control areas," as neighboring slums are more likely to share similar characteristics. A list of VIMO field-workers who serviced the 151 claims in our initial sample was generated and used to search the total claims database for other claims from neighboring areas that had been serviced by the same field-worker. This method identified a total of 3,645 claims from these "control areas." To reduce processing costs, a simple random sample of 510 control claims was obtained using the RAND function in Microsoft Excel (Microsoft Corporation, Redmond, WA). Claims from the additional "control slums" were grouped with claims that occurred prior to upgrading in "intervention slums" in order to define clear trends in overall claiming behavior. The appropriateness of grouping these claims together was demonstrated by conducting *t*-tests to compare the characteristics of claims coming from control slums and intervention slums prior to intervention. No significant difference in age, sex, or fraction of claims for waterborne illness was found between the two samples. We concluded that the pattern of claims before upgrading from the intervention slums had been similar to claims from the control slums, indicating that the outcome would not have had differential time trends in these areas.

Each claim was then coded as binary according to whether or not diagnosis of illness reflected a disease that was waterborne or mosquito-borne versus not waterborne or mosquito-borne. This variable serves as the dependent variable of interest in subsequent regression analysis, indicating claims due to waterborne diseases broadly defined. A more "conservative" specification of this variable was also constructed in which mosquito-borne diseases were coded as null, to distinguish claims due only to waterborne diseases. Claims that were unclear as to whether they reflected a waterborne or mosquito-borne illness were coded as null in the "conservative" analysis, and as positive in the "broad" specification to check for robustness. The data were then analyzed to examine differences in the fraction of waterborne illness claims within slums before and after the upgrade intervention.

Using STATA SE 10.0 (StataCorp, College Station, TX), the nonlinear probit regression method was employed using the following equation: $Yi = \alpha + (\beta_1 \times Ti \times Ci) + (\beta_2 \times Vi) + (\beta_3 \times Ci) + \varepsilon i$. In this model, each observation *i* is a micro-insurance claim. Outcome variable *Yi* is coded binary as to whether the claim is waterborne or nonwaterborne. Treatment variable *Ti* is coded according to whether the claim was made before or after the intervention; variable *Ci* represents whether the claim came from an intervention or nonintervention slum; and variable *Vi* represents the year in which the claim was made, to capture an overall time trend. The value β_1 represents the likelihood that a claim will be for a waterborne illness.

Thus, with each individual claim as an observation, the binary health outcome indicator was regressed on the binary intervention indicator while controlling for each claim's admit year and whether or not an observation came from an intervention slum. While the small sample size prohibited inclusion of slum-level fixed effects, standard errors were clustered around slums, as health outcomes within slums are likely to resemble each other. This model allows one to detect the existence of a differential time trend in claiming behavior as a direct result of the slum-upgrading intervention. Including both waterborne and non-waterborne claims in the construction of the dependent variable allows one to control for changes in overall health insurance utilization behavior exogenous to the slum-upgrading intervention. This assumes that the intervention does not affect incidence of hospitalization for non-waterborne claims, which was validated in the data using subsequent linear regression analyses.

RESULTS

The regression results indicate that the slum-upgrading intervention causes a statistically significant decrease in waterborne illness claims (table 13.2). The analysis shows that the likelihood of claiming for a waterborne disease as opposed to a nonwaterborne illness in a treatment slum decreased from 32 percent before the intervention to 14 percent after the intervention (table 13.3, "broadly defined" model). Using the more conservative specification of waterborne illness by excluding potentially mosquito-related illnesses, the results still show a statistically significant reduction in waterborne illness from 25 percent to 10 percent (table 13.3, "conservative" model). Regression 1 details the results of running the aforementioned empirical model. The coefficient on the slum upgrading treatment indicator is statistically significant and negative, indicating that slum upgrading is associated with a reduction in the probability that a claim is due to a waterborne illness. The coefficient on the claim admit year is not significant, even at the 20 percent level, indicating that there was no major increase or decrease in claiming for waterborne disease during this time. The coefficient on the variable indicating whether or not a claim was from a treatment slum or an added control slum is also not significant (table 13.2). This indicates that, before the intervention, the probability that a claim is associated with a waterborne illness is not different between control slums and treatment slums. This lack of difference further supports the assertion that the outcome would not have

TABLE 13.2 REGRESSION ANALYSIS OF EFFECT OF SLUM UPGRADING ON WATERBORNE-ILLNESS CLAIMS

Insurance claim variables	Waterborne illness (broad definition)	Waterborne illness (conservative specification*)
Slum upgrading	-0.6218	-0.6131
[Standard error]	[0.303]	[0.295]
(p value)	(0.025)	(0.017)
Intervention slum	-0.0131	-0.00588
[Standard error]	[0.311]	[0.0719]
(p value)	(0.966)	(0.883)
N	637	637

*Conservative specification does not count claims as positive for mosquito-borne diseases.

TABLE 13.3 MAGNITUDE OF SLUM UPGRADING'S IMPACT

Regression specification	Regression coefficient on slum upgrading (p value)	Probability of waterborne illness claim before upgrade (%)	Probability of waterborne illness claim after upgrade (%)	Decrease in probability (%)
Standard model (broad definition) (p value)	-0.6218 (0.025)	31.63	13.57	18.06
Conservative model (p value)	-0.6131 (0.017)	24.71	9.74	14.97

had differential trends in program and nonprogram areas, further validating the use of the difference-in-difference approach in this regression model.

DISCUSSION

This study provides rigorous statistical evidence to show that slum upgrading in Ahmedabad is associated with improved health outcomes. It supports findings from previous surveys while eliminating the self-reporting bias inherent in them. Using claims data allows easy patient follow-up over extended periods of time, is low cost, and limits reporting bias.[33] The empirical approach using micro–health insurance claims as a proxy for illness episodes demonstrates that a slum-upgrading intervention results in a statistically significant decrease in the incidence of hospitalized waterborne illness. This intervention led to an 18 percent decrease in the fraction of claims due to waterborne illness in an average year.

This decrease is likely an underestimate of the true impact, as health insurance claims of hospitalization for waterborne illness are a form of passive surveillance that can capture only the most severe forms of waterborne disease. Also, given that most waterborne illness is treatable at home or without admission to a hospital, insurance claims likely underrepresent the actual incidence of waterborne illness while overrepresenting nonwaterborne illness, relatively, in this analysis. Future research characterizing the rates of a variety of preventable medical conditions (designated as the "ambulatory care sensitive conditions") in this claims database could help quantify distortions in representation of actual waterborne illness identification.

There are many other positive outcomes that this study is unable to measure. The study does not measure the impact of this intervention on other health problems. While waterborne illness is an outcome more directly associated with improved water and sanitary infrastructure and better health, other direct and indirect health measures could also be used. Improved water and sanitation should reduce many infectious diseases that contribute to morbidity and mortality among children, including infant and neonatal mortality, two other MDG targets. Indirectly, mental health improvements have been positively correlated with improvements in living conditions. Reduced diarrhea may also result in reduced malnutrition in children. The analysis also does not measure possible positive health spillovers into neighboring slums. One would expect that this intervention would reduce waterborne illnesses in neighboring slums, as they are highly communicable.

The study has several limitations. The basic infrastructure improvements of this intervention were coupled with health education, including organization of community health education, health clinics, pharmacy services, and day care centers. However, anecdotal evidence suggests that most of this ancillary health intervention did not persist after the construction of the basic infrastructure, a period during which observations were dropped. It was also not possible to identify the exact timing of the intervention, given the imprecise dates of implementation in the MHT history file. The six-month window of construction used in this study is an approximation, but likely appropriate for most slums based on aggregate MHT data. In the future, a more precise time frame for the intervention implemented in different slums would be more effective. Also, the impact captured in this study shows that this intervention was successful only in the context of Ahmedabad and may lack generalizability. Many of the stakeholders who helped implement this intervention work only in Ahmedabad. Thus, the findings of this study may not be externally valid to implementations of slum upgrading in other cities. Nevertheless, the study does demonstrate a statistically sound proof of concept for slum upgrading in this context. Policy makers in other cities should consider the details of the implementation in Ahmedabad as guidance before implementing slum upgrading in other contexts.

As described in this chapter's introduction, information on health insurance claims has long been used as a proxy for health outcomes in clinical research, but it has clear limitations as a measure of disease incidence. To represent disease incidence, the health insurance system must capture all disease. For the purposes of this study's comparative analysis using waterborne and nonwaterborne illnesses claims, the insurance claims must simply capture all illnesses at similar rates. The study is thus predicated upon the assumption that the capture rate for all illnesses changes little over time. Furthermore, this analysis assumes that there was no significant increase in rates of nonwaterborne illness.

While the importance of clean water and sanitation is known, this study demonstrates that a simple infrastructure upgrade can produce positive health results even in the face of other health hazards specific to urban slums. Further research is needed to fully understand the benefits of such interventions, such as the health spillovers and the nonhealth benefits in savings, productivity, education, and overall well-being. Given that this study measured waterborne illness outcomes and that these illnesses are a large contributor to the morbidity and mortality of slum populations, longitudinal data would bear out the direct value in achieving reductions in infant and under-5 morbidity and mortality. Infrastructure upgrade also removes the distances some women travel to obtain water, thus improving their safety in urban slums. The savings in time spent on these activities, as well as the fewer days of missed work for illness episodes and costs incurred in seeking care, may all lead to increased productivity and wealth. A reduction in illness episodes is accompanied by a reduction in health spending, which among the poor in India is usually financed through debt.[34] In addition, infrastructure improvements such as this may have a direct effect on the social determinants of mental health in urban slums. Finally, children with fewer illness episodes should also have better school attendance, yielding a measurable positive effect on education. Further research should also focus on other interventions to affect illnesses and health risks concentrated or exacerbated by urban slums, as their cumulative positive outcomes far outweigh their costs.

This chapter invites further research on using micro–health insurance claims to measure the impact of public health interventions. Many developing countries are beginning to adopt public health insurance to address the health care financing needs of the poor. India is currently piloting the Rashtriya Swasthya Bima Yojana, a national health insurance scheme inspired in part by VimoSEWA's model, to provide individuals living below the poverty line with financial protection from catastrophic health expenses. Claims data from the implementation of micro–health insurance on a national scale provide a tremendous opportunity for public health researchers. Further research using claims databases in developing countries can not only perfect this new methodology in public health but also contribute to the evidence base that will inform public health practitioners in the field.

Finally, public–private partnerships such as that described above may allow governments paralyzed by the magnitude of this problem and lacking resources to effect positive change. This model in particular, cited as a successful case study by the Center for Sustainable Development and the World Health Organization, and armed with the study results above, argue for widespread scaling.[35] The Indian central government in India and international bodies such as WHO should coordinate large-scale slum upgrading based on this model.

If declines in health and the potential for outbreaks in this growing population are to be prevented, governments must act now. The findings above provide a role for governments in improving the health indicators of a rapidly increasing but ignored population. This study provides strong evidence for carrying out an urban slum upgrade in order to meet the Millennium Development Goals.

NOTES

Reprinted, with permission, from *Social Science and Medicine* 71 (2010):935–40.

1. United Nations Human Settlements Program (UN-Habitat) (2008). *Annual report, 2007*. http://unhabitat.org/books/annual-report-2007/ (accessed January 4, 2016).

2. United Nations Populations Fund (UNFPA) (2007). State of the world population 2007: Unleashing the potential of urban growth. New York.

3. UN-Habitat. (2003). The challenge of slums: Global report on human settlements 2003. Geneva.

4. UN-Habitat (2009). *Annual report, 2008.* http://unhabitat.org/books/annual-report-2008/ (accessed January 4, 2016).

5. Department of Economic and Social Affairs (2008). *The Millennium Development Goals report, 2008.* New York: United Nations. http://mdgs.un.org/unsd/mdg/Resources/Static/Products/Progress2008/MDG_Report_2008_En.pdf (accessed January 4, 2016).

6. UN-Habitat. (2003). *Water and sanitation in the world's cities: Local action for global goals.* London: Earthscan.

7. Department of Economic and Social Affairs (2008).

8. Gupta, N., Jain, S.K., Ratnesh, Chawla, U., Hossain, S., & Venkatesh, S. (2007). An evaluation of diarrheal diseases and acute respiratory infections control programmes in a Delhi slum. *Indian Journal of Pediatrics* 74(5):471–76.

9. Singhal, P.K., Mathur, G.P., Mathur, S., & Singh, Y.D. (1990). Neonatal morbidity and mortality in ICDS urban slums. *Indian Pediatrics* 27(5):485–88.

10. Awasthi, S., & Pande, V.K. (1997). Prevalence of malnutrition and intestinal parasites in pre-school slum children in Lucknow. *Indian Pediatrics* 34:599–605.

11. African Population and Health Resource Center (2002). Population and health dynamics in Nairobi's informal settlements. Nairobi, Kenya.

12. Kreiger, J., & Higgins, D. (2002). Housing and health: Time again for public health action. *American Journal of Public Health* 92(5):758–68.

13. Fewtrell, L., Prüss-Üstün, A., Bos, R., Gore, F., & Bartram, J. (2007). *Water, sanitation and hygiene: Quantifying the health impact at national and local levels in countries with incomplete water supply and sanitation coverage.* WHO Environmental Burden of Disease Series, No. 15. Geneva: World Health Organization.

14. Curtis, V., & Cairncross, S. (2003). Effect of washing hands with soap on diarrhea risk: A systematic review. *Lancet Infectious Disease* 3(5):275–81.

15. Semenza, J., Roberts, L., Henderson, A., Bogan, J., & Rubin, C. (1998). Water distribution system and diarrheal disease transmission: A case study in Uzbekistan. *American Journal of Tropical Medicine and Hygiene* 59(6):941–46.

16. Zwane, A.P., & Kremer, M. (2007). *What works in fighting diarrheal diseases in developing countries? A critical review.* World Bank Reserve Obs. Washington, DC: World Bank.

17. Northridge, M., Sclar, E., & Biswas, P. (2003). Sorting out the connections between the built environment and health: A conceptual framework for navigating pathways and planning healthy cities. *Journal of Urban Health* 80(4):556-68.

18. Harpham, T. (2009). Urban health in developing countries: What do we know and where do we go? *Health and Place* 15(1):107–16.

19. Yach, D., Mathews, C., & Buch, E. (1990). Urbanisation and health: Methodological difficulties in undertaking epidemiological research in developing countries. *Social Science and Medicine* 31(4):507–14.

20. Birnbaum, H., Cremieux, P., Greenberg, P., LeLorier, J., Ostrander, J., & Venditti, L. (1999). Using healthcare claims data for outcomes research and pharmacoeconomic analyses. *Pharmacoeconomics* 16(1):1–8.

21. Garbe, E., LeLorier, J., Boivin, J.F., & Suissa, S. (1997). Inhaled and nasal glucocorticoids and the risk of ocular hypertension and open-angle glaucoma. *Journal of the American Medical Association* 277:722–27.

22. Mitchell, J.B., Bubolz, T., Paul, J.E., Pashos, C.L., Escarce, J.J., Muhlbaier, L.H., et al. (1994). Using Medicare claims for outcomes research. *Medical Care* 32(7 Suppl.):JS38–JS51.

23. Motheral, B., & Fairman, K. (1997). The use of claims databases for outcomes research: Rationale, challenges, and strategies. *Clinical Therapeutics* 19(2):346–66.

24. Adler, N.E., & Ostrove, J.M. (1999). Socioeconomic status and health: What we know and what we don't. *Annals of the New York Academy of Sciences* 896:3–15.

25. Adler, N.E., & Newman, K. (2002). Socioeconomic disparities in health: pathways and policies. *Health Affairs* 21(2; March–April):60–76.

26. Zwane, A.P., & Kremer, M. (2007).

27. Nohn, M., Sinha, T., Patel, F., & Bhatt, B. (2007). *NIUA study on the habitat and employment of Ahmedabad's poor.* New Delhi: National Institute of Urban Affairs.

28. Abelson, P. (1996). Evaluation of slum improvements: Case study of Visakhapatnam, India. *Cities* 13(2):97–108.

29. Verma, G. (2000). Indore's habitat improvement project: Success or failure? *Habitat International* 24(1):91–117.

30. Mahila Housing Trust, Self Employed Women's Association. (2006). *Under one roof: A comprehensive report on activities and impact of Gujarat.* Ahmedabad, India.

31. Ranson, M.K., Sinha, T., Chatterjee, M., Acharya, A., Bhavsar, A., Morris, S.S., et al. (2006). Making health insurance work for the poor: Learning from the Self Employed Women's Association's (SEWA) community-based health insurance scheme in India. *Social Science and Medicine* 62(3):707–20.

32. Field, E., & Kremer, M. (2006). *Impact evaluation for slum upgrading interventions.* In Doing Impact Evaluation Series No. 3. New York: World Bank.

33. Wennberg, J., Roos, N., Sola, L., Schori, A., & Jaffe, R. (1987). Use of claims data systems to evaluate health care outcomes: Mortality and reoperation following prostatectomy. *Journal of American Medical Association* 257(7):933–36.

34. Mohanan, M. (2008). *Consumption smoothing and household responses: Evidence from random exogenous health shocks.* Working Paper Series, Center for International Development at Harvard University, No. 23. Cambridge, MA: Harvard University.

35. Mercado, S., Havemann, K., Nakamura, K., Kiyu, A., Sami, M., Alampay, R., et al. (2007). Responding to the health vulnerabilities of the urban poor in the "new urban settings" of Asia. Center for Sustainable Urban Development, for the Rockefeller Foundation Global Urban Summit, 2007. http://csud.ei.columbia.edu/files/2012/04/Week3_Health_Asia_Mercado.pdf (accessed January 15, 2016).

PART V

Knowledge Gaps and Future Considerations

In the final section of this book, we identify some of the gaps in knowledge regarding slum health and describe our thoughts on what still needs to be done to fill the gaps. We focus on four areas that we believe require further consideration: (1) research focused on specific health issues expected to increase in prevalence in urban slums, (2) development of new metrics specifically designed to assess the disease burden in slums, (3) policy changes that need to be implemented to effect good health in slum dwellers, and (4) training in research and advocacy targeting urban slum health. Some of these issues were touched upon in parts of the previous chapters, but they were not explicitly summarized as targets of further studies. Slums and their associated health issues will continue to evolve, and we are likely to encounter many health problems never previously observed. We must be prepared to address them with new ideas, approaches, and action.

CHAPTER 14

Toward Slum Health Equity

Research, Action, and Training

JASON CORBURN AND LEE RILEY

As this book helps highlight, slum health is not a static state measured through discrete diseases, but rather is an ongoing process of understanding and improving the determinants of well-being among the urban poor. Much is still unknown about the biology, exposure pathways, and efficacy of particular interventions—whether they be microbiologic, clinical, environmental, social, or some combination of all of these. What we recognize, however, is that scientific uncertainty is no reason not to act for slum health today. The issues and challenges are too great to delay. In addition, the science of slum health is only improved through a combination—a coproduction—of different types of disciplinary inquiry, analytic methods, professional and lay expertise, and learning by doing.

As every part of this book highlights, slum health demands active participation by slum dwellers, their representative organizations, scientists, and policy makers. No one group alone can accomplish slum health. We are particularly concerned with increasing the role of the urban poor and their organizations in slum health action-research. As we show, when research and intervention agendas are set without a meaningful role for the urban poor themselves, the research and policy often fail to improve the health and well-being of slum dwellers. In short, local knowledge is essential, and while it is not the only type of expertise needed to improve slum health, the experiences and knowledge of the urban poor are too often an afterthought in global health research and policy making. While global health efforts are increasingly working to change international organizations and national governments, urban slum health often depends on negotiation with local, municipal governments that can provide or stymie life-supporting services, from water and sanitation, to land tenure and gender rights, to education and health care.

We also show that slum health is achievable only when urban slum dwellers are offered the right to remain in place, not evicted or displaced. Slum health ought, then, to be thought of as an in situ process whereby the urban poor are integrated into the services and benefits of their larger urban context. An in situ slum health approach allows the urban poor to keep their existing social networks; improve the physical, social, and economic environment of urban places; and build upon the social, physical, and other investments already made by slum dwellers.

In this concluding chapter, we reflect on our experiences in the field and the laboratory to offer suggestions for improving slum health. We divide our comments on future needs for slum health into four sections: research, measurement, policy, and training. Research needs in slum health include further articulation of the coproduction of health using a systems science approach, the contributions that laboratory research can make to disease identification, and the complex interactions between noncommunicable and infectious diseases in urban poor communities.

Measurement is important, since we often act on what we appraise. Yet more and "bigger" data are not necessarily helpful for slum health. We explore specific ways data can more accurately characterize the burden of disease in slums and the social and physical determinants of health in slums while empowering local communities and slum dwellers to define health priorities and participate in decision making. Data and democracy must be linked for the future of slum health.

Policy making remains a great challenge for slum health. Declarations such as those by the World Bank's Cities Alliance for "Cities without Slums" and some slum upgrade national programs have rarely prioritized health or, if they have, have tended to focus narrowly on single diseases and improvements to primary care. We suggest that slum health policy must include an integrated approach whereby city governments are given discretion by their national ministries to design and implement improvements for the urban poor. By "integrated," we mean policies that are not fragmented by traditional sectors—medicine, transport, housing, environment, and the like—but rather that emphasize the ways infrastructure, transport, medical care, economic opportunities, quality living conditions, and nondiscrimination in accessing such social goods as education all interact to produce or stymie opportunities for the urban poor to be healthy. In addition to the examples explored in depth in this book, we recognize that such programs as Programa Urbano Integral (PUI; integral urban program) in Medellin, Colombia, and Favela Bairro/Morar Carioca in Rio de Janeiro, Brazil (mentioned in chapter 5), represent this integrated approach to urban well-being and are important models to explore for discovering whether and how they address health inequities in these cities.

Finally, we acknowledge that universities cannot continue to train public health, medical, and other professionals in the same ways if we are to meet the twenty-first-century challenge of slum health. Narrowly trained experts often fail to see the broad and intersecting determinants of urban health, and those with too-general training often fail to understand the complexity and nuance of disease burdens, such as how environmental exposures interact with molecular biology and immune system function to ultimately determine clinical outcomes. We briefly sketch what such a global slum health training program might look like and build upon our own experiences teaching undergraduates, graduates, and postdoctoral fellows.

FUTURE RESEARCH

Generating New Knowledge through the Coproduction of Research

The scientific foundation supporting the coproduction approach to slum health research is systems science— an interdisciplinary approach to scientific discovery based on the study of *systems*. What is the nature of systems and what systems exist in slum health? Applied to slum health research, systems science must compare and identify systemic differences between urban slum and nonslum communities that determine health outcomes. Chapter 8 unmasked differences at the cellular level of bacterial strains that cause pharyngitis in slum versus nonslum children residing in the same city. Such differences were then hypothesized to determine the prevalence of rheumatic heart disease (RHD) in the two populations in Salvador, Brazil.[1] In this example, the systems revealed and characterized included (1) the transmission dynamics of bacterial pathogens that cause pharyngitis, as deciphered through a molecular epidemiology approach; (2) the slum social network that affected the pathogen's pathways of transmission; (3) the structural characteristics of housing that determined population density and probability of transmission;

(4) the socioeconomic factors that influenced people's choice of location of residence, education, and opportunities for employment; and (5) the public health infrastructure that determined how, who, where, and when infected individuals would receive appropriate care for the pharyngitis. These systems need to be further analyzed to better understand the distribution of RHD in Salvador. For each disease and disease complex in urban slums, relevant systems-based approaches need to be developed. The challenge is in identifying and then analyzing the systems to generate knowledge that could then be used to devise new systems-based control of these health outcomes.

Laboratory-Based Research to Characterize Proximal Causes of Disease in Slum Communities

The goals of laboratory-based research applied to slum health must also incorporate basic systems science concepts. Three general goals of such approaches can be considered: simple, affordable diagnostic and prognostic test development; tools to diagnose and monitor noncommunicable chronic diseases; and identification of new therapeutic and preventive modalities designed to include slum dwellers.

Simple, affordable point-of-residence (in addition to point-of-care) diagnostic and prognostic test development

In developed countries, it is currently fashionable to talk about point-of-care (POC) diagnostics. POC, of course, could comprise a variety of entities. To be meaningful in the context of slum health research, POC must take into consideration not just the site and ease with which a diagnostic test is performed, but other relevant issues as well. These include, among others, (a) factors associated with reluctance or willingness of patients to seek medical attention, (b) the time between the onset of illness and health care provider visit, (c) ready access to the diagnostic test site, (d) timeliness of reporting the test results to patients, (e) timeliness of the decision to initiate treatment or intervention based on test results, and (f) the number and cost of the tests needed to identify a patient with the disease the test is designed to detect. If any of these other issues become hindrances, as they often do in slum communities, then POC serves little purpose. If, however, a diagnostic test can be developed that is so simple that it can be incorporated into a national public health care program (such as the Bolsa Familia of Brazil) and the test can be performed during household visits (point-of-residence, or POR), then an intervention can be made more efficiently and comprehensively. Laboratory-based research to develop such tests will therefore need to be based on understanding the epidemiological, anthropological, socioeconomic, environmental, and biological features of the health problem for which the test is being developed.

Better tools to diagnose and monitor noncommunicable chronic diseases at POR

Several devices for diagnosing and monitoring chronic noncommunicable diseases (NCDs) at home already exist, such as the portable electronic blood pressure–measuring device and the blood glucose self-monitoring meter. Although these blood glucose–monitoring meters can be used by diabetic patients at home, they require puncturing the skin to access capillary blood. Affordable noninvasive tests are still needed to maintain good blood glucose control to minimize complications of diabetes. Screening for common cancers, such as cervical carcinoma, breast cancer, and lung cancer, in urban slums requires tests that are simpler and more accessible than Pap smears, human papilloma virus (HPV) testing by polymerase chain reaction (PCR), mammography, or bronchoscopy. One example of such a simple test is the visual inspection of the cervix swabbed with acetic acid or vinegar (called the VIA test), which has been implemented in some urban poor communities in developing countries to screen for cervical carcinoma.[2] Such screening can greatly reduce mortality caused by this second–most common form of cancer in women in developing countries. Research is needed to develop similar screening tests for other forms of NCDs.

Identification of new therapeutic and preventive modalities designed to include slum dwellers

Chapter 8 discusses how the newly developed experimental vaccine against Group A *Streptococcus* infections would provide widely different levels of effectiveness if administered to slum versus nonslum children in Salvador. Laboratory research focused on slum dwellers is essential to make sure that new drugs and vaccines will provide the same level of effectiveness that they will for non–slum dwellers. Of course, they must also be made affordable for slum residents. The latter goal involves not just laboratory science but also knowledge of auxiliary issues, including intellectual property, financing of drugs and vaccines, and other operational science aspects involved in providing these products—sometimes referred to as implementation science.

Analysis of the Impact of Climate Change on Slum Health

Climate change in cities in low- and middle-income countries (LMICs) makes vulnerable populations even more susceptible to disease, displacement, and death. What can a focus on slum health do to make these populations less vulnerable to both disease and climate change variability? The Fourth Assessment Report of the Intergovernmental Panel on Climate Change states that urbanization and climate change may work synergistically to increase disease burdens. Uncertain but severe rain events are already linked to climate change. As preceding chapters show for urban Brazil, Kenya, and India, a significant share of ill health in slums stems from poor access to and quality of sanitation, drinking water, and housing. Lack of planning for the urban poor in LMICs has created flood-prone areas, latrines, and septic tanks that are key reservoirs for infectious diseases and are likely to increase in number with a rise in uncertain weather events related to climate change. The urban poor are forced to build houses made of weak, inadequate materials, often on steep slopes, in flood plains, and on other vulnerable land, all of which increases the physical, social, and economic vulnerabilities of slum dwellers.

Climate change is also expected to bring more frequent and longer droughts to many urbanizing parts of the world, and water scarcity for the urban poor is already contributing to poor health outcomes and violence as regions compete for this scarce resource. As urban temperatures rise, slum dwellers become more vulnerable to heat events due to their lack of ventilated housing. Slum dwellers are also frequently forced to live near roadways, railways, and urban industrial activities, increasing their exposure to outdoor air pollution, especially particulate matter and ozone. As urban temperatures increase, the concentration of ground-level ozone also increases, low-level ozone is associated with premature mortality and increased respiratory diseases including pneumonia, chronic obstructive pulmonary disease, and asthma.

There is an urgent need to ensure global efforts aimed at climate change mitigation and adaptation address the needs of the urban poor. Climate change adaptation has to be treated as a cobenefit of equitable and inclusive urban development. By addressing housing stability, infrastructure, social and health care services, and other priorities already identified by residents and community organizations based in informal settlements, climate change risks can be reduced. Thus, climate change adaptation needs to work with the urban poor most at risk from storms, floods, heat waves, and other hazards associated with climate change.

Urban dwellers can be and are local risk analysts, managers, and reducers. As we show, slum dwellers already have knowledge and capacity to identify and reduce those risks. Slum savings groups, as we show in Part III, about Nairobi's slum dwellers, help very low–income women manage risk and increase their resilience to shocks, including sudden and extreme weather events that can damage their homes and livelihoods. Slum savings groups have supported many initiatives—building or improving homes, building and managing community toilets and washing facilities, and carrying out censuses in informal settlements to generate the data needed to design and implement upgrading schemes.

As we note throughout this book, effective research and action for the well-being of the urban poor must include partnerships with academics, local governments, and NGOs. Top-down solutions, no matter how well intentioned and how advanced the technologies they use, are likely to fail since they do not involve those who must implement and live with the intervention, rarely account for place-specific and cultural nuances, and unfairly treat the urban poor as passive victims. Thus, we suggest that international and national climate change adaptation funds should first be channeled into planning processes that include the urban poor, not rushing to build citywide projects. Instead of national climate change adaptation funds and projects, each urban center should be allocated funds whose use has to be determined in cooperation with community organizations with transparency in how funding priorities are determined and supported. One precedent here is Brazil's national health system (Sistema Único de Saúde, or SUS), in which each municipality implements the program and budget priorities are set by a local council that includes NGOs and others.

MEASUREMENT

Development of new metrics and quantitative methods for assessing the disease burden is a major component of the coproduction approach to slum health research and action. Surely the point of gathering data in urban health is to make sure it assists (and even empowers) those in need in obtaining what they lack. Yet most official data sets used to assess disease and unmet health needs rarely capture accurate information within urban slums. Most national data, such as the Demographic and Health Surveys (DHSs) in many emerging-economy countries disaggregate data only by urban and rural, and not urban slum, populations. DHSs collect a wide range of objective and self-reported data with a strong focus on indicators of fertility, reproductive health, maternal and child health, mortality, nutrition, and self-reported health behaviors among adults.

Multidimensional Metrics

As we show for Salvador, Nairobi, and Ahmedabad, slum dwellers in partnership with scientists can collect relevant, informative, and significant data. For example, data collected in Nairobi provided detailed information on multiple health risks and vulnerabilities across the Mathare informal settlement. The community-generated data, when owned and controlled by local organizations, also supported democratic discussions of intervention priorities as to which healthy development investments were needed and where.

We suggest the need to develop more robust composite measures for slum health. A commonly used composite index is the United Nations Human Development Index (HDI), which measures a country's average achievement in three basic aspects of human development: health (life expectancy), education (expected years of schooling and mean years of schooling), and income (gross national income per capita). The Global Multidimensional Poverty Index (MPI)[3] is another measure of poverty designed to capture the multiple deprivations that each poor person faces simultaneously with respect to education, health, and other aspects of living standard. The MPI reflects both the incidence of multidimensional poverty (the proportion of people in a population who are multidimensionally poor) and its intensity (the average number of deprivations each poor person experiences at the same time). The MPI relies on three main data sets that are publicly available and comparable for most developing countries: the Demographic and Health Survey (DHS), the Multiple Indicators Cluster Survey (MICS), and the World Health Survey (WHS). Under the MPI, a household is identified as multidimensionally poor if, and only if, it is deprived in some combination of indicators whose weighted sum is 30 percent or more of the dimensions. The dimensions, indicators, and deprivation criteria include:

1. Health (each indicator weighted equally at 1 out of 6)

    Child mortality: if any child has died in the family

    Nutrition: if any adult or child in the family is malnourished

2. Education (each indicator weighted equally at 1 out of 6)

    Years of schooling: if no household member has completed five years of schooling

    Child school attendance: if any school-aged child is out of school in years 1 to 8

3. Standard of Living (each of the six indicators weighted equally at 1 out of 18)

    Electricity: if the household does not have electricity

    Drinking water: if water does not meet Millennium Development Goal (MDG) definitions, or is more than a 30-minute walk away

    Sanitation: if sanitation does not meet MDG definitions, or the toilet is shared

    Flooring: if the floor is dirt, sand, or dung

    Cooking fuel: If household members cook with wood, charcoal, or dung

    Assets: if the household does not own *at least one of the following:* radio, TV, telephone, bike, motorbike, or refrigerator and does not own a car or truck

A strength of composite indicators such as the MPI is that they summarize many determinants of health as a single number that can assist researchers in tracking and comparing change across places. However, the summarizing of measures into one index is also a weakness of composite indicators. When it comes to slum health, composite measures run the risk of washing out the nuance and differentiation that can be so important for understanding what specific exposures and diseases are important for improving health in specific slum environments and for different population groups.

Metrics for Chronic Noncommunicable Diseases and Their Interaction with Infectious Diseases

The need for quantitative assessment of the burden of infectious diseases on noncommunicable diseases (NCDs) and on the people who have an

NCD requires development of new instruments for obtaining data as well as new metrics for analyzing them. The development of new instruments with which to gather data related to NCDs is a component of the future laboratory-based research described above. However, analyses of the data obtained from the application of these instruments will require a more fundamental shift in methodology. As discussed in chapter 2, the current practice of disease reporting based on disease classification systems, such as the International Classification of Diseases (ICD), greatly underestimates the burden of infectious diseases, especially when these diseases cause death in individuals who have NCDs. For NCDs, reports of mortality used for research or policy purposes based on hospital-based surveillance or Global Burden of Disease (GBD) surveys do not usually indicate the number or the proportion of the mortality that is directly attributable to infectious diseases. Those statistics are included in the reports of mortality caused by NCDs. Infectious diseases that occur in NCDs deserve a category of their own and need to be included in reports used for research and policy purposes. The same ICD classification scheme can be used to describe the illnesses, but the reports of mortality or morbidity associated with the infectious disease complications of NCDs must be reported as an entity in itself. That is, there should be a category of NCD-associated infectious diseases included in mortality/morbidity reports in future disease surveillance systems. Only in this way can the burden of infectious diseases be accurately quantified. This is particularly relevant for slum dwellers, among whom such an interaction of infectious diseases with NCDs is quite common.

The 2010 GBD survey covered 291 diseases and injuries, with 67 risk factors for mortality and the burden from these diseases in 187 countries.[4] The total global disability adjusted life years (DALYs) in 2010 was 2,482 million, compared to 2,497 million in 1990.[5] Based on increase in population size over this period, DALYs should have increased by nearly 38 percent, but they actually decreased by 0.6 percent. Such an observation indicates progress in reducing DALYs, especially those attributable to communicable diseases, which predominantly affect children. By the same token, as the world's population became older, DALYs and years living with disability (YLD) caused by NCDs increased. Globally, ischemic heart disease increased from the rank of 4 in 1990 to being the top cause of DALYs in 2010.[6] Diabetes mellitus (DM) DALYs increased from the rank of 21 to 14. In Brazil, the rise in the prevalence of both DM and hypertension is associated with a parallel rise in obesity prevalence.

Three-quarters of deaths due to NCDs worldwide each year are estimated to occur in LMICs.[7,8] The epidemiological transition of decrease in the occurrence of communicable diseases with increase in NCDs is particularly evident in emerging-economy nations. In Brazil between 1990 and 2010, years of life lost (YLL) caused by DM increased by 95 percent (rank change from 17 to 7), while diarrheal diseases decreased by 90 percent (rank change from 3 to 24). In India and China, YLL caused by DM increased by 92 percent and 71 percent, respectively, over the same period (Institute for Health Metrics and Evaluation, http://www.healthdata.org/results/country-profiles).[9] Thus, at the national level, this epidemiological transition indeed appears to be occurring in these large emerging-economy nations.

The GBD metrics described above represent aggregate data from an entire nation or regions. Studies of the NCD burden in subpopulations in high-income countries show a higher prevalence among marginalized populations.[10, 11, 12, 13] Similar data for subpopulations within LMICs are not yet widely available.[14] Although in 2011 the Brazilian Ministry of Health initiated a population-based program called the Strategic Action to Tackle Non-communicable Diseases, it is not clear whether this program includes any component that targets NCDs that occur in vulnerable populations.[15] The transitions described above will certainly vary according to different subpopulations within a nation; hence the metrics described above may not accurately reflect the burden of communicable diseases versus NCDs in subpopulations within a nation or even within a large city.

For example, the population residing in the slum communities of Rio de Janeiro has a demographic profile distinct from that of nonslum populations in the same city.[16] The slum communities have a proportionately greater number of late teens and young adults in the age group 15–29 years.[17] This simple difference in age structure can contribute to a great difference in the incidence of NCD morbidity and mortality associated with firearm-related interpersonal violence.[18] Firearm-related mortality progressively increased in Brazil between 1980 and 2010, most of the deaths occurring among youths and young adults.[19]

However, the unequal distribution of NCD occurrence in communities is only part of the story. In the example from Rio de Janeiro, what is not known is what happens when NCDs like firearm-related morbidity occur in urban slums. What is not addressed is the infectious disease complications associated with firearm-related and other forms of interpersonal violence. Violence, especially when committed in the context of illegal activities, may lead to injuries that may not be immediately cared for.

Such injuries are more likely to progress to infection, and even death from infectious complication of the injury, among slum than among nonslum dwellers. Officially, these infections may not be recorded as infections, but as interpersonal violence-associated injury or death. Without review or reports of the proximal causes of death or secondary morbidity following violence-related injuries, the impact of infectious diseases on slum dwellers is underestimated or ignored.

The occurrence of NCDs in urban slum settlements where infectious diseases still prevail creates a new disease phenomenon: *NCD-associated infectious diseases* (NCDAIDs). As described above, DM, especially type 2 DM, is rapidly increasing in prevalence in large emerging-economy countries, including Brazil, China, and India. DM is a major risk factor for the development of tuberculosis (TB).[20, 21] In Brazil, the reported number of TB cases with DM increased from 337 in 2001 to 5,426 in 2011, even though the overall TB incidence decreased during this period. Brazil reports the highest incidence of TB in the Americas;[22] China and India together accounted for nearly 40 percent of the estimated total of new TB cases in the world. Using the World Health Survey, Goldhaber-Fiebert and colleagues estimated the relationship between DM and TB adjusting for demographic and socioeconomic characteristics.[23] They found that in lower-income countries, individuals with DM were more likely to develop TB than nondiabetics.[24] Thus, this rapid rise in the prevalence of type 2 DM combined with a high TB burden in the same regions is bound to create a new disease epidemic—an NCDAID—not previously seen in the world. Subpopulations within high–TB burden countries that have the highest incidence of TB are the slum dwellers. At this time, little is known about the burden of DM and TB in these subpopulations.

The negative effect of DM on NCDAIDs is not limited to TB. The noninfectious disease complications of DM, including chronic kidney disease (CKD) and microvascular disease, engender many other types of infectious diseases. They include skin and soft tissue infections (SSTI), foot ulcers, osteomyelitis, pneumonia, and recurrent urinary tract infections (UTIs) and blood stream infections. Patients requiring hemodialysis due to DM-induced CKD are at high risk for sepsis. These infections frequently recur in diabetics and predispose them to develop drug-resistant forms of these infections, including infections such as methicillin-resistant *Staphylococcus aureus* (MRSA), diabetic foot ulcers,[25] and multidrug-resistant UTI.[26] Risk factors for these complications include poor blood glucose control and lack of proper clinical monitoring of the DM status. These risk factors are, of course, more likely to be prevalent in slum dwellers. Again, little is known about the burden of these other infectious disease complications of DM in slum communities.

NCDAIDs occur in association with many other NCDs, including chronic obstructive pulmonary disease (COPD),[27] asthma,[28] autoimmune diseases such as rheumatoid arthritis,[29] CKD associated with hypertension or cardiovascular disease,[30] liver cirrhosis,[31] and cancer. Cancer is now the leading cause of death in most developed countries and the second–most common cause of death in developing countries.[32] However, the most common proximal cause of death from cancer is infections.[33] Both the disease and treatment of the disease itself (e.g., immunosuppressive chemotherapy, bone marrow transplantation, radiation, biologics) contribute to infectious complications and mortality. Most formal disease-reporting systems attribute deaths that occur in these individuals with NCDs to the NCDs themselves, even when their direct cause of death was an infectious disease. In this way, the high burden of infectious diseases on those with NCD is underrecognized and underappreciated.

Infections themselves can cause NCDs or exacerbate the NCD conditions. We discuss rheumatic heart disease (RHD) in chapter 1 as an example of a chronic NCD triggered by an infectious disease process. Group A *Streptococcus* has been hypothesized to contribute to exacerbation of symptoms of obsessive compulsive disorder, a neuropsychiatric disorder in children.[34] The association of cancer with infectious diseases occurs in the other direction as well. It is estimated that nearly 16 percent of all cancers globally are attributable to infectious agents.[35] These include *Helicobacter pylori,* which is associated with peptic ulcer disease and stomach cancer; hepatitis B and C viruses, which cause liver cirrhosis and hepatocellular carcinoma; and human papilloma virus (HPV), which causes anogenital warts, cervical dysplasia, and cancer. All of these infections are more common in low-income communities of LMICs. Cervical cancer is the leading cancer-related cause of death in women in low-income countries. The lack of screening services in urban slums contributes to a greater burden of advanced stag cervical carcinoma among women living in such communities. Undoubtedly, many other cancers will ultimately be attributed to infectious agents.

In 2011, the UN General Assembly held a high-level meeting to discuss the prevention and control of NCDs.[36] The declaration that emerged from the meeting included no recommendations or discussion regarding examination of the impact or interaction of NCDs with infectious diseases. The *Lancet* series that focused on NCDs in 2013 did not include any discussion of NCDAIDs.[37] As described above, infectious diseases contribute to a substantial burden on individuals who have chronic NCDs, especially when the NCD occurs in marginalized populations. There is a great need to fill this gap in knowledge regarding NCDs and NCDAIDs in urban slum communities, especially of emerging-economy nations where life expectancy has dramatically increased in the past 20 years. We cannot assume that the DALY transitions observed by the GBD 2010 survey apply to all populations inside these nations. Appropriate allocation of health resources and implementation of policies require quantitative measures of the NCD and NDCAID burden in the most vulnerable subpopulations. Quantitative measures of the burden of these diseases require better understanding and assessment of the biology of the interaction of NCD with infectious agents (cell), but also the environmental, structural, legal, economic, and political influences on the people who develop NCDs (street). Only then can we begin to make a difference in slum health.

POLICY

As we suggest in chapter 5, slum upgrading holds the potential to promote health equity in slums without widespread displacement of the urban poor. International agencies such as the World Bank, UN-Habitat, and the World Health Organization have all recognized that we can't treat our way out of the disease burden in urban slums. Instead, slum upgrading that recognizes slum dwellers' right to exist, improves their living conditions, and provides services, including universal medical care, is the route toward slum health.

Thailand offers one such example of a national program in both slum improvement and universal health care that takes account of local cultural conditions. The results since about 2002, when both the national slum-upgrading program called Community Organizations Development Institute (CODI) and the health care program called Universal Coverage Scheme (UCS) came into effect, suggest great achievements in reducing health for everyone and inequalities between socioeconomic class and regions. Infant mortality in Thailand is now about 11 per 1,000, and life expectancy is close to 74 years at birth. The programs are also beginning to reduce historic health disparities between richer and poorer regions and districts across Thailand, though more progress is sorely needed. CODI has provided housing loans, infrastructure improvements, and land rights negotiation for millions of residents in urban informal settlements. The idea is that both national programs—health care and slum upgrading—are needed and that both need to be explicitly attentive to specific community needs and historic inequalities and need to empower residents to help solve the challenges they face for being healthy.

Neither slum upgrading nor universal health services alone are sufficient policies to promote slum health; both together are necessary. However, few countries have begun to integrate slum upgrading into their national health care or public health systems. This policy innovation is sorely needed since health services often account for a large national expenditure but frequently ignore the living and working conditions that are making populations ill in the first place. Yet some countries, such as Thailand, are seeing the combination of health care and community development as the strategy for improving the lot of everyone, not just the urban poor.

Health care and slum upgrading are both labor-intensive programs, but an untapped and underutilized work force is exactly what most countries with large slum populations have. So, although low-income countries may not have adequate financial resources to implement universal health care and support urban slum upgrading, they often do have a knowledgeable labor force. National and universal programs—in both slum upgrading and health services—are crucial to avoid regional and population inequities. Thus, innovative health and slum-upgrading policies should be seen as generating employment and as smart investments in the future of emerging economies.

TRAINING

Our schools of public health, city planning, and related fields are currently not organized to meet the twenty-first-century challenges of slum health. It is rare to even find a course dedicated to urban health at the undergraduate or graduate level at universities in the United States, Europe, or emerging-economy countries. Training students from emerging-economy countries in how to work for slum health is crucial. We also suggest that training and retraining professionals in rich countries and in global institutions intended to support urban/slum health is also critical for twenty-first-century health equity. Below, we offer brief suggestions for how universities and others might address the training needs for slum health.

Curriculum Dedicated to Slum Health in Academic Institutions and Professional Schools

We suggest that a new curriculum needs to be developed for training students in the interdisciplinary methods and approaches needed to address slum health. As we emphasize throughout this book, narrowly trained professionals are unlikely to have the tools or know-how necessary to address the complex, interdisciplinary challenges of slum health. This new curriculum will need to situate students in fields of history and social sciences so that they may understand the forces that have often created and perpetuated slums; public health, biology, and other sciences so that they may understand the multiple ways slum dwellers are burdened with toxic exposures and diseases; and public policy, engineering, city planning, and other, related fields so that they may explore the set of interventions that might work in particular places.

Yet this professional training cannot happen within academic and other professional institutions alone. As we show through the coproduction model, partnerships between university scientists, clinicians, community organizations, local governments, and others are essential. Thus, professionals working for slum health must learn how to build ongoing, engaged research and action partnerships. We have found that the best way to do this is through learning by doing. One mechanism for learning by doing, often used in schools of architecture and planning, is the studio course, in which students and instructors partner with clients to address real-world problems. Students in cities of the global South and North might come together to share resources and experiences to address slum health issues. This is the model we used for some of the work in Nairobi's slums discussed in part III.

In the Nairobi Studio (see http://nairobistudio.blogspot.com), faculty and students from the University of California, Berkeley, and the University of Nairobi built a partnership with the NGOs Shack/Slum Dwellers International (SDI), Pamoja Trust, Muungano wa Wanavijiji, and Akiba Mashinani Trust in Kenya. The partners jointly designed a studio class in 2009 focused on slum upgrade plan making in Nairobi's Mathare slum. The students met with slum dwellers and their organizations, held community planning meetings, collected survey and mapping data, and jointly drafted slum-upgrading proposals. Three additional studio courses involving all the partners were held between 2010 and 2014, each building on knowledge gained and projects proposed in the previous studio. New water service delivery, food security, sanitation, and urban policy making were proposed through the courses, and almost all proposals managed to gain financing and political support for intervention.

Students in the studios came from a range of disciplines, including biology, journalism, public health, architecture, city planning, and engineering. The Berkeley students learned about working in a different culture with Nairobi University students, and the University of Nairobi students learned how to work with—not for—slum dwellers and their organizations. Discussions during studios included awareness of colonialism and Western/white privilege; the appropriate roles for technology, local knowledge, and research; how to prevent displacement while improving a poor community; how women can take a leading role in improving the well-being of themselves and the entire community; and other slum health issues. The studios offered a space for experiential learning about the complexities of slum health and other issues, learning that came from being inside a slum and from on-the-ground, face-to-face interactions with slum dwellers. Among the lessons learned were that residents are not to blame for their situation; there are limits to international aide and development projects; slums are not just places of crime, violence, and social degradation; and the poor health of slum dwellers is not inevitable.

A model for action-oriented research that involves students and community residents is also illustrated by the field research work, described in Part II, in Pau da Lima, Salvador, Brazil. In this project, focused on leptospirosis, the team included professional researchers, academics, students, and residents of the slum community. Many of the peer-reviewed publications resulting from this project benefited not only the academic careers of US and Brazilian professional researchers, but also the community residents, who learned new skills that enabled them to pursue their education in Brazil—an opportunity they may not have had otherwise. These publications also served as models and guides for other studies performed elsewhere in Brazil, serving as training materials for conducting slum health research as well as advocacy work. Thus, training for action and advocacy is coproducing slum health.

Action-research and the studio course act as core experiences in UC Berkeley's concurrent master's in public health (MPH) and master's in city planning (MCP) degree program (see http://healthycities.berkeley.edu). In this program, students spend three years earning two graduate degrees. Students fulfill the core requirements in both public health and city planning, but take targeted courses, attend a yearlong seminar, and pursue research and internship positions all at the intersection of urban planning and public health. The graduate program has a special emphasis on addressing health inequities and slum health. Faculty from both disciplines, as well as law, public policy, engineering, medicine, environmental science, geography, anthropology, and other disciplines ensure that the academic experience reflects the transdisciplinary knowledge that professional practitioners need to address twenty-first-century urban health challenges.

Training Grants Dedicated to Slum Health Research

The National Institutes of Health (NIH) have recognized systems biology research as a new discipline to fund. However, the NIH have yet to recognize slum health as a research discipline based on systems science that should be funded. Although a new cadre of computational biology researchers has been successfully created in the world, there are still very few investigators who conduct research in urban slums. Of course, the NIH fund many research projects focused on specific diseases more prevalent in urban slums. However, it is not obvious that the disease-focused research projects that the NIH have supported over past decades have made a substantial dent in the disease burden in urban slums of LMICs. If anything, some of these diseases have actually increased in prevalence, including Ebola, MDR tuberculosis, dengue, drug-resistant Gram-negative bacterial infections, health care–associated infections, to name a few infectious diseases; and diabetes, cervical cancer, mental disorders, homicide, and interpersonal injuries, to name a few NCDs. All of these diseases have increased in prevalence largely in the types of populations discussed throughout this book.

The 2014 Ebola epidemic in West Africa is a case in point. Despite numerous suggestions about the reasons for this epidemic's unprecedented magnitude (more than 28,636cases and 11,315deaths, as of January 14, 2016), there was very little discussion in the international discourse about the most obvious reason—that in 2014, for the first time, the Ebola virus entered the overcrowded slums of large urban centers of these countries.[38] The population of Sierra Leone, Guinea, and Liberia increased by more than threefold since Ebola's first outbreak in 1976 in Zaire, and more than 90 percent of most urban centers of these countries can be described by UN-Habitat standards as slums. To this day, there is no discussion about the need to address the slum conditions that have fostered such an explosive epidemic. The Ebola epidemic is only one of many infectious diseases to explode in urban slums. The Zika virus epidemic that began in Brazil in 2015 is a prime example.

Without funding specifically dedicated to training in research that deals with slum-related conditions that engender diseases like Ebola, no amount of research spent on drugs or vaccines to combat these diseases will make an impact. Health science funding agencies such as the NIH, along with global health funding organizations such as the Wellcome Trust and Gates Foundation, generally funds projects that are disease-specific, based on the traditional model of reductionist science. Health science research, however, is increasingly recognized as requiring a systems science approach to make a difference. This is particularly evident for those who conduct slum health research. Funding to support training in such new efforts requires a major change in thinking on the part of the NIH and other funding agencies.

Training related to coproducing slum health involves not just research but action and advocacy as well. Until recently, in many academic institutions, advocacy and action were not encouraged as components of student training, and researchers in academia were usually not recognized or rewarded for advocacy-related activities. However, this is changing, especially with the recognition of a new academic discipline called implementation science. Implementation science translates discoveries made through research into actionable products. It is a science dedicated to scaling up innovations and new ideas into real-world settings. Action can be taught and learned. Advocacy can be taught and learned.

TOWARD SLUM HEALTH

On an urban planet, slum health is vital. This book shows that action-research that links the microbe to the conditions in communities and that involves a range of experts in this process can contribute to greater health equity in urban slums. We have not aimed to reify centuries-old negative connotations of urban slums as dirty, unhealthy, and filled with undeserving minority groups. Rather, slums and slum dwellers are the majority of the population in many cities in emerging-economy countries, and unless their health is made a priority, inequities between rich and poor will grow, and arresting the spread of preventable disease and unnecessary suffering will be that much more challenging. A sustainable planet must include a healthy population and livable and vital places for all. We suggest the importance of a new approach toward slum health for our twenty-first-century planet of cities.

NOTES

1. Tartof, S.Y., Reis, J.N., Andrade, A.N., Ramos, R.T., Reis, M.G., & Riley, L.W. (2010). Factors associated with Group A *Streptococcus emm* type diversification in a large urban setting in Brazil: A cross-sectional study. *BMC Infectious Diseases* 10:327.

2. Satyanarayana, L., Asthana S., Bhambani, S., Sodhani, P., & Gupta, S. (2014). A comparative study of cervical cancer screening methods in a rural community setting of North India. *Indian J Cancer* 51(2; April–June):124–28. doi: 10.4103/0019-509X.138172.

3. See the Oxford Poverty and Human Development Initiative at http://www.ophi.org.uk/multidimensional-poverty-index/.

4. Murray, C.J., & Lopez, A.D. (2013). Measuring the global burden of disease. *N Engl J Med* 369(5):448–57.

5. Ibid.

6. Murray, C.J., & Lopez, A.D. (2013).

7. Schmidt, M.I., Duncan, B.B., Azevedo e Silva, G., Menezes, A.M., Monteiro, C.A., Barreto, S.M., et al. (2011). Chronic non-communicable diseases in Brazil: Burden and current challenges. *Lancet* 377(9781):1949–61.

8. Lozano, R., Naghavi, M., Foreman, K., Lim, S., Shibuya, K., Aboyans, V., et al. (2012). Global and regional mortality from 235 causes of death for 20 age groups in 1990 and 2010: A systematic analysis for the Global Burden of Disease Study 2010. *Lancet* 380(9859):2095–128.

9. Ibid.

10. Di Cesare, M., Khang, Y.H., Asaria, P., Blakely, T., Cowan, M.J., Farzadfar, F., et al. (2013). Inequalities in non-communicable diseases and effective responses. *Lancet* 381(9866):585–97.

11. Mackenbach, J.P., Stirbu, I., Roskam, A.J., Schaap, M.M., Menvielle, G., Leinsalu, M., et al. (2008). Socioeconomic inequalities in health in 22 European countries. *N Engl J Med* 358(23):2468–81.

12. Espelt, A., Borrell, C., Roskam, A.J., Rodriguez-Sanz, M., Stirbu, I., Dalmau-Bueno, A., et al. (2008). Socioeconomic inequalities in diabetes mellitus across Europe at the beginning of the 21st century. *Diabetologia* 51(11): 1971–79.

13. Marmot, M.G., Shipley, M.J., & Rose, G. (1984). Inequalities in death: Specific explanations of a general pattern? *Lancet* 1(8384):1003–6.

14. Lozano, R., et al. (2012).

15. Brazilian Ministry of Health (2011). Strategic action plan to tackle noncommunicable diseases (NCDs) in Brazil, 2011–2022. Brasilia.

16. Snyder, R.E., Jaimes, G., Riley, L.W., Faerstein, E., & Corburn, J. (2014). A comparison of social and spatial determinants of health between formal and informal settlements in a large metropolitan setting in Brazil. *J Urban Health* 91(3):432–45.

17. Ibid.

18. Weiselfisz, J.J. (2013). Mapa da violencia: Mortes matadas por armas de fogo. Centro Brasileiro de Estudos Latino-Americanos.

19. Ibid.

20. Reis-Santos, B., Locatelli, R., Horta, B.L., Faerstein, E., Sanchez, M.N., Riley, L.W., et al. (2013). Socio-demographic and clinical differences in subjects with tuberculosis with and without diabetes mellitus in Brazil: A multivariate analysis. *PLoS One* 8(4):e62604.

21. Goldhaber-Fiebert, J.D., Jeon, C.Y., Cohen, T., & Murray, M.B. (2011). Diabetes mellitus and tuberculosis in countries with high tuberculosis burdens: Individual risks and social determinants. *Int J Epidemiol* 40(2):417–28.

22. Reis-Santos, B., et al. (2013).

23. Goldhaber-Fiebert, J.D., et al. (2011).

24. Ibid.

25. Eleftheriadou, I., Tentolouris, N., Argiana, V., Jude, E., & Boulton, A.J. (2010). Methicillin-resistant *Staphylococcus aureus* in diabetic foot infections. *Drugs* 70(14):1785–97.

26. Geerlings, S.E. (2008). Urinary tract infections in patients with diabetes mellitus: Epidemiology, pathogenesis and treatment. *Int J Antimicrob Agents* 31(Suppl 1):S54–S57.

27. Lange, P. (2009). Chronic obstructive pulmonary disease and risk of infection. *Pneumonol Alergol Pol* 77(3):284–88.

28. Jackson, D.J., Sykes, A., Mallia, P., & Johnston, S.L. (2011). Asthma exacerbations: Origin, effect, and prevention. *J Allergy Clin Immunol* 128(6):1165–74.

29. Crowson, C.S., Hoganson, D.D., Fitz-Gibbon, P.D., & Matteson, E.L. (2012). Development and validation of a risk score for serious infection in patients with rheumatoid arthritis. *Arthritis Rheum* 64(9):2847–55.

30. Tonelli, M., Wiebe, N., Culleton, B., House, A., Rabbat, A., Fok, M., McAlister, F., Garg, A.K. (2006). Chronic kidney disease and mortality risk: A systematic review. *J Am Soc Nephrol* 17:1757–58.

31. Fernandez, J., & Arroyo, V. (2013). Bacterial infections in cirrhosis: A growing problem with significant implications. *Clinical Liver Disease* 2:102–5.

32. American Cancer Society. (2011). Global cancer: Facts and figures. 2nd ed. Atlanta.

33. Inagaki, J., Rodriguez, V., & Bodey, G.P. (1974). Proceedings: Causes of death in cancer patients. *Cancer* 33(2):568–73.

34. Swedo, S.E., Leonard, H.L., Garvey, M., Mittleman, B., Allen, A.J., Perlmutter, S., et al. (1998). Pediatric autoimmune neuropsychiatric disorders associated with streptococcal infections: Clinical description of the first 50 cases. *Am J Psychiatry* 155(2):264–71.

35. De Martel, C., Ferlay, J., Franceschi, S., Vignat, J., Bray, F., Forman, D., et al. (2012). Global burden of cancers attributable to infections in 2008: A review and synthetic analysis. *Lancet Oncol* 13(6):607–15.

36. UN General Assembly. (2011). Political declaration of the High-Level Meeting of the General Assembly on the Prevention and Control of Non-communicable Diseases. New York: United Nations.

37. Horton, R. (2013). Non-communicable diseases: 2015 to 2025. *Lancet* 381(9866):509–10.

38. Snyder, R.E., Marlow, M.A., & Riley, L.W. (2014). Ebola in urban slums: The elephant in the room. *Lancet Glob Health* 2(12):e685.

Contributors

SIDDHARTH AGARWAL, MD, Executive Director, Urban Health Resource Centre, New Delhi, India

AURELIO N. ANDRADE, Hospital São Rafael-Monte Tabor, Salvador, BA, Brazil

NEEL M. BUTALA, MD, Massachusetts General Hospital, Boston, Massachusetts

MARÍLIA S. CARVALHO, Escola Nacional da Saúde Pública, Fundação Oswaldo Cruz, Ministério da Saúde, Rio de Janeiro, Brazil

JASON CORBURN, PhD, MCP, Associate Professor, University of California, Berkeley

GUILLERMO DOUGLASS-JAIME, Department of City and Regional Planning, University of California, Berkeley

RIDALVA D. M. FELZEMBURGH, Centro de Pesquisas Gonçalo Moniz, Fundação Oswaldo Cruz, Ministério da Saúde, Salvador, Brazil

KIRSTEN HAVEMANN, Ministry of Foreign Affairs, Denmark

CHANTALL HILDEBRAND, graduate student, University of California, Berkeley

KIMANI JOSEPH, organizer, Muungano wa Wanavijiji, Nairobi, Kenya

IRENE KARANJA, former director, Muungano Support Trust, Nairobi, Kenya

ALBERT I. KO, MD, Professor and Chair, Epidemiology of Microbial Diseases, Yale University School of Public Health, Yale University, New Haven, Connecticut; Centro de Pesquisas Gonçalo Moniz, Fundação Oswaldo Cruz, Ministério da Saúde, Salvador, Brazil

JACK MAKAU, Director, Shack/Slum Dwellers International, Kenya

ASTRID X.T.O. MELENDEZ, Centro de Pesquisas Gonçalo Moniz, Fundação Oswaldo Cruz, Ministério da Saúde, Salvador, Brazil

SUSAN MERCADO, Director, Division of NCD and Health through the Life-Course, World Health Organization

SHARIF MOHR, Centro de Pesquisas Gonçalo Moniz, Fundação Oswaldo Cruz, Ministério da Saúde, Salvador, Brazil

BENSON ERICK OSUMBA, former chair, Muungano wa Wanavijiji, Nairobi, Kenya

RONAK BHAILAL PATEL, MD, Clinical Assistant Professor, Emergency Medicine, Stanford School of Medicine, Stanford University, Stanford, California

ADRIANO QUEIROZ, Centro de Pesquisas Gonçalo Moniz, Fundação Oswaldo Cruz, Ministério da Saúde, Salvador, Brazil

REGINA T. RAMOS, Department of Pediatrics, Federal University of Bahia School of Medicine, Salvador, BA, Brazil

ROMY R. RAVINES, Escola Nacional da Saúde Pública, Fundação Oswaldo Cruz, Ministério da Saúde, Rio de Janeiro, Brazil

JOICE N. REIS, Faculdade de Farmácia, Universidade Federal da Bahia, Salvador, BA, Brazil; Gonçalo Moniz Research Centre, Oswaldo Cruz Foundation, Brazilian Ministry of Health, Salvador, BA, Brazil

MITERMAYER G. REIS, Gonçalo Moniz Research Centre, Oswaldo Cruz Foundation, Brazilian Ministry of Health, Salvador, BA, Brazil

RENATO B. REIS, Centro de Pesquisas Gonçalo Moniz, Fundação Oswaldo Cruz, Ministério da Saúde, Salvador, Brazil

GUILHERME S. RIBEIRO, Centro de Pesquisas Gonçalo Moniz, Fundação Oswaldo Cruz, Ministério da Saúde, Salvador, Brazil

LEE RILEY, MD, Professor and Chair, Division of Infectious Disease and Vaccinology, School of Public Health, University of California, Berkeley

MOJGAN SAMI, PhD, University of California, Irvine

FRANCISCO S. SANTANA, Centro de Pesquisas Gonçalo Moniz, Fundação Oswaldo Cruz, Ministério da Saúde, Salvador, Brazil

ANDRÉIA C. SANTOS, Centro de Pesquisas Gonçalo Moniz, Fundação Oswaldo Cruz, Ministério da Saúde, Salvador, Brazil

HEENA SHAH, doctoral student, University of California, Berkeley

ALICE SVERDLIK, MS, doctoral student, University of California, Berkeley

SARA Y. TARTOF, School of Public Health, University of California, Berkeley

WAGNER S. TASSINARI, Escola Nacional da Saúde Pública, Fundação Oswaldo Cruz, Ministério da Saúde, Rio de Janeiro, Brazil; Universidade Federal Rural do Rio de Janeiro, Rio de Janeiro, Brazil

HIROSHI UEDA, World Health Organization, Kobe, Japan

ALON UNGER, MD, MsC, Assistant Professor, Division of Hospital Medicine, Departments of Internal Medicine and Pediatrics, University of California, San Francisco

MICHAEL J. VAN ROOYEN, Professor, Harvard Medical School and Harvard T.H. Chan School of Public Health

JANE WAIRUTU, Muungano Support Trust, Nairobi, Kenya

Index

Note: Tables and figures are indicated by *t* or *f* after the page number.